The Sebastopol Project is a charitable endeavour aimed at inspiring the public with stories of the diverse and courageous acts of men and women awarded the Victoria Cross and George Cross.

On Courage

Stories of Victoria Cross and George Cross Holders

The Sebastopol Project

CONSTABLE

CONSTABLE

First published in Great Britain in 2018 by Constable
This paperback edition published in Great Britain in 2020 by Constable

3 5 7 9 10 8 6 4 2

A CIP catalogue record for this book is available from the British Library.

ISBN: 978-1-47212-919- 2

Typeset in Electra LT Std by SX Composing DTP, Rayleigh, Essex
Printed and bound in Great Britain by Clays Ltd, Elcograf S.p.A.

Papers used by Constable are from well-managed forests
and other responsible sources.

MIX
Paper from
responsible sources
FSC® C104740

Constable
An imprint of
Little, Brown Book Group
Carmelite House
50 Victoria Embankment
London EC4Y 0DZ

An Hachette UK Company
www.hachette.co.uk

www.littlebrown.co.uk

Dedicated to all those who have had the courage to put themselves in harm's way selflessly to help others. May we continue as a nation to cherish the loyalty, discipline and commitment of those who serve.

The Sebastopol Project

CONTENTS

FOREWORD

It gives me great pleasure to write the foreword to this inspirational book. Following the publication of the first authorised volumes, *The Victoria Cross* and *The George Cross: The Complete History*, it is wonderful to see the stories of the lives and deeds of some of these most gallant recipients now brought to life in this work. In many cases, it is the ordinariness of a life that demonstrated such extraordinary courage that really serves to inspire. The humanity and character of these most brave individuals has been brought to life by setting their deeds of selfless valour within the wider context of their lives.

This volume brings together stories of courage borne out of the horrors of war and also domestic tragedy. The common thread is the steely commitment of the recipient of the award, to putting their own safety second to saving or protecting the lives of others.

Courage in the face of appalling adversity will never fail to make an impact. In reading these stories of men and women from many walks of life, experience and cultures, I hope that their remarkable examples of selfless courage will continue to inspire.

Field Marshal The Lord Bramall KG GCB OBE MC

SERGEANT JOHN BASKEYFIELD VC

Introduced by Mark Pougatch

One can only imagine what the father of 'Jack' Baskeyfield must have felt when George VI pinned his son's posthumous VC to his chest on 17 July 1945. Equally, we can but imagine how we ourselves would have reacted in the circumstances in which Sergeant Baskeyfield found himself during the Battle of Arnhem ten months earlier. Baskeyfield was a twenty-one-year-old butcher from Stoke-on-Trent who commanded two anti-tank guns in a battle later immortalised in the film A Bridge Too Far. *Ignoring his own injuries, outmanned and outgunned and under intense fire, he would surely have known what his own fate was to be, but his courage and commitment were unwavering. I would suggest this is not a well-known story outside army circles but it is an extraordinary one nonetheless.*

Operation MARKET GARDEN, the attempt by Allied airborne troops to seize a succession of river crossings and thereby open a road corridor though Holland, across the Rhine and into the heart of Germany in September 1944, was one of the boldest missions of the war. The hardest task, seizing and holding the great road bridge over the Lower Rhine at Arnhem, was given to the 10,000 or so men of the British 1st Airborne Division. These so-called Red Devils were told they would be relieved after forty-eight hours; they eventually fought a more numerous and better-armed opponent for eight days before the remnants were ordered to withdraw. More than 7,500 were killed or captured.

Acts of heroism during this week of desperate fighting at Arnhem were commonplace, but only five were thought worthy of the highest award for gallantry, the Victoria Cross. Four were given to officers and one to a non-commissioned officer, twenty-one-year-old Lance Sergeant Jack Baskeyfield of the 2nd Battalion, The South Staffordshire Regiment (or 2nd South Staffs). Baskeyfield's example of courage and self-sacrifice on 20 September 1944, the fourth day of the battle, was among the most extraordinary of the whole war.

Born in the Potteries town of Burslem, Stoke-on-Trent, on 18 November 1922, Baskeyfield was one of three sons of Daniel, a sliphouse worker, and his wife Minnie. He was educated at St John's and Corbridge Church Day Schools before starting work as an errand boy in the local Co-op Butchers Shop. An ambitious young man, he studied at night school while also working as a butcher, and his dedication paid off when he was appointed manager of the Co-op Butchers Shop in Pitshill, north of Burslem, at the age of just eighteen. A few months later, in February 1942, he was called up for military service and joined the South Staffordshire Regiment.[1]

Baskeyfield's first posting was to the 11th South Staffords, a training unit. But in early February 1943, by now a lance corporal, he switched to his regiment's regular 2nd Battalion that, eighteen months earlier, had become part of the newly formed 1st Airlanding (or glider-transported) Brigade. The inspiration for these first British airborne troops was the successful use of German paratroopers during the Wehrmacht's invasion of the Low Countries in May 1940. Within weeks of Winston Churchill declaring in June that 'we ought to have a corps of at least 5,000 parachute troops', a jump school was established at RAF Ringway, near Manchester.[2]

The 1st Parachute Brigade became operational in January 1942. By then it had been nominally joined by the 1st Airlanding Brigade to form the 1st Airborne Division. However, the lack of troop-carrying gliders hampered the 1st Airlanding Brigade's training, and it was not ready for battle until after Baskeyfield had become an airborne soldier in February 1943. His airborne instruction would have included fitness, insertion techniques, familiarity with weapons and tactics. To be issued with the famous maroon beret was to be confirmed as the member of a *corps d'elite*. Nothing could have prepared Baskeyfield for his first glider journey into action. A fellow airlanding soldier recalled: 'Who would like being cooped up in a confined space for hours wearing full kit with vomit sloshing around their feet, providing a nice slow target for ground fire, awaiting the crash landing – and then having to fight a battle?'[3]

After his own terrifying experience of glider warfare, American war correspondent Walter Cronkite wrote: 'If you've got to go into combat, don't go by glider. Walk, crawl, parachute, swim, float – anything. But don't go by glider!'[4]

In May 1943, the 1st Airborne Division was shipped to North Africa to prepare for the invasion of Sicily, its first operation. It was now composed of three parachute brigades – the 1st, 2nd and 4th – and Baskeyfield's 1st Airlanding Brigade.

In the forthcoming operation, the glider troops were given the vital task of seizing the Ponte Grande, a bridge at Syracuse. With British transport in short supply, they would be flown in 136 American Waco CG-4 gliders, better known as the 'Hadrian', and still in their packing cases when they reached North Africa. Described by one pilot as 'a dark green blunt-nosed dragonfly', the Waco was of steel, wood and fabric construction, forty-nine feet long and with a wingspan of eighty-four feet. It could carry thirteen men, a jeep and its crew or cargo.[5] It was wholly unfamiliar to the men from the Glider Pilot Regiment who were to fly them into Sicily; nor had these pilots trained in night flying, though the landing was to take place in darkness, and in a location crisscrossed with rocks and stone walls. When the chief pilot pointed out the risks to the commander of 1st Airborne, he was told to get on with it or resign. He opted for the former.

'Unsurprisingly,' wrote the author of one of the foremost books on the development of Britain's airborne troops, 'the landing on the night of 9–10 July 1943 was a fiasco, partly due to light winds, alert anti-aircraft defences and a light mist over the landing area'. Of the 144 gliders sent on the mission, 78 ditched in the sea after their inexperienced pilots released them too early, 2 diverted to Malta and Tunisia, 10 returned to base and 42 landed along a twenty-five-mile stretch of the Sicilian coast.[6]

Baskeyfield's glider – designated Chalk 54A – was among the seventy-eight that crashed into the water. One of those on board reported: 'Bumpy flight. Glider released 2230hrs at unknown height. Pilot said, just after releasing, "We are at 600 feet", next moment glider landed in sea about 8 miles from the coast. All men got out of glider, but both pilots and 7 ORs missing.' Only seven of the fifteen occupants survived, Baskeyfield among them, after waiting eight and a half hours to be rescued by a naval launch.[7] The brigade as a whole suffered 313 fatalities, including 225 drowned in ditched gliders; a further 101 of the 272 pilots were killed, wounded or missing.[8]

In December 1943, after a short time on the Italian mainland, the bulk of 1st Airborne Division – bar the 2nd Parachute Brigade which remained in the Mediterranean as an independent formation – returned to Britain. Incredibly, the man now appointed to command the division, Major General 'Roy' Urquhart, was a distinguished infantry officer but with no airborne experience. He was given the job because he was a protégé of General Sir Bernard Montgomery who would command the D-Day landings.

Baskeyfield's 1st Airlanding Brigade, billeted in Rutlandshire and south Lincolnshire, spent much of the next few months absorbing and training new recruits. Some historians have criticised the 1st Airborne's parachute brigades for not training as hard as they could have during the first half of 1944; but not the glider troops. 'By the end of May 1944,' wrote William F. Buckingham, '1st Airlanding Brigade had carried out no less than eight tactical exercises, seven of which involved most or all of the brigade, and at least two of which used large numbers of gliders.'[9]

4

On 20/21 March, for example, Baskeyfield's 2nd South Staffs carried out Exercise Goshawk with the 7th King's Own Scottish Borderers (KOSB), and towards the end of the month acted as enemy for 4th Parachute Brigade's Exercise Silk. The average member of the 1st Airlanding Brigade 'spent almost twice as much time engaged in tactical training as his parachute counterparts and participated in twice as many separate exercises'. Events at Arnhem would show, moreover, that 'parachute machismo was a poor substitute for the systematic training undertaken by 1st Airlanding Brigade'.[10]

It was also during this period that the 1st Airlanding's Infantry battalions reorganised their heavy weapon Support Companies. Henceforth these companies were equipped with quick-firing 6-pounder anti-tank guns (towed by jeeps), Vickers heavy machine guns and 3-inch mortars. Promoted in quick succession to full corporal in June 1944 and lance sergeant a month later, Baskeyfield was given command of a section of 2-pounder guns in the Anti-Tank Platoon of his battalion's Support Company. Manned by a team of six men, each one of these guns was capable, with its new armour piercing rounds, of knocking out even the heaviest German tanks at close range.[11]

Between D-Day, 6 June, and 5 September 1944, the 1st Airborne Division was considered for no fewer than fourteen operations. All were cancelled. The fifteenth – originally named COMET, and later MARKET GARDEN – was scheduled for 8 September, but later postponed so that more troops could be assigned. The key meeting was between US General Dwight D. Eisenhower, the Supreme Allied Commander, and his British subordinate Field Marshal Sir Bernard Montgomery, commanding the 21st Army Group, at the latter's headquarters at Laeken in Belgium on 10 September. At this meeting, Montgomery persuaded Eisenhower to let him implement a narrow thrust into Holland as far as Arnhem, and thus open a 'back door' into Germany. To do so he would use three and a half airborne divisions – the US 82nd and 101st and the British 1st Airborne Divisions, and the 1st Polish Parachute Brigade – to seize a succession of river crossings and open a corridor for the tanks, followed by the infantry, of the British Second Army. Once across the Rhine at Arnhem, Montgomery's troops could wheel east, outflank the fortified Siegfried Line and penetrate the German industrial region of the Ruhr.

With the conference over, Montgomery spoke to Lieutenant General Frederick 'Boy' Browning, Deputy Chief of the First Airborne Army, from which the three divisions would be drawn. He told Browning that his paratroopers and glider forces would have to secure, intact, five major bridges – including (from south to north) crossings over the Rivers Maas, Waal and Lower Rhine – over a distance of sixty-four miles between the Dutch border and Arnhem.

'How long will it take the armour to reach us?' asked Browning, pointing to the most northerly bridge at Arnhem.

'Two days,' replied Montgomery.

'We can hold it for four,' said Browning. 'But, sir, I think we might be going a bridge too far.'[12]

In truth, both Montgomery and Browning had a vested interest in this risky operation taking place: the former because he was determined to wrest back from his US rival, General George C. Patton, the initiative for the Allied advance into Germany; and the latter because he lacked operational experience and needed to establish his credentials as an airborne commander before the war ended. It was for this reason that Browning downplayed viable intelligence reports that two battered SS panzer divisions – the 9th and 10th – were refitting in the Arnhem area and refused to include them in intelligence summaries sent to the airborne troops.[13]

1st Airborne Division, with the 1st Polish Brigade under its command, was given the task of capturing the most northerly objective: the great concrete and steel bridge over the Lower Rhine at Arnhem (a railway bridge and pontoon bridge were also to be secured). Once a nearby airstrip had been taken, the 52nd (Lowland) Division would be flown in as reinforcements, giving a total of 35,000 troops. However, because of a shortage of both powered aircraft and gliders, and the refusal of US pilots to fly more than one lift a day, it would take three days to transport all these troops to Arnhem. Even then, without tanks or heavy artillery, they would be extremely vulnerable to counter-attack.[14]

The mission became even tougher when RAF planners refused to allow drops close to the bridge at Arnhem because of inaccurate reports that German flak defences were too strong and the land to the south was marshy and unsuitable for gliders. So Major General Urquhart, the new and inexperienced commander of 1st Airborne, was forced to choose landing and drop zones on heathland and pasture to the west and north-west of Arnhem, a distance of between seven and nine miles from the bridge. It was a fatal decision that would give 'the German defenders ample time to deduce 1st Airborne's objective and react accordingly, and thus robbed the comparatively lightly armed troops of their sole advantage of surprise'; and it would prove to be 'the single most significant factor in the failure of Market Garden'.[15]

Urquhart's final plan was for two brigades to land on D-Day, 17 September 1944: Brigadier 'Pip' Hick's 1st Airlanding Brigade would guard the drop zones, while Brigadier Gerald Lathbury's 1st Parachute Brigade hurried in to Arnhem to secure its road, railway and pontoon bridges. Spearheading this assault would be Major Freddie Gough's motorised Reconnaissance Squadron of 275 men with jeeps and motorcycles. Their job was to hold the bridge until the rest of the brigade arrived.

Brigadier John ('Shan') Hackett's 4th Parachute Brigade and the balance of the 1st Airlanding Brigade would arrive the next day, followed by Major General Stanisław Sosabowski's 1st Polish Parachute Brigade a day later. From the start, Sosabowski thought the 'mission cannot possibly succeed' and that it 'would be suicide to attempt it'. Browning reassured him: 'But, my dear Sosabowski, the Red Devils and the gallant Poles can do anything!'

At 9.45 a.m. on Sunday 17 September, the first of more than 2,000 planes, gliders and tugs – carrying 20,000 men, 511 vehicles, 330 artillery pieces and 590 tons of equipment – took off from twenty-three airfields in southern England. They had been preceded before dawn by 1,400 Allied bombers. Escorting these huge formations were nearly 1,500 fighters and fighter-bombers. In three columns, each ten miles wide and 100 miles long, the huge armada headed towards Holland. It was the greatest air operation in history.[16]

Sergeant Baskeyfield and the men of the 2nd South Staffs assigned to the first lift – Battalion HQ, B and D Companies, and part of the Support Company – were towed in plywood Horsa gliders, sixty-seven feet long and with an eighty-eight-foot wingspan, by Albemarle bombers from RAF Manston in Kent. The Horsas could deliver twenty-five soldiers, combinations of jeeps, trailers and guns, or up to three and a half tons of cargo. Private William Hewitt of the 2nd South Staffs' Mortar Platoon recalled:

12 noon: all gliders airborne. We could see people leaving their homes and churches to watch this great 'armada' . . . At 2.00 pm our pilot called 'Tow rope released' – height was about 1500 feet – our first glide down was to 500 ft. Pilot now drops wing flaps which all but brought us to a halt in mid-air – the pilot must now pick his landing 'spot' (no second chances) and no time to hang about. Quickly we disembark – 'first' out take up defensive positions around their glider to protect the other Airborne troops, as I did. Unloading took place – hand-carts [containing the mortars and their ammunition] being pushed to the nearest 'cover' at the edge of the field . . . A little time to assess our position – and no enemy gunfire (good). We noted that some gliders were not so lucky, some crashed into trees or turned over – medical orderlies helping where necessary. It appeared most of the 2nd South Staffs landed ok and it is our task to protect the landing area for the 'second drop' and supplies to take place at 10.00 am 18th Sept.[17]

8

By mid-afternoon, 5,191 men of the 1st Airborne's two spearhead brigades had landed safely. But thirty-six of the 320 gliders had failed to arrive, and among the missing equipment was the transport for one of the four troops of Major Gough's Reconnaissance Squadron. Gough therefore set off with just three troops, leaving the fourth to follow on foot. Also converging on Arnhem by separate routes were the three battalions of Lathbury's 1st Parachute Brigade. But they soon ran into units of the 9th SS Panzer Division which, as early as 1.30 p.m., had been ordered to secure the Arnhem road bridge and destroy the enemy troops to its west. Only Lieutenant Colonel John Frost's 2nd Battalion, The Parachute Regiment (or 2nd Paras) was able to fight its way through this blocking force to the northern end of the road bridge where, shortly after 8 p.m., it was joined by some of Gough's troops, a platoon from the 3rd Paras and Brigade Headquarters (minus Brigadier Lathbury, who had linked up with the bulk of the 3rd Paras), a total of 700 men. But Frost was effectively cut off from the rest of the division and German armour was on its way.[18]

General Urquhart should have assigned fresh troops to reinforce Frost, but a loss of radio contact had caused him to leave 1st Airborne HQ at Landing Zone Z in the late afternoon to assess the situation with his forward units, and he was forced to spend the night of 17/18 September with Brigadier Lathbury and the remnants of the 3rd Paras on the edge of Oosterbeek, a village on the outskirts of Arnhem. So responsibility passed to the next senior officer, Brigadier 'Pip' Hicks of the 1st Airlanding Brigade, who assigned the 2nd South Staffs to attempt a breakthrough to the bridge the following morning.

Though only at half-strength – the remaining portion was due to arrive later that day in the second lift – the battalion left its position north of the village of Wolfheze at 10.30 a.m. and moved towards Oosterbeek with the jeeps and light armour in the lead, followed by the rifle platoons and the mortars. But the going was tough and, harassed by German fighter planes, snipers and machine guns, the 2nd South Staffs took around seven hours to cover the six miles to a point close to St Elizabeth's Hospital on the outskirts of Arnhem where they joined the remnants of the 1st Paras. 'For some reason we halt here for the night,' recorded Private William Hewitt. 'This stop, I feel, was a mistake by a our Commander, for whilst we lay all night at the roadside, the enemy was moving in more troops and armour between us and the bridge.'[19]

The halt did, however, give the 11th Paras and the remaining portion of the 2nd South Staffs (A, C and the balance of the Support Companies), newly arrived from the UK, the chance to catch up. This time the 2nd South Staffs had taken off from Broadwell airfield in Oxfordshire in Horsas towed by Wellington bombers. A machine-gunner in the Support Company, Lance Corporal Jack Bird, recalled:

> The sky seemed full of gliders on either side of us, and we swept along in formation; the weather being perfect . . . Then we were over the Dutch coast (the time being about one o'clock) and below could be seen the flooded areas, and of course down went one or two gliders. We were encountering flak and it could be seen coming up at us, but luckily our glider was not hit. We carried on to our DZ which we reached at about two o'clock, and after being cast off by our tug plane . . . Gliders lay all over the place – many had come to grief and some were on fire, but the majority seemed to have comedown OK. Out we jumped and took up defensive positions around the glider whilst the kit was unloaded.

Once on the ground, the 2nd South Staffs were sent after the rest of their battalion. Bird 'was struck by the colourful and picturesque appearance of the houses, which from the air had a doll's house look'. He added:

> The Dutch people were genuinely glad to welcome us and greeted us with cheers and showered us with fruit and pointed out the direction that the Germans had taken. All along the road were signs

of a hasty retreat by Jerry – kit and equipment all over the place. Saw a German staff car wrecked at a crossroad, the four occupants inside dead, one sprawled grotesquely out of the door which he must have flung open in an attempt to get out.[20]

Among the dead was General Friedrich Kussin, Arnhem's town commandant, whose staff car had been ambushed on the 17th by men of the 3rd Paras.

As Bird and the other reinforcements approached Arnhem, they were targeted by snipers and had to move 'warily'. They finally made contact with the tail of their battalion near the hospital at around midnight.[21]

The following morning, 19 September, by which time a small German withdrawal had allowed General Urquhart to rejoin 1st Airborne's new HQ in the Hotel Hartenstein in Oosterbeek, all three battalions at the hospital made a final attempt to reach the bridge. None got through. The 2nd South Staffs got as far as the Municipal Museum, 600 yards from their start point, before intense fire from mortars, assault guns and tanks stopped their advance. 'By late afternoon,' writes Buckingham, 'it was all over and the South Staffs had been destroyed piecemeal, apart from one company which had been held back near the 11th Parachute Battalion's lines after its commanding officer was killed. Most of the remainder were taken prisoner . . . although some scattered groups and individuals managed to escape to the west.'[22]

Among the survivors was the machine-gunner Lance Corporal Bird who remembered hitching a lift on a jeep, part of 'a long column of vehicles pulling out of Arnhem in the direction of Oosterbeek'. When the column was fired on, Bird continued on foot to Oosterbeek where a defensive perimeter was being formed around the Hartenstein Hotel. 'There,' he recalled, 'in a dugout on the bank of a stream in front of the old village church, I met up with some of my mob. I decided to "muck in" with them as I could not see any sign of my platoon. Everybody was "digging in" and didn't need any encouragement either. Personally, the deeper the better.'[23]

Sergeant Baskeyfield and his two anti-tank guns had been kept back from the final advance on the bridge and missed the debacle at the museum. Like Bird, they were ordered to join the defensive screen east of the church, under the command of Major Dickie Lonsdale of the 11th Paras, a total force of around 400 men.

Early on Wednesday, 20 September, the remaining 2nd South Staffs in 'Lonsdale Force' were withdrawn a couple of hundred yards back to the main defensive perimeter, leaving the battalion's machine-gunners and anti-tank guns to assist the 11th Paras in the defence of a T-junction on the Benedendorpsweg. Baskeyfield's two guns faced up the Acacialaan, a road that joined the Benedendorpsweg from the north, and covered any enemy approach down this road and from open ground to the north-east. His right flank – to the east – was guarded by another anti-tank gun. Most of the paratroopers were posted in nearby houses.[24]

Soon after the departure of the riflemen, the Germans attacked Baskeyfield's position with infantry, tanks and self-propelled guns. Acting with 'coolness and daring', and with 'complete disregard for his own safety', the twenty-one-year-old former butcher allowed the tanks to advance down the Acacialaan to within 100 yards of his guns before ordering his crews to open fire. They eventually knocked out 'two Tiger tanks and at least one self-propelled gun', but the counter-fire killed and badly wounded the crews of both guns, and Baskeyfield himself was severely wounded in the leg. Despite this, he 'refused to be carried to the Regimental Aid Post and spent his time attending to his gun and shouting encouragement to his comrades in neighbouring trenches'.

After a short interval the Germans attacked 'with even greater ferocity than before, under cover of intense mortar and shell fire'. Manning one gun 'quite alone' – loading, aiming and firing it, a task normally carried out by six men – Baskeyfield 'continued to fire round after round at the enemy until his gun was put out of action'. His action, according to his citation, 'was the main factor in keeping the enemy tanks at bay', and 'the fact that the surviving men in his vicinity were held together and kept in

SERGEANT JOHN BASKEYFIELD VC

action was undoubtedly due to his magnificent example and outstanding courage'. Again and again, 'enemy attacks were launched' and then 'driven off', thanks to Baskeyfield.

Even after the gun he was manning was rendered useless, the badly wounded young sergeant would not withdraw from the fight. Instead he 'crawled, under intense enemy fire, to another 6-pounder gun nearby, the crew of which had been killed, and proceeded to man it single-handed'. As he was about to engage a Stug III self-propelled gun – a 75mm cannon mounted on a tank chassis – another soldier 'crawled across open ground to assist him but was killed almost at once'. Undeterred, Baskeyfield 'succeeded in firing two rounds at the self-propelled gun, scoring one direct hit which rendered it ineffective'. This extraordinarily brave man was about to fire a third shot when a shell fired from another tank exploded near his gun, killing him instantly.[25]

Shortly after Baskeyfield's death almost all the houses occupied by the paratroopers were now ablaze, and Major Lonsdale withdrew the survivors to the main perimeter. They were covered by fire from Baskeyfield's comrades in the support arms of the 2nd South Staffs. 'It was a near run thing,' noted the battalion war diary, 'as the last 6 pdr passed the road junction . . . as a Tiger tank approached 25 yds away to the north.'[26]

That evening, in an epic assault, the US 82nd Airborne Division and the tanks of the British Guards Armoured Division captured the road bridge over the River Waal at Nijmegen (the railway bridge was also captured intact). But instead of pressing on – with the 10th SS Panzer Division in temporary disarray and the eleven-mile stretch of road to Arnhem open – the leading tanks were halted while infantry support was brought forward.

By the time they got underway, the following morning, the 2nd Paras' heroic stand at the north end of Arnhem's road bridge had come to an end. More than half of the defenders had been killed or wounded, and most of the survivors were captured. Asked to hold the bridge for forty-eight hours, they had managed to do so for three days and four nights. No sooner was it back in their hands than the Germans rushed reinforcements over the bridge to form a defensive line at Elst, four miles to the south.

Later that day Polish parachutists were dropped south of the Lower Rhine, opposite Urquhart's defensive perimeter at Oosterbeek. Only 250 men made it across the river to bolster the defence. Under constant shell and mortar fire, weakened by persistent attacks from infantry, tanks and self-propelled guns, the pocket held by the 1st Airborne was constantly diminishing. The end came during the night of 25 September when the able-bodied survivors of Urquhart's command were paddled across the river to safety. Of the 10,005 men who had been deployed on the north bank, only 1,741 officers and men of the 1st Airborne, 422 glider pilots and 160 Polish parachutists escaped. Total casualties were 1,200 killed and 6,378 missing, wounded and captured. German losses were 3,300 men, including 1,100 dead.[27]

Baskeyfield's body was buried in a temporary grave but never found after the war. He is commemorated on the Groesbeek Memorial, Netherlands, and on the Burslem War Memorial in Stoke-on-Trent, Staffordshire. His posthumous Victoria Cross was pinned on his father by King George VI on 17 July 1945. It currently resides in the Museum of the Staffordshire Regiment at Lichfield. The citation concludes: 'The superb gallantry of this N.C.O. is beyond praise. During the remaining days at Arnhem stories of his valour were a constant inspiration to all ranks. He spurned danger, ignored pain and, by his supreme fighting spirit, infected all who witnessed his conduct with the same aggressiveness and dogged devotion to duty which characterized his actions throughout.'[28]

2

SECOND LIEUTENANT DONALD BELL VC

Introduced by Sir Bobby Charlton CBE

I feel very honoured to introduce the story of Donald Bell VC. The quickest players I played against were Willie Johnston (Rangers and Scotland), Arthur Duncan (Hibernian and Scotland) and Steve Kindon (Burnley and Wolves). They were fabulous players but their names are now largely lost in time. Donald Bell VC was a very fast defender several generations before me but I hope his name will never be forgotten. When I read this story I saw the way he used his lightning speed to cover the ground and I felt humbled and inspired. I sincerely hope you may feel something of this, too.

When people think of football and the First World War, they usually think of the Christmas Day truce of 1914. This was an early and illusory moment of peace in the Great War – the early recruits signing up in the belief they'd be home by Christmas were now discovering the harsher realities of a conflict with no immediate end in sight. With the weather crisp and cold, the singing of carols on both sides of the trenches was followed on Christmas Day by a meeting in no man's land and a sharing of gifts. The playing of football, rather than being a large or organised game, was more of a succession of smaller kickabouts – a spontaneous moment that over the years has developed in the public consciousness into a single match (such as in Paul McCartney's 'Pipes of Peace' video or Sainsbury's Christmas advertisements). In fact, the kickabouts were anything but organised: generals, concerned it might lead to questioning among the troops about the war, swiftly decreed that anyone involved in something similar again would be court-martialled.

It wasn't only in no man's land that football was brought to a halt. Following on swiftly from the declaration of war had come the start of the 1914–15 season back in England. This divided opinion sharply. In a piece for football periodical *The Blizzard* in 2016, Alexander Jackson describes how some, such as manager Tom Maley, thought that football 'fulfils a function and purpose useful'.[1] Others – described by one football writer as 'political cartoonists, kill-joys, conscriptionists, anti-sports and many others whom the deadliness of the fighting had somewhat unbalanced'[2] – wanted the league stopped. By the end of the season, the FA decided that continuing the league was not viable in the circumstances and suspended professional football until the end of the war.

Even within this one season of football during the First World War, the game wasn't quite the same as it had been before. One club in particular that had been looking forward to the new season, before world events took over, had been that of Tom Maley's Bradford Park Avenue. Formed as recently as 1908, the club had won its first ever promotion to the First Division, the Football League's top tier at the time. However it was a season that they would start at less than full strength as they, and many other clubs, found their squads depleted by players wanting to sign up and fight. One player who went to war was Joseph Maley, the son of the aforementioned Bradford manager. He would be killed by shrapnel on a trench raid in May 1915.

Another was the defender Donald Simpson Bell. 'At the outbreak of war,' Maley remembered, 'he spoke strongly about those who could go, ought to, and didn't. When he learned that my son had joined up he was mighty pleased.'[3] Bell's own footballing career was only just beginning when he went to war and he had yet to make his mark. Yet he remains one of the most well-known footballers of the period for somewhat different reasons: he is the only professional footballer to have been awarded the Victoria Cross.

Rather than the usual First World War tale of soldiers playing football, then, this is the converse: the story, rather, of a footballer who became a soldier, and one whose bravery resulted in his being awarded the highest of honours.

* * *

Donald Bell's prowess as a footballer was apparent from an early age. Born in Harrogate, Yorkshire, in December 1890, his sporting ability was noticeable at both his first school, St Peter's, and then at Knaresborough Grammar School, where he also won colours at cricket, hockey, rugby and swimming. Football, though, was his passion and he had a combination of physical attributes to help him. Archie White, a schoolboy friend who would also go on to be awarded the Victoria Cross in the First World War, said of his friend that 'he had the build of a hammer thrower; he could never have been a runner. Yet he had a unique gift of acceleration; he could start from zero on the centre line, be in top gear in two strides, and cover thirty, forty and fifty yards at the speed of a sprinter on a running track. That is what made him so valuable as a footballer.'

Another fellow pupil, A. A. Thompson, also wrote about Bell and his schooldays in his book *The Exquisite Burden*. There may be an element of artistic licence in his descriptions, and, indeed, Bell, like the others in the book, is given a pseudonym (Tom Leyland). But the essence of the person he is describing echoes that of White's description:

> It was not strange that small boys held their breath, for this was the great Tom Leyland himself, a genial giant and already, at sixteen, a figure of heroic legend. He bestrode the petty world of school football like a colossus, only turning out for the First Eleven on Wednesday; on Saturdays he played full-back for the town team. His physical strength was enormous, so was his cheerful good nature.[4]

This description would later be voiced by his Bradford manager, Tom Maley: 'he was about six feet tall and when fit about 13 st. 8lbs. With it all he was most gentle.'[5]

Even from a young age, Bell's career was shaped by a combination of sport and education. While at school, the teenage Bell also played for local sides Starbeck, Mirfield United and most noticeably Bishop Auckland (then one of the strongest teams in the Northern League). Then, while at Westminster Training College, studying to be a teacher, he turned out for Crystal Palace (at the time in the Southern League First Division, which after the war became the third tier of the Football League).

Having completed his teacher training, Bell went back north to Harrogate, where he had a job at Starbeck County School as assistant master. His fledgling football career now took him to Newcastle United. Newcastle were one of the powerhouses of English football in the early twentieth century, winning the league three times between 1904 and 1909 and reaching the FA Cup Final five times between 1905 and 1911. For Bell to play for the team as an amateur, then, was testament to his abilities, even if his time there confirmed his role as a defender: in one match, he was played up front to make the most of his pace, but after missing a number of opportunities was reshuffled back to his usual position for the second half.

It was in defence that Bell excelled, and it was this skill that led to him joining Bradford Park Avenue for the 1912–13 season. Bradford Park Avenue, nestled firmly in the Second Division, weren't as high flying as Newcastle, but the offer came with two important caveats: first, they offered more 'boot money' than Newcastle (£10 a month); and, second, it allowed Bell to play rugby and cricket alongside his teaching. It also meant that he was joining a team who were on the up. Bradford had hired Tom Maley as manager in 1910, two years after the founding of the club. Maley had a strong track record, winning the Second Division title and the FA Cup as manager of Manchester City. Changing the club's kit to the same green and white hoops of Glasgow Celtic, he was also in the process of turning the club around as well, guiding them to the First Division by 1914.

Bell played for Bradford for two seasons, the second as a full-time professional, having decided to quit teaching to focus on his football. In this second season, when the club were pushing for promotion (they eventually finished runners-up), Bell's own season was more mixed. At the start of the campaign, he was kept out of the team by another right-back. However, when he got his opportunity to play – first against Leicester Fosse and then Wolverhampton Wanderers – he was particularly impressive: Bradford won the first match 3–2, pushing them up to fourth; against Wolves, one of the promotion favourites, they lost by a single goal, but their defence was praised in the subsequent match reports. Bell would repeat this form away at Notts County in January: County were the league leaders and Bradford came away with an important draw. This came at a personal price for Bell, however: he picked up an injury that ruled him out for the rest of the season. As one newspaper noted, 'Had it not been for an accident he would probably have secured a regular place in the side. Indeed, some of those displays, particularly those in the matches with Notts County at Trent Bridge and Wolverhampton Wanderers at Molineux, were good enough for any country.'[6]

With Bradford promoted, Bell was set to test himself against the best players in the land and see if his displays justified the praise. Events on the Continent, though, were to take his life in a different direction. 'I have given the subject some very serious thought,' he wrote to the club, 'and have now come to the conclusion I am duty bound to join the ranks. Will you therefore kindly ask the directors of the Bradford Football Club to release me from my engagement?' The club agreed, and Bell became the first professional footballer to enlist.

* * *

To begin with, Bell's war experience echoed the frustration of many of those recruits desperate to serve. Having joined A Company of the 9th

Battalion, the West Yorkshire Regiment, Bell found himself in Wisley, Surrey, where the battalion was based, and stuck in a seemingly endless cycle of training exercises.

In May 1915, the regiment was at camp at Belton Park, Grantham, when Bell came across his old schoolfriend Archie White. White, too, had enlisted at the outbreak of war and was now a junior officer in the Yorkshire Regiment (The Green Howards). Aware of his friend's qualities, he was surprised to find that Bell hadn't been commissioned and insisted on introducing him to his Commanding Officer, Lieutenant Colonel E. H. Chapman. 'Colonel Chapman took one look at him,' White later recalled, 'and was so impressed that he recommended him for a commission on the spot.'[7]

Bell, who by this point was a lance corporal, began his officer training. He originally hoped to join White in the Yorkshire Regiment's 6th Battalion, but timing worked against him. By the time he had completed his training, the 6th Battalion, who had been on standby to go to the Dardanelles, were already in Gallipoli. Bell instead was posted to the 9th Battalion as temporary second lieutenant. He would never see his schoolfriend Archie White again.

Bell finally made it to France in August 1915. Arriving in Boulogne, the battalion went first to Northbécourt and then Vieux-Berquin, where training continued until the end of September. From here, the battalion continued on to Bois Grenier on the Armentières front, their base for the next six months. Here, the battalion mixed moments of duty with periods of calm and training – the front was a comparatively quiet one, and action was relatively infrequent. One of the first real tastes of action came early on 1 January 1916, when a raiding party made up of men from the 10th Battalion, the Northumberland Fusiliers and the 9th Battalion raided the German trenches at Rue-du-Bois. Bell was not one of the 100 men from the 9th Battalion chosen for the attack, but spent the raid manning the trenches: this turned out to be the more dangerous of the two roles, with heavy bombardment leading to four men being killed and another twenty wounded (by contrast, the raiders returned relatively unharmed).

Two months later, Bell's unit was transferred south again, this time to the Souchez sector, where they took over from French troops at the Notre-Dame-de-Lorette spur. In May, Bell was granted ten days' leave, which he took to look after important business back at home: marrying Rhoda Bonson in the town of Kirkby Stephen, Cumbria, on 5 June. Upon his return, his unit had moved south again, along with the rest of the entire 23rd Division (the 9th Battalion was part of the 69th Brigade, which, together with the 68th and 70th Brigades, made up the division). This was in preparation for the 'big push' at the Somme. Having arrived at Longueau by train on 24 June, the battalion marched to St Sauveur, a village near Amiens, where they spent the next week in preparation for the British attack.

* * *

The story of the Battle of the Somme is well documented, but even a century later the shock of the numbers of those lost reverberates as strongly as ever. On the opening day of the assault, 1 July 1916, when 100,000 troops were sent over the top, 19,000 soldiers lost their lives in the single bloodiest day in the history of the British Army – deaths at the rate of one every five seconds. The Battle of the Somme would continue until the middle of November, but that opening day remained the worst in term of casualties. The Germans, who had prepared for the assault for the best part of two years, were more than ready to face whatever the British could throw at them.

The 23rd Division was initially there as a back-up unit to III Corps and for the 34th Division in particular. Such were the casualties on that opening three days, the 34th Division lost a total of 6,591 men, and, as one account put it, 'ceased to exist as an effective fighting force'. Thus Bell's brigade was brought into play. They were assigned part of the line to the south of La Boisselle. The goal was to make it as far as the village of Contalmaison, where the Germans were heavily entrenched. It was a position that was protected by an area known as Horseshoe Trench. As the name suggests, this curved stretch of defence was just under a mile in length and had a machine gun that was well concealed and deadly to any advancing troops.

July the 4th, the first day of the assault by the 9th Battalion and 11th West Yorkshires, proved futile. At four o'clock the following morning, it was the turn of the 11th West Yorkshires and 10th Duke of Wellingtons. As 5 July wore on, it wasn't until late afternoon that any sort of progress was made: at this point, the order went out for Bell's 9th Battalion to attack over open ground. The hostility of the German defences aside, the weather made conditions for such an attack appalling: heavy rain had reduced the battlefield to something approaching a quagmire.

As the battalion attacked, they came under fire from a machine-gun position, suffering heavy casualties. It was here that Bell stepped up, taking it upon himself to deal with the gunner. Followed by two colleagues, Corporal Colwill and Private Batey, Bell made his way carefully along a communications trench, until they were within thirty metres of the gunner. It was here that the acceleration so noted in Bell's football career came into play. Dashing full speed across open ground, Bell managed to shoot the machine-gunner with his revolver before he could swing round and return fire: then, with a carefully aimed Mills bomb, he took out the machine-gun unit once and for all. The three of them continued to throw their bombs into the trench, and by the end of their attack more than fifty Germans had been killed. Bell's brave actions allowed the battalion to take Horseshoe Trench, both strategically crucial and saving myriad lives in the process.

It was the decisive moment in a terrible couple of days' fighting. As Archie White later wrote in the *Regimental Gazette*: 'Probably no one else on the front could have done what Bell did. Laden by steel helmet, haversack, revolver, ammunition and Mills bomb in their pouches, he was yet able to hurl himself at the German trench at such speed that the enemy would hardly believe what their eyes saw.'[8]

'When the battalion went over,' Bell wrote in a letter to his mother two days later after the attack:

> I, with my team, crawled up a communication trench and attacked the gun and the trench, and I hit the gun first shot from about 20 yards and knocked it over. We then bombed the dugouts and did in about 50 Bosches [sic]. The GOC has been over to congratulate the battalion and personally thanked me. I must confess that it was the biggest fluke alive and I did nothing. I only chucked one bomb but it did the trick. The CO says I saved the situation for this gun was doing all the damage. I had a grand little lad with me, only 19, who did all the work and I think both he and I will be recommended for something.[9]

That something was the Victoria Cross. The citation, published a couple of months later, announced that the award was:

> for most conspicuous bravery. During an attack a very heavy enfilade fire was opened on the attacking company by a hostile machine gun. 2nd Lt. Bell immediately, and on his own initiative, crept up a communication trench and then, followed by Corpl. Colwill and Pte. Batey, rushed across the open under very heavy fire and attacked the machine gun, shooting the firer with his revolver, and destroying gun and personnel with bombs. This very brave act saved many lives and ensured the success of the attack.

* * *

Bell never received the award in person. Nor, indeed, was he ever aware of it. As the citation goes on to say, 'Five days later this gallant officer lost his life performing a very similar act of bravery.' By 10 July, Bell's success at Horseshoe Trench had helped the British reach their goal of the village of Contalmaison. The Germans, however, were countering strongly, and Bell was among a number sent to assist 8th Battalion, who were under strong attack. According to one account,

> Bell dashed forward with an armful of bombs, and started to clear out a hornet's nest of Huns who were ready to take toll of our advancing troops. He advanced with great courage right up to where the enemy were posted. He took careful aim, and bowled out several of the Germans. Unfortunately he was hit . . . for a while he fought on, but was hit again. He got weaker and weaker and had to relax his efforts. He collapsed suddenly and when we reached him he was dead.[10]

It was decided by Bell's father that it should be his widow, Rhoda, who should accept the award: they had been married just over a month when Bell was killed. On 13 December 1916, she received a first-class rail warrant and made her way from Cheshire to London, where she was presented with the medal by King George V at Buckingham Palace.

The actions of Donald Bell continue to be remembered to this day. That is true of his former regiment, where the Green Howards Regimental Museum includes, among other items, the helmet worn by Bell when he was killed. And it's true of the football world, too: Bell's Victoria Cross resides today at the National Football Museum. A memorial to Bell where he died – now known as Bell's Redoubt – was unveiled in 2000 by Major General Richard Dannatt, then Colonel of the regiment. The project received funding from the Professional Footballers' Association, the Football Association and the Football League.

One of the most moving memorials to Bell came in a letter to Rhoda from his batman, Private John Byers. In November 1916, he wrote to Rhoda in response to her request for more information about her husband's death:

Believe me, dear madam, what I told my wife was just the truth,
if there is any debt, it is on my side and that is a very deep debt
of gratitude, also all my Company that were left. They worshipped
him in their simple, wholehearted way and so they ought, he saved
the lot of us from being completely wiped out, by his heroic act.
We have lost the best officer and gentleman that ever was with the
Battalion and we have lost some good ones.[11]

GROUP CAPTAIN LEONARD CHESHIRE VC

(later Baron Cheshire of Woodhall)

Introduced by John Simpson CBE

Human beings are almost never just one thing – evil, stupid, saintly, heroic. We're too complex to be summed up in a single word. All the same, I've come across two genuine heroes in my time, people whose heroism just seemed to pervade their whole character. One was Nelson Mandela. The other was Leonard Cheshire VC.

It was in 1989 that I met Leonard. A BBC programme wanted an interview with him, and I drove to his house at Cavendish, in Suffolk, to see him. His wife, Sue Ryder, a hero in her own right, brought us a tray of tea and biscuits. 'If I leave you to it you're likely to get more out of him. But nobody really succeeds, you know!'

Leonard certainly wasn't hostile: quite the reverse. But he was shy, which didn't make things easy, and above all he was amazingly modest. And it was clear to me that this was genuine, not assumed for effect. He had a charming, quizzical look, with his eyes twinkling under his thick eyebrows, and instead of grinning he would purse his lips while the rest of his face seemed to glow with amusement.

As for the extraordinary feats of courage which won him his VC, I failed utterly to get anything of broadcastable value. 'I don't think I ever did anything the rest didn't do,' he countered. Then he would purse his lips in his anti-smile once again.

A friend of his from the war had told me that what he admired most about Cheshire was the way he'd insist on going out on the most dangerous missions with young air crew who were brand new to the job. As a Wing Commander, he certainly wasn't obliged to put his life in such regular danger, and his superiors disapproved. But there was no stopping Cheshire.

'Why did you do that sort of thing?' I asked him in our interview. It was the only time in our interview that he talked about his feelings.

'I felt really sorry for some of these kids. They were scared stiff, but they didn't want to show it. It just seemed natural to give them a bit of support. I'm glad I could do it.' And he smiled his brilliant smile.

Even among the rare group of individuals who have been awarded the Victoria Cross, there remain some men whose life story stands out. Such is the case of Leonard Cheshire. While most awards of the medal cite a specific date or incident, such was Cheshire's contribution in the skies of the Second World War that his citation stretches from 1940 through to 1944: 'In four years of fighting against the bitterest opposition he has maintained a record of outstanding personal achievement, placing himself invariably in the forefront of the battle. What he did in the Munich operation [an air assault in April 1944] was typical of the careful planning, brilliant execution and contempt for danger which has established for Wing Commander Cheshire a reputation second to none in Bomber Command.'

These outstanding achievements form only part of Cheshire's remarkable life. In the aftermath of the Second World War, he was at the forefront of providing help and recognition for the disabled. The Leonard Cheshire Disability charity that he founded in 1948 has grown both in the UK and beyond, becoming an international network providing care and support in more than fifty countries.

Voted thirty-first in a 2002 BBC poll of the 100 Greatest Britons, Cheshire has been described by the London *Evening Standard* as 'the outstanding Englishman of his generation' and by as notable a figure as Jawaharlal Nehru as 'the greatest man I have met since Gandhi'. Sir Alec Guinness, who like Cheshire was received into the Catholic Church at Petersfield, Hampshire, once commented that, 'In good time, I suppose the process will start which will lead to him being called Blessed; and eventually, I hope, his canonisation.'

As such, an attempt to capture such an extraordinary life in a few thousand words can only begin to scratch the surface of Cheshire's many achievements. It is to be hoped that this brief essay will give a flavour of the man as an individual, and encourage those interested to explore his life in more detail.

* * *

It seems fitting that at the time of Leonard Cheshire's birth in Chester on 7 September 1917 his father, Geoffrey, was away serving with the Royal Flying Corps. Unlike his son, Geoffrey Cheshire was never a pilot himself – his poor eyesight ruled him out – but instead was a military observer, rising high above Arras and Ypres in a kite balloon to help direct artillery shelling.

Two years before the war, Geoffrey had been made a fellow in law at Exeter College, Oxford (earlier he had gained a first at Merton), and so, after the war, he returned to his post, a position he would hold until 1944. The family – Geoffrey, his wife, Primrose, and their sons Leonard and Christopher – lived on the Woodstock Road until the end of the 1920s, when they moved to Cothill in Berkshire. In 1925, Leonard was sent to The Dragon School in Oxford where, rather than spotting his future greatness, it marked him as being 'not terribly good at anything'. He remained at The Dragon until 1931, before gaining a scholarship to Stowe School in Buckinghamshire, then a relatively new public school. Here he had the good fortune to be taught English by the celebrated novelist T. H. White.

Cheshire did not stand out at Stowe either. His headmaster, John Roxburgh, later described him as 'very successful in the ordinary sense of the word' and said, 'I cannot remember that Leonard made more impression on his generation than several others did.' Cheshire's father wanted his son to follow in his footsteps and study jurisprudence at Merton. Writing a reference for him in 1935, Roxburgh gave him a mixed report: 'Young Cheshire is an excellent boy. As a scholar he is tasteful and hard-working but not very gifted.' Despite this less than ringing endorsement, Cheshire won a place and went up to Oxford in October 1936. His last summer before university was spent in Potsdam, Germany, where he stayed at the house of a retired admiral, Ludwig von Reuter. It would have been an interesting time to have been in Germany, and von Reuter sounds an intriguing host (each of his sons was named after a different German warship), but accounts differ on how much Cheshire actually saw of the politics of the time – from not very much at all to getting into trouble for refusing to give a Nazi salute at a Hitler rally.

Either way, armed with near-fluent German, Cheshire returned to Oxford to begin his degree. Here, too, stories abound of a high-spirited student lifestyle, what actually happened mixed, no doubt, with the apocryphal: downing an entire bottle of whisky in one go; winning a bet of a pint of beer that he couldn't hitch-hike to Paris with only a handful of change in his pocket, racing cars by running in front of them down the Iffley Road. At the same time as these high jinks, however, there is a strong sense of Cheshire growing and maturing as a young man as well.

This period also saw the beginning of Cheshire's flying career, when he swapped the Officer Training Corps (OTC), which he hated, for the Oxford University Air Squadron (OUAS), which he loved. Cheshire showed a natural talent for flying, though not everyone was convinced: Wing Commander Herbert, the chief flying instructor in 1937, considered him 'a sort of ne'er-do-well', and if he'd had his way would have thrown him out of the OUAS. Cheshire, though, continued to train hard, both regularly at OUAS's base in Abingdon and also on the longer camps in the summer vacation. Now everything seemed to happen at once: a frenzied revision for final examinations in June 1939; the declaration of war on 3 September; acceptance onto an RAF training course, beginning in early October.

Cheshire took this course at Hullavington in Wiltshire. Preliminary training took place between October and Christmas, the intermediate section, weather permitting, between January and March. He passed comfortably, with the comments in his Service Record describing him as 'an average pilot who can be relied upon to do good work. Instrument flying exceptionally steady and accurate. Should make good leader with experience.' From here he went to the No. 10 Operational Unit (OTU) at Abingdon where he began training on flying the Armstrong Whitworth Whitley, a vehicle used for long-range bombing raids. After taking further courses in armament training and flying by night, his training was finished, just as the withdrawal from Dunkirk was complete.

* * *

In June 1940, Cheshire became part of 102 Squadron, based at Driffield in Yorkshire. As a novice pilot, he was initially assigned to a crew and it wasn't long before he was sent out on his first sortie – a bombing raid to blow up a road bridge at Abbeville in northern France. The crew was led by Pilot Officer Frank Long, who let Cheshire fly the Whitley over England, before taking over once they left the Sussex coast behind. For Cheshire, watching as the bombs were dropped over France, it was a sobering experience. 'Somehow it had not quite been what I expected,' he wrote in *Bomber Pilot*, 'not enough glamour, and too much to learn.'[1]

In his first fifteen days, Cheshire flew on five sorties. It was on his next, on a mission to bomb a nitrogen plant at Ludwigshafen-Oppau, that seems the most important; here Cheshire found himself under attack for the first time as anti-aircraft fire shook the Whitley. He was relieved to see how he responded: 'God knows I have suffered real, hopeless fear,' he later wrote, 'but I am not afraid of ack-ack . . . It is nothing to be proud of, but it is something to cash in on.'[2]

After six weeks, Cheshire had flown twenty operations under Long and was considered ready to take charge of his own crew: sorties to Cologne, Frankfurt and Milan soon followed. Other experiences came closer to home when an enemy counter-raid identified Driffield as its target, Cheshire fleeing for his life as the Luftwaffe bombed the airfield, killing fifteen and destroying ten Whitleys in the process. The remainder of 102 Squadron went to RAF Leeming, where they were assigned to 15 group Coastal Command, helping to escort convoys. Compared to the bombing raids, this felt routine work and Cheshire was relieved when the squadron was moved to Linton-on-Ouse and the attacks on the European mainland – the 'real' job – could begin again. Attacks on Pretzch, Lunen and Ruhland followed.

On the night of 12/13 November, Cheshire's war almost came to a premature end. On a mission to Wessling to bomb the synthetic oil plant there, low cloud led to Cheshire switching the target to nearby Cologne. Richard Rivaz, Cheshire's tail gunner, describes in his book, also called *Tail Gunner*, what happened next:

> I remember a deafening explosion and a blinding red flash which seemed to be inside my head and behind my eyes. I was falling through darkness . . . I felt I was still in my turret, but could not see it; everything was dark and silent and the engines had gone. I knew we had been hit and I imagined the shell must have burst somewhere behind my turret and blown it from the aeroplane . . . I crawled forward through the smoke and flames. God, what a mess! The fuselage door had gone and most of one side of the fuselage as well. Desmond [Coutts, second pilot] was there, working like a maniac, with his blond hair shining in the light of the flames . . . sweat was pouring off his face and he was hurling flares, incendiaries

and spare ammunition out of the gaping fuselage. I started to do the same . . . he shouted at me to go back and get my parachute as the plane would probably break in two.[3]

Cheshire, meanwhile, was trying to keep his cool. As Rivaz and Coutts put the fire out, he focused on keeping the plane together, which, miraculously, was still just about holding up. After the heat from the fire, freezing wind was now an issue. Davidson, the wireless operator, who was on his first operation, had been hit in the blast and his face was badly burned: Rivaz describes putting his fingers in his mouth and breathing on them to try to keep them warm. The wind, too, had blown away the Whitley's maps. So, having dropped their bombs (Cheshire was not going home without fulfilling his mission), getting the aircraft back involved five hours of flying purely on memory, instinct and good fortune. It was a miraculous return and for his efforts Cheshire was awarded the DSO (Distinguished Service Order), the first junior officer in Bomber Command to be decorated at this level since the beginning of the war.

Promoted to flying officer (and to flight lieutenant six months later), Cheshire was moved to 35 Squadron, where he had a new plane to master: the Halifax. It was a bigger, better, more sophisticated plane but one still relatively hot off the production line and still in need of fine-tuning. Cheshire didn't fly a mission in one until April 1941 and when problems with the undercarriage were discovered, he was seconded, along with a fellow pilot, G. S. Williams, for Atlantic ferrying duties. There followed a journey by boat to Canada and a confused arrival in Montreal, where no one seemed to know what they should be doing. Put on standby, Cheshire and Williams headed for New York.

Here, among the days of partying, Cheshire met the American actress Constance Binney. Older than Cheshire and twice divorced, she had found fame during the silent movie era. The two quickly hit it off and were swiftly engaged; despite his parents' wishes, they were married on

15 July. Six days into the whirlwind romance, Cheshire was heading back to the UK, his wife set to follow him.

Returning to base to find the Halifax in better working order, Cheshire continued his raids – Berlin (three times), Cologne, Karlsruhe, Duisberg and Gelsenkirchen were just some of his targets in the coming weeks. At the end of August, Cheshire found himself taken off 'ops', his second tour complete (the longer a tour went on, so the theory went, the less the chance of survival). Cheshire was promoted to squadron leader and flight commander, but would rather have been back flying missions. He did, though, take the chance to write a book about his experiences: *Bomber Pilot* would become a bestseller.

After a brief period with 1652 Conversion Flight at RAF Marston Moor – during which he took part in Bomber Command's Millennium campaign of attacks by 1,000 aircraft – Cheshire was promoted to Wing Commander and became the youngest commanding officer of 76 Squadron on his third tour. Here, Cheshire showed great leadership, not only boosting the morale of the men under him at a time when their Halifax planes continued to be temperamental, but getting stuck into the mechanics of making them better flying machines. He completed his third tour successfully and in March 1943 became group captain at RAF Marston Moor: he was a bombing chief at the age of just twenty-five.

It was a considerable honour, but Cheshire missed operational duties and was desperate to get back into the air again. The opportunity came up when a vacancy appeared as commander of the celebrated Squadron 617. Cheshire's delight was matched by his wife Constance's disappointment at her husband being away and putting himself in danger again. The squadron had previously been under the command of Wing Commander Guy Gibson, set up to attack the dams of the Ruhr. The squadron flew Lancaster bombers and by the time of Cheshire's command a new weapon was being developed in the shape of Tallboy, a huge bomb that worked by burying itself into the ground and exploding beneath its target. Using the newly developed Stabilized Automatic

Bomb Sight (SABS), these could in theory be dropped with precision from a height of 13,000 feet.

As Cheshire started his command, it was clear the squadron's bombing was not as accurate as it could have been. The answer, developed by Cheshire, was for marker planes to fly in low and, essentially, lay down a pyrotechnic guide for the other Lancasters to aim at. On 7 February 1944, Cheshire put the plan into action on a bombing raid on Limoges. Piloting one of the advance planes, Cheshire flew in low – 'almost scraped the factory roof' was how one observer put it – and laid his markers. The Lancaster bombers were called in, with Cheshire's markings guiding them to a perfect hit.

More attacks followed using the new system, including factories at Albert, St-Etienne-la-Ricamarie, Clermont-Ferrand and Bergerac. Cheshire's marking role saw him switch planes to the Mosquito, lighter and faster, both of which qualities were crucial when flying in so low. On 22 April, the squadron took part in a huge raid on Munich, with 617 teaming up with 83 and 97 Squadrons to form a fleet of some 250 Lancaster bombers. Cheshire in his Mosquito was marker leader. It was both a daring raid and an extremely dangerous one – Cheshire found himself taking the plane straight down from 5,000 feet at speeds touching 480mph to set his markers. The flames created by the bombing could be seen from hundreds of miles away.

On 13 June, Cheshire led an attack on the German fleet at Le Havre. The ships, rather than being spread out between three ports, as they should have been, were temporarily crammed into one – Le Havre. In total 200 Lancasters took part in the attack: their precisely dropped Tallboys did the necessary damage. The raids continued, culminating in an attack on Mimoyecques in the region of Pas-de-Calais in northern France on 6 July, home of one of Germany's V-weapons sites. As with many other of the 617 attacks, it was almost routine in its success, but turned out to be significant for another reason: it was the end of Cheshire's fourth tour and the last of the hundred sorties he had flown over the previous four years.

When Leonard Cheshire's Victoria Cross was announced in September 1944, *Tatler* put him on the front cover and hailed him as 'the greatest bomber pilot in the world'. The *Evening Standard* concurred, calling him 'the greatest bomber pilot of them all'. Back at his old school, Stowe, his former headmaster declared a school holiday in honour of his achievements.

Cheshire's war was almost over. He took a placement in India with Air Command South East Asia (ACSEA). This did not go down well with Constance, who returned to New York. Barely had she arrived before she became seriously ill, and Cheshire flew to the USA to be with her. He felt bad about leaving his post in India, but he knew he should be with his wife. A position was found for him as part of the RAF delegation in Washington, allowing him to stay on in the country. Cheshire and Constance would divorce in 1951, with Cheshire remarrying in 1959 (his second wife was the humanitarian Sue Ryder).

In mid-July 1945, the US successfully tested an atomic bomb at Alamogordo, New Mexico. Two weeks later, Cheshire found himself on the tiny Western Pacific island of Tininan as preparations got underway to use the weapon against the Japanese. He was there as the British observer, to watch the atomic bomb in action. On 9 August he was taken up in one of the American B-29s en route to Japan. The original target was Kokura, but cloud cover meant a switch to a second target: Nagasaki. Cheshire watched from the bomber as the bomb was dropped.

In his biography of Cheshire, Richard Morris wrote:

> When Cheshire turned to face it, the fireball had already risen several thousand feet. Dust and smoke rocketed heavenward, blooming like some 'large piece of silk that had been compressed and then suddenly released, just expanding and unwrapping and unrolling' . . . Cheshire was bewitched by the symmetry of the ascending cloud. He sketched it. At its base was a boiling blackness: above, a turbulent stem of smoke, ash and dust which had an 'evil kind of luminous quality', not white, 'the colour of sulphur'.[4]

After the war, Cheshire, like so many, found it difficult to adjust to normal life. He tried to do something about this, setting up VIP (Vade in Pacem), a community where people could live and work together, both helping those who had fought in the war and trying to recapture some of the communal spirit that had seen them win it. It was a laudable idea, but arguments among those living there and financial difficulties brought the project down. He sold most of the estate of Le Court, a Victorian mansion in Hampshire that he had bought for the project, keeping the house and little else.

One of those who had been a member of VIP before its disbandment was Arthur Dykes. Dykes was dying of cancer and, having no home to go to, Cheshire took him in. Almost by chance, he had found a new purpose and he nursed Dykes until he died. This led to Cheshire wondering if there were others in a similar position who also needed help. It became clear that there were. Soon, more patients arrived, those suffering with TB, with disabilities, those who were dying. So, too, came people who wanted to help. Having been empty for so long, Le Court was suddenly full and thriving. Cheshire's charity work, which would dominate the second half of his life, had begun.

GENERAL SIR WALTER CONGREVE VC AND
MAJOR WILLIAM CONGREVE VC

Introduced by Michael Whitehall and Jack Whitehall

This is a very touching story about a father and son which particularly resonated with us, as they, like us, ended up 'working' together, although in their case in much more extreme and dangerous circumstances. We both identified with the fact that they clearly enjoyed each other's company and spent a lot of time together, and even when circumstances kept them apart they kept in touch daily, just as we do today. An inspiring story of courage and bravery, Walter and William Congreve, father and son, are a shining example to us all.

For a father and son to be awarded the Victoria Cross is exceptional. It has happened just three times since the introduction of the award: Major (later General) Charles Gough (1857) and his son, Major (later Brigadier General) John 'Johnnie' Gough (1903); Lieutenant (later Field Marshal Lord) Frederick Roberts (1858) and his son, Lieutenant Frederick 'Freddy' Roberts (1899); and Captain (later General) Walter Congreve (1899) and his son, Major William 'Billy' Congreve (1916). Tragically, in each case the son met an untimely end. Freddy Roberts and Billy Congreve were awarded their VCs posthumously, while Johnnie Gough was killed visiting trenches in 1915.

The last father and son to be awarded the Victoria Cross hailed from a family that was synonymous with the British Army. Sir William Congreve (1742–1814) had revolutionised British artillery through a reform of gunpowder production and storage. His son, also Sir William (1772–1828), was the pioneer of the famous 'Congreve Rockets' of the Napoleonic Wars, a weapon immortalised in the American national anthem.* Subsequent generations served in the 3rd Light Dragoons and 9th Foot. Walter, born on 20 November 1862, was always destined for military service. He joined the Rifle Brigade at the comparatively late age of twenty-three and was immediately nicknamed 'Squibs' in reference to the rocket of his illustrious ancestor.

Walter stood out as a 'true iron man' in an army that prided itself on physical and mental toughness. His wife remembered Walter's 'great dislike of luxury of any sort. Dislike is too mild a word – he had a horror of it. A meal in a smart restaurant was a misery to him.' His fit, wiry frame concealed the fact that he suffered from chronic asthma and he was prone to severe bouts of bronchitis. But he regarded the handicap, which would have barred him from entry into the modern military, as a challenge that could be overcome 'by sheer force of will'. His capacity for pushing himself through pain was legendary and drew the quiet admiration of officers and men.

Walter was a keen sportsman and was particularly fond of football. In 1895 he played in a notorious game between the officers of the 4th Battalion, the Rifle Brigade and 2nd King's Own Scottish Borderers. It was described at the time as 'a spirited and sporting football match', but a spectator remembered, 'Spirited the play certainly was, for the charging which took place would have struck dumb with horror the manager of a present-day professional football team'. In the second half, 'the charging became even more vigorous still, and the ground at times presented the appearance of a battlefield, which roused the spectators to a high pitch of

---

* 'And the rockets' red glare, the bombs bursting in the air'. The lyrics are a reference to the bombardment of Baltimore during the war of 1812.

enthusiasm'. The crowd was 'as pleased when one of their own officers was "grassed" as they were when one of their opponents took a toss'. The Rifle Brigade eventually emerged with a 2–1 victory.

At the outbreak of the Boer War (1899–1902), Walter was posted to the 2nd Battalion, the Rifle Brigade in South Africa, Unfortunately, upon arrival in the country he discovered that the unit he was meant to join was trapped in the besieged garrison town of Ladysmith. Without a post, Congreve attached himself to the headquarters of the British commander General Sir Redvers Buller VC and was given the unfancied position of press censor.

Buller commanded the Natal Field Force which was marching to lift the siege of Ladysmith. The Boers, led by future president of South Africa Louis Botha, intended to block the advance and had dug in on the far bank of the Tugela River opposite the village of Colenso. It was an extremely strong defensive position. But Buller, conscious that every day wasted brought the garrison of Ladysmith closer to starvation, could not afford to delay. He had little choice but to make an immediate attack. A frontal assault over the narrow fords that crossed the river was a daunting task and Buller called upon his artillery to soften up the enemy lines. Unfortunately, the gunners were deceived by Boer dummy trenches dug along high ground and directed their fire against this empty position. It inflicted virtually no casualties on the defenders, who were concealed along the riverbank, and merely alerted them that an attack was imminent.

On the day of the assault, Buller ordered Colonel Charles Long of the Royal Artillery to bring his guns forward to provide close-range support for the infantry. Long was an unpopular officer. He was notoriously arrogant and, although known for his physical bravery, his conduct in battle was often reckless. At 6 a.m. on 15 December he rode at the head of 14th Battery and 66th Battery as they trotted forward to take position. Unfortunately, Long seriously miscalculated his ranges. He later claimed that he had intended to come into action between 2,000 and 2,500 yards away from the Boer line, but that he had misjudged the distance due to the deceptive atmospherics of South Africa. Others felt that his impetuosity had got the better of him and that he had rushed ahead without any care for the consequences. Whatever the cause, he had gone too far forward and deployed in open ground approximately 1,200 yards from a Boer earthwork known as Fort Wylie.

The Boer riflemen at Fort Wylie had been lying in ambush awaiting the British infantry to march into range. The sudden appearance of Long's guns was an unexpected gift and they immediately opened fire. Both batteries were swept by fire as they unlimbered. 66th Battery managed to deploy with only a few casualties among the horses, but 14th Battery was flayed by fire. Several men were killed and two limbers were brought to a stumbling halt as their teams were shot down. Nevertheless, all twelve guns managed to get into action and valiantly returned fire. But the contest was an unequal one. Although the Boer riflemen were firing at long range, they compensated for diminished accuracy with sheer volume of bullets. A Boer 75mm gun added its weight to the action and fired with 'great accuracy'. Casualties swiftly mounted. Colonel Long was cut down by shrapnel and severely wounded. Moments later his second in command was disabled by a rifle bullet. One gun of 14th Battery was wrecked by a direct hit from a Boer shell. By 0700hrs, it was clear the position was untenable. Third in command Major C. W. Balward ordered the surviving gunners to cease fire and fall back. He envisaged this as a temporary move and gave no orders to spike the guns to disable them. The weapons were abandoned in open ground.

The British were on the brink of a military disaster. The Royal Artillery regarded their guns with the same gravitas that the infantry did their battle standards. To allow the enemy to seize a single gun was an intolerable disgrace. Yet at Colenso *twelve* guns were lying abandoned in the field and at risk of capture. Furthermore, Long's batteries represented more than a quarter of the Natal Field Force's total artillery strength. For moral and practical reasons, the guns had to be recovered.

General Buller took charge of the rescue operations. Walter Congreve accompanied his commander as they approached the site of the disabled batteries. Even though the headquarters party was about 2,000 yards distant from enemy lines, it was far from safe. Buller was struck by a spent shrapnel ball, a Royal Army Medical Corps officer standing between Buller and Congreve was killed by a sniper, and Walter's walking cane was shot out of his hand. But the fire directed at the distant officers paled in comparison to the storm of lead that swept the ground between British lines and the abandoned guns. It was clear that the extraction of the batteries would be a Herculean challenge. As Captain Harry Schofield of the Royal Artillery assembled the horses and limber teams, Buller turned to his staff and said, 'Some of you go and help'. Walter Congreve and Lieutenant Frederick Roberts, the latter the only son of Field Marshal Lord Roberts VC, stepped forward without hesitation.

The officers and artillery teams rode into a hail of fire. Congreve recalled what happened next:

I have never seen, even at field fire, bullets fly thicker. All one could see was little tufts of dust all over the ground, and one heard a whistling noise and a 'phut' where they hit, and an unceasing rattle of musketry somewhere in front. My first bullet went through my left sleeve and just made the point of my elbow bleed; next a clod of earth caught me no end of a smack on the other arm; then my horse got one; then my right leg one, my horse another and that settled us, for he plunged and I fell about a hundred yards short of the guns we were going to. A little nullah* was close by, and into that I hobbled and sat down. It was not much shelter, however, and I had not been in it a minute before another bullet hit my toe, went into the welt, travelled up and came out at the toe-cap two inches from end of toe. It did not scratch me even, but I shifted my quarters to a better place.[1]

---

* A dry watercourse that only runs during heavy rain.

Congreve's leg wound was painful but missed his major arteries. The bullet had struck his shin about three inches below his knee, torn through his leg and exited from the back of his calf. Fortunately, a medical officer, Major William Babtle, had ridden forward to the nullah to assist the wounded and dressed Congreve's injured leg. While Congreve was being treated, Schofield managed to limber up two guns and drag them back to British lines.

Congreve was desperate to know the fate of Freddy Roberts, who he had last seen 'cantering alongside those limbers, laughing and talking and slapping his leg with his stick as though we were on the Mall at Peshawur again'. Peering over the banks of the nullah – which was only three feet high and constantly being struck by bullets – he saw the gravely wounded Roberts lying about twenty yards short of the guns. Despite his own injuries, Congreve insisted on going out to rescue his friend. Hobbling as best he could on a 'very stiff and painful leg', he managed to reach Roberts and called for help to carry him to safety. Three officers who were sheltering in the nullah ran out and the four men managed to carry Freddy into cover.

Although relatively safe from Boer fire, the survivors endured an ordeal from the elements. Congreve recalled:

> We lay in the donga from eleven to four-thirty, no water, not a breath of air, no particle of shade, and the sun which I have never felt hotter even in India; a knife could not be held in a bare hand. It was the most beastly day I ever spent, and seemed interminable, and what it must have been for the badly wounded I hardly like to think . . . My jacket was taken to shade Freddy's head, and what with blood and dirt I was a pretty object by the time I got out.[2]

Three more attempts were made to retrieve the guns over the course of the day, but all of them failed, with severe loss of life. As dusk fell over the battlefield, the Boers came forward and captured the remaining artillery pieces. It was the worst loss of guns suffered by the British in battle since the Napoleonic Wars. The Boers discovered Congreve and his companions in the nullah but, as he and Roberts were wounded, the victors allowed them to be returned to the British lines rather than taken prisoner.

Sadly, Freddy, mortally wounded, died on 17 December 1899. Yet he and Walter's efforts were not entirely in vain and had resulted in the recovery of two guns. For their valiant attempts to rescue the artillery, Congreve, Roberts and Schofield were awarded the Victoria Cross.* Corporal George Nurse and Private George Ravenhill, who were part of Schofield's limber teams, received the same award.† Major William Babtle was also awarded the Victoria Cross for tending the wounded under fire.

In keeping with his ascetic character, Congreve attached little importance to his Victoria Cross and despised the 'celebrityship' that was associated with it. He was outspoken in his opinion of the award and believed, 'I should give none to officers on the supposition that they all deserve them, and are only doing their duty, but to NCOs [non-commissioned officers] and men only. My views are not likely to be adopted.'[3] Later in the war he wrote admiringly of the men under his command:

> Every day the Mounted Infantry do things far more deserving of the VCs than anything anyone did at Colenso. Every time they go out scouting they go in cold blood, with their lives in their hands, for every tree and stone may have a bullet behind it, and yet they go

---

* An interesting controversy surrounded the award of the Victoria Cross to Harry Schofield. He was initially awarded the Distinguished Service Order, while Congreve and Roberts received the VC, even though all three had been part of the same effort to recover the guns. In some ways, Schofield had done more, for it was under his direction that two guns were limbered up and brought back to British lines. A technicality was to blame for the differing awards. It was argued that, because Congreve and Roberts had volunteered to go to the guns, whereas Schofield had been ordered to do so, the latter was only eligible for the lesser award of the Distinguished Service Order. This injustice was noted at the War Office and led to a controversy that went to the very top of the British Army, ultimately involving both the Commander-in-Chief and the Secretary of State. It was not resolved until August 1901. Congreve played a key part in this process and it was his definitive account of the incident that convinced the War Office that Schofield deserved the Victoria Cross.

† George Ravenhill was incorrectly named as 'Charles Ravenhill' in his VC citation.

quite cheerily and nearly every day someone of them gets killed or fearfully wounded. I would give them all VCs. Grand, dirty, thieving fellows they are, but I admire them more than all the VCs in the British Army.[4]

As the war dragged into its second full year, Congreve found the guerrilla fighting 'depressing', and felt British scorched-earth tactics were counter-productive: 'I feel, though, were I a Dutchman and saw my home laid waste, I should not come in and make peace, but stay out and shoot all I could.'[5]

One of his few pleasures in the period was writing letters to friends and family. He took particular delight in writing to his children, especially his eldest son, William, whom he called 'Bildie'. Billy, as he was always known, had been born in 1891 and shared a lively correspondence with his father on the events of the war and the wildlife of South Africa. He was a restless child who longed to follow in his father's footsteps by joining the Rifle Brigade. Billy found life at Eton tedious and was a decidedly average scholar. He required the services of a crammer to pass the entrance exam to Sandhurst, but once there he excelled and came second in his class. To the delight of his father, Billy was commissioned into the 3rd Battalion, the Rifle Brigade in 1911.

Both Congreves travelled to France at the outbreak of the First World War. Walter commanded 18th Brigade and Billy marched with 3rd Rifle Brigade. Both father and son saw much intense action in 1914 and 1915 and distinguished themselves as officers. Despite the pressures of war, they maintained a close relationship, it being noted by an unnamed officer of the 1st Battalion, the Rifle Brigade that 'Father and son were particularly devoted, and seldom failed to write to one another on days upon which they were unable to meet.'[6]

Walter's iron resolve was demonstrated throughout the first years of the war and earned him the nickname 'Old Concrete' among his soldiers. He was a firm believer that officers should understand the hardships endured by the men and frequently visited the front line. He summed up his approach to command as: 'Be just, yet severe, never overlook a fault, yet be human. Keep up your dignity, but at the same time enter into your men's joys and sorrows and be their friend. See to their comforts before your own, which entails knowing what they should receive in rations, clothing, etc.' His approach won the admiration of his soldiers. Congreve's ability was also recognised by senior command and he was promoted to command 6th Division in February 1915, and then XIII Corps in November of the same year. Walter found the later promotion bittersweet as it separated him from the soldiers who he had, in some cases, commanded since the very start of the war.* He confessed, 'Dear, dirty fellows, how I do hate leaving them all the discomforts and dangers of those parts.† If only I could have brought them with me.' The feeling was mutual. Billy witnessed his father's farewell address to 6th Division and recalled: 'I was filled with pride and then almost reduced to tears when hundreds and hundreds of men rushed out along the road and cheered him – *real* cheering. It made me quite miserable and I think he nearly wept – lieutenant-generals can weep!'[7]

While his father was earning promotion, Billy had established a reputation as an outstanding young officer. He was famous for maintaining an ice-cold calm no matter how hot the fighting became. Although he served as a staff officer, Billy was never far from the front line and was drawn towards action like a moth to a flame. His father did not approve of such adventures and he felt it 'very wrong of him to be out on such work' but softened the criticism by adding, 'bless him'. He was awarded the Military Cross and the *légion d'honneur* for bravery during the fighting at Hooge in September 1915, and had been mentioned in dispatches three times by the end of that year.

---

* 18th Brigade, which Congreve had commanded at the outbreak of war, was part of 6th Division.

† Congreve refers here to leaving 6th Division in the Ypres Salient. This was a notoriously 'active' sector characterised by ceaseless sniping, shellfire and trench raids.

Yet his outward calm masked inner fire. Billy was appalled by the sight of ruined towns and pitiful refugees. He despised the Germans for starting the war and was enraged by their use of poison gas at the Second Battle of Ypres in 1915. Some idea of the depth of his feelings can be gathered from events that occurred in December 1915. He planned 'a gorgeous Boche strafe for Xmas Day – just to show him how much we can really "hate"'.* But his plans came to naught, for on Christmas Eve: 'a wire came in from the division this morning, saying: "No action to be taken by us on Xmas Day which is likely to provoke retaliation on the part of the Germans." Was *ever* such an order given before? I expect the corps commander† is leaving off trousers and putting on skirts.'

However, Congreve's disappointment was short-lived. Although he was especially annoyed at this 'awful rot', he consoled himself with the fact that his artillery plans 'will do for New Year's Day!'.

One of Billy's most famous escapades occurred in early April 1916. The 67th Brigade was engaged in ferocious fighting around the St Eloi mine craters. The sector was notorious for its underground war as British and German tunnelled beneath the battlefield and planted vast mines to destroy the trenches above. The resulting craters became the focus of incessant combat.

On 3 April, the brigade was fighting for control of a position known as Crater No. 5. Congreve observed the position and noted that some Germans had hoisted an empty sandbag on the end of a stick and were waving it from side to side. This appeared to be a sign of surrender, but Germans elsewhere in the crater were still firing furiously. Congreve surmised that some of the garrison wanted to surrender, while others were determined to carry on fighting. Having gathered a small party of an officer and four men, he decided to investigate further. The advance was nerve-wracking and Congreve 'expected a bullet' at any moment. Some

---

* Congreve refers here to the fact that artillery bombardment was known as 'hate'.

† Lieutenant General H. D. Fanshawe, V Corps.

rifle shots were directed at the party but all went high. Billy reached the lip of the crater unharmed and peered inside, expecting to find a group of broken Germans:

> Imagine my surprise and horror when I saw a whole crowd of armed Boches! I stood there for a moment feeling a bit sort of shy, and then I levelled my revolver at the nearest Boche and shouted 'Hands up, all the lot of you!' A few went up at once, and then a few more and then the lot; and I felt the proudest fellow in the world as I cursed them.[8]

Billy's audacious bluff was a success. He and his small party captured five German officers and seventy-seven men, and ensured that Crater No. 5 was taken. He was recommended for the Victoria Cross but was eventually awarded the Distinguished Service Order, which was presented to him on 16 May 1916. The early summer was a happy time for the young officer. His wedding to Pamela Maude came a mere fortnight after receiving the DSO.

As June progressed, the British Army prepared for its greatest offensive of the war so far. The Battle of the Somme was imminent. Walter Congreve's promotion had placed him in charge of XIII Corps and he now faced the daunting task of preparing the formation for an assault on the German line at the Somme. Walter worked hard to ensure his attacking divisions were trained, equipped and properly prepared. His meticulous approach was frowned upon by some officers. His superior, General Sir Henry Rawlinson, of Fourth Army, was especially critical and bluntly told Congreve he did not believe he was fit to command. But Walter stuck to his principles and their value was proved on 1 July 1916. On the blackest day for the British Army, only Congreve's XIII Corps achieved significant success. His leading divisions pierced the German line and captured all their objectives. The German defenders were driven back in disarray and there was an opportunity to drive on much further. Perhaps even capturing the undefended village of Longueval and the lush woods of Mametz. It has been claimed that Congreve wanted to press forward and telephoned Rawlinson to ask for permission. Rawlinson refused. The opportunity vanished and in the coming weeks the British Army would suffer tens of thousands of casualties trying to capture positions that were there for the taking on 1 July.

By the middle of July the village of Longueval – now reduced to smouldering rubble and shell holes – had become a key British objective. Walter continued to direct the operations of XIII Corps and received reinforcements that included Billy's 76th Brigade. Father and son had no time to comment on the unusual twist of fate that had brought them together. The Battle of the Somme was raging all along the line. The fighting was incessant. The air was thick with bullets and the ground shuddered under the impact of artillery bombardments. Billy Congreve was at the heart of this maelstrom; issuing commands, writing orders, carrying out reconnaissance and even assisting the wounded. He was continuously engaged from 6 July and found himself 'suffering severely from gas and other shell effects'. Observers noted he was 'pale and drawn' from lack of sleep.

In the early hours of 20 July 1916, 76th Brigade attacked Longueval once more. In the darkness the assault miscarried. Units advanced piecemeal and were mown down by German fire, not to mention the 'friendly fire' of their own machine guns which mistook them for the enemy. As dawn broke, Congreve went forward with a party of officers to reorganise the line. The battlefield was a labyrinth of shell holes, devastated trenches and hastily dug foxholes. Proper reconnaissance was vital in this maze and Congreve spent some time seeking out a suitable vantage point. He eventually took up position in an abandoned German gun pit and began studying the enemy lines with his binoculars. A nearby officer, Major G. C. Stubbs of the 2nd Suffolks Battalion, had come forward with Congreve and suddenly felt anxious for him. He warned Billy to keep his head down for fear of the enemy snipers that infested the area. Congreve responded with a 'small laugh' and returned to his reconnaissance.

After completing his study of enemy lines, Congreve climbed from the gun pit and entered a newly constructed British trench. He began to talk with the men, but as Sergeant Sheen recalled: 'Just as he spoke the word "work" he was hit. He stood for half a second and then collapsed. He never moved or spoke, and he was dead in a few seconds.'

The admiration the officers and men of 76th Brigade had for Billy Congreve was proven in the aftermath of his death. They made a 'spontaneous request' that he be nominated for the Victoria Cross for his consistent courage during the Battle of the Somme. The award was confirmed 'For most conspicuous bravery during a period of fourteen days preceding his death in action.' His wife Pamela, pregnant with their child, received the award on 1 November 1916.

The death of Billy was a terrible blow to his father. Walter learned of the news amid battle and had no time to grieve. An observer remembered: 'When I told him what had happened he was absolutely calm to all outward appearances, and, after a few seconds of silence, said quite calmly, "He was a good soldier"[9]. In private the emotion was raw. He saw his son in the mortuary on the day of his death:

> I saw him and was struck by his beauty and strength of face . . . I felt inspired by his look and know that he is 'helping' me, as he used to say, and that he will always do so. I never felt so proud of him as I did when I said goodbye to him. A lot of flowers were sent by kind people, amongst them wild mallows from the fighting line by some of the men. I myself put in his hand a posy of poppies, cornflowers and daisies . . . and with a kiss I left him . . . I know I shall see him again.[10]

The war was not over for Walter Congreve. He served with distinction as XIII Corps Commander until he contracted cholera from contaminated water in August 1916. After a period of recuperation, he returned to command and led the Corps through the Battle of Arras (April–May

1917). In June 1917 Congreve was seriously wounded during a visit to the trenches. A contemporary noted: 'His personal courage was extraordinary. He was always amongst the front-line troops, and was a magnificent example to the men of a complete disregard of shelling or any other form of Boche hatred.' Unfortunately, his luck ran out and he was caught in a shell blast which virtually severed his left hand at the wrist and left him 'a good deal cut and knocked about'. An officer who was with him at the time bound his wrist with a handkerchief as they went to the first aid post. Congreve returned it 'and apologised for making it such a mess!'. Walter's hand had to be amputated and was eventually replaced with a hook. He was the third in the family to be afflicted this way: Lt. Col. Ralph Congreve lost his left arm at the Battle of Almanza in 1707, and Lt. William Congreve lost his left hand in 1730. The iron resolve of the Congreve family was in evidence soon after the incident. Walter wrote to his commander, General Sir Henry Horne, beginning the letter, 'DEAR GENERAL, – Barring the loss of a left hand I am much as usual.'[11] Recovery kept Congreve in England for the remainder of 1917.

Walter returned to France in January 1918 and commanded VII Corps. By now his asthma was crippling and frequently confined him to bed. Yet, despite his failing health, he commanded his formation with courage and skill when it was struck by the great *Kaiserschlacht* (Kaiser's Battle) Spring Offensive – Germany's last-gasp effort to win the war – on 21 March 1918. VII Corps conducted a desperate fighting retreat over the coming week. Congreve's conduct drew praise and eventually the German advance was brought to a standstill.

It was to be the last major act of Congreve's war. In May 1918, General Headquarters decided to relieve Congreve of command due to his failing health. Congreve thought 'it is all nonsense' and was eager to continue active service, but his friends agreed that the hardships of war and the loss of Billy 'had told on him'. He returned to England with honour and was promoted to full General and knighted for his services. He spent the last years of his life as Governor of Malta, where he found the warm climate and the sea breeze eased his asthma. He died in 1927 and was buried at sea off the coast of the island.

Walter spoke little of his lost son. In the 1920s, biographer L. G. Thornton asked him for an epitaph for Billy. Walter replied, 'He would have made a good Rifleman.'[12] For a man who was so deeply proud of his regiment, there could be no higher praise.

TOM CREAN AM[1]

Introduced by Bear Grylls

The story of Tom Crean is both incredibly moving and inspiring, and part of its magic is because his conflict was with the raw power of Mother Nature rather than against the forces of mankind. Tom faced the worst conditions imaginable, and an epic march across the frozen Antarctic wasteland, in a time when Antarctica had never been explored and from which there was no hope of rescue. He made the extraordinarily brave decision to strike out alone for a supply depot in an inspiring attempt to save his companions. He had two biscuits and a little chocolate to sustain him and the bare minimum of supplies, and he faced the overwhelming likelihood of death. Yet his motivation to save the lives of his friends drove him on against all odds. He finally succeeded, and showed, once again, just what the human spirit is capable of when the odds are heavily stacked against you. I have no doubt that you will be in turn horrified and amazed by his humbling story of courage and determination.

In the entrance hall of Dulwich College in south London sits a small wooden boat. Measuring just seven metres long, to the untrained eye the open boat might seem remarkably nondescript. Indeed, every time the school bell goes for a change of lesson, the present generation of pupils file past the boat, giving it barely a second glance; to many it was just part of the school furniture.

The *James Caird*, as the boat is called, might look ordinary, but the journey it took in the South Atlantic was one of the remarkable sea travels of all time. On Easter Monday, 24 April 1916, the boat set out from Elephant Island in the direction of South Georgia, some 800 miles away across some of the most violent, turbulent sea passages anywhere in the world. It was the last throw of the dice of the failed Imperial Trans-Antarctic or Endurance Expedition that had begun two years earlier. Led by Ernest Shackleton, the expedition's ship, the *Endurance*, had become first stuck in the Weddell Sea pack ice, and then after drifting on the ice for several months, finally sank. The crew made it in three lifeboats to Elephant Island, where the men were faced with the choice of waiting – more in hope than expectation – that a passing ship would rescue them. The alternative, which Shackleton eventually decided upon, was to take one of the boats to South Georgia, where a call for rescue could be arranged.

It was far from the easy option. Shackleton selected five men to go with him: Frank Worsely, Jack Vincent, Timothy McCarthy, Chips McNeish and the Irishman Tom Crean. The journey, as Worsely describes it, was 'ordeal by water', with the boat battling waves that rose fifteen metres in height: 'These blue water hills in a very heavy gale move as fast as 27 statute miles an hour but striking the banks probably attain a speed of 60 miles. The impact of hundreds of tons of solid water at this speed can only be imagined.' Navigation was everything: such was the pull of the ocean's current that, get the direction fractionally wrong, and South Georgia would be overshot, with no way of tacking back and no further land for thousands of miles.

Conditions were appalling. Freezing temperatures and constant waves crashing over the boat led to the accumulation of ice; this had constantly to be chipped off to stop the vessel from becoming heavier and sinking. Eating and drinking was another challenge. Tom Crean, who acted as cook, had to double over the primus stove when he cooked as there wasn't the space to sit up straight; when eating, the men were similarly cramped, which made swallowing difficult. Not that the rations were anything to write home about: such was the swell that even experienced sailors such as Crean and Shackleton were affected; if that wasn't enough, hair from the rotting reindeer skin sleeping bags made its way into every meal, and the water supply, despite the best efforts, turned brackish.

That the *James Caird* made it to South Georgia is remarkable. But reaching land was not the end of the story: such was the ferocity of the weather that the boat landed on the opposite side of the island to the whaling station where rescue could be raised. Even though they had made it to land, the sea had not finished with the men. As they slept in a cave on the beach, decorated with fifteen-foot icicles, Crean who had been assigned the middle of the night watch, watched with horror as the boat slipped its moorings. Without thinking, he dived straight into the ice-cold water after the rope, up to his neck in the freezing sea before anyone stirred to help him.

The journey to the whaling station was a thirty-mile trek up and over the Allardyce range of mountains that dominated the centre of South Georgia at an average peak of 1,500 metres. As one account describes it, 'the rugged interior is a jumble of rocky cliffs, snow fields, treacherous crevasses and steep icy slopes'. The journey was a crossing that had never previously been attempted. Shackleton, Crean and Worsely took the journey on, a thirty-six-mile trek with the barest of equipment. Brass screws from the boat were hammered through the men's boots to act as crampons. A sledge made from scraps of wood had to be abandoned because it was too heavy. The three men had no tent or, indeed, any form of shelter; if they didn't reach the whaling station, there was no way they would survive.

Setting off at 2 a.m. in moonlight on 19 May 1916, the trio narrowly missed the edge of a huge crevasse as fog came down around dawn. The three men roped themselves together, Shackleton at the front, Crean in the middle and Worsely at the rear. There continued a deadly day of reaching one mountain peak after another. Visibility remained poor and such were the heights that the trio had to stop every twenty minutes, gasping for breath. As daylight began to fade, the men found themselves high up and facing a night of sub-zero temperatures without shelter (or sleeping bags, which they had abandoned with the sledge). The decision was made to abandon the toboggan down the glacier on which they were. Their solution was to coil the rope they had into a makeshift toboggan, the three of them clasping each other tightly as they hurled down at high speed. It was a risk they had to take, but one that came off. Luck was with them – not only did they land softly in deep snow, but soon after the moon rose, allowing them light to continue the journey through the night.

In honour of one of these three men who first crossed this spot, the place is today named Crean Glacier, a fitting testament to one of the more unsung heroes of Antarctic exploration. Crean, together with Shackleton and Worsely, eventually made it to the whaling station and were able to rescue first their companions from the *James Caird* and then the rest of the *Endurance* crew on Elephant Island. It was an epic journey, but such was the bravery of Tom Crean that it was just one adventure of many. Indeed, it was on an earlier expedition that Crean's heroics led to him being awarded the Albert Medal for courage – saving the life of a fellow explorer who would otherwise have undoubtedly perished but for Crean's bravery.

* * *

Thomas 'Tom' Crean's career in polar exploration began quite by chance. Born in the farming country of Gurtuchrane, near Annascaul, in County Kerry on 20 July 1877, he was one of ten children and grew up speaking Gaelic and English. At fifteen he left his rural childhood behind and enlisted in the Royal Navy. Having trained on HMS *Impregnable* at Devonport, Plymouth, he slowly made his way up the ranks via a series of ships; Boy First Class on HMS *Devastation*, ordinary seaman on HMS *Royal Arthur* and Able Seaman Crean on HMS *Defiance*. Promoted to

Petty Officer Second Class, Crean was assigned to HMS *Vivid*, HMS *Northampton* and then the torpedo vessel HMS *Ringarooma*.

Ringarooma was part of the Australia–New Zealand squadron and it was when the ship was in the New Zealand harbour of Lyttleton that opportunity arose for Crean. In late November 1901, the ship *Discovery* arrived in port. This was the vessel of Robert Falcon Scott and his forthcoming Antarctic expedition. Lyttleton was the ship's last port of call before heading for the White Continent, and as such the Admiralty had told both the *Ringarooma* and another squadron ship, HMS *Lizard*, to give *Discovery* whatever help she required in preparation for the expedition.

This work included sorting *Discovery*'s rigging and also finding the cause of an ongoing leak. Over the next few weeks, working parties from *Ringarooma* were regular visitors to *Discovery*. Crean, it appears, was part of this group and, as such, became acquainted with the ship, the mission and the crew. At this point, just days before the ship was due to leave, fate intervened in the form of *Discovery* seaman Harry J. Baker. Scott explained what happened in a letter to the Royal Geographical Society (who, together with the Royal Society, were behind the expedition): '[Baker] struck a Petty Officer and learnt from me that I could not afterwards keep him in the ship – in consequence of which he ran away. I immediately issued a reward for apprehension, but he has not yet been found.' History does not relate what became of Baker, but what happened to the vacancy he created is clear: Scott went to Captain Rich of *Ringarooma* for help and Crean volunteered to take Baker's place.

The first of Crean's Antarctic expeditions is the least well known of the three, though it laid the groundwork for much of what was to come. One such aspect was the creation of Hut Point, where *Discovery* landed in McMurdo Sound and would become both a key base for future expeditions and also play its role in Crean's subsequent mission. Perhaps most crucially, it gave Crean his first experience of Antarctica and allowed him to begin to build a wealth of knowledge and understanding of the continent and its conditions: interestingly, Crean would go on to spend more time on the ice and snow of Antarctica than either Scott or Shackleton. Crean was part of the team that for a brief while held the record for travelling further south than anyone had gone before; accompanying Lieutenant Michael Barne, the team had set out ahead of Scott, Shackleton and Edward Wilson, placing a line of supply depots for the trio to pick up on their journey back to the ship.

Scott had been impressed by Crean's contribution and had earmarked him for his next journey to the Antarctic. Following the expedition, Crean returned to naval service, first on HMS *Pembroke* and then HMS *Vernon*. Scott, meanwhile, spent the best part of a year writing his book, *The Voyage of the Discovery*. He sent a finished copy to every member of the ship's crew, but in Crean's copy placed an additional note, asking him to join Scott as coxswain. This he did on board HMS *Victorious*, HMS *Albemarle*, HMS *Essex* and HMS *Bulwark*. It was in 1909 that Scott decided the time was right to return to the Antarctic. He and Crean happened to be waiting for a train to London when Scott read the news of Shackleton's failed Nimrod Expedition (Shackleton had got closer than anyone to the South Pole before having to turn back). Running down the platform holding the newspaper he had just bought, Crean showed Scott the news, to which he replied, 'I think we'd better have a shot next.'

* * *

Scott's Terra Nova Expedition of 1910–13 was to succeed where Shackleton's mission had failed (he reached the South Pole, albeit one month after the Norwegian mission of Roald Amundsen). But it also tragically failed where Shackleton succeeded; as Shackleton later remarked to his wife Emily, 'a live donkey is better than a dead lion'. While Shackleton returned, defeated but alive, Scott succeeded in reaching the Pole but failed to live to tell the tale.

Crean's heroics on the expedition first came to light early on, during the setting up of One Ton Depot, one of the main supply points en route to the South Pole. On the way back to Hut Point with the ponies, Crean was with Lieutenant Henry 'Birdie' Bowers and Apsley Cherry-Garrard (who would later write about the expedition in his book *The Worst Journey in the World*). The three of them made it to the edge of the Great Ice Barrier (now called the Ross Ice Shelf) and onto the sea ice. Here they camped, only to wake in the middle of the night to discover that the ice had broken up, leaving them adrift on a thirty-foot floe, floating out towards sea in mist and darkness. There began a desperate attempt to jump from ice floe to ice floe to safety, together with their sledges and terrified ponies. Just to add to their problems, in the water between the floes appeared a succession of killer whales, creatures known to upend an ice floe in the hope of sending their prey into the water.

As the trio progressed across the floes, they got closer to the Barrier, which was by this point just that: a wall of ice some twenty feet high. It was at this point that Crean volunteered to go ahead and help. The other two watched as he continued his hazardous journey, until at last he came across a thicker ice floe, allowing him the opportunity, with the aid of a ski stick, to scramble up the Barrier face and get help. Although Crean had saved the day, he remained modest about his achievements. Frank Debenham, who wrote a book about Crean and spoke to him about the incident, recalled, 'As always, he made light of his feats in extricating himself from trouble and all I ever got out of him was, "Oh, I just kept going pretty lively, sorr, them killers wasn't too healthy company."'

Now the proper expedition to the South Pole began. The main polar party set off on 1 November 1911, traversing 400 miles across the Barrier to the foot of the Beardmore Glacier. Reaching this on 9 December, the remaining ponies were shot and the ongoing explorers continued by man-hauling. The Beardmore Glacier rises up to 3,000 metres, and this 120-mile rise is then followed by a final 350-mile stretch to reach the Pole. The expedition was now split into three teams of four: first one team headed back on 21 December and then on 3 January 1912,

168 miles from the Pole, Scott announced who would be going with him, and which team would head back. He chose Henry Bowers, Edgar Evans, Lawrence Oates and Edward Wilson to accompany him. Crean, along with William Lashly and Edward Evans, was to turn back.

For Crean and the others not chosen, so close to the goal, it was a heartbreaking moment. 'Poor old Crean wept,' Scott noted in his diary. But according to Michael Smith's biography of Crean, *An Unsung Hero*, the Irishman's tears were not just for himself. 'Many years later, Crean told members of his family that his tears were both for himself and for Scott, who he realised had taken a huge risk in adding an extra man to the polar party. With his experience of ice travel, it may well have struck Crean that Scott's decision smacked of desperation.'[2] Certainly, for many polar historians, the split of the teams into a five and a three was a fateful one.

Crean, Evans and Lashly now faced a demoralising 750-mile journey back to base. The fact that they were a man short made this difficult journey even harder: 'I soon realised that the ceding of one man from my party had been too great a sacrifice,' Evans later wrote, the only navigator among them. Evans, like Lashly, had been considered 'stale' by Scott after the previous two months' exhaustion; he, too, unbeknownst to any of them at the time, was already beginning to suffer from the early signs of scurvy.

Evans worked out that in order to get back on full rations they needed to travel at an average of seventeen miles a day (this while pulling a 180kg sledge). This meant a march of ten to thirteen hours solid, a length of time he attempted to mask by winding his watch forward an hour in the morning and setting it back again in the evening. Bad weather and snowblindness led to them veering off course, to the point that when they reached the start of the descent of the Beardmore, they were miles from where they should be and above the Shackleton Ice Falls. Deducing that it would take three additional days to track around them and that they didn't have the rations to do so, Evans made the decision they should take the risk of glissading down. Crean was unconvinced: 'Captain Scott would never do a damn fool thing like that,' he told Evans. 'Captain Scott is not here,' Evans replied. 'Now get on board.'

Just as Crean, Shackleton and Worsely would later do during the crossing of South Georgia, the slide into the unknown, at 60mph with no way of braking, was a huge risk. 'How we ever escaped entirely uninjured is beyond me to explain,' Evans later recalled. But escape they did, descending 2,000 feet in the process. The difficulty of the journey, however, refused to let up. Having reached one depot (Mount Darwin) and restocking, they found the way to the next one marked by huge crevasses. One gulf they crossed on a bridge of hard snow, which Crean described as being like 'the crossbar to the H of Hell'. So narrow was the bridge and so concerned were the men of it collapsing that they sat astride it, nervously inching their way across, the sledge precariously balanced on its apex.

Having made it down from the Glacier, the three men should have now reached the easiest part of the journey. Instead, the final stretch proved the most difficult of all. Evans now clearly had scurvy and was suffering badly. He was passing blood and no longer able to take his share of the sledge pulling, putting a greater burden on the other two in the process. Two days after passing One Ton Depot and with 100 miles still to go, Evans could no longer stand and had to be strapped to the sledge. The pace of the march was slowing: even discarding all but the most essential equipment, Crean and Lashly were unable to pull more than ten miles a day. Time and food were running out. Evans, now fading, told the others to leave him and save themselves. They disobeyed his orders and carried on, cutting their food ration in half.

On 18 February 1912, thirty-five miles from Hut Point, the men had to make a choice. In their present condition, it would take Crean and Lashly four or five days to get to Hut Point. They had enough food for three meals, which was enough to sustain them for less than half that time. Something had to give.

It was here that Crean stepped up to take the decision that would lead to him being awarded the Albert Medal. He volunteered to go on ahead alone, to raise the alarm, leaving Lashly behind to tend Evans. It was an all-or-nothing mission: as with the later trek across South Georgia with Shackleton, Crean had no shelter with him. He had nothing to help him navigate, and just three biscuits and two sticks of chocolate to sustain him. If he did not make it to Hut Point, he would not survive.

Setting out at ten in the morning, Crean walked for sixteen miles without a break. He stopped for five minutes, ate two of the biscuits and the chocolate, and carried on. By midnight he had made it to the edge of the Barrier. The sea was not firm enough to allow him to cut across it, so round the edge he went. He had his final biscuit and a piece of ice. Now the clock was really ticking. A blizzard was approaching and, as the wind picked up, Crean knew he had to reach the hut before it arrived. Stumbling on, he made it just in time, getting to the hut at 3.30 a.m., just as the storm whipped up. Within half an hour, the blizzard was in full flow and would continue all next day and well into the night. Inside the hut Crean found Dmitri, the Russian dog driver, and Edward Atkinson, the doctor. Once the blizzard had died down, they set out to find Lashly and Evans on 20 February. This they achieved, bringing them back to be reunited with Crean at the hut.

It was a remarkable escape, made possible solely by Crean's bravery, courage that would go on to be recognised once the tragic end of the expedition had been played out, Crean being part of the search team that discovered what had happened to Scott. Returning first to New Zealand and then back to Britain that summer, the surviving members of the expedition were invited to Buckingham Palace. Here, where everyone was given an Antarctic Medal, Crean and Lashly were also awarded the Albert Medal for their part in saving Evans' life. 'After a march of eighteen hours in soft snow', the citation read, 'Crean made his way to the hut, arriving completely exhausted. Fortunately Surgeon Edward L. Atkinson R.N., was at the hut with two dog teams and the dog attendant.

His party, on February 20th, effected the rescue of Lieutenant Evans and Lashly. But for the gallant conduct throughout of his two companions Lieutenant Evans would undoubtedly have lost his life.'

* * *

Crean's Antarctic exploits were not over: there was the small matter of his role in Shackleton's Endurance Expedition to come. But he declined a further expedition with Shackleton and, after a short return to the navy, was invalided out in 1920 after a fall.

Instead, Crean returned to Ireland. While others from the era of Antarctic exploration made their money from books and exhibitions and speaking events, Crean never talked of his exploits again. Whether that was modesty or an awareness of having been on Imperial expeditions in what was now a staunchly republican part of Ireland, Crean opened a pub, the South Pole Inn, and declined to speak about his adventures. He gave no interviews and, should anyone bring the topic up (people would travel long distances to the pub to try to talk to him), he would either change the topic of conversation or excuse himself.

Crean, now living a simple family life, died in hospital in 1938 of a perforated appendix, leaving behind his wife, Nell, and two daughters, Mary and Eileen. While Crean hasn't the recognised name of a Scott or a Shackleton, the naming of the Crean Glacier in South Georgia and Mount Crean in Antarctica are proof that his exploits are not forgotten; there is also a memorial to him in the church at Grytviken in South Georgia. His was a heroism of the quieter sort and one that, in its modesty, has a power all of its own.

LIEUTENANT MAURICE DEASE VC

Introduced by Will Greenwood MBE

A brisk one-minute walk would take me from my boyhood home to the Lady Statue, whose gaze directs the visitor along the Stonyhurst avenue, with its slight gradient undetectable to the casual visitor, but infamous to those generations of pupils who have battled along it in training for myriad sports. The vista from here never fails to drop the jaw and widen the eye of the newcomer, while swelling the heart and fervour of those who live, study and work here. Stonyhurst tradition has it that all those returning from trips, tours or matches should spontaneously break into a lusty rendition of Neidermeyer's Pater Noster, as their coach swings to the right onto the avenue to bring the College into view. When a tear pricks the eye of the Stonyhurst leaver, it is memories such as these which will cascade it down the cheek.

My roots at Stonyhurst were laid deep at an early age. My parents taught there for many years and my father, Richard, former England rugby captain, was bursar for a time also. Life at Stonyhurst is all-absorbing and not confined to the office and classroom, allowing plenty of opportunity for outside activities, particularly sport. Stonyhurst families not only work together, but play together, too, and this broadened and deepened their attachment to the school. It was on the fields of St Mary's Hall, the preparatory school to Stonyhurst, that my own rugby journey began.

Ninety years before my connection with Stonyhurst, Maurice Dease walked the same galleries, fields and pathways and I do not doubt for a second that he, too, would have been imbued with the same pride and enthusiasm shared by his linear pupil descendants. His portrait in the school seems to cast a caring watch upon them and they, in turn, are aware of him and of his fellows, who were also awarded the Victoria Cross. Pupils at Stonyhurst have a clear perception that they can be 'heroic' in the small events of everyday life, particularly in the service of others and, if their talents allow, in great things, too.

On the sunlit afternoon of 22 August 1914, men of A Company, 4th Battalion Royal Fusiliers, took the weight off their weary feet, unbuttoned jackets and webbing and relaxed in the Grand Place in the centre of the city of Mons. They were photographed as they did so, with the grainy image showing tired men, their hats pushed back from sweaty temples, chatting to mates through a haze of relaxing tobacco smoke, gazing ahead in unfocused, thoughtful stares or simply glancing in bemused fashion as the photographer wandered over from the crowd of inquisitive local inhabitants to capture the moment. Theirs had been a welcome reserved for heroes and people felt they could now go about their business confident that the German invader would be ousted from Belgium by these gritty, hardened professionals and driven without ceremony back to Germany.

The British High Command had been true to its word to have the bulk of the British Expeditionary Force (BEF) mobilised and transported to France within twelve days of the outbreak of hostilities and, to that point, the war for them had been a poor imitation of a summer holiday: journeys by boat and train, followed by a long walk in pleasant weather through beautiful countryside. And yet the *pavé* had played a discordant tune with men's feet as hobnails slipped between cobbles and blistered soles and heels, particularly of the reservists called back to the colours at the outset of war, sung painfully to the tunes drummed out by new boots.

The photograph taken that afternoon is an enduring, haunting image and begs the viewer to imagine the thoughts and hopes of these soldiers, who expected to engage at a moment's notice an enemy, whose strength they did not know, whose exact position had so far eluded their scouts and who had swept all before them since the invasion of Belgium had begun. History tells us that, before the bells of Mons had tolled out twenty-four hours, the death knell would have sounded for many of them.

Although he does not actually appear in the photograph, with them, and perhaps not far out of shot, would have been the commander of their machine-gun section, Lieutenant Maurice Dease. He and his men would play a prominent role in the events which were about to unfold, and his name would be etched deeply into the annals of the BEF. Dease did not stand on ceremony as a commissioned officer and certainly did not flinch from participating in the hard labour he often had to inflict on the fusiliers under his command. In fact, only a few hours before battle was joined, he was to be seen with sleeves rolled up filling sandbags alongside his men. This, and his affable sense of humour, which brightened many a sweaty, slogging route march, did not diminish his natural authority. In return, these hardened, gritty soldiers, many of whom were from a background of grinding poverty, held him in the highest esteem and affection.

On 28 September 1889, Maurice Dease was born to Edmund Fitzlawrence Dease and Katherine Dease (née Murray) in Gaulstown, County Westmeath. The Dease family were high society among the Irish Catholic elite and could boast an impressive lineage, with Maurice's grandfather being the Vice-Lieutenant of Cavan. For Maurice, early childhood was happy and comfortable, with plenty of opportunity for fun and adventure in and around their family residences. Keen on hunting and fishing, the young Maurice was also a proficient rider and owned a striking grey pony called Kitty.

At the age of nine, education in England beckoned and Maurice arrived at St Basil's, Frognal Hall, a preparatory school in Hampstead. There, he met a distant relative, Aidan Liddell, whose uncle had married Maurice's aunt, and they got along famously. Their educational paths would continue to cross[1]. We have a glimpse of the young Maurice's character and humour from a postcard sent home in October 1900, when he was eleven. His news is brief and mirrors the approach typical of a young boy preferring excitement with friends to mundane duties such as writing to father: 'Thank you very much for your letter and chocolates you sent me for my birthday. We played football yesterday morning and it was a very good game. I have very little news to tell you now as I told it all to mother yesterday. MD.'[2]

Maurice was very attached to his uncle Gerald Dease, who had served in the Royal Fusiliers and had reached the rank of major. As Gerald had no children, Maurice was heir to his Turbitston estate and there is no doubt that he was greatly influenced by his charismatic and accomplished relative.

In 1903, Maurice was sent to Stonyhurst College, run by the Society of Jesus, and met up once more with his friend Aidan Liddell, who had been a pupil there for two years. To avoid the attentions of the government of Elizabeth I, the College had been founded in 1593 at St Omer in France by Father Robert Persons SJ for the education of the sons of Catholic gentry and a grant from Philip II of Spain had given the establishment its primary impetus. Throughout its time on the Continent, the school had remained essentially English and, although often treated with suspicion, was held in affection by Louis XIV even when the armies of John Churchill, Duke of Marlborough, had repeatedly trodden on his military corns. Political and religious circumstances precipitated moves to Bruges, then Liège, before the French Revolution levered the community back onto English soil and into the beautiful countryside of the Ribble Valley in Lancashire. Stonyhurst Hall had been made available to the Jesuits by Thomas Weld, a former pupil and by the time of Maurice's arrival, the school had been in operation there for over a century.

Bleak on rainy days, stunningly beautiful in the sunshine of all seasons, Stonyhurst made a great impression on Maurice and he invested himself deeply in all aspects of its life. Proud of its long history, the school embraced the ideals of the nation, which were encapsulated in the words of General Sir Edward Bulfin, an Old Stonyhurst who had a distinguished career in the Great War. In a short preface to the *Stonyhurst War Record*, which was published in 1927 as a memoir to the Stonyhurst fallen, he writes: 'May I be allowed to suggest to those who follow after, a careful study of those words of the great Apostle: "Honour all men, love the brotherhood, fear God, honour the King." To my mind, these contain the essentials to make us worthy of Stonyhurst and citizens of our glorious Empire.'[3]

The school motto *Quant Je Puis* (As Much As I Can) demanded the best of effort in all things and, in the margin alongside the heading and the date, each piece of written work (studies, in Stonyhurst parlance) was opened with AMDG (*Ad Maiorem Dei Gloriam* – To the Greater Glory of God) and concluded with LDS (*Laus Deo Semper* – Praise God Always). The tradition exists to this day. Many of the staff were Jesuit priests and so daily Mass, night prayers and Benediction became routine for the boys at the school. In fact, contemporaries recalled a touching memory of Maurice: 'To see old Father Myers, then a man of no small weight, limping slowly along to say Mass, leaning on the arm of his favourite server, Maurice Dease, was an object lesson in the respectful and thoughtful sympathy of the right-minded boy for venerable old age.'

It was a measure of the boy and eventually the man. This brief glimpse into Maurice's education helps us to elucidate his character and perhaps allows us to crack the mask of the inscrutable look we witness in his portrait. Maurice had risen to the challenge of the Stonyhurst ethos in his everyday life as a pupil of the school and, imbued with this, was left with a profound conscience, an unswerving sense of duty and a deep regard for leadership in the service of others.

In June 1907, Maurice left Stonyhurst and, that September, entered the Army College, Wimbledon. From there, it was to Sandhurst, where he received his commission into the 4th Battalion, Royal Fusiliers (City of London Regiment), on 25 May 1910. Once his decision to join the army had been made, he could only have followed his beloved Uncle Gerald's footsteps and become a Royal Fusilier.

Maurice trained hard and drew the attention and accolade of his commanding officers. Promoted to lieutenant, he was given the charge of the battalion machine-gun section of two Vickers-Maxim guns, served by twelve men. Each Maxim had a maximum rate of fire of 500 rounds per minute, so was the equivalent of around forty well-trained riflemen and, with the cauldron of war simmering, it was increasingly important to hone skills and bring routine to a peak of efficiency.

In addition, route marches were common, consisting of a twenty-mile grind at four miles to the hour, in full kit and with 200 rounds of ammunition. Very few fell out, and those who did caught up quickly. Feet were toughened to the assault of leather and hobnail, muscle and sinew tightened with drill and army fare and Maurice would have been in close attendance, ensuring that his section was drilled to perfection.

On the range, Maurice instructed his men in the use of the .303 Short Magazine Lee Enfield rifle, considered to be the finest weapon of its time. Shooting was taken very seriously and Musketry Regulations dictated that subalterns (first and second lieutenants) should practise on the range along-side their companies – and woe betide the officer who was not a first-class shot – giving Maurice the additional opportunity to cement his relationship with the men directly under his command. The musketry scores of the army of 1914 were nothing less than remarkable, with the majority of Battalion Commanders able to boast that 50 per cent of their men were marksmen. During the 'mad minute', every man in the army could put fifteen rounds into a target two feet in diameter at a range of 300 yards and many could double that rate. Men grew attached to their rifles, 'and spent hours in the barrack room practising loading with drill rounds, checking their point of aim with the help of a mate and they even balanced a penny on the forward sight to ensure the trigger was squeezed gently: jerk the trigger and down goes the penny.'[4] With such intensive preparation, life would be made very difficult for an enemy appearing before them within 600 yards' range.

While life was tough and expectations high, many of the soldiers might have been heard to mutter that for the man who was cut out for it, army life before the war was actually enjoyable.

Recognising the importance of his role as the battalion machine-gun officer, Maurice approached the training of his men with optimism and encouragement. He scrutinised the performance of each and decided that the most constructive policy would be to pair the best with the worst in the hope that the skill of the former would bring on his partner. This had particular success in accurate range-finding, crucial to the art of the machine-gunner, when Privates Godley, Russell, Godman and Marshall, particular causes of concern, were set alongside Lieutenant Harvey and Private Walker. Private Godley's consistency had lain in his unswervingly poor performance, though Maurice had kept him in the section because he had excelled at 'tactical handling'. The policy paid off and Maurice recorded that Godley and Godman made great strides forward; Godman would rise to become a first-class machine-gunner, although Godley would continue to tax the seemingly limitless patience of his section commander. Indeed, one of the sergeants quipped to Godley that, 'as a machine gunner, he would make a bloody good bus conductor'[5]. Maurice was quick to recognise that Godley's many talents lay in other directions; as a talented footballer and cricketer, Godley's proven athleticism and good-humoured optimism meant that he was the man for the team should the going get tough.

Ensuing events would now cast Lieutenant Maurice Dease, Private Sidney Frank Godley and the machine-gun section of the 4th Royal Fusiliers into the teeth of the gale.

Germany's refusal to leave Belgian territory by midnight on 3 August 1914 was the gauntlet thrown down in the face of the British ultimatum and war was declared the following day, a Bank Holiday Monday, where the sun drew crowds to railway stations in the hope of a day at the seaside. They were to be disappointed in many cases as the cheap excursion trains had all been cancelled.

* * *

At this time, the 4th Royal Fusiliers were based at Parkhurst on the Isle of Wight and Maurice's diary reveals that he had been tasked with the purchase of horses, a job he had found irritating, owing to the inefficiency of local civilian buyers. Yet the tedium was perhaps broken by Mollie Hewitt, whom he had met the year before and who shared Maurice's love of horses. Married, though separated from her husband, Rupert, Mollie had a three-year-old son and lived in a large house close to Battalion HQ. Conventions of the time, Maurice's sense of honour and the fact that he was a devout Roman Catholic mitigated against the relationship becoming anything more than friendship, but he undertook to write to her once the battalion was on the move.

The *War Book*, a tome of encyclopaedic proportions, which cascaded orders into all areas of the establishment, civil and military, had got the show on the road. Maurice, as every subaltern in the BEF, knew exactly what mobilisation would now entail, the content of orders expected from his superiors and how to marshal his section and all its equipment. Maurice jotted details briefly in his diary.

Monday 11th August
The Reservists went down to the range today to have some practice. I believe the shooting was good.

Tuesday 12th August
The Battalion paraded at 11 am and did drill for an hour, after that the battalion and all the transport went for a route march around the forest about 8 miles. A lot of men – about 120 – fell out, the day was very hot and it was a long march. We got in at about 2 pm. The transport went along very well.

Wednesday 13th August
The CO addressed the battalion this morning giving them final advice and saying what would be required and expected of them. We received the order tonight to be ready to move tomorrow.

Just time for a letter home.

12/8/14

My Dear Daddy

We are still here but expected to be moved tomorrow. This however is secret and must go no further than mother.

I think I have now paid all my bills except tailor's – you might pay this sometime out of the £60. I don't know how my accounts stand just at present as I have written some cheques and have packed up my account book I enclose my will, they say it will save you trouble if I don't return.

Dandy [Maurice's beloved pet dog] is not now going home. Blake is going to look after him, but I have told him that if he is a nuisance to send him home.

Our address when we leave will be 4th Bn. Royal Fusiliers, 9th Infantry Brigade, 3rd Division.

Goodbye and best of love to you,

your loving son Maurice[6]

And from then on, it was all go.

On the morning of 13 August, Maurice and his machine-gun section joined A and B Companies as they marched to Cowes encouraged along by enthusiastic locals and an enormous gable-end painting of John Bull proclaiming 'The Dawn of Britain's Greatest Glory'. A short voyage took them to Southampton, where they boarded the steamer *Martaban* and headed for Le Havre. Maurice adhered to procedure and stopped writing his personal diary, but others resisted and took advantage of quiet times away from the gaze of superiors to jot down their thoughts. It is these invaluable sources which allow us an insight into the whirlwind of events about to envelop them.

Lieutenant 'Kingy' Tower, a good friend of Maurice, writes of the voyage, saying they were 'packed like herrings' sitting in the darkness 'with a thousand thoughts of the future crowding through our brains'. Lieutenant Frederick Longman, another of Maurice's friends, was 'as pleased as anything to get a move on'. The French population were ecstatic in their welcome and the fusiliers responded with waves and greetings, especially for the pretty *mesdemoiselles*, who demanded cap and shoulder badges as souvenirs. The fusiliers whistled the Marseillaise and then sang 'Hold Your Hand Out, Naughty Boy!', a popular music-hall ditty; the French locals doffed their caps in deference, thinking this was the British national anthem.

The weather was against them for the first couple of days, with an enormous thunderstorm ensuring that every man and every piece of equipment was soaked and spattered with mud. On to Rouen by train and then to Landrecies and billets in Noyelles. It is here that Longman notes that Maurice was not billeted with them, but at HQ with 'the Col', as he was known to the junior officers. Lieutenant Colonel Norman Reginald McMahon, DSO, had been Chief Instructor of Musketry for the best part of a decade and it was he who had devised many of the practices, including the 'mad minute' which had generated in the BEF a proficiency with the rifle universally unmatched. Known as the 'Musketry Maniac', McMahon took a special interest in Maurice, knowing that the firepower under his command would be crucial during the coming battle and, if McMahon had had his way, battalions would have had six machine guns at their disposal rather than two, though his requests had been shelved for the exigencies of finance.

On 21 August, a march of ten miles took them to Longueville and here another friend gave Maurice photographs of a tea party they had attended only ten days before. It is not clear if the relaxed conviviality included Mollie, but Maurice was prompted to write:

My Dear Mollie

We are getting on grand out here but cannot let you know where we are or what we are doing on account of censorship . . . Write me a line when you have time . . .

Best love,

Maurice[7]

As the 4th Royal Fusiliers and the BEF probed the western borders of Belgium, to the east General von Kluck's First Army on the right of the German advance was bowling along through town, city and countryside. The Belgian field army had been shepherded into Antwerp and Brussels had been entered on 19 August. It had not been plain sailing for the Germans as the Belgians fought tooth and nail for every brick and every blade of grass. General von Moltke would comment that, 'our advance through Belgium is certainly brutal', though these sparks of admission would be fanned to flames of terror as tales of atrocities reached the ears of the populace who stood in the path of the German juggernaut.

The BEF was now poised on the left of the French Fifth Army to challenge the German right, though it was now expected that they would turn south and so the threat would not extend to menace them directly. General Joffre launched the French offensive on 20 August, when Maurice and his battalion were heading with 4th Division for Longueville and the French 1st Cavalry Corps had been ordered up from the Ardennes to support the British left flank. General Sir John French, commander of the BEF, could be content that prospects seemed positive at that point and that the German advance, although more incisive than anticipated, would now be blunted and broken. However, the German cut into Belgium had run deep enough to necessitate a frequent reassessment of objectives and then, on the 21st, when the Royal Flying Corps (RFC) spotted a large body of cavalry and guns much further to the west than had originally been anticipated, adjustments were made and the line along the canal north of Mons from Nimy to Pommerœul would now be held. First blood was drawn the following day in a cavalry skirmish between the 4th (Royal Irish) Dragoon Guards and the German 4th Cuirassiers and Corporal Edward Thomas fired the first shot by the British Army in a European theatre for ninety-nine years, felling a German cavalry officer from 400 yards.

Bad news was soon to wing its way to General Sir John French and GHQ. Lieutenant Edward Spears was charged with finding General Lanrezac, commander of the French Fifth Army on the British right to ascertain progress: he was met by streams of wounded men and bedraggled, leaderless troops in full retreat. The Fifth Army had been dealt a crippling blow and, as a consequence, the BEF was now dangerously exposed, with its right flank up in the air. Lanrezac requested that the BEF should now fall back to cover his left flank, but General French thought that such a move would be folly, trapping the BEF in a pincer movement between the German First and Second Armies. He politely refused and added that he would hold the line of the canal for twenty-four hours.

With the French Third and Fourth Armies all but routed in the Ardennes and the Fifth Army checked at Charleroi, German High Command had every right to feel bullish and confident. General von Kluck, commanding the German First Army, with orders direct from the Kaiser 'to exterminate the treacherous English and walk over General French's contemptible little army', had expected to find the BEF much further south and was surprised to learn that both I and II Corps were at Mons. He intended to continue his wide sweep to the west, ignoring the possibility that the BEF actually lay directly in his path. Surprise would be his gamble and speedy victory a safe bet.

The BEF was also unaware of the strength of the hammer blow that was about to fall upon them and reports from fleeing citizens, spies and the RFC were considered exaggerated. However, General Sir Horace Smith-Dorrien, commander of II Corps, sensed that hasty preparations along the vulnerable line of the canal should be undertaken as a matter of urgency, with a fall-back position established south of Mons. Demolition plans were now put into effect to topple the eighteen road and rail bridges which could lead the Germans across the canal and into the BEF positions, though this was an enormous task to achieve.

The war diary of the 4th Royal Fusiliers records that they crossed the Belgian border on 22 August and camped at Malplaquet, close to the site of the Duke of Marlborough's bludgeoning, bloody victory two centuries before. As they tramped into the town of Mons, they were met by an exuberant, ecstatic crowd of well-wishers and Maurice and his fellow officers had difficulty in prising their men away from the gifts showered upon them. As Lieutenant Cundy-Cooper wrote, 'A multitude of inhabitants appeared and gave the men all sorts of things – eggs, fruit and drinks. We, the officers, had great difficulty in preventing the men from getting drunk, which would have been exceedingly bad for them after a long march under the hot sun, with entrenching etc. before them.'

It was here that the men of A Company were photographed in the Grand Place and this convivial scene lasted only a few more minutes before it was hastily brought to a conclusion. As it happened, Maurice and his fellow officers had no need to muscle in, as Lieutenant Cundy-Cooper explains: 'Suddenly there was an alarm among the inhabitants that the Germans were coming, and, within a minute, there was not one inhabitant to be seen, all the shutters were up . . .'

Sharp instruction got the men to their feet, many with pockets full of fruit and sticky delights to assuage future pangs of hunger, and readied them to move off when the order came through. An hour later, they were en route for the line of the Mons-Condé canal, where they would entrench and prepare for whatever the Germans might throw at them.

Standing today on the railway bridge at Nimy, which is accessed by an often undignified scramble up a steep earth and scree pathway, leaves one in no doubt as to the vulnerability of the position where Maurice and his highly trained machine-gunners set up their emplacements. The original bridge would be demolished to halt advancing armies (as would a number of its descendants) with the modern incarnation boasting a superstructure not present in August 1914. The canal is wider now at 100 feet than the 64 feet of the time, though its depth at seven feet remains the same, precluding the possibility of wading across. As I braved the occasional din and slipstream from an intercity of Belgian Rail, I was struck profoundly by the enormity of the task which lay ahead of Maurice and his men. Jet skiers on the canal seemed only a touch out of reach and the lad in a red shirt, who had paused for a breather on his bike on the far side of the canal would have turned had I called him; a punt from a proficient rugby player would have landed the ball effortlessly in his arms.

Down to the left, the canal takes a turn, forming a knee bend in the position and, for the 4th Royal Fusiliers, this imposed a dangerous salient, which the Germans would attempt to exploit. I skittered once more to the canal level, all too aware that Maurice had done the same dozens of times throughout the course of the battle (with far greater dexterity and athleticism) as he heartened his men and ensured the machine guns of his section were supplied and working. The position here is largely unchanged and known to this day as the Quai des Anglais; with good reason. Behind the concrete pathway on which I was now walking, the 4th Royal Fusiliers and the 4th Middlesex to their right hacked their trenches to a depth of two feet during the night and into the early morning of 23 August and waited for battle to be joined.

As the men of the battalion scraped away, Maurice and his men prepared the position, with a machine gun on either side of the railway tracks and fortified their emplacements with railway sleepers and sandbags, which Maurice helped to fill. It was the measure of Maurice as their superior officer, that, if he had encouraged and cajoled his men in training, shared their successes and failures on the range, the aches of the route march and as confidant to their lives in general, it was quite right that he should muck in with them in mundane soldiering, especially on the eve of battle. It certainly endeared him to them and they held him in the highest affection. Later, Captain Kingy Tower recalled a convivial gathering in the shadow of the machine-gun emplacements. In a letter to Maurice's sister, Maud, he wrote: 'We sat together (Maurice, Ashburner, Steele and I) on the bridge all cheerful and happy and drank some awfully good coffee. Old Maurice then lay down and had a real good sleep, which must have done him all the good in the world.'[8]

On the heels of darkness arrived a torrential storm which left the men on the canal bank wet and miserable. Dawn broke with mist over the canal and the Tommies' eyes smarted as the smoke from barges, burned to prevent the Germans constructing makeshift bridges, hung in the air. As the bells in Nimy and Mons rang out for Sunday Mass, the men along the canal stretched weary limbs and stamped feeling into cold feet. Rations were plentiful, with fresh bread from local boulangeries and tins so rusty that many quipped they had been left over from the Crimean War. They opened to reveal bacon, pilchards or herring, or even apple dumpling – it was pot luck. Time for a Woodbine and a slurp or two of hot, strong army tea.

Quiet descended. The canal settled. Not a ripple. A mirror. Then the first Germans appeared on the opposite bank. It was a patrol of cavalry, probing cautiously forward down the Nimy road in the direction of the canal.

A barked order rent the silence. 'At five hundred yards – five rounds rapid – FIRE!'[9]

With a composure that mirrored practice on the range, the line erupted with a storm of withering fire and then ceased as sharply as it had begun. Tommies craned necks, ears still ringing, to watch the German patrol retreat in consternation.

At this point, a little boy and girl came onto the bridge with rolls and coffee, which they offered to Private Sidney Godley; he was clearly moved by this simple gesture of kindness. When the first German shells crashed into the position, he was immediately concerned for their welfare and, with an almost paternal affection, said, 'You'd better sling yer 'ooks now, otherwise you might get 'urt!' With only body language to interpret, they left.

It was at 9 a.m. that the battle now began in earnest.

German artillery ranged in on the British positions from open ground to the north and pounded the canal for about an hour. It was an unpleasant

77

business for men in shallow defences, and a company of the 4th Middlesex, at Obourg to the right of Maurice's position, lost its commander and second in command. British artillery was hampered by the spoil heaps and buildings south of the canal and, although four guns had been brought up in support of the West Kents, the majority had been held back to deal with an attack on the left flank. For Maurice and the 4th Royal Fusiliers, there would be no artillery support.

On the tail of the bombardment came the German infantry, massed in columns, who attacked the 4th Royal Fusiliers on one bend in the canal and the 4th Middlesex on the other, hoping to break into the salient at its weakest point. The response from the opposite side of the canal was immediately devastating as every man fired as if he were back on the range with umpires counting the shots. The German columns reeled under the torrent of lead. As Captain Osburn of the 4th Dragoon Guards later wrote, 'I shall not easily forget the overture of that extraordinary battle: a crackling sound, exactly like that of an October bonfire into which a cartload of dry holly boughs had been suddenly thrown.'[10]

Corporal William Holbrook of the 4th Royal Fusiliers was positioned slightly behind Maurice's position: 'Bloody Hell! You couldn't see the earth for them there were that many. Time after time they gave the order *"Rapid Fire"*. Well, you didn't wait for the order really! You'd see a lot of them coming in a mass on the other side of the canal and you just let them have it . . . I don't know how many times we saw them off. They didn't get anywhere near us with this rapid fire.'[11]

Captain Walter Bloem of the 12th Brandenburg Grenadiers, a writer who had seen the call to arms in Germany as an effort 'to meet the demands of the "tear season"' (Bloem's own way of describing the effects of war and its devastation), described the experience of being on the receiving end of this murderous firepower: 'The enemy must have been waiting for this moment to get us all together at close range, for, immediately the line rose, it was as if the hounds of Hell had been loosed at us, yelling, barking, hammering, as a mass of lead swept in amongst us.'[12]

On the bridge, the machine-gun section of the 4th Royal Fusiliers, under the watchful eye of its commander, Lieutenant Maurice Dease, was working with desperate efficiency. One of Maurice's men later wrote that they had spotted German soldiers between the houses across the canal. Maurice then told Private Guines to 'lay the gun on the space between the houses and when we saw the Germans again to open fire'. Sidney Godley, who had been carrying supplies of ammunition and spares up to the machine guns, would later recall, wandering back to events seared into the depths of his memory, which decades later would cause him to pause in the telling, 'The Germans came over in large formation and . . . er, . . . we opened fire. The old order came "15 rounds rapid fire!" The lads let 'em have it. Of course, the British troops, with this great volume of fire – 15 rounds rapid, which we'd been highly trained in – was very effective.'

On the bridge, the machine-gun teams were also in action and worked like modern Formula One pit crews to keep their guns in working order. A constant watch would be made to ensure optimum efficiency: the water jacket, equipped with a pipe to run off condensation into a petrol can, would need to be refilled at regular intervals as the barrel temperature rose with constant firing; belts of 250 rounds would be brought up constantly, as the Maxims would hammer through two of these in a minute. Jamming must be avoided at all costs and experts were on hand to clear the action, should this occur. Maurice supervised his teams with typical efficiency and calm, running from one gun to another in full view of the advancing Germans, encouraging his men and then dashing back to bring up ammunition and spares as they were needed.

The machine guns wreaked havoc and, prominent as they were in the fusiliers' position, drew in a storm of bullets, shrapnel and high explosive. If the Germans were to get across the bridge, the machine guns would have to be neutralised and they now concentrated their fire power on them to do just that. Privates Marshall and Guines responded to Maurice's calm encouragement and their fire dominated the approaches to the railway bridge, keeping the Germans away from the hastily constructed barbed wire obstacle placed there by the fusiliers' outpost guard only a short time before. Guines reeled as a bullet struck his head. Maurice told him to get it bandaged and replaced him with another fusilier from the section.

The German 84th Infantry Regiment (IR 84) now adopted the tactic of attacking in companies, rather than in column, which had presented such a tempting target to the Tommies on the canal bank. Concentrating their fire on the railway bridge, there was a certain amount of cover afforded by trees, but to venture there would invite the wrath of Vickers-Maxims, well placed on the far side. Maurice's position now became the focal point of their attack and accurate shrapnel and rifle fire soon began to take its toll.

The correct posture for the man firing a Vickers is to sit upright, straight-backed and not hunkered over to squint along the sight, as one would imagine, so as a consequence he was exceptionally vulnerable. Private Marshall had kept this gun in action for nearly an hour before he was wounded and, having been ordered by Maurice to the aid post, fell again to a shrapnel bullet (small lead balls contained in a shell casing). As Maurice stood to help him, he was toppled by a shot in the leg. Lieutenant Francis Steele, also of the 4th Royal Fusiliers and a close friend of Maurice's since their days at Sandhurst, was there: 'Poor Maurice got shot below the knee (or thereabouts) at about 9 am [sic] while he was attending the machine gun on the left side of the bridge. Ashburner and I begged him to go off and get fixed up at the hospital but he refused. He continued to direct the fire of his guns, although obviously in great pain.'

Maurice's concern was for his men and his guns and so he fought through the pain as a rudimentary dressing was applied, constantly asking if the position was properly supplied with men and ammunition. As the German attack intensified, his guns were vital in keeping them at bay. He could hear the machine gun to the left of the tracks working away, but the one on the right had stopped. He immediately yelled for a machine-gunner and crawled over to the emplacement, in spite of entreaties from his men to retire to safety. As Maurice reached the gun, he was struck down by a bullet in the side. 'Gunner!' he yelled.

Dragged a short distance away, Maurice was desperate to get back to his men, but was told by Steele to lie still, assuring him that all was well with the guns and that his expert crews were dominating the battle. Around this time, the machine gun to the left of the tracks was put out of action, its water jacket riddled with bullets, so the crews salvaged any useful kit and concentrated on the remaining gun. So did the attackers and men in the section begin to fall. Sergeant Haylock was wounded in both arms and in the chest, another had an arm shattered and so Corporal Palmerton, on the orders of Haylock, grabbed ammunition and made for the remaining gun. Finding the gunners dead or wounded, he dragged them from the position and, joined by Steele, worked desperately to get the gun in action once more.

Steele had reassured Maurice that all was well, but the silence from the position and the lack of the tell-tale rattle of the Maxim told him this was clearly not the case. He dragged himself towards the emplacement, demanding, 'How are the machine guns getting on?' and, as he raised his head to look, he was shot in the neck. The gun was working again, however, and Steele heard Maurice say, 'That's good. Let them have it.' Steele returned to Maurice and reported him to be 'much more happy', though he noticed Maurice had been wounded again while he had been working on the machine gun.

The situation was now becoming desperate all along the canal bank as the Germans rained in shrapnel and high explosive, and the machine-gun position continued to be deluged with fire. When the remaining machine gun fell silent once more, Maurice called out, 'Why isn't the gun firing?' and crawled over to check. Once the wounded man had been replaced, Maurice began to help with the ammunition belts to keep the gun in action. When the next gunner was hit, Maurice, in spite of his wounds, dragged him clear and rolled him down the canal bank to a place of relative safety. Maurice then took his place and poured a steady stream of fire into the advancing Germans.

Maurice, having seen the effects of the German fire concentrated on the position, could have been under no illusions about the outcome of firing the gun himself, yet he blazed away regardless to support the fusiliers on the towpath below and kept the enemy off the bridge. Then he was struck on the head by a bullet, but refused to leave the position until a replacement was found and insisted on staying with him to keep the ammunition flowing. 'Gunner!' yelled Maurice as the new man fell and, as he crawled over to clear the position, he fell forward as a German bullet struck him in the chest.

Corporal Palmerton approached the machine gun and saw Maurice lying on the sandbags, mortally wounded. Palmerton got the gun working once more and concentrated fire on the advancing Germans on the far bank. Wounded in the head himself, he rolled backwards down the embankment into the path of Private Sidney Godley, telling him it was suicide up on the bridge. Lieutenant Steele, who was now in charge of the company, asked if there was anyone else who knew how to fire the machine gun. Private Godley stepped forward, got the gun back into action and followed his orders from Lieutenant Steele to keep it firing to cover the retreat which had now been ordered. Godley recalled: 'I managed to carry on, on my own. I was on my own at the latter end of the action. Of course, Lieutenant Dease lay dead at the side of me and Lieutenant Steele retired with his platoon. I was there for a couple of hours or more on my own. I remained on the bridge and held the position.'

Desperately wounded by shrapnel and by a bullet which lodged in the top of his skull, Godley, under orders from Lieutenant Steele, who had returned to the bridge, crawled back to the main road and was taken to hospital by two civilians. He was later captured and spent the rest of the conflict as a prisoner of war.

Lieutenant Francis Steele knew that there had been few survivors to witness the actions on Nimy Bridge that day and, in spite of the desperate pace and constant dangers precipitated by what now became the Retreat from Mons, recorded his account and sent it to the commander of the 4th Battalion Royal Fusiliers. Lieutenant Colonel McMahon, who had insisted that Maurice should be billeted with him and his staff only a few short days before, then sent a strong recommendation to the War Office that Maurice and Sidney Godley should each be awarded the Victoria Cross.

Maurice's award came through first and a citation was sent to his parents, stating:

'FOR VALOUR'
War Office
16th November, 1914
HIS MAJESTY THE KING has been graciously pleased to approve of the grant of the Victoria Cross to the under-mentioned Officer for conspicuous bravery whilst serving with the Expeditionary force:
Lieutenant Maurice James Dease,
4TH Battalion, The Royal Fusiliers
Though two or three times badly wounded he continued to control the fire of his machine guns at Mons on 23rd August until all his men were shot. He died of his wounds.

Private Sidney Godley's award of the Victoria Cross was approved by the King a week later.

The portrait of Maurice Dease hangs in the Top Refectory at Stonyhurst College, with portraits of six other old boys who were awarded the Victoria Cross and side by side with that of Aidan Liddell, his old schoolfriend, who was himself to receive the VC, posthumously, a year later. It is a magnificent room and, in part, hails back to the original sixteenth-century building, into which Oliver Cromwell had once stomped, booted and spurred, before the Battle of Preston in August 1648. The table on which he slept that night is still there, unobtrusive and practical, usually adorned by a bunch of flowers and covered in texts and dictionaries during exam times. The sun often pours cascades of colour through the stained glass onto the white marble floor below and, in quiet times, when the demands of exams, school functions and weddings are distant echoes, it is a place where a moment of reflection is always possible. A refectory during Maurice's time, the present school community follows the demands of timetables and bells, and bustles through here under his gaze to games, studies and class in much the same way he would have done just over a century ago.

The actions of Maurice Dease at Mons are Stonyhurst folklore, but, had he survived, he may well have categorised them quite simply and modestly under the challenge of his old school motto – *Quant Je Puis* – 'As Much As I Can'.

ADMIRAL SIR MARTIN ERIC DUNBAR-NASMITH VC

Introduced by Dame Katherine Grainger DBE

Several years ago when visiting my parents, I was persuaded to watch the film Das Boot. *Although I seemed to have spent most of my adult life in a boat, I wasn't convinced the tale of a U-boat in the Second World War would grip me. I was wrong. The tense, claustrophobic, heroic and nail-biting action was riveting. I thought of that film when I read about the bravery of Martin Eric Dunbar-Nasmith as he commanded a submarine during the Gallipoli campaign in the 1914–18 war. His actions were every bit as gallant, valiant and daring as in the film I'd watched. Only more so.*

Dunbar-Nasmith's task was made much more challenging because he was involved in very early submarine action. This was an age when instructions were written in pencil and delivered via a dinghy. Apart from his skill commanding his ship – sinking an almost unbelievable number of Turkish ships during the short Gallipoli campaign – he was also responsible for many ingenious inventions including developing the retractable periscope and the Attack Teacher, a forerunner of the modern simulator. He also showed originality by making his torpedoes capable of floating so they could be retrieved and reused if they missed their target. My favourite image of him is stripping off, grabbing a spanner and diving in to make a torpedo safe so it could be reused. Obviously very much a commander who led from the front.

My admiration increased even more when I decided to seek out more information about this early Action Man. Not content with destroying enemy ships in the Dardanelles, he entered Constantinople harbour and blew up a cargo ship in front of a reception party waiting to greet it. He also demonstrated himself as a man of principle. He made great efforts to avoid harming civilians and often, when they were endangered, he carried them back to the safety of the shore on the submarine. Another story that made me warm to him was when he captured a cargo of Turkish Delight and then handed over boxes of it to the civilians he had rescued as he ferried them to shore.

I read this chapter about Martin Eric Dunbar-Nasmith immediately after going through the Sunday papers. They made depressing and sad reading that day. The aftermath of a terrorist attack was the main story. The papers also discussed the petulant brinkmanship of two world leaders. I also read how, in actions approaching genocide, a whole race was being hounded from their homes and having to seek shelter in an overwhelmed neighbouring country. Disheartening and dispiriting events. I then turned to read about Martin Eric Dunbar-Nasmith and my spirits were lifted. Inventive, daring, fearless; also humane, enlightened and compassionate. It made me feel confident that, while men and women like him exist in the world, there is reason to be optimistic that good can, and will, prevail.

On the morning of 16 December 1914, Britain was under attack on home soil for the first time during the First World War. Under darkness, a fleet of German ships had navigated the minefields of the North Sea to launch a surprise assault on the seaside towns of Scarborough, Whitby and Hartlepool. In the fierce bombing that followed – 1,100 shells were fired on Hartlepool in just forty minutes – 130 people were killed in Hartlepool, 18 in Scarborough and a further 7 in Whitby. With the main British fleet in Scapa Flow, the only thing stopping the German ships from a clear run back to their base on the River Weser was the smattering of submarines on patrol in the North Sea.

One such craft was *E11*, under the command of Lieutenant Commander Martin Eric Nasmith (later Sir Martin Eric Dunbar-Nasmith). His day had started quietly – 'sat on bottom for cocoa and rest' read one logbook entry. Then a searchlight in the sky had signalled 'Eighth Flotilla close': this was the Eighth Submarine Flotilla, under the command of Commodore Roger Keyes. Nasmith made contact with Keyes, who was on board the destroyer HMS *Lurcher*, and who sent him instructions, written in pencil, via dinghy: the German Fleet was at sea and on its way back to the Weser; Nasmith was to head there and attempt to intercept them.

The following morning, three large columns of ships came into sight: eleven in total, including three battleships. Nasmith attempted to hit one of the battleships, but, as the sights were coming on, the ship changed course towards him and the torpedo fired at it, missed, going underneath it. He then attempted to hit the next battleship, but, again, it turned straight in his direction. Nasmith ordered the submarine to dive and only just escaped being struck: *E11* hit the ground as the battleship roared past overhead, shaking the submarine (the gap between the top of the submarine and the bottom of the battleship was no more than a few metres). By the time he surfaced, the chance had gone.

One of the other members of the crew commiserated with Nasmith on the missed opportunity. 'It's just as well I missed,' Nasmith replied. 'She was too close. We would have both gone up together. But I'll tell you this, I won't smoke or drink till I've sunk an enemy warship.'

* * *

Martin Eric Nasmith was born on 1 April 1883 in Richmond, Surrey. He went to school at Eastman's Royal Navy Academy in Winchester and in 1898 joined the navy as a cadet, on board the training ship *Britannia*. After being posted to various battleships, he joined the fledgling Submarine Service as a lieutenant in 1904 and the following year he was given the command of his own craft, the *A4*, at the age of just twenty-two.

His time on the *A4*, however, was to prove short-lived. On a training exercise to practise underwater signalling (a somewhat rudimentary system in those days, involving a flag and a bell), rough conditions led to water getting in through the ventilator shaft. As *Fleet* magazine described the incident, 'A plunging submarine diving at an angle of 40 degrees, in utter darkness, water rushing in through the open ventilator with ever increasing volume as she descended and the pressure got greater, the fumes of chlorine gas rapidly developing, every particle of metal sparking and giving off electric shocks when touched.'[1] Yet somehow Nasmith managed to hold it together and bring the submarine back to the surface (it later sank, with no one on board, while being towed back to dry dock).

Because the submarine was sunk, a court martial followed for Nasmith, but not only was he cleared of any blame, his heroics were rewarded with a Naval Signal from the Commander-in-Chief sent to the whole fleet:

> The Commander in Chief having read the minutes of a Court Martial held on the officer in command of submarine A4 wishes to make known to all officers and men of the Fleet that he is deeply impressed with the behaviour of the officers and crew on the occasion which led to that Court Martial. Their pluck and devotion to Duty under the most trying of circumstances was most commendable and aptly described by the President of the Court in his report.[2]

Two years later, Nasmith took charge of a second submarine, *C4*, before in 1911 taking command of the *D4*: this new submarine was the first to have a gun which folded away into the ship's casing. Nasmith kept the shell casing of the first shot fired from the weapon (and hence the first shot fired from a submarine) as a memento. At Weymouth in 1912, as part of a series of naval manoeuvres, he found himself tasked with taking a number of very important passengers for a trip across the bay underwater – King George V, Prince Albert (the future George VI) and the then First Lord of the Admiralty, Winston Churchill. Thankfully for both the future of the monarchy and British political leadership, no incident like that on *A4* occurred and he returned them to shore safely.

Such was Nasmith's experience on submarines that in 1912 he became the lieutenant in charge of the Submarine Attack School, training others in the art of underwater tactics. Here, he came up with numerous inventions, most notably the Attack Teacher, a forerunner of a modern simulator, comprising a periscope and model ships, the latter of which were moved around according to the student's orders. He also developed the retractable periscope as well as a torpedo course finder (known as the 'Is-Was' or Nasmith Director).

When war broke out it was therefore assumed, not least by Nasmith himself, that he would have an important role to play. But assigned the command of a brand new submarine, *E11*, the early months of his war experience were a mixture of near misses, such as that following the Scarborough attacks, and mechanical failures. In October 1914, he and two other submarines, *E1* and *E9*, were assigned to go via the Kattegat – the straits between Denmark and Sweden – to the Baltic Sea, in order to attack the supply of iron ore from Sweden to Germany. While the other craft made it through the passage unscathed, Nasmith's submarine had engine failure and, following on a day later, found the Germans ready for her: as she was hunted by a combination of destroyers and seaplanes, she had no choice but to turn around and return to base.

In spring 1915, therefore, Nasmith was determined to make amends when his submarine was assigned to the Eastern Mediterranean, along with fellow submarines *E14* and *E15*. Once again, the plan was to disrupt enemy supply chains – this time Turkish ones across the Sea of Marmara to the Gallipoli peninsula. Once again, *E11* found mechanical failure leaving it lagging behind. By the time the submarines reached Malta, it was clear that *E11* had problems with both its port motor and clutch – with its starboard intermediate shaft fractured all along its length. With no suitable spare parts available, Nasmith had no choice but to wait for the replacement equipment to be sent out from Portsmouth. As *E14* and

E15 set off without him, Nasmith tried to save time by overseeing some basic repairs before heading for Mudros harbour on the Greek island of Lemnos (where he asked the replacement shaft to be sent directly). But there was no way of shortening the repair time – once the part arrived, it would take three weeks of engineers working day and night before the sub would be ready for battle.

Ahead of Nasmith, his fellow Allied submarines had enjoyed mixed fortunes. Firstly, *E15* ran aground and was shot up by Turkish troops. Next, an Australian submarine, *AE2*, made it through to the Sea of Mamara, but, even as news of its arrival was beginning to spread to the Anzac troops on Gallipoli, it too was sunk by a Turkish gunboat shortly after. That left *E14*, which not only made it to the Sea of Mamara but succeeded in both sinking two Turkish gunboats and one large military transport and returning to Mudros intact (its commander, Boyle, was later awarded the Victoria Cross for his efforts). By the time *E14* returned to safety, *E11* was finally seaworthy and ready to go. Nasmith took his craft to Kephalo, where, on board *Lord Nelson*, he had a final briefing with Boyle, Commodore Keyes and Admiral de Robeck. Robeck offered Nasmith a glass of sherry – an offer that, given his pledge after his failed assault on the German fleet by the River Weser, he declined.

* * *

On 19 May 1915, Nasmith and *E11* finally set off for the Sea of Marmara at just after one in the morning. To say that the journey there was dangerous would be an understatement. To get there, the submarine had to traverse the Dardanelles, the narrow passage of water thirty-eight miles long and between one and four miles wide that runs between the Turkish mainland and the Gallipoli peninsula, linking the Mediterranean and the Sea of Mamara, which, in turn, is linked to the Black Sea via the Bosphorus. Known as the Hellespont in ancient times, the Greek expedition against Troy had seen a princess sacrificed to get a wind strong enough to sail against the current. In 448 BC, Xerxes had similar struggles in his invasion of Greece, attempting the cross the strait by building a bridge of boats, that the current proceeded to whip away.

Part of the challenge of traversing the Dardanelles were its currents: while there was a surface current coming out of the strait, beneath the surface a second, strong, undercurrent travelled in the opposite direction. On top of this, the Turkish forces had not only mined the strait, but were on the lookout for enemy shipping. Rather than being able to stay submerged for the whole journey, *E11* did not have the power to make the entire journey submerged, but would need to spend time on the surface in order to recharge the batteries that powered the craft.

It was a tense, nervous journey, punctuated by the scraping of wires against the craft, positioning the minefield above them – each time, *E11* had to carefully extract herself for fear of dragging a mine down on top of her. Nasmith was concerned that the submarine wouldn't be able to fight against the current, but to his surprise the journey was quicker than anticipated, and without the need for surfacing. This was probably just as well: when the craft raised its periscope just before Nagara Point, it was immediately spotted and shot at: in total, there were three destroyers following *E11*'s progress and trying to predict where the sub might be. The cat and mouse game continued until at 1.30 p.m., Nasmith nervously pushed the periscope up to discover, with huge relief that they had made it.

Now the mission proper began. Nasmith began his search for enemy ships, while they continued their search for him. All along the headland he could see a series of lit beacons, a warning system to ships that a submarine was in the area. The first ship they came across was a Turkish dhow, which Nasmith used to mask the submarine, ordering the Turkish captain to sail alongside, blocking the view of *E11* from the shoreline. By the morning of Sunday 23 May, Nasmith was just short of Oxia Island, beyond which, in the distance, they could see Constantinople spread out along the water's edge. Suddenly the targets came thick and fast: after stopping another sailing ship, they then spied a bigger prize in the shape of a steamer, in use for transporting soldiers and equipment to Gallipoli. This made it into the harbour before Nasmith could attack, but a Turkish gunboat patrolling the harbour offered an alternative prize. This *E11* successfully torpedoed, though at the expense of having her periscope hit. Retreating back to Kalolimnos Island for repairs, the crew celebrated with beer and cigars. Nasmith, having finally sunk his warship, allowed himself a beer to cheers from the crew.

The following day, *E11* came across a small steamer, which, on seeing the submarine, attempted to escape, but was unable to outrun its pursuer. As the crew and those on board attempted to leave the ship, either by lifeboat or throwing themselves overboard, Nasmith was surprised to hear an American voice calling out to him: it belonged to a journalist, Raymond Swing of the *Chicago Herald*, who told Nasmith the ship was bound for Chanak, carrying Turkish marines. A search revealed a stash of munitions as well. Nasmith's men set a charge on the ship and, as they watched it explode, one of them commented 'that, in the words of the prophet, was certainly some sink'.

Soon after, another steamer was spotted, bound for the port of Rodosto. *E11* gave chase and, as the ship docked, the crew pouring off, Nasmith took aim and torpedoed it, sinking the ship along with half the pier. A third steamer appeared, but this time Nasmith's effort to stop it were thwarted by, of all things, the arrival of cavalry on the shoreline, who opened fire on the submarine until it beat a retreat.

On Tuesday 25 May, Nasmith set course for one of the most daring raids of the entire operation – aiming to strike within Constantinople harbour, on the shore of the Bosphorus itself. Passing Oxia Island, *E11* headed for the Seraglio Bank, travelling just a mile offshore and on the lookout for potential targets. Clearing Old Seraglio Point, they could now see the harbour itself and the Galata Bridge. Nasmith settled on a large transport craft, the *Stamboul*, moored in front of Topkhana Arsenal, the main Turkish army barracks. The first torpedo struck Custom House Quay in the direction of the Galata Bridge; the second sank the *Stamboul*.

The explosions, meanwhile, caused huge panic in the city itself and led, temporarily at least, to the Turkish rerouting their supply lines to shorten the time out at sea.

Before Nasmith had set off, his orders had been 'to go and run amuck in the Marmara', and he continued to do just that. On the Friday, he spotted a convoy of a large ship flanked by four destroyers. Nasmith manoeuvred *E11* between them to get a clean shot at the main prize, which, once struck, sank in less than a minute. That afternoon, another large ship was spotted, heading for Panderma. Assuming it was full of soldiers, Nasmith fired a torpedo at it, but this time it didn't go off. Nasmith's disappointment turned to relief as he realised the ship was a civilian rather than an army vessel. The drama, however, wasn't quite over: with torpedoes limited in number, Nasmith was determined to retrieve the one that had missed: sailing up to it, he stripped off, grabbed a spanner and dived in, carefully making it safe by hand.

Such was the confidence of the crew that they even indulged in making a decoy periscope and watching with delight as a destroyer homed in on it, discovering that their prize was nothing but a fake, hiding only a weight, a long string and a bottle – the latter containing a note that read, 'Have you ever been had?' The following Monday, they returned to Panderma, sinking a large ship in the harbour that was clearly being used for transporting troops: two days later, patrolling the northern traffic route, a large supply ship was also sunk.

By now, *E11* only had two torpedoes left. The first of these was lost, attempting to hit a steamer; the second missed a larger ship escorted by two destroyers. Nasmith waited until the ships had disappeared before retrieving and rearming the second, errant missile. The mission, though, was coming to an end: a crack was discovered in the shaft between the engine and the motor, the same fault that had forced them to dock at Malta on the way in. Reluctantly, they headed back to the Dardanelles, though not without one last attack: having spotted an empty transport vessel at Moussa Bank, the sub U-turned and sank her with her final torpedo.

As the sub traversed the strait, the coxswain commented that the sub felt heavy: when Nasmith looked through the periscope, he could see why. The sub had snagged a mine and was dragging it along, just twenty feet behind them. Nasmith knew that there was no way he could surface to try and remove it, as they'd be spotted and shot at. Instead, they'd have to dive, drag the mine along with them and hope for the best. Not wanting to alarm his men, Nasmith kept the discovery to himself, gently guiding the sub as smoothly as he could through the rest of the strait. Once out the other side, he ordered the sub to go full astern and to his huge relief managed to shake the mine off.

* * *

From his endeavours commanding *E11* from 20 May to 8 June, Nasmith was awarded the Victoria Cross. His citation stated this was

> for most conspicuous bravery in command of one of His Majesty's Submarines while operating in the Sea of Marmora [sic]. In the face of great danger he succeeded in destroying one large Turkish gunboat, two transports, one ammunition ship and three storeships, in addition to driving one storeship ashore. When he had safely passed the most difficult part of his homeward journey he returned again to torpedo a Turkish transport.[3]

Nasmith was to take his submarine back to the Sea of Marmara for two further operations. Refitted to include a four-inch gun, *E11* continued to cause havoc. In total, the submarine spent ninety-six days in Marmara, bagging one battleship (in the shape of the *Barbarossa*), two gunboats, one destroyer, twenty-six steamships and a further sixty-four sailing vessels – a haul of ninety-four craft in all.

In 1920, Nasmith married Beatrix Justina Dunbar-Dunbar-Rivers, a descendant of the shipping magnate Duncan Dunbar. Family tradition stated that the estate had to be passed down the female line and that the surname had to be retained – after some discussion, Martin became Dunbar-Nasmith. Newly titled, he took command of the battleship HMS *Iron Duke* in 1921, and went on to become, among other awards, a knight, an admiral and Second Sea Lord. After the Second World War, during which he served as Flag Officer for London, he spent six years as vice chairman of the Imperial War Graves Commission, before passing away, aged eighty-two, in June 1965.

Martin Eric Dunbar-Nasmith's service for his country was exemplary throughout his long and distinguished career, but it will be for those achievements in late May and early June 1915 that he remains best known. As Winston Churchill, who had been treated to a submarine ride by Nasmith a few years earlier, commented, 'The Naval History of Britain contains no page more wonderful than that which records the prowess of her submarines at the Dardanelles.'[4]

LIEUTENANT COMMANDER
EUGENE ESMONDE VC

Introduced by Willie Carson OBE

In this short story it is possible to see the essence of bravery. Esmonde faced a series of choices on his last day: whether to take off, whether to await the fighter escort, whether to attack one of the smaller ships with less powerful anti-aircraft capability and, finally, whether to pull out of the attack.

Every one of those choices was conscious and deliberate and each one placed him in greater danger. I think this process of deliberately putting yourself in harm's way to execute a duty you have undertaken is the essence of bravery. I hope you enjoy reading this story as much as I did.

On Sunday 26 April 1942, a small boat was out in the Thames Estuary when its crew spotted something in the water. On closer inspection, it turned out to be a body, kept afloat by a half-inflated life jacket. The crew took it back to Sheerness dockyard, where the identity of the individual remained a mystery. The life jacket suggested that the man was a member of an air crew. There was an RAF post at Sheerness, and this was where the body was taken in the back of a small truck.

At the mortuary at RAF Sheerness, the man's sodden outer clothing was removed to reveal that initial suspicions that this was an airman were correct: underneath was the uniform of a lieutenant commander of the

Royal Navy. On his tunic sleeve was a gold wire badge, indicating that the man was a pilot. On the little finger on his left hand was a gold ring: inscribed on this was a single word: Jerusalem.

The ring was the first clue as to the identity of the dead man, as it appeared on the family coat of arms of a missing pilot. Just over a month earlier, the man's elderly mother had been at Buckingham Palace for an investiture ceremony, to receive the Victoria Cross on his behalf. Her attendance had been complicated in more ways than one: living in the neutral Republic of Ireland, she had to be driven from the family home in Drominagh, County Tipperary, to Dublin, then by train to Belfast, where a plane was waiting to take her to London. The aircraft, a De Havilland Dominie, was usually used by the Fifth Sea Lord, and the mother's wheelchair could not be stowed on board. When she eventually made it to Buckingham Palace, a bath chair had to be found for her to be wheeled in to meet King George VI.

It was one of those quirks of fate that the King had seen Mrs Esmonde's son more recently than she had. On 11 February that year, he had been at Buckingham Palace for an earlier investiture ceremony, that time to receive the Distinguished Service Order (DSO). That was impressive enough, but the very next day, 12 February 1942, this prestigious honour was superseded by an even greater award. As the citation for the Victoria Cross ended, 'His high courage and splendid resolution will live in the traditions of the Royal Navy, and remain for many generations a fine and stirring memory.'

* * *

Eugene Esmonde was born on 1 March 1909 at Huthwaite House, Thurgoland, Yorkshire, where his father, the GP Dr John Esmonde, ran his practice. Eugene was one of twins, his younger brother James following a few minutes later. Both boys were tiny – they weighed just six pounds between them – and, as a snowstorm blew around the building, James was originally thought to have died at birth. As Chaz Bowyer notes in his biography of Esmonde, 'his father picked up the frail little body, saying, "Give the poor little chap a chance," then proceeded to slap enough vigour into it to start James breathing. Eugene, after some anxious moments for his parents, gave ample evidence that he would survive without the need for such violent treatment.'[1]

Although Eugene Esmonde was born in Yorkshire, the Esmonde family were 'more Irish than the Irish' according to one historian, and their family seat in Wexford could be traced back to the tenth century. The Esmonde family had a long and celebrated history: in the seventeenth century Laurence Esmonde was given a peerage for his services to the crown: his son Thomas became a baronet. Two centuries later, another Thomas Esmonde received an honour of a different kind – taking part in the Crimean War and the Siege of Sebastopol, he was awarded the Victoria Cross just under a century before Eugene would receive the same honour.

With strong echoes of the levels of courage that his subsequent descendant would also go on to show, Thomas Esmonde's citation said that he received the award 'for having, after being engaged in the attack on the Redan, repeatedly assisted at personal risk, under a heavy fire of shell and grape, in rescuing wounded men from exposed situations; and also, while in command of a covering party two days later, after having rushed it with the most prompt and driving gallantry to the spot where a fireball from the enemy had just lodged, which he effectively extinguished before it had betrayed the position of the working party under his protection, thus saving it from a murderous fire of shell and grape.'

By the time of Eugene Esmonde's birth, the family seat had moved from Wexford to Drominagh, a Georgian mansion on the shore of Lough Derg in Tipperary. Not long after Eugene and James were born, their father inherited Drominagh and the family moved back to Ireland. He gave up medicine almost immediately, to become MP for Tipperary, though returned to his calling by enlisting in the Royal Army Medical Corps soon after the start of the First World War. Illness forced him to return to Drominagh and he died of a heart attack in April 1915, when Eugene was just six years old.

It now fell to Eugene's mother, Eily, to bring up her young family (as well as Eugene and James, there was also Owen, the eldest, Donal and John Witham, then, after the twins, Carmel and Patrick). After spending their early years in Ireland, the family moved to London, where Eugene and James went to the Jesuit School in Wimbledon, returning to Drominagh for the summer holidays. After four years of schooling, with several of the older children now working back in Ireland, Eily moved the remaining children back to the family home.

Eugene Esmonde's older brother Donal had joined the Mill Hill Society for Missionary Fathers, and Esmonde decided he wanted to follow suit and become a missionary himself. But after studying at St Peter's College in Freshfield, Lancashire, and Burn Hall in County Durham, he became less certain as to whether this was his calling. After several lengthy discussions with the college's spiritual director, he decided to give up his studies. It was a difficult decision, and, according to Chaz Bowyer, initially left Esmonde 'terribly depressed and troubled'[2] when he headed back to Drominagh.

* * *

Eugene Esmonde's true calling lay in the skies: in the late 1920s, he spotted an advertisement placed by the Air Ministry in London to join the Royal Air Force: qualified pilots would get five years' active and four years' reserve service, and the chance of a permanent commission.

In January 1929, Eugene began his pilot training at No. 2 Flying Training School at Digby in Lancashire. Upon completing this, he was posted briefly with 26 Squadron at Catterick before being moved to 43 Squadron at Tangmere in Sussex. The latter was considered one of the RAF's elite units of the time, which says something about Eugene's abilities as a pilot. Certainly, he was part of the unit's display team which used to wow crowds with their 'tied together' aerobatics – piloting their Siskin aircraft in 'V' or 'vic' shapes attached to each other by long rubber cords.

By June 1930, Esmonde had been promoted to flying officer and sent to RAF Gosport for training to join the Fleet Air Arm: this involved instruction in naval-air manoeuvres, such as landing and taking off from aircraft carriers. He was assigned to the carrier HMS *Courageous*, and, though he did well, in December failed the exam that would have led to a permanent RAF commission. Now the clock was ticking on his active service: Esmonde built up as much flying time as he could, which he hoped would stand him in good stead for his return to civilian life (he would still remain in the RAF reserves for another four years).

In 1934, Esmonde applied to join Imperial Airways, the government-backed airline formed a decade earlier that would go on to be merged with the British Overseas Airways Corporation (BOAC), which, after further mergers, would ultimately become British Airways. Esmonde joined as what was then called a first officer, the equivalent of co-pilot today, but was quickly promoted to captain. For the first two years of his time there, he was based in Karachi, primarily flying the route between there and Singapore. One engineer working at the time remembers him as 'widely travelled, with a good mind and a terrific Irish sense of fun'. From Karachi, Esmonde was relocated to Rangoon in Burma in 1936, where he flew floatplanes; a year later he returned to Hythe in Kent to learn how to pilot the airline's Empire class flying boats.

Esmonde now flew these from Hythe to India and Singapore (in those days a staging route). Then in January 1939, with war with Germany looming, he was offered what was initially described as 'a position of responsibility' in the Royal Navy's Fleet Air Arm: this was a commission as a lieutenant commander, with a guarantee of fifteen years' regular service. Coupled with Esmonde's own concerns about war and feelings that he should play his part, this was an offer he felt unable to turn down.

Following further training on Walrus amphibious aircraft and aircraft catapulting technique, Esmonde was appointed as commander of 754

Squadron in May 1939. The squadron, based in Lee-on-Solent, was a training unit and flew a number of craft, including the aforementioned Walrus, Fairey Seafoxes, Blackburn Rocs, Percival Protectors and Fairey Swordfish torpedo bombers. While Esmonde could see that helping train up fellow pilots was useful for the war effort, he was keen to have a more active role in taking on the enemy. This he got at the end of May 1940, when he was transferred across to take command of 825 Squadron. This squadron had been formed in 1934 and since 1936 had been flying the Fairey Swordfish torpedo bomber. The squadron had been embarked on the aircraft carrier HMS *Glorious* since October 1939, protecting shipping in the Indian Ocean, before returning to England prior to being used in the Norwegian campaign. By the time Esmonde joined, the squadron was based at RAF Detling in Kent, to be used for missions over the English Channel and bombing raids on German positions along the French coast.

In September 1940, the squadron's nine Swordfish were deployed on the aircraft carrier HMS *Furious*. *Furious* was bound for Norway and Esmonde's squadron were tasked with disrupting enemy shipping. Esmonde led night raids on Trondheim and Tromsø, both with mixed success: a number of aircraft were lost on both occasions, hampered by bad weather and, perhaps, too, Esmonde getting to grips with his new role. His observer, Lieutenant Cardew, recalled afterwards that Esmonde was determined to attack the enemy, even when the odds were against them. In Chaz Bowyer's biography of Esmonde, Cardew recalled what happened on reaching the coast on the Trondheim attack:

> the cloud base was down to below 1000 feet . . . there was no way we could reach the inner fjord as a co-ordinated strike force even if we could manage to miss the mountains. It would mean blind flying, blind navigation . . . we could not fly in through Trondheim fjord as this was heavily protected with guns and wires stretching across the fjord. Both ways in would be suicidal. Esmonde wanted to press on

over the mountains. We had a flaming row in the aircraft for about
five minutes. I could not pull rank on him but had to convince him
through experience that should he press on with the attack eighteen
very valuable aircraft and crews would certainly be lost.[3]

After returning to the UK for further training in Arbroath, Esmonde
then took his squadron back on HMS Furious for a trip to Takoradi
on the Gold Coast, where the ship was delivering a consignment of
Hawker Hurricane fighter aircrafts. Esmonde's squadron was there as an
anti-submarine protection force and the mission went smoothly with one
exception: Esmonde, Lieutenant Cardew and Leading Airman Russell
left on a sortie late one afternoon, but, due to extreme weather conditions
and navigation equipment packing up, were unable to find their ship as
darkness began to fall. It was a frightening moment but, as Cardew further
noted, 'Esmonde was a great help in giving me confidence, helping me to
analyse my navigation to try to find out where any mistakes might be. He
was very different from the dogmatic pilot I had on the Trondheim raid.'

In May 1941, Esmonde and his squadron embarked on the newly built
HMS *Victorious*. Now the focus was the Atlantic Ocean and the German
plans to disrupt Allied shipping routes – in particular the German navy's
largest battleship, the *Bismarck*. When this was spotted, *Victorious* was
one of the ships giving chase and Esmonde was tasked with launching
a bombing raid. They set off just after 10 p.m. on 24 May in appalling
weather and fading light. The odds were against a successful mission:
the *Bismarck*'s range of arms at its disposal were both huge and highly
accurate; the Swordfish, meanwhile, was not a fast plane, making them
easy to pick off. As Bismarck's guns started firing, the planes had to
abandon their formation.

Colin Ennever, Esmonde's observer that night, remembers:

I called out to Esmonde via voice pipe at one-quarter and one-half
mile positions until he considered position and sang out 'Going

Down' . . . Esmonde made a perfect drop at 800 yards or so . . . passing the bow, I saw a column of water jump funnel high on the starboard amidships side and black smoke issue from her funnel – a definite hit – followed by a smaller water column on the port side. I instructed our air gunner to wireless, 'One definite hit. One probable. Returning.'[4]

Esmonde's attack was the opening salvo against the *Bismarck*. Two days later, a second sortie of Swordfish, this time from the *Ark Royal*, succeeded in doing more damage to the ship, one torpedo jamming the ship's rudders. Now the Allied ships closed in for the kill, and the pride of the German navy was sunk the following day.

* * *

By the time Eugene Esmonde went to Buckingham Palace on 11 February 1942 to receive his DSO for his role in the attacks on the *Bismarck*, his 825 squadron had been relocated to an RAF forward airfield at Manston, Kent. They had arrived the week before, flying through a snowstorm and landing under a cover of secrecy, similar to their role there.

Esmonde had signed his squadron up to take part in Operation FULLER. This operation concerned the German warships *Scharnhorst* and *Gneisenau*, the 'ugly sisters' as the RAF had dubbed them, and which had been discovered on a reconnaissance mission at the port of Brest. Their presence here was both a threat and an opportunity: the Germans had plans to relocate the ships back north to protect Norway from a possible Allied invasion, but getting there meant travelling up the English Channel. For the British, this would give them a window of opportunity to attack them as they made their way through the Dover Strait, and take out some of the deadliest threats in the German fleet. Operation FULLER was therefore set up in great secrecy in readiness for the ships' movements.

Esmonde's squadron of Swordfish planes was included in the plans for the aircrafts' ability to attack at night: it was assumed that the German ships would make their journey under the cover of darkness and, though not the fastest planes at the Allies' disposal, the Swordfish could attack without the need of a fighter escort. The squadron's participation was voluntary, but when Esmonde heard the plans he was determined to put them forward for the role.

On the evening of 11 February, the *Scharnhorst*, *Gneisenau* and a third ship, the heavy cruiser *Prinz Eugen*, along with a number of smaller ships, left Brest, initially heading west under the pretence of being on exercise, and then switching round sharply to their true course. In the run-up to the departure, the Germans had been quietly jamming British radar signals, just enough for the radar controllers to assume this was caused by atmospheric interference. This had been ramped up in the preceding weeks, and, combined with the dark of night, they hoped it would give the ships enough chance to escape. Certainly, the movements had the effect of surprising the British: it had been assumed that the ships would attempt the Dover Strait at night – but the German plan had them arriving there about midday, with most of their journey completed.

Coupled with this, the British response was initially slow and confused. Such was the secrecy of Operation FULLER that, when the ships were finally spotted, there was difficulty in raising the alarm, as only a select few knew about the plan. It wasn't until 11.35 a.m. – a full fifteen hours after the ships had set off – that the Air Officer Commanding of Fighter Command's 11 Group, Air Vice Marshal Trafford Leigh-Mallory, finally executed the order (when the Spitfire pilots who had originally spotted the fleet tried to call him, they were told he was not to be disturbed).

The clock was now ticking. The German ships were just short of ten miles west of Calais and it wouldn't be long before they were out into the open of the North Sea. The original plan was for Esmonde and his squadron's attack to take place at the same time as an attack by destroyers and motor torpedo boats. Now, though, they faced the far deadlier task of attacking the ships in daylight. Even though Esmonde was told that they'd have a fighter escort to cover them, all their training had been done for a night assault. As Esmonde was waiting for the position of the ships, he received a call from Wing Commander Constable-Roberts at the Dover Castle headquarters: 'The Admiral wants to know how you feel about going in,' he was asked. 'He says it's to be your decision.' Esmonde told him he'd do it, but according to the controller at RAF Manston, when he put the phone down, 'he looked like a man torn apart inside'[5].

Having looked at the ships' positions, Esmonde's plan was to set off at 12.25: every minute beyond that, the window of attack got smaller, as the fleet would sail out of range. But as the squadron prepared for take-off, he was told that the fighter escort was late. Esmonde announced they'd take off anyway, and would 'orbit' the coast until they arrived. For a few minutes they waited, but, with no sign of the escort, Esmonde made the decision to press on with the attack before the ships escaped (part of the escort finally rendezvoused ten minutes later, but struggled to maintain visual contact with them).

By 12.50, the ships were in sight. Facing both a Luftwaffe air umbrella and the fleet's guns, Esmonde led his squadron of six planes on (together with the British fighter escort, it was estimated there were a total of a hundred aircraft in the air). Brian Kingcombe, whose 72 Squadron was part of the fighter escort, recalled later, 'I went down to 100 feet, clipping the bottom of the clouds, and we managed to keep most of the German fighters off them. The Germans were firing heavy guns which threw up great mountains of spray like water spouts. The Swordfish flew straight into them.'[6]

Esmonde, though, was not to be thrown off his target, the *Prinz Eugen*. He flew through the smoke screen and tracer fire thrown up by the outer boats and on towards the main battleships, all the while being fired on by cannon shells and machine-gun bullets from the Luftwaffe planes. Charles Kingsmill, flying one of the other Swordfish, describes how he 'saw Esmonde's plane jerk upwards in the midst of the tracers and I knew it must have been badly damaged. Then in the confusion I lost sight of it.'[7]

The tailplane of Esmonde's Swordfish was hit and set ablaze after being caught by fire from a German plane. Then it took a hit from the guns of the *Prinz Eugen*, ripping off one of its lower wings. Still, Esmonde flew on for the battleship. The German plane that had hit the Swordfish struck it again, this time hitting both Esmonde and his fellow crew members. As Chaz Bowker describes it in his biography of Esmonde, 'The Swordfish was seen to nose up slightly, its torpedo fell away – apparently released on the track for the *Prinz Eugen* by Esmonde's dying hand – then the shattered aircraft nosed down into the waves and disintegrated on impact.' It would be over two months before Esmonde's body was finally recovered.

* * *

Esmonde's heroics that afternoon were immediately apparent to all. Back at RAF Manston, Wing Commander Tom Gleave wrote in his report, 'the determination and gallantry shown by Lieutenant-Commander Esmonde and his crew is beyond any normal praise'. At Dover Castle, Admiral Bertram Ramsay concurred, adding, 'the gallant sortie of these six Swordfish constitutes one of the finest exhibitions of self-sacrifice and devotion that the war has yet witnessed'. Even the German sailors who witnessed Esmonde's attack were taken aback. Helmut Giessler, a navigator on *Scharnhorst*, said, 'such bravery was devoted and incredible. One was privileged to witness it . . . they knowingly and ungrudgingly gave their all to their country and went to their doom without hesitation.'[8]

In total, of the eighteen men who flew for Squadron 825 that day, thirteen died and three were seriously injured. Despite their brave actions, they and the rest of the combined forces of Operation FULLER failed to stop the fleet, which sailed through the assault relatively unscathed (indeed, the fallout from the failed operation, and the lack of support given to Esmonde's squadron, would rumble on for some time).

What no one doubted was the courage that Esmonde showed in

leading his men in the face of appalling odds. Back in 1940, he had written in a letter, 'I can think of no greater honour, nor a better way of passing into Eternity than in the cause for which the Allies are fighting the war.'⁹ That fateful February day, those thoughts were tragically and heroically realised.

9

BRIGADIER GENERAL
CHARLES FITZCLARENCE VC

Introduced by Margaret MacMillan, D.Phil.,
Warden, St Antony's College, Oxford University

We tend to think that bravery comes more naturally to the young. As you get older, the risks seem greater and life even more precious. Yet Charles FitzClarence won his Victoria Cross in 1900 when he was already thirty-five and died at the age of fifty-one leading his men in a critical battle in the opening stages of the First World War.

One of the reasons I like history so much is that I keep encountering other worlds than mine and other sorts of people. FitzClarence is unlike me in every way. We are divided by more than a century. I am a middle-class Canadian woman; he was an aristocratic British soldier. I hope never to be in a war. He longed for active service. He was brave in ways that I know I never could be. I am grateful I have had the opportunity to learn something of him.

He is of a type that has largely vanished from our world. Born in the mid-nineteenth century into the Anglo-Irish ascendancy, Charles and his twin brother were expected to be physically brave and to serve their monarch and her Empire. It seemed natural that they should both become army officers even though Charles's health was poor. Yet he was also more ambitious, more open-minded and more prepared to engage with changing technology and warfare than many of his fellows. He was fascinated by the

108

new machine gun and its possibilities and became a member of a special mounted unit. He longed for service, perhaps even more after his twin was killed in the Sudan in 1897.

In 1899 FitzClarence had his chance. He volunteered to go to Southern Africa where it looked as though a war was about to break out between the British Empire and the two independent Afrikaaner republics of the Orange Free State and the Transvaal. He was posted to a place few in Britain had ever heard of, the little town of Mafeking on the border between Britain's Cape Colony and the Transvaal Republic. Under the command of Colonel Robert Baden-Powell (later of Boy Scout fame) his challenging task was to take a motley crew of adventurers and frontiersmen and turn them into a fighting force. And fighting there was soon to be. What had seemed like an unequal struggle – the mighty Empire against irregular forces largely made up of farmers – was initially a humiliation for Britain. In the Black Week of December 1899, its army, poorly organised and badly led, with an outmoded strategy and tactics, suffered a series of defeats at the hands of the Afrikaaners.

Mafeking, in a critical strategic spot, came under attack from the start of hostilities and it was there that FitzClarence distinguished himself by his coolness under fire, his unwavering determination, his leadership and his personal courage. When the Siege of Mafeking was lifted in May 1900 Baden-Powell recommended Charles for his Victoria Cross.

I cannot imagine what it must be like to raid enemy trenches, fight hand-to-hand, carry on command even though severely injured – and what is more enjoy it as he seems to have done. There was, as his fellow soldiers spotted when they nicknamed him 'the Demon', something uncanny that possessed him in battle. Somehow I am not surprised that, even though he was a senior officer in 1914 and expected to stay in the rear, he insisted on leading a raid on German trenches. A German sniper picked him off and he was buried where he fell. His grave has never been discovered.

The Menin Gate in Ypres is one of the most famous military memorials in the world. It lists the names of 54,896 men of the British Empire who have no known grave. The sheer scale of the memorial can overwhelm visitors and only the most observant will have noticed the name of Brigadier General Charles FitzClarence VC. FitzClarence is the highest ranking officer commemorated upon the Menin Gate. To most modern visitors his name may appear as a curiosity, for his deeds have been long forgotten, a sad fate for a soldier who was lauded as the 'Man who Saved the Empire' in the 1920s. He had been awarded the Victoria Cross for his actions during the Siege of Mafeking in 1899 and he saved the British Army from disaster at the First Battle of Ypres in 1914.

FitzClarence was born to be a soldier. He and his twin brother Edward entered the world on 8 May 1865, in Bishopcourt, County Kildare, Ireland. Royal blood flowed through their veins, for their paternal grandfather was George, First Earl of Munster, an illegitimate son of King William IV. The FitzClarences were a military family and, following education at Eton and Wellington College, the twins joined the British Army. Charles joined the Royal Fusiliers as a second lieutenant in November 1886. A fit and lean figure, at six foot two FitzClarence looked every inch the soldier, but he was still filling out his frame. His army reports suggest he was prone to illness, particularly chest infections, and he was plagued with bouts of sickness, although this passed as he grew older. Lacking the robust constitution necessary for field operations, FitzClarence was assigned various administrative roles, an unwelcome duty for a man who was not at his best behind a desk. He was 'grievously disappointed' to miss out on active service[1]. His frustration was magnified by the fact that his twin brother saw action in the Sudan, although envy turned to sorrow with the tragic news that Edward had been killed at the Battle of Abu Hamed, on 7 August 1897.

Charles was not idle during the first decade of his career. It was noted by his fellow officers that he was 'anxious to get on in his profession'. He developed an interest in machine-gun tactics and took a training course to become a member of the Mounted Infantry. It was in the Mounted

Infantry that he first caught the eye of his superiors, who adjudged him to be 'first rate'. Yet it was not until the summer of 1899, thirteen years after he had first joined the army, that Charles had the opportunity to see action.

Tensions were mounting in South Africa. The British Empire had a long history of antagonism with the Boer republics of Transvaal and Orange Free State. Relations had become openly hostile after the disastrous Jameson Raid of 1895, an ill-advised and poorly executed British attempt to overthrow the Boer governments using a tiny force of mercenaries. By 1899 a full-scale war was expected before the end of the year. In anticipation of the coming conflict, 'Special Service' officers were requested to travel to the country and organise local militia to supplement the British garrisons. This was the chance FitzClarence had been waiting for and he immediately volunteered. He was posted to Mafeking, a dusty border town in north-west South Africa. Here he joined Colonel Robert Baden-Powell, who would later find fame as the founder of the Boy Scout movement, and set about mustering two units of mounted riflemen: the Rhodesia Regiment and the Bechuanaland Protectorate Regiment. FitzClarence was given command of 'B' Squadron of the latter formation. In total he commanded approximately eighty mounted riflemen.

This was FitzClarence's first field command and it was neither easy nor enviable. The members of 'B' Squadron were a strange mixture of settlers, drifters and freebooters. A handful had served in a British or European army prior to emigrating to South Africa, and some had seen action against the Zulu or Matabele, but the majority had no military experience. What these men possessed in abundance was the fiercely independent outlook born of life on the frontier. This made them resilient and resourceful, but also rowdy and scornful of authority. FitzClarence had his work cut out turning this disparate group of frontier toughs into a coordinated military unit. By his own admission, the squadron was 'only partially trained' by the outbreak of war on 11 October 1899[2].

'B' Squadron received its baptism of fire a mere three days later. On 14 October a British armoured train sallied forth from Mafeking to drive off a Boer patrol. The scouting party turned out to be the vanguard of a large enemy force that was advancing upon the town. The armoured train suddenly found itself in grave danger of being surrounded and derailed. The Boers poured fire onto the engine and its armoured compartments while a separate party galloped ahead to try and block the tracks. The train reversed course – a slow and laborious process – and the stokers desperately raised steam to outrun their nimble opponents. Seeing that the train was in danger of being derailed, Baden-Powell ordered FitzClarence and 'B' Squadron to cover the withdrawal.

FitzClarence 'rode hard' at the head of his squadron and took a dismounted position atop a ridge. This allowed him observation of the railway tracks and allowed his riflemen to surprise the Boers who were attempting to cut the line. The sudden fusillade cut down several of the enemy and scattered the remainder, but the battle was far from over. FitzClarence had to remain in position until the engine had made it to the safety of the Mafeking perimeter. The train made agonisingly slow progress as it puffed its way towards the British lines. The Boers, denied their original prize, turned their attentions to 'B' Squadron and directed 'furious fire' against the crouching riflemen. Bullets zipped through the air, ricocheting from boulders and striking shards of bark from the gnarled trees. Enterprising groups of Boers edged around the flanks, seeking to cut off the squadron's retreat. FitzClarence's riflemen returned fire as best they could, inflicting 'stinging losses' against the attackers. The battle intensified as more Boers joined the fight. Enemy fire grew hotter but FitzClarence kept his cool, it being noted that 'by his personal coolness and courage [he] inspired the greatest confidence in his men'.[3]

The situation demanded nerves of steel. If FitzClarence abandoned the position prematurely, the Boers would sweep down on the train and capture it. If he held it too long, his riflemen would be encircled and annihilated. After what must have seemed like an eternity, with 'B' Squadron under fire from the front and flanks, FitzClarence judged the train to be safe and ordered a withdrawal. Falling back in bounds, the fire of one group covering the movement of the next, 'B' Squadron executed that most difficult of military manoeuvres – a withdrawal under fire – with a level of skill that belied their limited training. The men returned to their horses, concealed at the base of the ridge, before galloping back to the safety of Mafeking. The Boers were left to lick their wounds atop the abandoned ridge. Total British casualties were two men killed and sixteen wounded; Boer casualties were unknown, but believed to be higher. FitzClarence had 'manoeuvred brilliantly' during his first engagement and won a valuable victory[4]. 'B' Squadron had proved themselves tenacious fighters and gained confidence in themselves and their commander.

In the days that followed the Boers surrounded Mafeking and placed the town under siege. Trenches and gun emplacements encircled the settlement. The British garrison was too small to break the siege but Baden-Powell recognised that his men could serve an important role by holding enemy forces in place and preventing their transfer to the critical battlefront in Natal. He sought to maintain an 'active defence' whereby he would deliver a series of 'kicks' against the besiegers to keep their attention. To this end, he ordered FitzClarence to prepare a night raid against enemy trenches.

At 9.30 p.m. on 27 October, FitzClarence and fifty-five men of 'B' Squadron clambered from the British lines and crept across no man's land towards the Boer position, guided only by a compass bearing. The inky blackness of the night meant that progress was slow and nerve-wracking. Men stumbled in the darkness and spat out muffled curses. Dropped equipment rattled with stentorian sound and at several points FitzClarence ordered his squadron to drop flat as he feared they had been detected. It took forty-five agonising minutes to cross the ground to the edge of the Boer position but fortunately the attackers were not observed. When 'B' Squadron was twenty yards from the enemy line, FitzClarence 'gave a who-oop and hurrah' and his men sprang into action. FitzClarence led the way and was the first man into the enemy trenches, coming face-to-face with a startled Boer sentry. The man raised his rifle to fire but FitzClarence promptly decapitated him with a single sword stroke. There followed 'such a pandemonium as you never saw' as 'B' Squadron fought hand-to-hand with the Boers[5]. The towering figure of FitzClarence was at the heart of the action and he personally dispatched three more opponents with his sword. After a short, violent struggle the defenders were slain and the Boer trench was taken. The bloody work done, FitzClarence gave a blast on his whistle to signal withdrawal. The Boers, having recovered from their initial shock, were unwilling to let the British escape unscathed and directed withering fire against the retreating raiders. A spent bullet struck FitzClarence in the ribs – some accounts say it was deflected by his compass case – leaving him with a painful but fortunately non-fatal wound. Despite the hail of fire, 'B' Squadron withdrew to safety having suffered total casualties of six men killed, nine wounded and two missing. The Boers certainly suffered heavier losses and were 'thoroughly unnerved' by the attack. They 'continued firing aimless volleys for some time after FitzClarence had retired'.

Baden-Powell was delighted with the results of these two actions. FitzClarence's skilful handling of his soldiers is more remarkable when one remembers that this was his first experience of active service and that he was commanding a half-trained unit of frontiersmen. It was clear that the fire of leadership burned brightly within the young officer. Yet there were also hints of something darker. His ferocity in combat earned him the enduring nickname 'the Demon', a decidedly unusual moniker in the straitlaced Victorian army, and one that suggests a love of battle that was out of the ordinary[6]. FitzClarence embraced this idea, writing to his wife soon after the engagement to rescue the armoured train: 'I feel that you will not be so pleased as I am when I tell you that I have at last been in action and what is better still in command of the fight'.[7]

The success of the October raid convinced Baden-Powell of the value of such actions. More were carried out at different points of the line in November before a lull settled over the siege in December. News of a series of British disasters in Natal – the notorious 'Black Week' of the British Army – buoyed the Boers and brought gloom to the garrison. The Boers were in a jovial mood as Christmas approached and offered a truce for Christmas Day. While he honoured the agreement, the restless Baden-Powell was determined to remind the Boers that the war was still being fought and planned an ambitious raid for Boxing Day.

Game Tree Fort was the target: a sandbagged blockhouse buttressed by eight-feet-high walls, each of which had three tiers of loopholes through which defenders could fire. The position anchored the Boer siege lines to the north and protected the approaches to an artillery emplacement. It was a 'worthy prize' but also a 'tough nut' that would be difficult to capture. Yet Baden-Powell had reasons for confidence. Reconnaissance of the position suggested that the Boers had reduced its garrison as their fighters went home on Christmas leave. It was antici-pated that the remaining defenders would be sleepy and vulnerable after their Christmas celebrations.

The attack was to take place on a much larger scale than previous raids. The armoured train – saved by FitzClarence at the opening of the war – was assigned to provide fire support and the garrison's handful of artillery pieces planned a preparatory bombardment. The initial attack was to be made by the Bechuanaland Rifles with FitzClarence and the Protectorate Regiment following close behind. The attack was to begin at 5.00 a.m.

Things went wrong immediately. The armoured train was unable to advance because the Boers had torn up the railway lines and therefore could not bring its weapons to bear. The 'feeble' artillery bombardment 'accomplished nothing'. The guns were meant to maintain their fire until the attackers were within 200 yards of the fort, but the commander of the Bechuanaland Rifles inexplicably ordered the bombardment to cease while his infantry were 1,200 yards away from their target. Worse still, the Boers were ready and waiting. They had observed unusual British activity opposite Game Tree Fort in the previous week and had anticipated the attack. They had secretly strengthened the defences and, far from reducing the garrison as Baden-Powell believed, had actually reinforced it. The fire of the defenders 'blazed up with a fury and intensity that appalled the onlookers', tearing through the Bechuanaland Rifles as they advanced 'over ground without a vestige of cover'[8].

Remarkably, the Rifles managed to reach the Fort but were unable to force their way inside. The effort came at a cost: all the unit's officers and half of its men fell killed or wounded. FitzClarence, seeing his comrades in dire straits, led 'B' Squadron into the attack. Accounts differ as to what happened next. One veteran recalled seeing FitzClarence climb atop Game Tree Fort and fire his revolver through a trapdoor before falling wounded. A journalist at the siege reported that he had somehow fought his way into the fort and had been engaged in hand-to-hand combat. A third account suggested that FitzClarence was shot down while charging but that, although lying flat on his back, he continued to fire his revolver at the Boers and roar encouragement to his squadron. What is certain is that FitzClarence was shot through both legs and severely wounded. His men had to carry him back to the safety of British lines.

Baden-Powell's 'kick' had come up against a brick wall. The attack was a complete disaster. It cost the British three officers and nineteen men killed, one officer and twenty-three men wounded, and three men taken prisoner. These were casualties the tiny garrison could ill afford. There were no further raids after this debacle.

In the coming months FitzClarence recovered from his wounds and by April he was fit enough to participate in garrison cricket matches. Although this period of the siege was characterised by stringent rationing rather than daring action, Baden-Powell remembered his subordinate's bravery. When the siege was finally lifted on 17 May 1900 FitzClarence was recommended for the Victoria Cross. Referring to his actions in October, the citation noted: 'Major-General Baden-Powell states that had this Officer not shown an extraordinary spirit and fearlessness the attacks would have been failures, and we should have suffered heavy loss both in men and prestige.' It also praised FitzClarence's 'coolness and courage' during the disaster at Game Tree Fort[9]. The award was confirmed and Field Marshal Lord Roberts VC presented FitzClarence with the Victoria Cross in October 1900.

With the siege of Mafeking over, FitzClarence became an officer in the Rhodesian Brigade. He served with distinction in this role and was mentioned in dispatches for his courage under fire. In February 1901 he left South Africa to join the newly formed Irish Guards, created in honour of the courage of the Irish contingents of the British Army. Having established a reputation in South Africa, FitzClarence's career blossomed in the years that followed. He passed Staff College in 1902 and subsequently served as a staff officer in 5th Brigade; from 1906 to 1908 he was the senior company commander in the 1st Irish Guards; and between 1908 and 1913 he took full command of the battalion. By 1913, now a lieutenant colonel, he was promoted to command of the full regiment. Although the Boer War had shown that he was a man of action, the years that followed revealed that he was also an excellent instructor. Fellow officers noted that he had 'the great gift of being able to teach others'. He demanded high standards from soldiers and was a stern disciplinarian who was 'both loved and feared by his battalion'[10]. By 1913 the Irish Guards were considered one of the best formations of the British Army and FitzClarence was described as 'the finest type of British officer'.

At the outbreak of the First World War FitzClarence was promoted to brigadier general and given command of the newly formed 29th Brigade. The promotion was bittersweet for FitzClarence, as it separated him from his beloved Irish Guards and deprived him of the chance to lead them into battle. However, he was soon called in action. In September 1914 he was assigned to take command of the crack 1st Guards Brigade in France. Although highly trained, the formation was battle-worn. It had been involved in heavy fighting as it fought to stem the tide of the German invasion in August and had endured a 'tremendous ordeal' at the Battle of the Aisne in mid-September.

FitzClarence's arrival boosted morale. One officer wrote home: 'Our new Brigadier is a great man. We are jolly lucky to have got him.' Within days of his arrival FitzClarence had taken stock of the situation and reorganised his weary troops. Observing that German trenches were surprisingly close to his line, and perhaps inspired by his own experiences of raiding in the Boer War, he organised the first British trench raid of the First World War. The assault was directed against a German position known as Fish Hook Trench and took place on the night of 4/5 October. The Germans were surprised and overwhelmed by a raiding party from the 1st Coldstream Guards led by Second Lieutenant Merton Beckwith-Smith, who was awarded the Distinguished Service Order for his role in the action. FitzClarence was delighted with the 'entirely successful' raid and planned further attacks for October 'to make the enemy's advanced trenches as uncomfortable as possible'[11].

FitzClarence did not have the chance to carry out this plan, for on 15 October 1st Guards Brigade was transferred north to Belgium, joining what became known as the First Battle of Ypres. Although deployed with the intention of advancing towards the besieged port of Antwerp, the British were soon forced onto the defensive by a major German drive that aimed to expel the Allies from Belgium and break through to the Channel coast. The stakes were high. If the Germans breached Allied lines they would be able to occupy the entirety of Belgium and seize the Channel ports which were essential to British supply lines. A German victory here might have brought the war to an end in a masterstroke worthy of Napoleon, or at the least ensured a war of Napoleonic duration.

British, French and Belgian forces fought tooth and nail to hold the line. Outnumbered, outgunned and under relentless pressure from German attacks, the British Army found itself fighting for its very life. Combat was continuous from 19 October to the last great German push on 11 November. The First Battle of Ypres was proportionally the bloodiest battle fought by the British Army in the entire First World War.

Victory or defeat depended on the slenderest of margins.

The chaotic battle demanded leadership of the highest calibre. FitzClarence rose to the challenge. He was described as 'the soul of the defence' and a 'superb example [of] a commander in battle'[12]. He spent much of his time in the front line inspiring his soldiers and organising their defences. His proximity to the action meant that at critical moments he could react quickly, sealing breaches and organising counter-attacks.

By 31 October 1914 the battle was reaching its height. The Germans were relentlessly battering their way towards the Belgian city of Ypres. In their path stood the tiny village of Gheluvelt. To continue the advance the hamlet needed to be captured. British defences in this sector were gravely overstretched. Although made up of experienced officers and veteran soldiers, the defenders were pitifully understrength and had been exhausted by weeks of constant fighting. The British had no fall-back position and the only reserves available were the 2nd Worcesters, a single battalion that had already been reduced to half-strength by the prolonged battle. If the line was broken then the road to Ypres, four miles beyond Gheluvelt, would be thrown wide open to the Germans. Senior British commanders were aware of the danger but the fighting was so ferocious and numbers so few that they could do nothing more but urge their men to hold on. As one officer recalled, 'The line that stood between the British Empire and ruin was composed of tired, haggard and unshaven men, unwashed, plastered with mud, many in little more than rags'[13]. Facing them was a powerful German assault force of several divisions backed by a startling concentration of artillery. Their plan was simple. A devastating preparatory bombardment would crush the British line, allowing the attackers to sweep through the ruined trenches and into the open country that lay beyond.

The Battle of Gheluvelt began at 6 a.m. on 31 October 1914. The Germans opened a bombardment with their artillery and followed it with a massed infantry advance. The British defenders gritted their teeth and repulsed this initial assault, but the Germans regrouped and, under the cover of the heaviest barrage of the battle, attacked once more. The 'murderous fire from their big guns' reduced the trenches to 'a broken and bloody shambles' and the sheer weight of the attack was too much for the thin British line[14]. It cracked and then crumbled as the Germans poured through. The Germans surged onwards to Gheluvelt, passing 'a scene that to the onlooker seemed to exhibit every element of disaster' being marked by dead and dying British soldiers, wrecked artillery pieces and abandoned equipment. The scale of this crisis should not be underestimated. In later years, British Commander-in-Chief Field Marshal Sir John French described the moment he heard the news of the loss of Gheluvelt as the 'worst' of his entire life, adding, 'I felt as if the last barrier between the Germans and the Channel seaboard was broken down'. Worse was to come. A crisis conference of senior British officers assembled at a nearby chateau to discuss responses to the loss of Gheluvelt, but the concentration of staff cars parked outside attracted the notice of a German spotter aircraft and soon afterwards the building was pulverised by German shellfire. Major General Sir Samuel Lomax, commanding 1st Division, was mortally wounded and Major General Sir Charles Monro, commanding 2nd Division, was concussed and would not recover for several hours. At the height of the crisis the British chain of command had been broken.

At the front the battle raged on. Gheluvelt had been reduced to smouldering ruins by artillery fire. A handful of British survivors, primarily men of the South Wales Borderers, clung on in the grounds of a chateau to the east of the village. The Germans, elated at their apparent victory, slowed their advance to deal with this stubborn remnant. It would prove to be a fatal mistake. Remarkably, a telephone line was still operational between the chateau and FitzClarence's command post to the north. The defenders alerted FitzClarence to the situation. For a moment, he considered withdrawing the survivors north and trying to form a new defensive line, but, recognising that this retreat would remove the last barrier to the German advance, he rejected it. Instead he 'decided that an immediate counter-attack was to be made'. The decision was entirely his own. With the chain of command broken there were no orders from above and no one to ask for instruction.

The only troops available for this attack were the 2nd Worcesters. Strictly speaking, FitzClarence did not have authority over this formation and its commander, Major Edward Hankey, was reluctant to accept orders from this unknown officer. It was only after FitzClarence had 'gone into things quite thoroughly' and explained the gravity of the situation that Hankey relented. After briefing Hankey on the ground and the objectives, FitzClarence then gave a formal order: 'Advance without delay and deliver a counter-attack with the utmost vigour against the enemy, who were in possession of Gheluvelt, and re-establish our line there'[15].

The task seemed hopeless. Hankey's battle-scarred force consisted of just eight officers and 370 men. It would have to cross a stretch of entirely open ground to reach the burning village. Once there, they would have to drive the Germans out at the point of the bayonet. It is unclear how many German soldiers occupied Gheluvelt at this stage, but they certainly outnumbered the Worcesters considerably. Wounded and broken men drifted past the unit as it prepared to advance, 'warning them that it was impossible to go on, and that it was murder to attempt it'[16]. The one advantage the attackers had was surprise. FitzClarence reasoned that the enemy would be 'in that dangerous state of relaxation' that occurs when troops feel the battle is won, and would not expect the British to mount a rapid counter-attack. It was a faint hope.

At approximately 2 p.m. the Worcesters began their advance. Hankey led from the front. His terse memories of the attack were 'deafening noise – retreating men – shouting commands'[17]. He and his soldiers sprinted across the open ground, passing underneath a hail of German shrapnel that claimed over one hundred casualties on the small force. Yet a combination of the pace of the attack, the thick smoke that clouded the battlefield and the fact that the Germans were concentrating their attention on the survivors at the chateau meant that the enemy did not see the Worcesters until it was too late. Bursting through the smoke and surging into the village, the British set about the surprised Germans with bayonets and rifle butts. A German survivor remembered the first he knew of the attack was hearing the cry of 'The British have forced their way back in!', immediately followed by disordered panic as his comrades reeled back from the sudden attack[18]. The surprise was complete. The Germans, startled by the violence of the assault and believing they were being attacked by a far larger force, were routed from the village in short order. The Worcesters linked up with the bloodied survivors at the chateau. Hankey met up with Colonel H. E. Burleigh Leach, commanding the South Wales Borderers, greeting him with a typically British, 'My God, fancy meeting you here'. The severely wounded Burleigh replied, 'Thank God you have come.'

Against all odds, the counter-attack had been a complete success. The German rout was so great that they were incapable of making any further attacks. In the early evening, conscious that his men could not hold the position indefinitely, FitzClarence ordered his troops to abandon the devastated village and withdraw to a new defensive line to the north-west.

There is no doubt that FitzClarence's decision and the bravery of the 2nd Worcesters saved the British Army from a devastating, and perhaps even war-ending, defeat. It halted the German tide at a critical point and hurled it back in disorder. It bought the British priceless time to reorganise their shattered defences and, when German patrols cautiously advanced into the ruins of Gheluvelt on 1 November, the prize availed them little. Although it was not immediately apparent to embattled officers and men, the fight for Gheluvelt was the tipping point of the First Battle of Ypres. The great assault of 31 October represented Germany's best chance to win a decisive victory and capture Ypres itself. The defeat knocked the wind from the German offensive. Although fighting continued for another three weeks, the tired and bloodied

Germans never again came so close to a breakthrough. The action would be immortalised in the silent film *Ypres* (1925) which portrayed FitzClarence ordering the attack.

FitzClarence would not live to enjoy his fame. On 11 November, the Germans launched a final, last-ditch assault against the British line, spearheaded by the cultural elite of the German army – the Prussian Guards. After a day of intense combat the attack was thrown back in disarray. During the storm-wracked night that followed, FitzClarence decided to make a surprise raid against the battered Germans to reclaim some lost trenches. To his delight, his force was assigned reinforcements in the form of his beloved 1st Irish Guards. FitzClarence could not resist leading his old unit into action and marched at the head of the column as they moved into position.

The weather was appalling and visibility near-zero. As the attackers advanced, a soldier of the Irish Guards stumbled and accidentally discharged his rifle into the air. The Germans in front responded with a nervous burst of fire into the darkness, prompting FitzClarence to halt the column and go forward to reconnoitre. As he did so, he was struck and killed by a single shot from a German sniper. The attack was abandoned. FitzClarence's body was carried back and buried in haste. Unfortunately, in the confused aftermath of battle, the precise location of his grave was lost and never rediscovered. 'The wondrous spirit that had inspired the 1st Brigade and made its influence felt far beyond his own battalions was stilled for ever.'

FitzClarence's death was a devastating blow to those who knew him and 'was felt and deplored far beyond his immediate command; his was a loss to the whole Army'. Even his foes paid him tribute. Prince Eitel Friedrich, second son of Kaiser Wilhelm II and commanding officer of the 1st Prussian Footguards, which had battled against FitzClarence's own 1st Guards Brigade on 11 November 1914, wrote soon after learning of his death: 'He was an opponent before whom we dip our swords in respectful salute'[19].

THE 'SIX BEFORE BREAKFAST'

Introduced by Joanna Kavenna

As a small child, I once asked my father how you earned the Victoria Cross. Was it for bravery? Weren't lots of people brave? My father was from a naval family, and he was knowledgeable and precise about military honours. He explained that when Queen Victoria established the VC in 1856 she actually refused a proposed inscription 'For the Brave' on the grounds that all her soldiers were brave. The final inscription was 'For Valour': the VC would honour those who exhibited 'most conspicuous bravery' and 'most distinguished and prominent personal gallantry'. In a highly significant moment in British history, the VC was also defined as 'an order of merit . . . to which every grade and individual from the highest to the lowest may be admissible'. Prior to this, only senior officers could receive military honours.

The story of the 'Six Before Breakfast' embodies these crucial aspects of the VC. On the morning of 25 April 1915, under intense fire at Cape Helles, Gallipoli, six soldiers from the Lancashire Fusiliers performed acts of such exceptional courage that each earned a VC. These extraordinary men were much-loved sons, brothers and husbands. They were far from home, in the Dardanelles, battling forces from the Ottoman Empire. As the author of this piece writes, they represented 'a slice of society, from the relatively privileged to the ordinary recruit' – some from English public schools, some from Lancashire collieries. They were Captain Cuthbert Bromley, Corporal John Grimshaw, Private William Keneally, Sergeant Alfred Richards, Sergeant Frank Stubbs and Captain Richard Willis.

They approached a strange, hostile coast at dawn, everything eerily quiet, as if in a dream, until hidden machine guns opened fire. The casualty rates were atrocious; the odds of survival were low. What passed through their minds, as they committed themselves to action, despite the unutterable carnage around them? Perhaps they 'balanced all, brought all to mind,' as W. B. Yeats wrote of an Irish soldier, and found: 'The years to come seemed waste of breath/A waste of breath the years behind/In balance with this life, this death.' Perhaps they saw their fellow soldiers suffering, unable to progress, being fired upon and crushed against barbed wire, dying in great numbers, and acted from extraordinary altruistic instinct. The 'Six Before Breakfast' clearly demonstrate, if any further demonstration were required, that unbridled courage makes no distinction between social class, background or military rank. They are conspicuous for their bravery, even among the conspicuously brave.

We might leave the final words to the British soldier and war poet Rupert Brooke, who died on his way to Gallipoli, on 23 April 1915 – from a sonnet he published only months earlier, The Dead IV:

> These hearts were woven of human joys and care,
> Washed marvellously with sorrow, swift to mirth.
> The years had given them kindness. Dawn was theirs,
>   And sunset, and the colours of the earth.
> These had seen movement, and heard music; known
>   Slumber and waking; loved; gone proudly friended;
> Felt the quick stir of wonder; sat alone;
>   Touched flowers and furs and cheeks. All this is ended.
>
> There are waters blown by changing winds to laughter
> And lit by the rich skies, all day. And after,
>   Frost, with a gesture, stays the waves that dance
> And wandering loveliness. He leaves a white
>   Unbroken glory, a gathered radiance,
> A width, a shining peace, under the night.

Early morning, 25 April 1915. Off the western end of the Gallipoli peninsula a flotilla of small boats rocked gently in the waves under the shadow of the HMS *Euryalus*. The boats were crammed with members of the 1st Battalion, Lancashire Fusiliers, part of the 86th Fusilier

Brigade, waiting for the signal to cast off and head for shore. The boats were packed into groups of four, each guided by a picket boat and each full of soldiers – 672 in total, laden with kit, rations and ammunition.

The Fusiliers had been on board, waiting since 4.30 a.m., watching as the dawn rose on the Turkish coastline. Their destination was known as W Beach, a small sandy cove on the stretch of coastline between Cape Helles and Tekke Burnu, 350 yards long and between 15 and 40 yards wide. Their immediate aim seemed relatively simple: A Company and B Company were to take the cliff-top trenches and capture the hill beyond; C Company were to take the trenches guarding the opposite side of the beach. Once this was achieved, D Company would also be landed, along with Major Bishop, the battalion's Commanding Officer, and the assorted headquarters personnel.

The landing was to be the first foothold in a much longer term Allied plan to defeat the Turks: by doing so, it would not only take out a key German ally, but in the process reopen links between Britain and France on one side and Russia on the other. The German Axis had essentially sealed this shut following the Turkish entry into the war in November 1914. Naval attempts to open up the Dardanelles (and thus, via the Sea of Marmara, through to the Black Sea) had failed the previous month: now the focus was on doing so by land.

It was unusual for an amphibious landing to take place in daylight (further up the coast the Anzac troops at Gaba Tepe arrived before dawn). The thinking was that what the attack lacked in darkness and surprise could be more than compensated for by naval firepower. For forty-five minutes, as the sun rose over the cliffs, the fleet of Fusiliers watched as the bombardment of the Turkish coastline continued. The response from the peninsula was non-existent: no troop movements, no return fire. It was eerie, almost as though there was no one there.

Captain Richard Willis was in charge of C Company that morning. 'The sea was like glass,' he was to remember later, but as the picket boats drew off to get into formation our boats heeled over dangerously, and one of the men remarked to the cox, 'I 'listed to get killed, not to get drowned . . .' When the water began to get shallow the picket boats called out 'Slip' for the tow ropes to be cast off, and we began to approach the shore under the oars of the naval ratings. There were five to each boat. Not a sign of life was to be seen on the Peninsula in front of us. It might have been a deserted land we were nearing in our little boats. Then crack! The stroke oar of my boat fell forward, to the angry astonishment of his mates. The signal for the massacre had been given.[1]

That morning, the Lancashire Fusiliers set out with twenty-seven officers and 1,002 other men. Within twenty-four hours of that first shot being fired they were reduced to sixteen officers and just 304 men: the horror of what followed is difficult to describe, a day (and a campaign) that anyone who took part in would never forget. But among the brutality and military mistakes that served to perpetuate the memories, there were moments of remarkable bravery by men placed under the most difficult of circumstances. Captain Willis was one of a number of many men whose character was put to the stiffest possible test that morning, and came out fighting. He and five of his colleagues were to be awarded the Victoria Cross for their endeavours over the next few hours – a multiple award that, even though the men had eaten in the early morning while on board HMS *Euryalus*, became known in army legend as the 'Six Before Breakfast'.

* * *

Richard Willis was born in Woking, Surrey, on 13 October 1876. His was a traditional officer route into the army, going to first Harrow School and then the Royal Military College at Sandhurst. Originally, he joined the Lancashire Fusiliers as part of the 2nd Battalion in 1897. After time in Quetta (today part of Pakistan), he went to Sudan, taking part in desert patrols under Lord Kitchener and the famous Battle of Omdurman in 1898. He then moved across to the 1st Battalion, serving in Malta, Crete, Gibraltar and Egypt. Promoted to captain in 1900, he spoke four languages, including fluent Turkish and Arabic, was the battalion's champion revolver shot and also excelled at polo and hockey. When the First World War broke out, he was serving with his regiment in India – returning to Nuneaton Barracks, then Alexandria in Egypt, before heading on for Gallipoli.

By way of comparison, Private William Keneally had a somewhat different upbringing. Born in Wexford, Ireland, on 26 December 1886, his father was a colour sergeant in the Royal Irish Regiment. When William was four, the family moved to Wigan in Lancashire, where his father, on completing his military service, had a job at a local colliery. William then followed his father's career path in reverse: joining another local colliery as a pit boy when he was thirteen and working down the mines for a decade before signing up. He joined the Lancashire Fusiliers in 1909: unlike Captain Willis, Gallipoli was to be his first real taste of action.

Sergeant Alfred Richards was seven years older than Keneally. Like Keneally, his father was also a colour sergeant, with the Lancashire Fusiliers, where he served for twenty-one years. Richards was born in Plymouth on 21 June 1879 and grew up in Newcastle upon Tyne. Skilled as a musician, he joined the Fusiliers in 1895 as a band boy before becoming a full drummer. Such was his talent that, despite training to go to South Africa in 1899, he was kept back by the adjutant for his 'musical abilities'. Richards was also a talented footballer and considered one of the best in the battalion. As with Captain Willis, Richards served in Malta, Gibraltar and Egypt. He left the army briefly in 1907, but after two months of civilian life returned to the battalion, becoming a sergeant in C Company and serving in India until the outbreak of war.

At twenty-two, Corporal John Grimshaw was the youngest of the six. Born at Abram, near Wigan, on 23 January 1893, he followed his father as a carpenter after leaving school, working for one of the Wigan collieries. He enlisted for the Fusiliers in 1912 and was in India for just a year before war broke out. Sergeant Frank Stubbs was, by contrast, a Londoner – born in Walworth on 12 March 1888. His father, Francis, was a clerk at Her Majesty's Stationery Office. He joined the army as a boy soldier and, like his fellow VCs, served with the Fusiliers in India.

Also born in London (Fulham) was Captain Cuthbert Bromley, on 19 September 1878. Like Grimshaw, his father, John, was a civil servant, in this case rising to become Principal Clerk in Charge of the Audit of Army Accounts and Accountant General to the Board of Education, for which he was knighted in 1908. By this point, his son had been in the Fusiliers for a decade. Cuthbert had been educated at St Paul's, but, while he hoped to follow his father into the civil service, his final report described him as 'only moderate' in most of his subjects, and he decided to enlist instead.

Here, Bromley rapidly rose through the ranks, being made lieutenant within the year and captain three years later. He served as part of the West African Frontier Force between 1901 and 1903, and then in the Irish Command as Captain of Gymnasia. He rejoined the Fusiliers where, according to regimental records, 'His influence for vigorous endeavour in every form of competition, work, sport or play was extraordinary.' In August 1914, he was made adjutant of the battalion.

Willis, Keneally, Richards, Grimshaw, Stubbs and Bromley were all quite different individuals: different backgrounds, different ages, different talents, different skills. Although they had served together in the Fusiliers, none of them were particularly close to each other. This wasn't a group of friends, but, rather, something that offers a snapshot of what made a battalion, a slice of society from the relatively privileged to the ordinary recruit. Together, they were to show how true courage can be found across the ranks, individuals pulling together not just for each other as fellow soldiers, but responding to that instinct to help your fellow man, whatever the consequences.

* * *

'Rapid fire, machine guns and deadly accurate sniping opened from the cliffs above,' Willis recalled later of the landing.

Soon the casualties included the rest of the crew and many men. The timing of the ambush was perfect; we were completely exposed and helpless in our slow-moving boats, just target practice for the concealed Turks and within a few minutes, only half of the thirty men in our boat were left alive. We were now 100 yards from the shore, and I gave the order 'Overboard'. We scrambled out into some four feet of water and some of the boats with their cargo of dead and wounded floated away on the currents still under fire from the snipers. With this unpromising start the advance began.[2]

War is never controlled at the best of times but the start of the Gallipoli campaign was particularly horrific and chaotic. As Alan Moorehead says in his book on the conflict, 'on both sides the opening phases of the battle were fought in the absence of the commanders-in-chief; each having made his plan stood back and left the issue to the soldiers in their awful collision on the shore'[3]. On the British side, General Sir Ian Hamilton stayed on the *Queen Elizabeth*, a large battleship too far out to sea to enable him to get a sense of what was really going on. Beneath him, Lieutenant General Aylmer Hunter-Weston had tactical authority, but, again, was all at sea, both literally and metaphorically, and lacking information as to the true situation on the ground. As Moorehead writes, 'Signalling arrangements on the shore began to fail as soon as the first contact with the enemy was made, and very soon each separate unit was left to its own devices. Thus no senior commander had any clear picture of the battle, and battalions divided by only a mile or two from the main front might just as well have been fighting on the moon for all the control the commanders exercised upon them.'[4]

For the men on the beach, consideration of tactics and who was to blame was secondary to staying alive. The first to stand tall was Captain

Willis. As another member of C Company recalled, 'I saw him stand up and everyone in the boats heard him above the noise of the bullets and guns shout: "Come on C Company! Remember Minden!" That was it. Whenever we were in trouble, whenever we looked like going under, the cry "Remember Minden!" brought us back to our senses. Captain Willis could not have timed it better.'[5] The Minden in question was a famous battle back in 1759 that was part of Fusiliers folklore. Willis' intervention helped to rally the troops for the task ahead.

One of the many problems that the landing troops faced was barbed wire. Another soldier, Captain Clayton, remembered afterwards that 'there was tremendously strong barbed wire where my boat was landed . . . there was a man there before me shouting for wire cutters. I got mine out but could not make the slightest impression. The front of the wire by now was a thick mass of men, the majority of whom never moved again.'[6] As Willis recalled, 'our wretched men were ordered to wait behind this wire for the wire-cutters to cut a pathway through. They were shot in helpless batches while they waited.'[7]

It was here that Richards and Keneally stepped up. Private Keneally put himself forward to attempt to cut the wire. Under heavy fire, and with no regard for his own safety, he crawled forward to try and help the men through. The cutters he had were faulty, his courage anything but. Sergeant Richards, meanwhile, had been hit as soon as he got to the beach. Such was the damage from the bullets that his right leg was almost severed. Even so, he had the wherewithal to realise that staying put would leave him and his fellow soldiers to be gunned down. Like Keneally, he crawled forward, this time out of both necessity and excruciating pain, leading the way and encouraging the other men to follow him through the wire.

Sergeant Stubbs, too, encouraged his men through the wire. His task that morning was to take his platoon off the beach and up the south side of the hill, hill 114, capturing it and meeting up with D Company. He urged his men on, in the face of some of the heaviest fighting. Not only did he lead his men off the beach and up onto the cliff, but also on up to the summit. Here, a single tree stood at its summit: cruelly, Stubbs was shot in the head. He died immediately, just short of his target.

Corporal Grimshaw's role that day was as a signaller, attempting to maintain contact between the troops on the beach and command back on board ship. In his book *VCs of the First World War: Gallipoli*, Stephen Snelling describes his survival in the assault as 'little short of miraculous . . . almost half the men in his boat had been killed or wounded before they reached the shore'[8]. Grimshaw recalled later that, as they landed, such was the ferocity of the gunfire they were facing, 'we couldn't do anything about the wounded at all. We had to leave everything. We didn't know if they were dead or wounded and even if we had known we couldn't stop.'[9] Grimshaw led the fight up the cliffs and on towards hill 114. He encouraged those around him and risked his life in the gunfire to try and send messages back to command about the situation.

Cuthbert Bromley, too, showed remarkable bravery, particularly as he was shot in the back on landing. But he refused to give up, and carried on: Snelling claims that Bromley 'perhaps did more than anyone to get the men through the wire and up the cliffs'. He quotes Grimshaw, too, who said of the captain: 'his personal example was unequalled by anyone. His bravery was superb, and he was admired by the whole battalion . . . he was one of the first men to reach to the top of the cliff.'[10]

* * *

If the bravery of these six men was placed together in a short, concentrated spell, their lives afterwards separated out in different directions.

Frank Stubbs was the only one of the six to die on the opening day itself. His mother collected his medal at the investiture ceremony on his behalf in May 1917. His name is one of more than 20,000 inscribed on the Helles Memorial, a large obelisk that looks down onto the strait below.

William Keneally survived that first day. He survived, too, three battles to try and take Krithia, the small village four miles in from the end of the peninsula. But on 28 June, two months after landing on the peninsula, he was involved in the Battle of Gully Ravine, a little further towards the coast. He was injured on the first day of the battle, and died from his wounds the following day.

Cuthbert Bromley was shot in the knee three days after the opening assault: 'I'm laid up with a bullet wound,' he wrote home to his mother, 'nothing serious at all, clean through the flesh and I'm as fit as can be.' In something of an understatement, he added, 'the regiment suffered rather heavily in the recent fighting. I quite enjoyed myself and hope to be about very shortly.'[11] Returning to the front line, he was promoted to major and led Keneally and the battalion in the Battle of Gully Ravine in June. This time, Bromley was shot in the foot, but struggled on, using a pair of Turkish rifles as crutches and refusing to leave until the battle was over. He was sent to Cairo for treatment and then convalesced on Cyprus. Six weeks later, he was on board the *Royal Edward* on his return to Gallipoli, when the ship was torpedoed by a German submarine and he drowned.

Alfred Richards, who had been shot so badly in the right leg, was sent to hospital in Cairo. His leg couldn't be saved and it was amputated: he returned to England and discharged as no longer fit for war service. He struggled on his return, initially living at the Princess Christian Soldiers' and Sailors' Home in Woking. With his parents having emigrated to Australia and his brothers serving with the Anzacs, he was nicknamed the 'Lonely VC'. But then he met Dora Coombs who nursed him in hospital, and they married in 1916. He served as a member of the Home Guard in the Second World War and died in 1953.

Richard Willis continued to lead C Company in the weeks after the landings: one account suggests that he used his fluent Turkish to get the enemy to surrender during one battle; on another occasion a bullet left a hole in his cap; on 4 June, commanding D Company, he was less lucky, hit by a bullet beneath the heart. He was evacuated to hospital in Egypt and then back to England. Promoted to major, he joined the 2nd Battalion in France, fighting at the Somme, Messines and

Passchendaele. After the war, he briefly took charge of the 2nd Battalion in India, before retiring from the army in 1920. He became a teacher and died in February 1966.

John Grimshaw lived the longest of the six, dying in July 1980 at the age of eighty-seven, leaving a widow, two daughters, eight grandchildren and eleven great-grandchildren. Having survived the landings and the battles that followed, he was evacuated after suffering frostbite. He was sent back to England to recuperate, and then posted to Hull as an instructor (and where he met his future wife, Maggie Stout). After serving in France, India and Ireland, he became an army recruiting officer in Cardiff and then chief recruiting officer in Northumberland and East Anglia, retiring from the army in 1960.

* * *

One hundred years after the events of April 1915, the 'Six Before Breakfast' found themselves reunited in a slightly different way. The Fusilier Museum in Bury wished to commemorate the hundredth anniversary of the battle by bringing all six VC medals together for the first time. Two of the medals already resided at the museum; three more were loaned from their regular display at the Imperial War Museum; the sixth, awarded to Cuthbert Bromley, required some cunning detective work to track it down.

Putting the six medals together, Sarah Stevenson, collections officer of the museum, told the BBC, 'It's quite moving when you realise what they did to deserve these medals, and here they all are on their hundredth anniversary. It's a very special moment.'

Allied parachutes and aircraft in the area around Arnhem, marking the beginning of Operation MARKET GARDEN.
© Popperfoto/Getty Images

Sergeant John Baskeyfield VC.
© Illustrated London News Ltd/
Mary Evans

Memorial of Donald Simpson Bell VC at
Bell's Redoubt, Contalmaison.
© Tom Stoddart Archive/Getty Images

Donald Bell VC as a
professional footballer.
© Ross Parry Collection/SWNS

Leonard Cheshire VC drinking a pint with
Jig Holloway at the Chequers pub,
Oxford after the Oxford Beer Challenge.
© Courtesy of the Leonard Cheshire Charity

Leonard Cheshire VC in the chapel of Le Court
his former home in Hampshire, 24 April 1954.
© Joseph McKeown/Picture Post/
Hulton Archive/Getty Images

Tom Crean AM with an armful of sledge
dog puppies during the Imperial
Trans–Antarctic Expedition, 1914–17,
led by Ernest Shackleton.
© Frank Hurley/Scott Polar Research Institute,
University of Cambridge/Getty Images

Tom Crean AM on Endurance, 1915.
© Scott Polar Research Institute,
University of Cambridge

William Congreve VC on his wedding day in May 1916.
(Walter Congreve VC, back row, right).
© Illustrated London News Ltd/Mary Evans

General Sir Walter Congreve VC.
© Topham Picturepoint/
Press Association Images

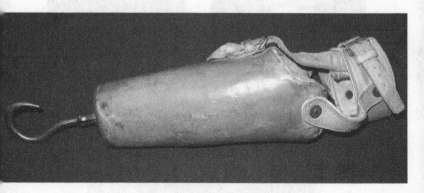

Walter Congreve VC's false arm.
© With permission of The Royal Green Jackets (Rifles) Museum, Winchester

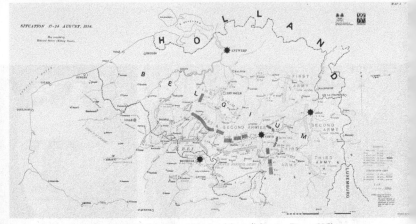

Situation 17–24 August 1914 at Mons (Maurice Dease VC).
© Imperial War Museum

Lieutenant Maurice Dease VC.
By permission of the Governors of
Stonyhurst College. © Photograph @
Geoff Harris 2nd Image Photography

Admiral Sir Martin Eric
Dunbar-Nasmith VC.
© National Portrait Gallery, London

E11 cheered as she leaves Dardanelles, 6 June 1916.
© National Army Museum

Charles FitzClarence VC.
© Image kindly provided by the family of
Charles FitzClarence VC

Charles FitzClarence VC (right) outside a dugout in Troyon, September 1914.
© Image kindly provided by the family of Charles FitzClarence VC

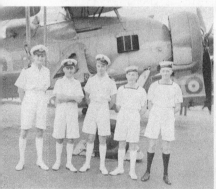

Lieutenant Commander Eugene Esmonde VC.
Esmonde (second left) after the sinking of the
Bismarck, October 1941.
© Imperial War Museum

William Hall VC.
© Image 75.100.1/Nova Scotia Museum

Lancashire Fusiliers at W Beach.
© Mansell/The LIFE Picture Collection/
Getty Images

First boatloads of Lancashire
Fusiliers landing at W Beach.
© Imperial War Museum

The cliff stormed by Lancashire Fusiliers at Cape Helles, Gallipoli.
© Imperial War Museum

Wing Commander Guy Gibson VC (left) and crew in
July 1943. © Imperial War Museum

Breached Mohne Dam, 16 May 1943.
© Illustrated London News Ltd/Mary Evans

Lieutenant Commander
Arthur Harrison VC.

The peppered and shredded HMS Vindictive after the raid.
© Photo 12/UIG/Getty images

An artist's impression of charging up the ramps at Zeebrugge.

Barbara Jane Harrison GC.
© PA Archive/PA Images

BOAC Flight 712 on the runway at Heathrow
after its emergency landing.
© Rolls Press/Popperfoto/Getty Images

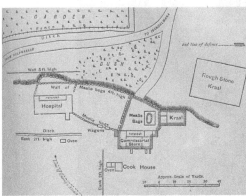

Plan of Rorke's Drift. © Print Collector/Getty Images

Private Henry Hook VC.
© Imperial War Museum

11

WING COMMANDER GUY GIBSON VC

Introduced by The Lord Fellowes of West Stafford

Like many of my contemporaries, I first became aware of Guy Gibson when my school ran a print of The Dam Busters, *the 1955 film depicting the mission to blow up the Mohne and Eder dams at the height of the war in 1943. Gibson himself was played by Richard Todd, a rather uncompli- catedly heroic star of many of the British films of my youth, who brought his own brand of devil-may-care charm and insouciance to the role, and, of course, there was a measure of truth to his portrayal. Gibson was a dash- ing, handsome fellow, with a taste for beer in the company of fellow fliers, for showgirls (he married one) and fun generally, and a dog with a name so politically incorrect that I see it is not even mentioned in this essay. It apparently had a habit of relieving itself against the other servicemen's legs which Gibson thought hilarious, although I do not remember that this fea- tured in the film. But, as so often proves to be the case, the truth was both more complicated and more interesting.*

Guy Gibson found his gifts and even his personality in war. He was not a pupil of great promise at his various schools, nor was he much remarked on by his contemporaries. Until the war, that is. To start with, he flew far, far more missions over enemy territory than he was obliged to, and even when he had been given a well-earned desk job he found a way to fly again until, inevitably and even perhaps fittingly, he crashed and died during a raid on Bremen in September 1944. He was twenty-six years old.

During his time in the air force he had consistently demonstrated extraordinary courage, never more so than during the historic raid on the dams, using Barnes Wallis's newly invented bouncing bombs. Around and around he flew, encouraging all his team of fighters to have their turn, switching on the lights of his own aeroplane to take the flak from the anti-aircraft guns of the Germans; again and again he took incredible risks in an attempt to achieve the mission's goals but also to protect the members of his team. When it was over he was summoned to Buckingham Palace to receive a bar for his DSO, and the Victoria Cross, from Queen Elizabeth (the King was in Africa), making him the most highly decorated serviceman in the country.

But what makes all this so peculiarly admirable, so praiseworthy, so profoundly touching, is that Gibson was not one of those men of steel who feel no fear, who plunge among the enemy with their hearts soaring. Not at all. He was prey to terror all his flying days, by his own account, from the start to the finish. Each flight meant he had to take control of his fear, suppress it, deflect it, until he was in a position to do his duty. Another period might have judged him harshly for this, but not our own. For us, it surely makes him even more remarkable. How much richer is his final achievement in serving his country's interests so fiercely and so continuously, when he paid in terror for every flight he made? For me, this is a real hero. Not some fool who had no understanding of danger, but a normal, sensible and sensitive fellow, who had to conquer his fear to serve his country. I salute him, and I would finish by quoting Sir Arthur Harris's description of Gibson in his book The Enemy Ahead. *He was 'as great a warrior as this island ever bred'.*

No one is awarded a Victoria Cross who does not deserve it, although there is no exact science when it comes to analysing extreme bravery. Character is also rarely taken into account, and, although there is an old adage about there being no such thing as an atheist when shells are falling around a foxhole, some people really are psychologically better equipped to deal with danger than others. Think of extreme sportsmen; for them, danger is a compulsion. In the Second World War, there were men who relished battle and who really did not feel much fear. I remember interviewing George Jellicoe, who had served in the SAS and commanded the SBS, and who, with one other man, had captured Athens on a bicycle. He had loved the adventure and adrenaline-charged action of war. For him it had been like Boy Scouts with guns. Then there was the remarkable reconnaissance pilot Adrian Warburton. Those who flew with him repeatedly said he felt no fear; certainly, the risks he took were enormous and all done with a breezy nonchalance of one hardly struggling with terror.

Most, though, when faced with the prospect of imminent death, do, understandably, feel extreme terror and it is their ability to overcome this that is so remarkable. Bomber crews had to repeatedly conquer these fears, and with rapidly diminishing odds every time they flew; death, often random, lurked at every moment of a mission. This had an understandably debilitating effect on those flying operations over enemy territory, which was why, in Bomber Command, no one was expected to fly more than thirty missions without a protracted break and then only a further twenty in all. After fifty missions, if they were still alive, the operational careers of Bomber Command crews were over.

Some years ago I was talking to the legendary test pilot Captain Eric 'Winkle' Brown, and the conversation turned to Guy Gibson. The two had met during the war and Winkle recounted a conversation they had had. 'Do you ever feel scared when you get inside a cockpit?' Gibson had asked him. Winkle had replied that, no, he did not. He liked to make sure he was properly briefed and had done his homework and then took off feeling untroubled. Gibson had thought about this for a moment and then had said, 'I feel absolutely petrified every time.'[1]

'I admit,' Winkle told me, 'I was surprised about that.'[2] By the time of their meeting, Gibson was one of the most celebrated pilots in the RAF, with a VC, two DSOs and a further brace of DFCs – and certainly many more than fifty bomber missions to his name.

His first operational mission had come on the very opening day of Britain's war, Sunday 3 September 1939, when he was the pilot of one of twenty-seven crews sent by RAF Bomber Command to try and find and bomb the German fleet. Back then, he had been a twenty-one-year-old flying officer fresh back from leave. He and five other crews from 83 Squadron had been told they would be taking their twin-engine Hampdens on this first bombing mission of the war soon after Prime Minister Neville Chamberlain had announced the declaration of war that morning with a scheduled take-off time of 3.30 p.m. For Gibson, the wait had seemed interminable. Even then, he was terrified at the prospect; just a few days before he'd been in Cornwall enjoying the beach, but now was about to head off to war. He was so nervous, he kept heading to the lavatory and when he finally boarded his plane he realised his hands were shaking like a leaf. 'Good luck, sir,' one of the ground crew had called to him. 'Give those bastards a real hiding.'[3] Gibson had smiled weakly and then begun his take-off.

His fears had abated a little once airborne but it had still seemed utterly surreal that he and his fellows should be flying off in an act of war. As it happened, the mission was something of a damp squib. Thick cloud covered the German fleet and although they saw faint smudges of orange as enemy anti-aircraft fire opened up, the formation leader decided this was not a good enough target marker and so banked and turned for home. Gibson duly followed, the entire formation safely touching back down again on friendly soil some time later.

Two and a half years later, however, Gibson was still flying and had an astonishing 154 operational sorties under his belt, including ninety as a Beaufighter night-fighter pilot and sixty-four bomber raids. By that time, he could and should have been grounded permanently, training new recruits or safely flying a desk, but instead was a twenty-four-year-old Wing Commander and CO of 106 Squadron, and one of the brightest young commanders in Bomber Command, known for his determined 'press on' attitude and apparent cool imperturbability.

On the night of 16/17 January 1943, Bomber Command were sent to attack Berlin, the first time in over a year, and 106 Squadron were among those briefed to take part. Gibson was also due to be flying that night and had been entrusted with taking a journalist along for the ride. Richard Dimbleby had been given complete and unprecedented free access to make a powerful report on the battle being waged by Bomber Command and had been determined to experience just one bombing raid himself. They took off without incident but, as they crossed the Dutch coast, flak opened up 'in little winking flashes'[4], but none hit them and they pushed on until they eventually neared Berlin. Dimbleby was mesmerised by the searchlights that crisscrossed the sky but horrified by the amount of flak that caused the Lancaster to jolt and jerk around the sky. That night, Gibson's Lancaster was carrying just one large 8,000lb bomb but there was cloud about on the first bomb run and so the bomb-aimer could not see his target. Round they went again, with more flak bursting nearby, but having survived the second run they still couldn't see the target and so Gibson flew them in a wide circle yet again. This third time, they finally dropped the bomb, then Gibson quickly pulled away, corkscrewing the mighty Lancaster to shake off any enemy night fighter or searchlights, and which caused Dimbleby promptly to throw up.

'A good trip and fairly successful,'[5] Gibson had jotted in his logbook once they had safely touched back down again at RAF Syerston, while Dimbleby went on to pay tribute to the bravery and skill of the crew. 'Perhaps I am shooting a line for them,' he said, 'but I think somebody ought to. They and their magnificent Lancasters, and all others like them, are taking the war right into Germany. They have been attacking, giving their lives in attack since the first day of the war.'[6] That was most certainly true of Guy Gibson.

Despite his outward imperturbability, Gibson was, however, struggling badly by this time. That fear he had felt on the first day of the war had never been conquered and later that day, 17 January, he had driven over to the military hospital at Runceby to see Corporal Maggie North, a nurse there with whom he had begun an intense, albeit platonic, relationship. They had met a few weeks before in December when Gibson's great friend and mentor, the station commander Group Captain Gus Walker, had lost an arm when a Lancaster had exploded on the runway.

Gibson was married to a dancer, Eve Moore, eight years his senior, with whom he had become infatuated during the autumn of 1940. There had never been any great meeting of minds but he had felt certain he would die, Eve was very alluring and so he had persuaded her to marry him. Because of their separate professional commitments, however, they had spent little time together. He had instantly clicked with Maggie North, however. As CO of 106 Squadron, Gibson always put on an act: to his men, he was the indefatigable, cheery and gung-ho bomber commander, flying by example and always willing to have a beer with his men, but also something of a martinet, too. Men came and went, but Gibson never betrayed more than the obvious regret of a commander. He knew that he, above all, had to set the right example. With Maggie, however, he could be himself because she understood what he was going through; he did not need to hide his insecurities or fears.

That day she found him sitting in his car waiting for her, staring into space and chewing on an unlit pipe. He was also shaking uncontrollably.

'Please hold me,' he asked her and she did so, in silence, until the shaking stopped.

'Ops last night?'[7] she asked him. Gibson nodded in reply, but mentioned nothing of the Berlin raid nor the fact that two of his best friends and most experienced crews had been shot down and killed just a few days earlier.

* * *

By March 1943, Gibson's operational career was finally coming to an end – for the foreseeable future at any rate. However, there was one more raid to undertake before he bade farewell to 106 Squadron. It was his seventy-second and the target was Stuttgart. They took off at 10.20 p.m. and, avoiding the coastal flak, were making good progress towards the city when suddenly his flight engineer reported trouble from the port outer engine. Gibson glanced left across the wing and saw the propeller stuttering then felt it on the throttle, and then it shut down completely. This meant they were now on three engines and in the bomb-laden aircraft meant they needed to lose height, which in turn made them more vulnerable.

Gibson would have been entirely within his rights to turn around but instead he flew on, dropping out of formation and losing height. They managed to reach Stuttgart, by which time fires were already raging. Four miles above, the bomber stream was dropping bombs and one 8,000-pounder hurtled past his wing tip, narrowly missing them. Pressing on, they managed to drop their own bombs on target, then, with the Lancaster now dramatically lightened, headed home at just 4,000 feet. The journey back was physically and mentally exhausting for Gibson as he tried to counteract the asymmetrical torque caused by the loss of one engine and all the time in the knowledge that a crippled low-flying bomber was especially vulnerable to night fighters and flak. Three and a half hours after leaving Stuttgart, however, they made it, touching back down at Syerston in one piece.

Later that day, Gibson was recommended for an immediate bar to his Distinguished Service Order. 'Any Captain who completes 172 sorties in outstanding manner is worth two DSOs if not a VC,' wrote Air Marshal Arthur Harris, C-in-C Bomber Command. 'Bar to DSO approved.'[8]

Gibson was now looking forward to well-earned and desperately needed rest. For several months he had been showing clear signs of combat fatigue and was now physically and mentally extremely fragile. His relationship with Maggie North had come to an abrupt end after she had become engaged, and with his wife a virtual stranger there were few people he could now turn to for solace. Time off, however, would unquestionably help.

The promised leave, however, would have to wait. A few days after the Stuttgart raid he was summoned to Bomber Commander 5 Group HQ in Grantham to see Air Vice Marshal Ralph Cochrane. 'How would you like the idea,' Cochrane asked him, 'of doing one more trip?'

Gibson's spirits immediately fell and his mind thought of more flak and night fighters. 'What kind of trip, sir?' he asked.

'A pretty important one,' Cochrane replied, 'perhaps one of the most devastating of all time. I can't tell you any more now. Do you want to do it?'[9]

Gibson did not but felt he had no choice. He initially thought Cochrane meant for that same night, but in this he was mistaken. Rather, he was being asked to help form a brand new squadron especially to carry out one particular raid using a new and as yet entirely untested weapon. All this was to be done in the utmost secrecy and even the crews he was to help recruit were not to have a whisper of what it was all about.

Over the ensuing weeks, he alone from this new squadron, soon to be given the number 617, was allowed in on the secret. Barnes Wallis, the Assistant Chief Designer at Vickers Aviation, had invented a bomb that could bounce on water. This meant it could, in theory, skip over the vertical steel anti-torpedo nets that protected the largest of Germany's gravity dams. These dams, the Mohne especially, but also the Eder, were vital for supplying both drinking water for the large conurbations of the Ruhr industrial heartland and other areas, and also for industrial processes. Their collapse would also cause untold damage. The idea was that the bomb, codenamed UPKEEP, would skip over the nets, hit the face of the dam wall, sink and then explode. The effect of the detonation combined with the pressure of the water above would be enough to destroy the two largest dams in Germany. However, they had to hit their mark perfectly dead centre of the dam wall and at a time when the water level above was high enough to provide the ideal hydrostatic pressure to tamp the bomb. That meant before the beginning of June and realistically, since they would have to approach the dams at very low level, they would also need the light of a full or nearly full moon. It would have to take place in the middle of May.

Gibson arrived at RAF Scampton just north of Lincoln on 21 March, by which time he had barely any crews or any equipment and about nine weeks in which to get ready. Bomber crews usually flew out of close formation and at heights in excess of 18,000 feet, and then dropped their bombs on what they hoped was the right target. If they detonated within a mile or so they were doing well. Now, he was being asked to oversee the training of an entire squadron to operate at very low level and drop an entirely new type of bomb on a metaphorical sixpence, and with just eight weeks of training. It was a very tall order indeed.

By Sunday 15 May 1943, Gibson had pulled it off, although he had been ably supported by his best pilots and crews and by his experienced flight commanders. Nonetheless, many of the crews for this special high-risk operation were not all as experienced as he would have liked and not all had mastered the twin demands of very low-level flying and pinpoint bombing accuracy. He himself had had nothing like as much training as the rest because of other demands: repeated trips to meet with Barnes Wallis and senior commanders, as well as planning the raid itself, and also the normal day-to-day tasks of running a squadron, made worse because 617 was brand new and he and his staff had had to start from scratch. On top of that, he was suffering from exhaustion and painful and debilitating gout. The medical officer tried to take him off flying, but Gibson laughed and dismissed the notion. To make matters worse, his beloved dog and constant companion at Scampton was also run over and killed the night before – another blow with which he had to contend; now it wasn't just friends and colleagues being killed but his pet as well.

Despite this, Gibson was determined once again to lead by example. The squadron was split into three groups: the second wave of five Lancasters would attack the Sorpe dam, although it would take off first. The UPKEEP bombs were designed to smash gravity dams, but the Sorpe was an earthen type. However, Wallis reckoned it was still possible to break it if bombers dropped their UPKEEPs right on top by flying along the length of the dam. The first wave of nine aircraft in three 'vics' – arrowhead formations – of three were to attack the Mohne first and then the Eder. Finally, the remaining five were to form a reserve and strike either those dams not destroyed in the first and second waves or hit a number of lesser dams in the area. Gibson's Lancaster, *G-George*, was, like all the others, specially adapted to carry the UPKEEP, which would not fit in a normal Lancaster and which, in any case, needed to be rotating at 400 revolutions per minute at the moment it was dropped. Gibson was to be the lead aircraft in the first wave.

Lancasters weigh around thirty tons and UPKEEP a further four. The wingspan is 102 feet, but they were flying at under 100 feet all the way. This was because at that height they could benefit from the curvature of the earth and avoid radar detection. The flip side was that this gave pilots very little room for manoeuvre should they be hit by flak or if they suddenly came upon a rise in the ground or some other unexpected object. And although there was a full moon, they were flying at night, where the light was limited and the distance at which the human eye could pick out defined distance was less. It also made navigation much harder because the ability to see a wide expanse of ground was less and they were operating too low to use normal navigation aids of the day such as GEE, OBOE or H2S. Just getting to the target required immense skill and, above all, sustained concentration. Not all made it. At least two flew into power cables, while others were damaged and had to turn back or were shot down.

Of the first wave, however, eight made it to the target and Gibson and his crew were the first to reach the Mohne and they immediately came under heavier fire than they had expected. Gibson began by carrying out a dummy run, curling in low and flying straight over the centre of the dam at just sixty feet off the water directly towards the dam wall. Tracer pumped towards them, but then they were past and climbing, turned for what was now to be the actual bomb run. It was now 12.28 a.m. In they swept, tracer from multiple gun positions on and around the dam pulsing towards them and horribly close, too. At that height, any one of those shells could have finished them. In effect, it was like a man charging over open ground directly towards a machine gun. Gibson felt he was being dragged towards the target against his will. He was gripped with fear. Any moment, he thought, we will all be dead.

A few hundred yards from the dam, the revolving UPKEEP was released and skipped across the water to hit the dam wall as Gibson hurtled over and began climbing once more in a wide arc. Moments later, there was a huge explosion and a column of water erupted over a thousand feet into the sky. As the flume settled, however, the dam wall still stood firm.

Next up was John Hopgood and his crew. Hopgood was Gibson's closest friend from his time with 106 Squadron. He now told Hopgood he would fly alongside and try and draw off the flak. It worked in as much as Gibson's Lancaster was being targeted as well as Hopgood's but it was the latter aircraft, *M-Mother*, that was hit, although not before the UPKEEP had been dropped and bounced over the dam wall and exploded on the power station below on the far side, destroying it in the process. Hopgood's plane was doomed, however. Three managed to bail out, although one did not survive, but Hopgood and the rest of the crew were killed as the Lancaster crashed and exploded into a million pieces.

Having watched his best friend die, Gibson then turned for a fourth run as Micky Martin began his run in *P-Popsie*. The Lancaster was also hit but survived although the UPKEEP sheered away to the left and exploded with the dam still solidly intact. Gibson now turned for a staggering fifth run as 'Dinghy' Young in *A-Apple* began his run. This time, Gibson ordered his own identification lights to be turned on and off as a further distraction. His machine guns were also fired at the defenders as Young swept in low and the fourth UPKEEP was dropped. After three good bounces it hit the wall perfectly, sank, then moments later came the high eruption of water. 'I think I've done it!' Young called out over the radio although, as the water subsided, the dam still appeared to be intact. Gibson now turned back for his sixth distracting run, although joined this time by Micky Martin as David Maltby and his crew prepared to make their run. As they sped across the water, however, the top of the Mohne began to crumble and as the next Upkeep was dropped, struck and exploded, so the whole dam was already collapsing. Suddenly, there was a vast breach, with water pouring through. Gibson thought it looked like stirred porridge in the moonlight. Below, millions of cubic metres of water were now hurtling down the valley, sweeping all before it. Circling overhead, he now ordered Martin, Maltby and Young to head for home, while he joined the rest of the first wave and headed east to find the Eder.

It was Gibson's crew that found it. I flew the same route many, many years later and even at 500 feet it was easy to get lost. At night, with valley mists building all the time, it must have been almost impossible. There was no flak at the Eder, but it was technically much harder to fly over and extremely dangerous at the low heights the operation demanded. Here there were steep wooded hills and the lake snaked awkwardly. Gibson waited, circling, encouraging his remaining crews, and on the third attempt this mighty edifice was also breached. It was a truly extraordinary feat. Only then could he finally turn and make the run home.

Elsewhere, the Sorpe was hit twice, and badly damaged – so much so that it had to be drained completely to be repaired – but it was not breached. Nonetheless, the two main targets had been, and spectacularly so, although for the returning crews the same dangers faced on the outward leg faced them on the return. Several more were shot down, including Dinghy Young's crew as they crossed back over the Dutch coast. In all, eight of the nineteen crews did not make it.

Yet Gibson and his crew did make it home. Somehow, he had survived again, and this time, at long last, he was finally given the leave he so badly deserved – and needed. He and all the surviving crews were also rightly feted for their considerable achievement, one that had caused untold damage to the German war effort and which would require a massive diversion of resources and barely comprehensible cost to repair and at a time when Germany could in no way afford such catastrophic damage. Gibson himself was awarded the Victoria Cross and his and his men's achievement hailed around the free world.

He was sent to the United States to promote the war effort, something he loathed. He drank too much and returned in December assuming he would return to active service. This was refused and so he spent the next few months writing a memoir, *Enemy Coast Ahead*, as requested by the Air Ministry. The original draft was too brutally honest for their liking, but an amended version in which he came across as the cheery, indefatigable type he had always tried to portray was duly published. He was then given a staff post at 55 Base at East Kirkby, the hub of three squadrons. Racked by guilt for not flying, he started up with Maggie once more and began unofficially flying. He took the place of a Lancaster pilot from 630 Squadron on a raid on a V1 missile site and then was posted to 54 Base HQ at Coningsby. There he made himself master bomber on 19 September 1944 for a raid on Rheydt. This time, though, he was at the controls of a twin-engine Mosquito, a plane for which he had not received proper briefing or training. Driven by a kind of manic madness, it was certainly an unnecessary and foolhardy decision. It remains unclear exactly what happened, but the expectation of death, which had followed him since that opening day of the war, finally came true. His Mosquito crashed near Steenbergen in Holland, killing both Gibson and his navigator. It was terrible, tragic and pointless but, somehow, an inevitable end for one of Britain's truly great war heroes.

Gibson could be arrogant and he was opinionated and not without a malicious streak. Like all great heroes, he was flawed, but his achievements truly were Herculean. At school he'd not showed any great intellectual aptitude, nor was he particularly good at sports or widely popular; there had been nothing about him that had marked him out for greatness. Yet somewhere, deep inside, there was an extraordinary inner resolve, a steel core that enabled him, despite his bouts of intense fear, despite clear signs of mental illness and combat fatigue, to dig deep and somehow drive himself and others forward. His leadership was always impressive but on Operation CHASTISE, as the Dams Raid was officially called, he surpassed himself. Although ill enough to be grounded, he led those nineteen crews from the start to the end and in doing so pulled off one of the most extraordinarily daring and outrageous air operations ever mounted. At the time, he had been still only twenty-four.

Wing Commander Guy Gibson, VC, DSO and bar, DFC and bar – deserving of all those awards, and not least the Victoria Cross. A truly remarkable, yet deeply tragic, man.

12

PETTY OFFICER, FIRST CLASS
WILLIAM HALL VC

Introduced by Frank Bruno MBE

As a child I wanted to be a world champion in my chosen sport of boxing. My sporting hero was Muhammad Ali but, when I look through these stories, what I thought was hard work getting to the top of my chosen occupation is nothing compared to what these people in this book did. My reward was financial, and world recognition; these people did their various historic deeds not for the medal or the recognition but because it was their duty. In a current world where to be on TV, not achieving anything in life, makes you an overnight celebrity I humbly ask that, if there is another plateau higher than 'celebrity' or the overused word 'legend', then these people fully deserve the respect and almost reverence we must give them. Let's tell our children about them – may they never be forgotten. This brings me to William Hall VC.

I had never heard about William Hall VC but I'm glad I know about him now because his whole life was a story of courage winning against the odds. The story you are about to read is in two parts.

The first describes the Victoria Cross action which shows William using his physical strength and endurance to keep the cannon firing against overwhelming odds. It was a four-man job to fire that cannon, but William did it all alone after he witnessed the death of all his friends and with incoming rifle and artillery fire all around. A lesser person would have collapsed in a heap on the floor, but William was strong and kept going.

The wider story tells of a family who escaped slavery and staggered north to Canada in fear and dread. William later joined the navy in Liverpool and was alone in race and nationality when he did so, which must have caused him hardship on every level, but this is a life of triumph. In the narrow story he was amazingly effective in keeping up the fire and saved the day. In the wider story he must have inspired respect and admiration among his shipmates and officers. Why else would they have recommended him for the Victoria Cross and promoted him to Petty Officer, First Class?

William Hall VC ignored the abuse he must have suffered, showed what he was capable of and what kind of man he was. This makes him an inspiration to me and, I hope, to you, too.

In the archive of the library of King's College in Halifax, Nova Scotia, rests a small wooden cross, a replica of a much larger stone monument. It is a Celtic cross on a stepped base of three wooden squares and the wood it is made from comes from a particular house in Cawnpore, India: the base from the doors and the cross from a tree in the property's interior square. The house in question became famous for tragic reasons, as the inscription on the front of the cross makes clear: 'In memory of the / women and children of H.M. 32nd Regt. / who were slaughtered near this spot / 15th July A.D. 1857 / This memorial was raised by 20 men of the same Regt. who were passing through Cawnpore / Nov. 21st 1857'.

The massacre at Cawnpore was one of the defining moments of the Indian Mutiny. The uprising of Indian troops in the Indian army was triggered by the use of the new gun cartridges for the Enfield rifle, which were purported to be greased with fat from pigs and cows – offensive to both Muslims and Hindus. Whether the cartridges were indeed greased in this way is unclear: according to Saul David's *The Indian Mutiny*, it was a mixture of 'five parts tallow, five parts stearine (putrified fatty acids) and one part wax . . . But the [Bengal Army's Ordnance] Department made the fatal, and unforgiveable, error of not specifying what type of tallow was to be used'.[1] Later on, 'the officer in charge of the Fort William arsenal testified that no one had bothered to check what type of animal fat was used'.[2] Whatever the truth, the story quickly spread through the Indian troops – with dangerous and explosive results.

One person who took advantage of this was Nana Sahib, the adopted son of Baja Rao II, the last Peshwa of the Maratha Confederacy. The British had stopped his pension; this uprising was the perfect opportunity for revenge. The Nana decided to take Cawnpore, a military base by the shores of the Ganges, 700 miles upriver from Calcutta. The British troops there, despite being heavily outnumbered, held out for three weeks, before accepting a deal of safe passage downriver to Allahabad. The deal, however, turned out to be a trap – and having been ambushed, 125 women and children were taken back to a house in Cawnpore, where they were massacred (the logic being to dissuade the British from returning to take the city).

A few weeks before the 32nd Regiment arrived in Cawnpore, a fellow Nova Scotian arrived in the town as part of an earlier force. By the time they arrived, William Hall had become the first black person, the first Nova Scotian and the first Canadian sailor to be awarded the Victoria Cross. Hall was part of the Naval Brigade, a select group of individuals from HMS *Shannon* who, under the orders of Captain Peel, had arrived to bolster the British Army forces, led by Sir Colin Campbell. Although Cawnpore had by now been recaptured, the marks of the massacre were all too apparent: 'the blood of the helpless women was still upon the walls', Hall later recalled.

The battleground in the conflict had now shifted to Lucknow, the capital of Oudh. Here, General Havelock and his men had taken shelter in the Residency: trapped for six weeks and surrounded by Indian mutineers, they were running out of supplies and desperate for relief. Breaching the city was a stiff military challenge: one of the main obstacles was the Shah Najaf, a mosque with thick, twenty-foot walls, which was well protected and heavily armed. Capture this, and the route to the Residency was clear.

Captain Peel's Shannon Brigade had at their disposal six 24-pounders, and a pair each of 8-inch howitzers and rocket tubes. On the afternoon of 16 November 1857, the attack began. For several hours, Peel's battery bombarded the walls from a distance of several hundred metres, 'as if he had been laying the *Shannon* alongside an enemy's frigate'[3]. But with little impact, it was clear that the guns would have to be moved closer – and in easy range of the enemy's own weapons.

As Peel gave the order for two of his 24-pounders to move much nearer to the Shah Najaf, it became clear that one of the crews was a man short. It was at that point that Hall stepped forward to volunteer his services.

'I guess I will go in with you,' he told the captain of the gun.

'You had better not,' was the captain's reply. 'It means almost certain death.'

Hall, though, was not to be moved in his decision. 'I will take the chance, sir,' he replied.[4]

* * *

Precisely when and where in Nova Scotia William Hall was born is sometimes the subject of debate. Depending on which account you read, it could be Horton Bluff, Kings County, in 1824; Hantsport in 1825; Avonport, Kings County, in 1826; Horton Bluff again; or Newport, Hants County, in April 1827; or Summerville, Hants County in 1829 or 1832. This uncertainty is partly because of a lack of information and statistics kept by the provincial government of the time, and also different dates. However, the Victoria Cross and George Cross Association, having consulted with a number of historians, put his birth as 28 April 1827, in Horton.

What is generally agreed, however, is that Hall's parents, Jacob and Lucy, were former slaves who escaped to Nova Scotia as a consequence of the War of 1812 between the United Kingdom and the United States.

Jacob and Lucy were both slaves in St Mary's County, Maryland, and escaped from their respective masters, Robert Duncanson and George Locker. Again, accounts differ as to which ship they escaped on, but the most reliable suggest that they managed to get on to HMS *Havannah*, and eventually arrived at Halifax, Nova Scotia, on board HMS *Ceylon* in May 1815.

Jacob initially found work in a shipbuilding yard in Summerville belonging to Abraham Cunard (his son, Samuel Cunard, would found the British and North American Royal Mail Steam Packet Company in 1840, which in turn would become the Cunard Line). At some point in the early 1820s, the family moved to Horton Bluff, Kings County, with Jacob presumed to be working at one of the shipyards in nearby Hantsport, owned by J. B. North or Ezra Churchill, as a rigger and a caulker.

Horton Bluff was a small village on the shores of the Avon River, with the house high on a hill where, today, the Horton Bluff lighthouse sits. This was where William Hall was brought up and, as the aforementioned article by Charles Bruce Fergusson describes it, 'from this windswept hill of his boyhood he could look down on the one hand on the farms and marshes of Avonport and the fertile meadows of Grand Pre, and on the other on the Mouth of the Avon and the broad expanse of the Basin of Minas, guarded by its faithful, brooding sentinel, Blomidon. White sails daily passing before his eyes carried him in imagination beyond Cape Blomidon around which they disappeared.'[5] William Hall was one of seven children – alongside older brothers Jacob Henry and Charles Gideon, and sisters Margaret Maria, Lucy Ann, Mary Jane and Rachael Clara. Both family and home were clearly important to him: in later years, as we shall see, he returned to Horton where his lived with his two youngest sisters.

Hall's education is assumed to have been fairly limited. At this time there was no provision for free schooling and there was no school within several miles of the family home. Certainly, there is no record of Hall having attended any of the local common or grammar schools. There was an African School established in Halifax by the Protestant Gospel

School in autumn 1835, and it is possible that Hall went here, staying with a relative to study. One of the subjects taught here to the young black students was navigation, which would clearly have stood him in good stead for his subsequent career.

Whether it was being inspired by watching ships from his family home, his father's work or possibly what he studied at school, Hall was destined for the sea. Records suggest that he first shipped the mast of a small boat out of Hantsport in 1844 (aged fifteen, depending on which birth story you believe). The following year, 1845, he joined the merchant navy, where he would remain as a merchant seaman for the next years. As part of the crew of the *Kent* of Kentville, Nova Scotia, he sailed to London and Boston, Massachusetts.

It was in Boston in the autumn of 1847 that Hall joined the United States Navy. He began his time serving as an ordinary seaman on board the *Franklin*, a guardship. From here, he was transferred to the frigate USS *Savannah*, the flagship of the Pacific Squadron, sailing around Cape Horn and landing in San Francisco in summer 1848. From here, in August 1848, he joined the battleship *Ohio*, and served alongside midshipman John Taylor Wood, who would perform heroically for the Confederacy during the American Civil War. Between 1846 and 1848, the US was involved in the Mexican–American War and although some accounts suggest Hall took part in this, it appears that his time on the various ships just missed active service: certainly, the US Navy refused his request for a war pension on the grounds that his service was just after.

Hall left the US Navy in 1849, and, after some time working on ships out of Boston, sailed to the UK on board the clipper *Tam O'Shanter*, arriving at Liverpool in early 1852. It was here, in February 1852, that he enlisted in the Royal Navy at the recruiting office in Red Cross Street. At a talk given to the Royal Nova Scotia Historical Society in 1993, David W. States described the recruitment policy of the Royal Navy at the time, and its somewhat dubious classifications:

The presence of persons of African descent in the merchant service or Navy of Great Britain was not a rarity as some historians may suppose . . . blacks were considered 'foreigners' who were willing to serve in the Royal Navy and came from every nation in the world . . . Blacks had fought in the Navy of Great Britain during both the Revolutionary War and the War of 1812, and were therefore not a new phenomenon when Hall joined . . . a regulation cited in a history of the recruitment of the British Army of the 1840s describe the practice in force when William Hall enlisted in 1852: 'The enlistment of foreigners is permitted, provided that in every regiment, battalion or corps, the number shall not exceed the proportion of one to fifty of natural born subjects.'[6]

Hall was initially drafted on to HMS *Rodney*, a ninety-gun ship under the command of Captain Charles Graham. After two years as part of the Channel Fleet, in 1854, the *Rodney* was sent to the Mediterranean and on to the Black Sea, passing through the Dardanelles and Bosphorus, to play its part in the Crimean War. For Hall, this was to be his first experience of being part of a Naval Brigade, being one of the men from the *Rodney* chosen to support the regular soldiers, under the command of George G. Randolph. Hall was tasked with manning the thirty-five guns in the siege batteries.

Hall's brigade took part in a number of key episodes of the campaign, including the Siege of Sebastopol, the Battle of Inkerman and the attacks on the Redan. He himself was captain on one of the Lancaster guns in Green Hill. Conditions were extremely difficult, both in terms of the heavy casualties suffered from the fighting and also the appalling weather – a hurricane-force wind ripping through the camp and the winter faced with lack of clothing after the ship providing them was sunk. Disease was widespread, and not helped by a severe lack of rations and food: Hall recalled later how Captain Lushington, one of those in command of the Naval Brigade, managed to secure himself a steak, only for another desperate, starving soldier to steal it, while it was cooking. Lushington called the man a 'd—d scoundrel' and, despite the soldier having had no food all day, ordered the man to be flogged four dozen times as punishment for his theft.

In the midst of this hardship and deprivation, Hall was also witness to the rarest sort of courage. That came from Acting Mate William Hewett, a member of Hall's battery, who found himself under attack from the Russians and was given the order to retreat. Hewett, however, refused, saying that he would only take orders from Captain Lushington. He proceeded to hold firm and used his gun to successfully hold back the enemy advance. For his endeavours, he would be one of the 111 men fighting in the Crimean War to be awarded the Victoria Cross.

Following the war, for which he was awarded both the Crimea Medal (and Turkish Medal and also the Inkerman and Sebastopol clasps), Hall continued to serve on the *Rodney* until 1856. Here he switched briefly to service on HMS *Victory*, before joining HMS *Shannon* in October 1856. *Shannon* was captained by Captain William Peel, the son of the former prime minister Sir Robert Peel. She left England for the China Station in March 1857, travelling down to Simon's Bay in South Africa by May, Singapore by June and then, finally, Hong Kong. By the time *Shannon* had arrived, however, the Indian Mutiny was in full swing. She was ordered, along with several other ships, to travel immediately to Calcutta, to give assistance to the embattled British troops.

Having arrived at Calcutta – a journey that saw Hall save the life of a fellow seaman from drowning in the Ganges – Peel created his Naval Brigade of some 400-odd men, along with the armoury mentioned earlier. This brigade and weaponry then made its way first to Allahabad and then on to Cawnpore. Having defeated the mutineers here, the brigade then moved on to Lucknow and the attack on the afternoon of 16 November.

The events this day were to see considerable bravery – in total, eighteen Victoria Crosses were awarded for endeavours that day. But even among this remarkable bravery, Hall's actions stand out. Having been warned of the danger in volunteering to take the place of the missing man on the guns aimed at the Shah Najaf, Hall rose to the challenge regardless. Peel's warnings were to prove sadly prescient: within minutes, the entire crew of one of the two guns had been killed by gunfire from within the mosque's defences. On the second crew, only Hall and Lieutenant Thomas James Young were still alive – and with the latter wounded, too. Yet somehow Hall continued, doing the work that normally required a whole crew, finding the strength to repeatedly sponge and load the weapon, and, despite being continually under fire, sent shell after shell smashing into the mosque wall. His courage was to bring immediate results, successfully breaching the wall where all previous attempts had failed. The waiting Highlanders were able to climb up and scramble inside, running round to open the main gates. The mutineers fled, and the battle had turned: the following day, the British troops reached the embattled Residency.

Hall is said to have remarked afterwards, 'We would have liked to go in with the soldiers, but the gun's crew had to stay with the gun.'[7] But he had already more than made his mark in the battle. Captain Noel Salmon described him as 'a fine powerful man and as steady as a rock under fire'[8]. For their heroics, Hall and Young were both awarded the Victoria Cross, Hall eventually receiving his from Rear Admiral Charles Talbot in October 1859, at a ceremony in Queenstown Harbour in Ireland.

By this point, Hall was serving on HMS *Donegal*: he'd left the *Shannon* the previous year, having risen from able bodied seaman to leading seaman, captain of the mast and captain of the foretop. Hall spent three years on the *Donegal* before joining HMS *Hero* is June 1862, and then spending further service on the *Kangsoo*, HMS *Bellerophon*, HMS *Impregnable*, HMS *Petrel* and, finally, the *Royal Adelaide*. This was to be his last ship, finishing his long and distinguished naval career in July 1876, as Petty Officer, First Class.

The story has it that Hall was offered a post in Whitehall, but turned it down, saying, 'I want to spend my days in the old place, the land of my birth.'[9] He returned to Canada, and to Horton Bluff in particular, where he took up farming on a plot close to where he had been born – and where he lived with his sisters Mary and Rachel. His farm boasted a two-acre orchard, and also cattle and poultry.

In 1900, Hall was tracked down by a journalist, D. V. Warner, who found him in the fields sharpening his scythe. Hall had to have his exploits teased out of him, but eventually led Warner into the farmhouse, where he showed him his medal: a previous visitor had taken the blue ribbon it was normally attached to, and Hall had fixed it to a watch chain instead. 'It's nothing to have a cross now,' Hall somewhat disingenuously told the journalist, 'they're as thick as peas.'[10]

Hall died on 25 August 1904, and was buried without honours in an unmarked grave at Stoney Hill Baptist Church Cemetery in Lockartville. His sisters, left in debt by his death, sold his medals to the Nova Scotia Historical Society to raise funds. Hall himself became something of a forgotten hero for the next few decades, until, in the mid-1930s, interest in his exploits was rekindled. Hall's grave was located and, after a campaign to give him a proper burial, his remains were disinterred and reburied in the churchyard of Hantsport Baptist Church, along with a more fitting memorial.

In 2010 he was again remembered, when a Canadian postage stamp was issued in his honour. Then in 2015, it was announced that Hall was to be remembered with another sort of memorial, when the Canadian government revealed that a new Royal Canadian naval ship would be named after him. Present at the announcement in Africville were a number of Hall's descendants. Phillip Safire, a sergeant in the Canadian forces, remembered that 'growing up, we heard lots and lots of stories [about Hall] . . . this was just our aunts and uncles and grandparents talking, but I never learned about it in school . . . Canadian history is made up of a lot of different groups . . . recognising a part of that history that is not well known is a great day.'

Sharon Rivest, Hall's great-niece, described the naming of the ship after him as 'healing and overwhelming. I'm just thankful that he will not just go and disappear in history. Every time someone steps on the ship, they are going to ask what the story is. That's all we want.'

13

LIEUTENANT COMMANDER
ARTHUR HARRISON VC

Introduced by Bill Beaumont CBE DL

I am humbled to have been asked to write about Arthur Harrison, the only England international rugby player to be awarded the Victoria Cross. It was his inspired leadership and courage during the First World War that prompted Stuart Lancaster's England team in 2014 to name a bravery award after him.

When you read about Harrison's selfless bravery in leading his troops at the Zeebrugge raid on 23 April 1918, it is obvious why he was also a great leader of rugby players – especially when you learn how he continued to lead his troops from the front, despite being seriously injured.

To quote the captain of his ship that day: 'Harrison's charge down that narrow gangway of death was a worthy finale to the large number of charges, which, as a forward of the first rank, he had led down many a rugby football ground.'

The dropping of the atomic bombs on Japan in August 1945 marked a crucial turning point in world history. In the flattened remains of Hiroshima and Nagasaki, a new age of warfare had arrived in which the vast conscript armies of the two world wars would never again be repeated. Science and technology, which had transformed warfare over the previous fifty years, had taken another giant leap forward. Even today, with the end of the Second World War still within living memory, it seems incredible that those two global conflicts could have affected the lives of every man, woman and child of every major combating nation so completely. By the Second World War, Britain was more dependent on technology and mechanisation – 'steel not flesh' – than it had been a generation earlier, but, even so, every fit and able young man was expected to do his bit for the war effort, and very often that meant donning a uniform and fighting, either on land, or, increasingly, in the air or at sea.

No one was exempt. Imagine if today's footballing or rugby and cricketing superstars suddenly found their careers cut dramatically short and having to swap sports kit for uniforms and weapons. It's hard to picture it, yet that was exactly what happened. I once talked at length to the late Sir Tom Finney of Preston North End (his only club) and England, knighted for his contribution to English football and still one of the finest strikers to play for his country. His career was not only delayed by the Second World War but he ended up in North Africa and then inside a tank fighting the Germans in Italy. Fortunately, he was still young enough at the end of it all to resume his playing career.

He also emerged unscathed: more than could be said for the vast majority of front-line combatants in the Italian campaign. In fact, although thanks to mechanisation the numbers of front-line troops in the British Army were fewer in the Second World War, the chances of coming through unscathed were even lower than they had been in 1914–18. On the other hand, the sheer scale of British manpower thrust into the front line in the First World War remains hard to comprehend, even to this day. What's more, during that war, sportsmen were expected to do their patriotic duty just as Tom Finney would be a generation later. Between 1914 and the armistice of November 1918, footballers, cricketers, athletes and a host of other sporting stars not only volunteered but also gave their lives.

Many more were horribly maimed and never played sport again, but, proportionally, rugby unquestionably suffered the most. England alone suffered 27 international players killed in the war, Scotland 31, Wales 13, Ireland 9 and France 22. The Dominions of New Zealand, South Africa and Australia suffered similar losses. Most of those internationals killed had been playing and in the prime of life when war broke out in August 1914.

One of those was Arthur Harrison, who played only two Tests for England, before the war cut short his international career, as it did that of so many others. On St Valentine's Day 1914, he and his namesake, Harold 'Dreadnought' Harrison, were selected to strengthen the England scrum against Ireland and helped the side to grind down the Irish with a 17–12 victory. Both men then played in the season finale in Paris, which England won 39–13 on 13 April. The five tries scored had put a gloss on the England scoreline, but it was the English pack that had worked so much better than the French and which had enabled the backs to get away. That victory gave England the Grand Slam for the second successive year. They would not win it again for a further seven, and by then it was a very different team.

In those days rugby union was an amateur game and so most players had to earn a living outside the sport. Rugby was very popular in the armed forces in part because of its sheer physicality and so a disproportionate number of players had military careers, which goes some way to explain why an equally disproportionate number of rugby internationals fought in the First World War. Harrison, despite being the son of a colonel in the Royal Fusiliers, joined the Royal Navy, a career that was mapped out from a very early age. Born in the Devon coastal resort of Torquay in 1886, he had the sea in his blood. Packed off to school at Dover College at the age of nine, five years later he won a place at the Britannia Royal Naval College. With the Royal Navy indisputably Britain's Senior Service, there was no better place for an aspiring naval cadet to be educated. It was demanding, tough, academically challenging and physically even more so, and, back in 1901, when Harrison entered the college, it was not based at the magnificent buildings now in Dartmouth but aboard creaking and long out of service wooden hulks on the River Dart.

Harrison was more than equal to such rigours, however. By the age of eighteen, when he left Dartmouth as a sub-lieutenant, he had grown into an imposing young man, broad-shouldered, sturdy, physically strong, assiduous and intelligent and keen as mustard in all that he did. He was also blessed with a magnificent jutting chin that lent ballast to his character. He appeared destined to go far in the navy, a prediction that was borne out over the next few years: he sailed through his various exams in pilotage and gunnery and by 1908 had been promoted and given his first command in Portsmouth.

He had first played rugby at prep school and had continued to do so throughout his schooling and beyond, playing regularly for the United Services Club and also for Rosslyn Park in south-west London, one of England's premier clubs, whenever leave permitted. With Rosslyn Park he toured France and even Germany, in 1913, where they played two matches against Hanover sides. He also found himself selected for the Navy against the Army, an annual match heavy with international players, and his England call-up in the final Five Nations before war was declared seemed long overdue.

The Royal Navy came first, however, which was why he had been forced to miss the Scotland game between the Ireland and French Tests, and, with international tensions rising, Lieutenant Arthur Harrison was, swiftly after the victory in Paris, back on board his ship, the battlecruiser HMS *Lion*.

Harrison was soon thrust into the action. *Lion* was the flagship of the 1st Battlecruiser Squadron alongside the *Princess Royal*, *Indefatigable* and *Queen Mary* under the command of Vice Admiral Sir David Beatty. On 28 August, less than four weeks after the outbreak of war, the Royal Navy launched the war's first major naval action. With the war going badly on land, the navy had been encouraged to do something to restore both morale and British pride. It had been observed that German destroyers were patrolling off the Heligoland Bight near the German North Sea coast and so a plan of Nelsonian daring was hatched to try to ambush these patrols. Some thirty-one Royal Navy destroyers and two cruisers along with a submarine force were sent and duly attacked shortly after 7 a.m. German light cruisers swiftly emerged to investigate although, with the tide low, German heavy capital ships were unable to follow. The British destroyers were given extra support from a light cruiser squadron and from Beatty's 1st Battlecruiser Squadron, which quickly sank three enemy light cruisers at range along with a destroyer and two torpedo boats, and severely damaged a further light cruiser and three destroyers for no loss of their own. More than seven hundred German sailors were killed and almost five hundred captured and wounded for minimal British losses and just one cruiser damaged. It had been just the kind of dramatic naval victory the British had hoped for and prompted the Kaiser to forbid anything other than close patrols and insist that, from now on, his precious High Seas Fleet was not to engage without his prior consent. In a trice, the Battle of Heligoland Bight had ensured the enemy fleet would barely venture forth into open seas again for almost two years. It was hailed as a great British victory and Harrison was among returning seamen cheered by waiting crowds as Beatty's squadron returned to port.

However, on 24 January 1915 a German raiding force did venture into the North Sea. With German messages successfully intercepted and decoded, the Royal Navy was able to intercept and then chase and harry the enemy ships as they swiftly turned tail and fled. The 1st Battlecruiser Squadron opened fire at long range and first hit the *Blücher*, a German heavy battlecruiser. On board *Lion*, the leading British cruiser, Harrison was witness to extremely heavy return fire, much of which found its mark and which forced the ship to withdraw and limp for home. The rest of the force, however, rounded on the *Blücher* and eventually sank her, although not before the rest of the enemy force had made good their escape.

Lion was now out of action undergoing repairs for the next few months, but for his part in the battle Harrison was mentioned in dispatches and also promoted to lieutenant commander. Following the battle, the battlecruiser squadrons were formed into the Battlecruiser Fleet under Admiral Beatty but, while this reorganisation was taking place and while *Lion* was being repaired, the newly promoted Harrison was given leave to tour the country playing scratch games of rugby and exhibition matches to boost morale and help raise money for war charities. With the Imperial German High Seas Fleet now skulking in port, there followed a period of comparative inactivity for Harrison and his fellows, time that was spent on courses, patrol work and training.

Not until May 1916 was he back in action and that was playing a part in what became the largest naval engagement of the war and the only time both main battle fleets clashed. Some 250 warships were engaged off Jutland on 31 May and 1 June that year and Lieutenant Commander Arthur Harrison was in the forefront of that mighty naval battle.

Neither the British nor the Germans had really wanted the battle. As with the nuclear age just over a generation later, these huge fleets, which tied up enormous amounts of money and resources, were primarily a deterrent. In the case of the German High Seas Fleet, it was designed to compel the British to tie up vast resources, prevent the Royal Navy's Grand Fleet from offering merchant shipping protection elsewhere and keep the British from attacking German inshore shipping. The Royal Navy was the superior sized force – it was the largest in the world – and commander of the Grand Fleet, Admiral Jellicoe, had no intention of risking that dominance in a naval clash where weather, circumstances and ill-luck might throw away that superiority.

However, the German Admiral Scheer had taken over command of the German fleet earlier in 1916 and had begun putting his force out to sea once a month in an attempt to lure the British out into the open and, with luck, into a position where the German battleships might create some havoc. By way of riposte, the Grand Fleet began doing much the same. At some point, the two fleets were bound to make contact, and so they did on 31 May, when Admiral Scheer's First Scouting Group ventured out into the North Sea to sweep for British patrols and any merchant vessels. Thanks to British naval intelligence, Jellicoe's main Grand Fleet and Beatty's Battlecruiser Fleet knew of this foray and were already at sea, although unaware that the rest of the German fleet had also left port at Wilhelmshaven. Beatty's fleet were therefore dangerously ahead of Jellicoe's battleships and so came within range first of the German Scouting Group and then the main High Seas Fleet. It was the five battlecruisers of Beatty's force, including HMS *Lion* with Arthur Harrison on board, that bore the brunt of the first clash in the battle, later known as the 'run to the south'.

Unfortunately, Beatty's battlecruisers failed to exploit the superior range of their guns, found themselves silhouetted against the horizon and made the error of leaving the doors between the magazines and the gun turrets open to enable quicker loading. Suddenly large numbers of shells were hurtling across the sea as both sides opened up with their guns, the mighty ships lurching with each crashing salvo. Two of Beatty's battlecruisers, *Indefatigable* and *Queen Mary*, were struck multiple times and blew up and sank with almost all hands. *Lion* was hit no fewer than fifteen times, although, along with the remaining battlecruiser force, managed to turn north. The German High Seas Fleet pursued them, only to come within range of the British battleships, which were now in line between the enemy fleet and the German home ports. The battle continued to rage until the German High Seas Fleet finally managed to get away successfully behind a smokescreen and a charge by Scheer's battlecruisers and destroyers. In all, the British came off worst with fourteen ships sunk, including three battlecruisers, and 6,094 dead, while the Germans lost eleven, among them one battlecruiser and a battleship and 2,551 killed. Neither side, however, had lost their precious battle fleets and it was the Germans, not the British, who had withdrawn. It was nonetheless a bloody nose for the Royal Navy and Arthur Harrison found himself heading back to Rosyth, on the Firth of Forth, under the steam of a wounded *Lion* for the second time.

The Battle of Jutland was the last major fleet engagement of the war, frustrating for a man of action like Harrison. It was all very well playing charity rugby matches and continuing yet more training, but for almost two years after Jutland he found himself itching to return to the fray once more. A month after Jutland came the start of the Battle of the Somme; his fellow member of the England scrum, John Abbott King, was killed in that battle. Then came the offensive at Arras in the spring, followed by the Third Battle of Ypres – or Passchendaele as it became known – in the summer and autumn of 1917. Edgar 'Mobbsy' Mobbs, a former Northampton and England captain, was killed at Passchendaele.

Although the British and German fleets were doing little more than glaring at each other from across the North Sea, there was still plenty of action at sea, as the Germans now launched their major U-boat offensive. The Battle of the Atlantic of the Second World War is rightly considered a pivotal campaign in that conflict – possibly even the most important of all in the eventual outcome – but the same battle that raged during the First World War has, for some inexplicable reason, become an almost forgotten episode, even though it very nearly brought Britain to her knees and to the peace table but ultimately came to seal Germany's fate.

On 1 February, Germany proclaimed that the waters around Britain were now to be considered a prohibited area, which meant that any ship, regardless of its nationality, entered those waters at its peril. Most U-boat attacks occurred in the Western Approaches off the British Isles and very soon began to cripple Atlantic shipping especially. In January 1917, 153,666 tons of British shipping had been sunk but those figures began to rise dramatically: 313,486 tons in February, even more in March and a staggering 545,282 in April. In all, German U-boats sank 881,207 tons of shipping in April 1917, all of which was British or operating on behalf of the Allies. By this time, the chances of an ocean-going merchant vessel making it across the Atlantic were about one in four, the kind of figures that far exceeded the rate of replacement. In what became known as the 'black fortnight' of 17–30 April, the British lost almost 400,000 tons of shipping.

At no point in the Second World War did the Battle of the Atlantic reach such crisis proportions for Britain as it did in the spring of 1917. Clearly something had to be done to stop the rot and in very quick order, or else Britain would soon be facing defeat and in turn so would France. The answer was the implementation of the convoy system. Up until that point, ships had been sailing independently and for what, at the time, seemed like good reasons. The concern was that if U-boats intercepted a convoy a massacre would follow, and that arriving en masse would overwhelm ports and leave them idle in between. There was also concern that convoys could not be adequately protected. Nonetheless, convoying now had to be tried. The first trans-Atlantic convoy left on 10 May.

Thankfully for Britain and her allies, the convoy system quickly disproved the doubters. Of 5,090 ships convoyed in 1917, only sixty-three were lost. The truth was that convoys rather emptied the seas – the oceans were big places and twenty or even forty ships together were very hard for the U-boats to spot. Furthermore, if they were spotted, British naval intelligence was able to intercept successfully U-boat radio traffic and steer the convoys around the waiting enemy submarines. By autumn 1917, U-boat activity had encouraged the USA to send naval reinforcements to help with escort duty and then brought America into the war. Shipbuilding was further increased thanks to earlier shell and ammunition stockpiling, which released munitions labour to the shipyards. A corner had been turned and the U-boats, increasingly overextended, had been forced to focus their attentions on coastal cross-Channel shipping where the convoy system had yet to be introduced.

By the beginning of 1918, this had been rectified with convoys now travelling around British coastal waters. The Royal Flying Corps also increased the number of aircraft dedicated to anti-submarine operations. Their role was to hunt for U-boats, force them to submerge, at which point they dramatically lost speed, and report their sightings via on-board radio. Naval destroyers were by then better equipped to strike back, too. Typically, destroyers carried around four depth charges in the early part of 1917; a year later, they were carrying as many as thirty. As a result, a year on from the launch of the all-out U-boat campaign, the threat had diminished massively.

The campaign had not been crushed, however, and U-boats continued to sink Allied shipping. Especially threatened was the all-important cross-Channel shipping, that vital supply line that kept Britain's war on the Western Front going. Not only was British shipping responsible for transporting food, weapons and munitions across the Channel but also between 12,000 and 15,000 troops daily. The U-boats operating from Zeebrugge threatened that shipping. This was the backdrop against which the Zeebrugge Raid was planned.

The idea for the raid was conceived by Vice Admiral Sir Roger Keyes, the Director of Plans at the Admiralty at the end of 1917. It was known that the port of Bruges-Zeebrugge was a major U-boat base and was unusual because, unlike most harbours, access to it was via a comparatively narrow canal and lock system, which then fed into a much larger port system of quays and dockyards. Protecting the entrance to the canal was a curving mole, or jetty, a weather screen that was, at one and a half miles, the longest in the world. Keyes and his planners originally envisaged a simultaneous attack on Ostend, but this was abandoned in favour of a single attack on Zeebrugge both to block the canal entrance and blow the gates on the lock system. No one was in any doubt that such an operation was extremely risky and likely to prove incredibly difficult to pull off successfully.

Since it was such a vital port for the Germans, Bruges-Zeebrugge was extremely well defended, as was known to the British via extensive aerial reconnaissance. A dozen heavy guns, anti-aircraft guns, machine guns, concrete bunkers, barbed wire and accommodation for a 1000-strong garrison protected the harbour complex. The only way the British could pull off such an operation would be by a surprise attack and causing a diversion by making a landing on the mole. Under the cover of a smokescreen and with the enemy's attention focused – or so it was hoped – on the mole, blocking ships would then sail around the end of the mole and cover the half-mile to the canal entrance, where they would manoeuvre themselves across the width of the canal and scuttle themselves. It was a tall order, and, to make the raid even more difficult, the markers for the constantly shifting sand bars off the coast had been removed by the Germans. Navigation would be hazardous, to put it mildly.

Despite these innumerable risks and obstacles, the plan was given the go-ahead in January 1918 and, recognising the inherent dangers to the men who would be carrying out the raid, it was agreed that only volunteers should take part. As a result, a notice was put up at the Grand Fleet's base at Scapa Flow in the Orkneys asking for volunteers to take part in a 'show'. The only requirement was that they should be both single and athletic. Arthur Harrison was there at the time, saw the notice, knew he fitted the bill and offered his services. It had been a long time since Jutland and he was itching to get back into the fray.

Told to report to Chatham, there Harrison met up with other officers who had similarly answered the call and who, like him, had no idea what they were letting themselves in for. This was still not revealed at that point, although Admiral Keyes did tell them frankly it would be a vital but extremely dangerous raid and that at the end of it their best chance of survival was a German POW camp until the end of the war. 'With one exception only,' Keyes recalled, 'they appeared to be simply delighted and most grateful for the honour I had done them in offering such a wonderful prospect.' Lieutenant Commander Arthur Harrison was not that one exception.

Some 1,700 marines and sailors were detailed for the raid and although Harrison was a sailor and had spent the war serving on a battlecruiser, he was now to be transferred into the role of a marine officer for the raid: he would be part of the raiding party itself. He was also put in charge of physical training, while army instructors taught them about close combat and even martial arts. They were also issued with and taught to use naval cutlasses. Training took place near Dover on a replica position most guessed was some kind of ammunition dump. No one considered it might be Zeebrugge.

A task force of some seventy vessels was earmarked, although most were warships that would bombard the port. Three blockships, *Thetis*, *Intrepid* and *Iphigenia*, were detailed with the role of creeping around the mole and up to the canal entrance; these would carry a skeleton crew. The rest of the men were to be crammed into an old cruiser, HMS *Vindictive*, and two shallow-draught River Mersey ferry steamers, *Iris* and *Daffodil*, which would pull alongside the mole and take out the bunkers and defences along it and, most importantly, cause a diversion. Finally, three submarines, filled with explosives, were to blow up the viaduct that connected the mole with the shore. Harrison was to be aboard *Vindictive*, which was being hastily stripped and then re-equipped with a false deck the same height as the mole, sixteen steel gangways for hasty disembarkation as well as demolition equipment, extra shelter barricades on board and even boarding ladders as well.

In March the Germans launched their great spring offensive, stunning the British and pushing them back further than at any point in the war since the opening weeks of 1914. There was now an added imperative to the planned raid. Admiral Keyes had originally hoped to launch it on 2 April, but the wind direction changed at the last minute, which would have fatally affected the planned smokescreen and so it was called off. The Germans renewed their offensive on 9 April and the raid took on even greater importance. Winds, tides and moonlight all conspired to ensure the next opportunity would be the morning of 23 April, St George's Day.

The task force set sail from Dover just before 5 p.m. on Monday 22 April 1918. 'St George for England,' Admiral Keyes signalled[1]. Captain Alfred Carpenter on *Vindictive* replied, 'May we give the dragon's tail a damned good twist.'[2] The men aboard were in good spirits, Harrison included; a photograph taken of him and fellow officers on board *Vindictive* just before they set sail shows them smiling and looking relaxed. There is an easy confidence about them.

Any such confidence was, however, soon to be shattered. By 11.30 p.m. on the 22nd, the fleet was approaching Zeebrugge, although they were largely hidden by the smokescreens already created by a number of Royal Navy motor launches. These little craft certainly attracted the attention of the defenders who opened fire as they beetled about just off the mole, smoke canisters detonating and providing smoke so thick that even the beam from the harbour lighthouse could not penetrate it. Then the warships' guns opened fire; it was not the first such bombardment and it seems that the Germans set no great store by it. By now midnight was fast approaching and speeding towards the mole were *Vindictive* and the two Mersey ferries.

Just then, at 11.56 p.m., disaster struck, as the wind suddenly changed direction and the smoke swiftly dispersed. From the mole, the German defenders could now see *Vindictive*, still fifty yards away but bearing down on them. This meant she was both far enough away for the defenders to have time to react and close enough for them not to miss when they opened fire. Approaching at forty-five degrees, she presented an even bigger target for the battery guns and suddenly the ship was being raked with heavy guns and machine-gun fire. *Vindictive*'s own guns were answering, too, so that the din was earthshattering. Bullets, shrapnel and shells tore into the attackers lined up on the deck. Men went down like skittles and in moments the deck was a scene of carnage, of blood, limbs and body parts and the screams of the wounded and dying.

Vindictive kept going and finally drew alongside the mole just a few minutes after midnight, although some 300 yards further on from the battery and from where she had been due to moor. Most of the metal gangways had been destroyed – just two remained – and a succession of officers were mown down as they tried to get onto the jetty. Captain Halahan, the leader of the storming party, was killed, as were two other marine officers, Lieutenant Commanders Elliott and Cordner. Harrison had been on deck and had had his jaw smashed by a shell fragment. Knocked unconscious, he was taken below decks. The only remaining officer was Lieutenant Commander Bryan Adams, who charged up one of the surviving gangways followed by a number of his men. Only once he was on the mole did he realise just how far they had yet to go to reach the battery and so he hastened back to the ship to try and gather more men around him. There he was astonished to see Harrison, his jaw a bloody mess. Far from being dead, Harrison had come to, and, eschewing any attempt to dress his wound, had made his way up onto deck and called his surviving men around him. He then led them up onto the mole and personally led the charge along the mole towards the battery. Heavy machine-gun fire opened up and on that narrow width the attackers made an easy target, Very lights illuminating the scene so brightly it might have been daylight. Harrison was among the first to be cut down, killed in his tracks. Only two of his men reached the battery. It had been a slaughter.

Yet the sacrifice had achieved its aim. Duly distracted, the battery never opened fire on the three blockships, which successfully crept past the mole. *Thetis* was caught on anti-torpedo nets before reaching the canal, but both *Iphigenia* and *Intrepid* reached the canal entrance and were successfully scuttled. One of the submarines also managed to destroy the mole's viaduct. With the recall signal now given, the few survivors on the mole pulled the dead and wounded back on board and began to pull away. Enemy fire continued to rake the ships as they withdrew slowly; one shell hit the ferry *Iris*, killing seventy-five. *Vindictive* was now so peppered and shredded it seemed incredible it could still be floating let alone moving under its own steam. Some 188 had been killed and a further 384 wounded and sixteen missing out of a total force of 1,700. Of the dead, forty-nine had been left behind, one of whom was Arthur Harrison. His body was never found.

Despite the human loss, the raid was hailed as a major success and was unquestionably a timely boost to British morale, yet although the lock gates were broken and two ships lay across the canal's entrance there was still enough width for a U-boat to squeeze through. Once a channel had been dredged through the silt, U-boats were able to slip in and out of Zeebrugge just as they had before the raid. By then, however, the war had finally turned against Germany. The spring offensive had failed; the Germans had shot their bolt. A reinvigorated British Army, reinforced by the continued flow of supplies and supported by the Americans, now proved unstoppable. By November, the war was over.

The Zeebrugge Raid swiftly entered folklore as one of the most audacious actions ever mounted. Winston Churchill thought it 'the finest feat of arms of the Great War and an episode unsurpassed in the history of the Royal Navy'[3]. Eight Victoria Crosses were awarded, one of them to Harrison. 'Lieut.-Commander Harrison though already severely wounded and undoubtedly in great pain,' ran his citation, 'displayed indomitable resolution and courage of the highest order in pressing his attack, knowing as he did that any delay in silencing the guns might jeopardise the main object of the expedition.'[4] His men were cut down, too, but it was Harrison who had led them, who had urged them on, and it was his extraordinary dedication and self-sacrifice, when critically wounded, that had seen his men prepared to follow him. Of the England rugby internationals who served in the war, Harrison was the only one to receive the Victoria Cross. He was as worthy a recipient of Britain's highest award for gallantry as any.

14

BARBARA JANE HARRISON GC

Introduced by Miranda Hart

Most of us at one time or another have imagined ourselves in a moment of crisis and wondered how we would react. I mean really react. It is one of those deep-down questions that goes to the heart of who we are. We can never know until such situations arise, and most of us are lucky enough not to face such traumatic circumstances.

However, Jane Harrison, a twenty-two-year-old air stewardess from Bradford, did. She found herself in the middle of a crash-landing at Heathrow and became the only woman to have won the George Cross in peacetime.

Jane would have received much instruction and training about how to react in various situations, including a crash-landing. Being an air stewardess in the 1960s was glamorous but also, of course, far riskier than it is today.

It is clear from eyewitness accounts that Jane's training certainly kicked in. From the discovery of the engine fire and the emergency descent to the crash-landing, she acted with complete professionalism.

But this amazing young woman was tested one step further and reacted in an extraordinarily brave way that did indeed show who she really was: a woman of integrity, courage, selflessness and strength.

For me the most poignant moment was Jane standing at the aircraft door preparing to jump to safety. She had already gone back inside the plane several times to rescue passengers, some of whom she had physically pushed from the plane when they refused through fear to jump. Her priority was to rescue, in whatever way she could. Before she herself jumped, there was black smoke billowing from the plane, but something compelled her to stop, turn round and go back into the cabin one last time.

She put herself last, and in danger, and continued her brave instinct to help her fellow man. This bravery hit the papers in 1968 but remains as relevant today. At twenty-two, well, what a woman. Would I have jumped? Would I have gone back inside? I hope I never have to know. All I do know is, I salute you, Jane.

On the afternoon of 8 April 1968, Flight BOAC 712 was readying for take-off from Heathrow Airport for Sydney. It was a clear, sunny London day and, as the crew gathered, no one was expecting anything out of the ordinary. Captaining the flight was Captain Charles Wilson Ratcliffe Taylor, known to all as Cliff, who had just under 15,000 hours of flying experience under his belt: to add to this, he was being monitored during the flight, as one of the company's regular checks, by Check Captain Geoffrey Moss, who had just under 13,000 hours of flying experience himself.

Making up the cockpit team were First Officer Francis Kirkland, Flight Engineer Thomas Hicks and Acting First Officer John Hutchinson: Hutchinson's wife had given him a parcel for a homesick friend in Australia of home-made marmalade and freshly laid eggs from a local farm. These he managed to slip under his seat. Back in the cabin itself, the team of six was led by Chief Steward Neville Davis-Gordon. Alongside Neville was Delhi-based Jennifer Suares, who wore a tradi-tional turquoise silk sari (it was custom at the time for BOAC to have a member of cabin staff from a country where they were stopping over). Andrew McCarthy and Rosalind Unwin were assigned to first class, while in attendance in economy were Bryan Taylor and Barbara Jane Harrison, known to everyone as Jane.

The flight was significant for Jane in particular. She had suggested to Andrew that she was planning to stop flying and he thought this might be their last journey together. Her childhood friend Kay Golightly, meanwhile, thought that Jane had a boyfriend in Sydney, a pilot for Qantas. It was possibly because of him that she was considering applying to become a ground hostess in Australia.

Jane wasn't the only person on the flight thinking about a potential life in Australia: among the passengers were several families leaving the UK to migrate to the other side of world. In total, there were 115 passengers: some travelling all the way to Sydney; others to the various stopping-off points of Zurich, Tel Aviv, Tehran, Mumbai, Singapore and Perth. With everyone boarded, the attendants went through the usual pre-flight safety routine. Then, once completed, they sat down themselves as the plane prepared for take-off – Jane sitting next to Bryan in one of the jump seats at the back.

At 4.15, the plane left its stand and taxied down to the holding point, waiting for permission to take off. As it sat there, one of those emigrating to Australia, Fred Pagnell, heard a muffled bang. Fred was an electrical engineer by trade, and as he says in Susan Ottaway's *Fire Over Heathrow*, 'I spent most of my employment in testing electrical motors and generators, during which time I was tuned for unusual noises especially from machines.'[1] But Fred's sharp ears were not shared by those in the cockpit and nothing untoward was noted: instead, with permission given by the control tower, the plane made its way to the end of the runway, and made to take off.

At 4.27, flight BOAC 712 became airborne. Almost immediately, the plane wobbled and veered as it started to climb: there was a second loud bang, and this time you didn't need the training of an electrical engineer to realise that something was badly wrong.

* * *

Barbara Jane Harrison was born in Bradford on 24 May 1945, a fortnight after the end of the war in Europe. Her father, Alan, was a local policeman and her mother, Lena, had worked for the furriers Swears & Wells before having Jane and her older sister, Sue, who was born in 1941.

Lena suffered from rheumatoid arthritis, which made bringing up two children a difficult task. To begin with the family relied heavily on Lena's mother for help. But when her condition didn't improve, Alan decided to relocate to Scarborough, hoping that the sea air might help. Sadly, Lena's condition deteriorated – the drugs prescribed for her arthritis resulting in nephritis – and in the summer of 1955 she died at the age of just forty-one. Jane and Sue, who'd been sent away to stay with their aunt, returned to discover not only that their mother had passed away, but that the funeral had also taken place in their absence.

Inevitably, family life changed. Jane and her sister found themselves growing up fast as they took on much of the household work their mother had done: Sunday lunch became Saturday lunch instead, with leftovers eaten the following day to give everyone a break. A schoolfriend of Jane's, Margaret Jessop, told Susan Ottaway, 'I remember Jane at 11 having to take the washing to the launderette, do the shopping and generally grow up; things which I never had to do. I also remember her father once burning all her makeup for some reason; I'm sure he was out of his mind with the responsibility.'[2]

Yet for all the hardship, Jane emerged not just as a responsible individual but one full of fun, life and mischief. Passing her eleven-plus, she went to Scarborough Girls' High School where she fell in with friends Kay, Margaret and Sheila Turton, a group that the teachers seemed determined to keep a particular eye on. On one occasion, Jane and Kay were castigated in front of the whole school for stealing – their crime was filling their school berets with cherries from overhanging trees, unknowingly witnessed by a teacher. On another occasion the same pair borrowed Kay's mother's moped, and were caught riding it unlicensed along the seafront. Then there was the time the girls decided to experiment with dyeing their hair – Jane turning up at school with hers a particularly vibrant shade of green.

Having taken her O levels in 1961, Jane decided against staying on at school and got a job working for Martin's Bank (which would later become Yorkshire Bank). This turned out to be a temporary career. As a teenager, Jane had been a member of the World Friends group and spent many holidays abroad, including visits to Holland, Germany and Austria. Her friend Kay, who'd taken a job as a civil servant, had decided she'd rather be an air stewardess instead, something that Jane was tempted by as well.

Becoming an air stewardess was not as easy in the 1960s as it is today – with far fewer airlines, openings were more limited and the entry requirements were higher. For BOAC, applicants had to be over twenty-one, and were expected to have childcare or nursing experience, together with a fluency in at least one other language. In order to meet these requirements, Jane got a job as a nanny in Switzerland through her cousin, Patrick, who lived there. Here she was able to tick off the childcare experience and improve her French at the same time. After a similar position with a family in San Francisco, Jane applied to BOAC, and, having been accepted, began her new role immediately after her twenty-first birthday in 1966.

Over the next two years, Jane grew into her role and relished her work. She moved to London, living in a Kensington flat along with some other BOAC stewardesses. When she was away, she'd send postcards to friends and family of all the places she visited. Back in London, Jane also worked occasionally for Universal Aunts, an organisation that provided services from babysitting to looking after elderly people, housekeeping to gardening. On one occasion, she found herself babysitting for a boy named Jason Connery: to her delight his father and the then James Bond, Sean Connery, gave her a lift home in his sports car.

On 8 April 1968, Jane drove herself to Heathrow in her blue Ford Anglia. Parking in the staff car park, she met up with Rosalind Unwin – Jane told her she had asked to be put on this particular flight because she had been invited to a wedding in Sydney. As the two stewardesses stood in the sunshine, neither knew this would turn out to be a fateful request.

* * *

My desk in Windsor Castle looks eastwards towards London Airport. In the beautifully clear late afternoon of 8 April 1968, I noticed a Boeing 707 flying south, straight and level, between the Castle and Heathrow. It struck me as odd, since most flights taking off to the west climb quite steeply as they turn to the south, or they come fairly close past the Castle going west. I also noticed, what I first thought, was the sun being reflected from the side of the aircraft. It then dawned on me that it was not the reflection of the sun but that one of the engines was on fire.[3]

As he wrote in his foreword to *Fire Over Heathrow*, HRH The Duke of Edinburgh was one of many people who witnessed the brief flight of BOAC 712 that day. Fifteen-year-old Allan Blackman was out on a bike ride near his home in Colnbrook when he saw the plane in trouble. At the nearby Poyle Trading Estate, young draughtsman Roy Stannett heard 'a distant but audible bang. Upon looking out of the window I was astonished to see a Boeing 707 trailing a long orange flame that appeared to stretch as far back as the aircraft's tail fin.'[4]

In the nearby village of Thorpe, meanwhile, sand and gravel merchant Anthony de Marco was supervising work on one of his water-filled gravel pits. As local children played on the banks, he heard the noise of the plane and looked up in astonishment to see one of the aircraft's engines fall from the sky, landing in the pit just fifty metres from where he and the children were standing.

The engine wasn't the first part of the plane to leave the aircraft – when it had set off just moments before, the bang heard in the cabin were smaller parts of one of the engines falling off. Fred Pagnell told Susan Ottaway how his mother Vera had turned to him: 'Vera said to me, "Look out the window, the engine's on fire". I said, "Don't be silly it's probably burning off excess fuel" . . . Vera mentioned it twice more and I had another look. I said, "Shit, you're right". I immediately turned round and told the steward to look out of his window. He was reluctant at first until I shouted, "The engine's on fire". He took one look and ran up through the cabin to the captain.'

As the cockpit and the control tower became aware of what was going on, Cliff Taylor was told to turn around and head back for Heathrow. As the plane continued its anti-clockwise loop back towards the airport, the fire spread from the engine to the wing itself: attempts to put it out with the plane's fire extinguisher system had failed; in the cabin, meanwhile, the heat from the blaze could now be felt by those on the port side of the plane.

Check Captain Geoff Moss, who had the advantage of being able to see the fire from where he was sitting, told the captain that they wouldn't be able to reach the runway they'd taken off from. Radioing back to the control tower, Cliff Taylor repeated the advice and was told to make for runway 05R instead – this was a shorter runway than the main ones, and further away from the now-alerted emergency services, which were on the opposite side of the airport. But given the state the aircraft was in – having now lost the engine it was moving from side to side – it clearly needed to attempt to land as soon as possible.

All the while, the fire was creeping up. The cabin now had an orange glow – the windows on the port side were now too hot to touch and some were beginning to buckle. The passengers were told to prepare themselves for an emergency landing, while Jane and the rest of crew checked the doors and aisles were clear before strapping themselves in bracing themselves for impact themselves. By now, the plane's descent was being punctuated by explosions and bright flashes as parts of the port wing were falling off. Fuel was running down the side of the plane and smoke was beginning to seep into the cabin.

Somehow, Cliff Taylor managed to bring the damaged aircraft down. Interviewed in the *Evening News*, he was modest about what he had done: 'Bringing this plane down was a team job,' he said. 'There were five other people on the flight deck and I just happened to be in command.'[5] Even so, his landing was a formidable task: the aircraft was much heavier than its maximum landing weight (because of unused fuel) and missing one of its engines; the runway was short and in a crosswind.

But while Cliff Taylor's part in the drama was coming to an end, for Jane and the rest of the cabin crew their role was just beginning. Even before the plane had come to a halt, they were out of their seats and opening the emergency doors for the passengers to escape. For Jane and Bryan, only the door on the opposite side to the fire was usable: it was Bryan's job as the steward to open the door and for Jane to help the passengers to the exit. Having opened the chute, it immediately became twisted before anyone could use it. Bryan jumped down in order to straighten it, but, having done so, he couldn't get back up again. So while the other attendants worked in pairs to escort the passengers off, Jane was now left alone at the back of the cabin – and at the end where the fire was its greatest.

Time was now everything. The crosswinds the plane had landed in meant that the smoke was now blowing over the plane. Such was the thickness of the plume that it could be seen from ten miles away. The airport fire engines, when they finally arrived, turned out to be inadequate for containing the blaze, which was threatening to burn out of control. It wasn't just the fuel on board that threatened to blow – in the cargo hold was a consignment of radioactive material, Yttrium-90, on its way to Jerusalem's University Hospital. As Fred Pagnell slid down the chute, he was told by a fireman to run for it, as the plane was about to explode. Fleeing for his life with his son in his arms, he heard a huge explosion.

The chute at the back of the plane caught fire. For the remaining passengers on board, it was a horrible choice: to jump through the door-way onto the ground below or risk joining the longer queue of passengers for the other exit. For some of the passengers, neither was an option: seventy-year-old Esther Cohen had been brought on board with the assistance of a wheelchair and was unable to move by herself; her chair then trapped those sitting at the back of the aircraft alongside her.

At the front of the aircraft, Cliff Taylor and Acting First Officer John Hutchinson called out to see if anyone was still aboard. The smoke was now so thick that both visibility and breathing were all but impossible. With no response, they used a rope to climb out of the cockpit window. At the back of plane, Jane was still there, the one remaining member of the crew, alongside four passengers: Esther Cohen, Catherine Shearer, Mary Smith and Jacqueline Cooper. Several eyewitnesses on the ground recall seeing Jane standing in the doorway preparing to jump down, before changing her mind and disappearing back into the smoke and flames, never to be seen again.

Writing to BOAC after the incident, Jacqueline's father Brian said:

> Miss Barbara Harrison was a very brave and courageous young lady. The last I saw of her was desperately trying to throw and encourage other passengers to jump from the plane. She threw me out through the side of the plane, smoke and flames licking around her face. I had only landed but a few moments when my wife threw my son and then jumped herself. As I got them to safety, I turned to go back to the plane and I saw Barbara reappear, with another passenger, still with flames and explosions all around her, then complete blackness as she disappeared once more inside of the plane.[6]

* * *

The story of Flight 712 made headline news around the world, the media stories a mixture of relief that 121 people had somehow managed to survive, along with the sadness of the deaths of Jane and the four passengers. And while the early reports were quick to applaud the bravery of Cliff Taylor – the *Herald*'s headline JET PILOT SAVES 121 being typical of the coverage – as more became learned of the incident, it was

Jane's selfless behaviour that began to stand out.

Anthony Crosland, President of the Board of the Trade, began to receive recommendations from different parties for awards from various members of the crew. Having studied the role of Jane Harrison, Crosland was convinced her efforts should be recorded. He wrote, 'I feel strongly that Miss Harrison's lonely and courageous action in that part of the aircraft first to be affected by heat and smoke when the integrity of the cabin was breached by an explosion should be recognised. From the evidence available, it is known that without thought for her own safety she returned time and again to the cabin to push out a passenger before returning for another, until she went back into the aircraft and failed to appear. I believe that this devotion to duty, in the highest tradition of her calling, is worthy of recognition by the posthumous award of the George Cross.'[7]

* * *

Jane Harrison is just one of four women to have been directly* awarded the George Cross at the time of writing, and the only one to have been given the award in peacetime. When her father, Alan, made the difficult decision to sell the medal in 1987, to raise money for the children of his other daughter, Sue, it was bought by British Airways. The medal now resides, perhaps fittingly, at Heathrow Airport at the British Airways' heritage centre, along with a plaque at the airport's chapel, St George's: 'We dedicate this plaque', it reads, 'in thankful memory of Barbara Jane Harrison, to be a lasting memorial of she who faced the final challenge of humanity and was not found wanting.'

---

* As opposed to exchanging a discontinued Albert, Edward or Empire Gallantry Medal.

PRIVATE HENRY HOOK VC

Introduced by Sir Derek Jacobi CBE

It is not easy to separate the real Henry Hook from the figure portrayed in the film Zulu. *It is therefore tempting to see him as a drunken layabout who was continually under sanction for one breach of Queen's Regulations after another. It is obvious from this story that the real man was very different. Fighting for his own life and in immediate danger from Zulus who had infiltrated the makeshift hospital, he used his bayonet to break through mud-brick walls and helped drag sick and wounded comrades to safety when the building was in flames and under sustained attack.*

I was also moved by the image of him spending his days retired from the army as a cloakroom attendant at the British Museum. There is, in this, a deep insight into the nature of what are sometimes called 'ordinary people'. And there is, of course, no such thing as an ordinary person. The cloakroom attendant you next come upon may seem unexceptional but this story proves that appearances can be highly deceptive. I sincerely hope you enjoy reading this essay as much as I did.

'Everything was perfectly quiet at Rorke's Drift after the column had left,' remembered twenty-eight-year-old Private Henry Hook, a former farm labourer from Monmouth in the Welsh Borders, 'and every officer and man was going about his business as usual. Not a soul suspected that only a dozen miles away the very men that we had said "Goodbye" and "Good luck" to were either dead or standing back-to-back in a last fierce fight with the Zulus.'[1]

Hook was a member of B Company of the 2nd Battalion, The 24th Regiment of Foot (or 2/24th). Eleven days earlier, he and his comrades had been left to guard the supply depot and river crossing at Rorke's Drift while General Lord Chelmsford's Central Column of 4,700 men (including the balance of the 2/24th) crossed the Buffalo River from the British Crown colony of Natal into Zululand. The invasion was an attempt by the British to neutralise the military threat posed by King Cetshwayo's powerful warrior nation and, at the same time, incorporate it into a larger Confederation of South Africa. Chelmsford's plan was for three columns to converge on the Zulu capital of Ulundi, with himself leading the Central Column. His greatest concern was that the Zulus would withdraw into the interior and refuse to fight.

On 20 January 1879, nine days into the invasion, Chelmsford's column had set up camp in the shadow of Isandlwana Hill, a steep, rocky peak that resembled the Egyptian Sphinx. In the early hours of 22 January, Chelmsford received word that a large Zulu force had been sighted to the south-east of the camp, and he promptly left with the bulk of his force to investigate. But it was a Zulu ploy and, in Chelmsford's absence, the camp was attacked and overwhelmed by 20,000 warriors. Of the 1,700 men left in camp, only 55 Europeans and around 300 African soldiers survived. All 21 officers and 581 men of the 24th Foot – including more than a hundred men of Hook's 2nd Battalion – were killed.[2]

The first that Hook and his comrades knew of the disaster was around 2 p.m. when a sentry reported to Lieutenant John Chard of the Royal Engineers, the senior officer at the drift,[3] that two riders were approaching from the Zulu side of the river. Once across, they told Chard that the camp at Isandlwana had been attacked and taken by thousands of Zulu warriors who were, at that very moment, advancing on Rorke's Drift. Chard at once rode the half-mile from the drift to the supply depot – a requisitioned Swedish mission at the foot of a large hill known as the

Oskarberg – to consult Lieutenant Gonville Bromhead, the popular but unexceptional and partially deaf commander of Hook's B Company.

Chard arrived to find the camp a hive of activity as Hook and the other men put up barricades and loopholed[4] the two main buildings. Bromhead explained that he had just received a message from a staff officer at Isandlwana that the mission was to be held 'at all costs'.[5] But after a brief discussion, recalled Hook, 'orders were given to strike the camp and make ready to go, and we actually loaded up two wagons'. Clearly neither officer thought much of the tiny garrison's chances of repelling a Zulu attack. Most of the men agreed. 'There was a general feeling,' recalled Hook, 'that the only safe thing was to retire and try and join the troops at Helpmekaar.'[6]

Fortunately a cooler head was at hand. Acting Assistant Commissary James Dalton, a former NCO (non-commissioned officer) who had distinguished himself in the recent Cape Frontier War, could see no sense in flight. If they abandoned the supply depot, he told the officers, they would be caught in the open by faster moving Zulus 'and every man was certain to be killed'. This gloomy assessment brought Chard to his senses and, having consulted Bromhead, he ordered the work on the defences to continue. The men 'were never to say die or surrender'.[7]

The supply depot consisted of two main buildings: a thatched, single-storey brick and stone homestead that was fronted by a covered veranda; and a smaller storehouse, also thatched and with a veranda. They had been built by Jim Rorke, the son of an Irish ex-soldier who had acquired the 3,000-acre property in 1849. Three years after Rorke's death in 1875, the farm was bought by a Swedish missionary called Otto Witt. As the British prepared to invade Zululand, Witt put his property at Lord Chelmsford's disposal.

The house had since been converted into a makeshift hospital under the supervision of Surgeon James Reynolds and his small medical team. Hook was assisting them as the hospital cook. He bore a striking resemblance to Lieutenant Colonel Redvers Buller, one of the few

ON COURAGE

British officers who would emerge from the Zulu War with any credit. Yet their backgrounds could not have been more different: Buller came from Devon gentry, Hook from the agricultural poor.[8]

The son of a woodsman, Alfred Henry Hook was born in Churcham, Gloucestershire, on 6 August 1850. After a rudimentary education, he worked as a farm labourer and, from 1869 to 1874, was a part-time soldier with the Royal Monmouth Militia. At twenty he married a Herefordshire girl called Comfort Jones who bore him a son and two daughters. They were living in Monmouth when Hook, at the relatively late age of twenty-six, joined the 2nd Battalion of the 24th Regiment as a regular soldier. In the iconic 1964 film *Zulu*, Hook is portrayed as an old sweat who liked a drink and was constantly in trouble. In reality he was a teetotaler with fewer than two years' service with the Colours. More than half that time, however, had been spent in South Africa, including three months fighting the Gaika and Gcaleka tribes on the eastern Cape frontier.[9]

When word reached Rorke's Drift of the massacre at Isandlwana, Hook was making tea for the thirty or so invalids in the makeshift hospital. A few had been wounded in recent skirmishes in Zululand; but most were recovering from the fevers, dysentery, trench foot and minor injuries that were typical of any African campaign. They were lying on rudimentary beds – straw mattresses on wooden planks raised a few inches off the hard dirt floor by bricks – in the eleven rooms of Witt's house: five could be accessed only from doors on the outside of the building; the remaining six were split into two self-contained suites. Rorke had had an aversion not only to inside doors but also windows: five of his rooms were windowless.[10]

To prepare the hospital and the storehouse for the coming battle, therefore, Bromhead ordered the doors to be barricaded and the walls to be loopholed. He also ordered the construction of two walls – made from wagons and heavy sacks of locally grown Indian corn known as mealies – to connect the two buildings into a single defensive position.[11]

To defend this hastily constructed fort, Chard and Bromhead had around a hundred able-bodied British soldiers (while some of the thirty or so in hospital could also bear arms). Of more doubtful value was a company of the Natal Native Contingent (NNC) – a hundred African soldiers under a British officer – who had been left at the drift on fatigue duties. They were supplemented, shortly after 2.15 p.m., by a Lieutenant Henderson and eighty African horsemen who had escaped the Zulu encirclement at Isandlwana. At first Henderson agreed to help defend the post, but his men had gone through a terrible ordeal and were clearly jittery.[12]

Shortly before 4.30 p.m., Hook and his comrades heard gunshots from the far side of the Oskarberg Hill. Seconds later Henderson appeared at the gallop. Thousands of Zulus were approaching, he told Chard, and his men would not obey orders and 'were going to Helpmekaar'. He then rode away, ostensibly to rally his men; he never returned.[13]

This mass desertion caused panic among the remaining African levies who had done good work on the barricades. 'Instantly,' recalled Hook, 'they bolted towards Helpmekaar, and what was worse their officer and a European [NCO] went with them. To see them deserting like that was too much for some of us, and we fired after them.' The NCO, a Corporal Anderson, was shot and killed.[14]

The garrison had, at a stroke, been reduced to 104 fit men and those of their hospitalised comrades who had been issued with rifles and were willing to fight. In response, Chard ordered a wall of wooden biscuit boxes to be built across the middle of the defensive compound – between the edge of the storehouse and the middle of the mealie-bag wall – so that the soldiers could withdraw to a small defensive area in an emergency.[15] It was just two boxes high – and far from complete – when Private Frederick Hitch, perched on the roof of the storehouse, reported a huge Zulu column approaching.

'How many are there?' asked Bromhead.

Four to six thousand was the reply.

'Is that all,' muttered a wag below. 'We can manage that lot very well for a few seconds.'[16]

Moments later the Zulu vanguard of 600 warriors – carrying rifles, rawhide shields, knobkerries (wooden clubs) and assegais (short stabbing spears) – appeared at the run from the back of the Oskarberg and made straight for the south wall. 'Here they come,' shouted an Irish-born sergeant. 'As thick as grass and as black as thunder!'[17]

The defenders opened fire at 500 yards, shooting wildly at first but soon steadying their aim. Zulus fell in heaps, but their comrades kept coming, using the cover provided by the trees, banks and cookhouse ovens at the back of the post to approach to within fifty yards of the south wall. 'They were caught between two fires,' recalled Hook,

> that from the hospital, and that from the storehouse, and were checked . . . During the fight they took advantage of every bit of cover there was, anthills, a tract of bush that we had not had time to clear away, a garden or sort of orchard which was near us, and a ledge of rock and some caves (on the Oskarberg) which were only a hundred yards away. They neglected nothing, and while they went on firing large bodies kept hurling themselves against our slender breastwork.[18]

An even bigger force of Zulus veered to the left and attacked the end of the hospital and the north-west wall, where they were opposed by a group that included Bromhead and Dalton. A fierce hand-to-hand fight ensued, with Dalton saving the life of a corporal who was about to be stabbed. But eventually this stout defence, and the supporting fire from the hospital, forced the Zulus back behind a five-feet-high garden wall.[19]

A mass assault from all sides would probably have overwhelmed the tiny garrison. But it never came. Instead, during the remaining hour or so of daylight, the Zulus launched a series of piecemeal attacks against the hospital and the north wall. None succeeded. 'As if seized by a single impulse,' recalled Lieutenant Chard, they rose up in the bush as thick as possible, rushing madly up to the wall . . . seizing where they could the muzzles of our men's rifles, or their bayonets, and attempting to use their assegais and to get over the wall. A rapid rattle of fire from our rifles, stabs with the bayonets, and in a few moments the Zulus were driven back, disappearing in the bush as before, and keeping up their fire.[20]

At around 6 p.m., as daylight faded, the Zulu commander ordered simultaneous attacks on the south and north wall. With the garrison in danger of being overwhelmed, Dalton was an inspiration as he moved up and down the barricades fearlessly exposing himself and using his rifle to deadly effect. Private Hook would later describe him as 'one of the bravest men that ever lived'.[21]

It was now that Chard took the fatal decision to withdraw his men behind the biscuit boxes, thus reducing his defensive perimeter by two-thirds. He did so because he feared, as he put it, the 'Zulus would get in over our wall behind the biscuit boxes'. Yet in the process he marooned the six soldiers (including Hook) and twenty-four patients still in the hospital. The Zulus immediately occupied the far side of the mealie-bag walls that had been abandoned and used them to fire over. They also increased their attacks on the hospital.[22]

Since the start of the battle, Hook had been guarding the room on the south-east corner of the hospital. It contained two patients: Robert Cole, a nineteen-year-old private in F Company who was well enough to hold a rifle; and an African with a broken leg. Hook recalled:

Half a dozen of us were stationed in the hospital, with orders to hold it and guard the sick. The ends of the building were of stone, the side walls of ordinary bricks, and the inside walls or partitions of sun-dried bricks of mud. These shoddy inside bricks proved our salvation . . . We were pinned like rats in a hole, because all the doorways except one had been barricaded with mealie-bags, and we had done the same with the windows. The interior was divided by means of partition walls into which were fitted some very slight doors. To talk of hospital and beds gives the idea of a big building, but . . . this hospital was a mere little shed or bungalow, divided up into rooms so small that you could hardly swing a bayonet in them. There were about nine men who could not move, but altogether there were about thirty.[23]

For a time, Hook and Cole blazed away from their loopholes. But eventually – according to Hook – Cole lost his nerve and fled the room.[24] 'The helpless patient was crying and groaning near me,' recalled Hook. 'The Zulus were swarming around us, and there was an extraordinary rattle as the bullets struck the biscuit boxes, and queer thuds as they plumped into the bags of mealies. Then there was the whizz and rip of assegais.'[25]

Soon after Chard had withdrawn behind the biscuit boxes, the Zulus finally managed to set alight the western end of the hospital's thatched roof with flaming spears. It had taken some time because the thatch was damp from the recent rains. Hook wrote:

This put us in a terrible plight because it either meant we were to be massacred or burnt alive, or get out of the building. To get out seemed impossible; for if we left the hospital by the only door which had been left open, we should instantly fall into the midst of the Zulus. Besides, there were the helpless sick and wounded, and we could not leave them.[26]

As Hook's room began to fill with choking smoke, he broke through the flimsy inner door to the neighbouring room, leaving the injured African to an 'awful fate'. He could hear the Zulus questioning him before they killed him. But Hook's troubles were just beginning because in the next room he found nine unprotected sick and wounded men. Moments later he was joined in the room by Private John Williams, a twenty-one-year-old former labourer from Monmouthshire, who appeared through a hole he had made in the side wall and shouted: 'The Zulus are swarming all over the place. They've dragged Joseph Williams out and killed him.'[27]

The two Williams had been detailed to guard the four patients in the room next to Hook's original position. For an hour they fired away. But when their ammunition ran out, there was nowhere to go, the room having only one sealed-up door that led outside. Eventually the Zulus broke in and hauled out Joseph Williams and two patients. While they were killing them, John Williams and the remaining two patients used bayonets to break through the mud-brick partition into an empty inner room. From there they repeated the trick into Hook's new room.

The situation was still desperate. Hook and Williams now had eleven patients and one route of escape: through the wall and into the next room along. While Williams knocked a hole with a pickaxe, Hook held off the Zulus who were trying to get through the doorway from his original room. Assegais kept whizzing past him until, finally, one struck him on the peak of his white sun-helmet, causing it to tip back and leaving him with a minor flesh wound on his scalp. Fortunately the doorway was only big enough to allow one Zulu through at a time and, as each one appeared, Hook shot or bayoneted him. He wrote:

> A big Zulu sprang forward and seized my rifle, but I tore it free and, slipping a cartridge in, I shot him point blank. Time after time the Zulus gripped the muzzle and tried to tear the rifle from my grasp and time after time I wrenched it back because I had a better grip than they had. All this time, Williams was getting the sick through the hole into the next room, all except one, a soldier of the 24th named Conley [Private John Connolly of G Company], who could not move because of a broken leg. Watching my chance, I dashed for the doorway and, grabbing Conley, I pulled him after me through the hole. His leg got broken again, but there was no help for it. As soon as we left the room the Zulus burst in with furious cries of disappointment and rage.[28]

As so it went on, though in the next room Hook only had to defend a hole instead of a door while Williams picked away at the far wall. Again, once all the others were through, Hook dragged Connolly to safety.[29] Unwittingly he left behind Private Waters, the original occupant of the room, who was hiding in a cupboard with a wounded arm. Heat and smoke eventually forced Waters to leave the cupboard and, hidden by a dark cloak, he escaped the hospital and took refuge in the cookhouse. There he used soot from the chimney to blacken his hands and face and, incredibly, remained undiscovered until morning, though the Zulus were all around him and some even trod on him.[30]

Hook and Williams, meanwhile, had met up with Privates Robert and William Jones and six more patients in the small end room closest to the wall of biscuit boxes and safety. While the Jones pair guarded the entrances to the room, Hook and Williams lowered the patients out of a high window and onto the ground below. Most of them made it across the forty yards of open ground that separated the hospital from the biscuit boxes thanks to the efforts of Corporal William Allen and Private Frederick Hitch who risked their lives to provide covering fire. But one unfortunate, a Natal Mounted Policeman, was speared to death as he staggered across. His assailant was shot and killed.[31]

One other patient did not make it: Sergeant Maxfield. Delirious in bed, he refused to be moved and was assegaied by Zulus as Robert Jones made a final attempt to save him. Jones fled back into the end room where he and his namesake guarded the door. 'As fast as they came up to the door we bayoneted them,' he recalled, 'until the doorway was nearly filled with dead and wounded Zulus.' By now Robert Jones had three assegai wounds and was weak with loss of blood. Fortunately the spreading flames forced the Zulus back, giving the pair a chance to escape through the window. No sooner had they hit the ground – the last to leave after Hook and Williams – than the roof fell in, 'a complete mass of flames and fire'. Bullets whizzed past them as they raced over the neutral ground to safety.[32]

Thanks to the gallantry of Hook and five other men – Williams, both Joneses, Allen and Hitch – twenty-three of the thirty or so men stationed in the hospital when the battle began were saved. The sick and wounded were placed on the storehouse veranda where Surgeon Reynolds did what he could for them. Hook took his place on the biscuit-box wall where two men had already been killed. While he was there another was shot in the neck, the bullet coming through a gap between two biscuit boxes. 'Every now and then,' wrote Hook, 'the Zulus would make a rush for it and get in. We had to charge them out. By this time it was dark, and the hospital was all in flames, but this gave us a splendid light to fight by. I believe it was this light that saved us. We could see them coming, and they could not rush us and take us by surprise from any point.'[33]

The Zulus' failure to take or burn the storehouse, their dislike of night fighting and their mounting casualties all contributed to a decrease in serious attacks. They continued to line the abandoned walls and kept firing from all sides until midnight, but no actual attempt to break into the defensive perimeter was made after 9.30 p.m. After midnight there was desultory firing from both sides and the occasional false alarm. From 4.30 a.m. the firing stopped completely, though the garrison remained on the alert. When day finally broke the exhausted defenders were delighted and relieved to see the Zulus 'disappearing' the way they had come, round the southern shoulder of the Oskarberg. The garrison was down to its last box and a half of bullets.[34]

Patrols were at once sent out to collect the arms and ammunition of the dead.[35] Hook went out alone and almost paid the price when a wounded Zulu grabbed his rifle and tried to wrestle it from him. But after a short fight he knocked the Zulu to the ground and shot him.[36]

At 8 a.m. Lord Chelmsford and the remnants of the Central Column arrived at the drift. They were greeted with a hearty cheer. Expecting to find the post in ruins, Chelmsford was delighted to find it intact and thanked Chard and his men 'with much emotion for the defence we had made'.[37] On hearing of Hook's gallantry, the General asked to speak to him. Hook was in his shirtsleeves, making tea for the sick and wounded, when a sergeant ran up and told him to report to Lieutenant Bromhead. 'Wait till I put my coat on,' said Hook.

'Come as you are, straight away,' insisted the sergeant.

Hook recalled: 'With my braces hanging about me, I went into the midst of the officers. Lord Chelmsford asked me all about the defence of the hospital, as I was the last to leave the building. An officer took our names and wrote down what we had done.'[38]

Given the length and ferocity of the fight, the British casualties were comparatively light: fifteen dead and twelve wounded (though two mortally, giving a total of seventeen fatalities). The official number of Zulu dead was 351, most buried in two large pits in front of the hospital. But others had crawled away to die and the number of dead Zulus, a sergeant told his wife, was 'over 800'.[39]

Lieutenant Bromhead's official report of the battle mentioned six men who had 'especially distinguished themselves': Hook, Williams, the two Joneses, Hitch and Allen. Chelmsford recommended all six for the award of the Victoria Cross, and also added the names of Lieutenants Chard and Bromhead.[40]

The recommendations were eventually confirmed by Field Marshal HRH the Duke of Cambridge, the Commander-in-Chief, and appeared in the *London Gazette* on 2 May 1879.[41] Part of Hook's joint citation with John Williams reads: 'These two men together, one man working whilst the other fought and held the enemy at bay with his bayonet, broke through three more partitions, and were thus enabled to bring eight patients through a small window in the inner line of defence.'[42]

Hook was presented with his Victoria Cross by Lieutenant General Sir Garnet Wolseley, Chelmsford's replacement as commander of British troops in southern Africa, at Rorke's Drift on 3 August 1879, the only one of the VCs to be invested at the scene of the action.

Ten months after receiving his VC, partly for reasons of poor health, Hook purchased his discharge for the not inconsiderable sum of £18 and returned home to learn that his wife Comfort, thinking him dead, had sold his property and remarried.[43]

For a time he worked as a groom for a Monmouth GP, but in 1881 he moved to London and got temporary work as a labourer at the British Museum in Bloomsbury. The job became permanent in December 1881 after letters of recommendation were sent to the museum's Clerk of Works by both Lord Chelmsford and Major George Bromhead VC, the latter describing Hook as 'an honest and sober man'. He later became a cloakroom attendant.[44]

Hook also joined a number of different Volunteer Battalions as a part-time soldier and rose to the rank of Sergeant Instructor of Musketry. In 1897 he was married a second time: to Ada Taylor, the daughter of a well-to-do goldsmith. They had two girls. But in late 1904, with his health deteriorating, Hook retired from his job at the British Museum and, a month later, resigned from the Volunteers. He returned to Gloucester where he died of pulmonary tuberculosis on 12 March 1905 at the age of fifty-four.

He is buried in St Andrew's parish churchyard in Churcham, Gloucestershire, the place of his birth. His Victoria Cross is in the Museum of the Royal Welsh Regiment at Brecon.[45]

16

FLIGHT ENGINEER
NORMAN JACKSON VC

Introduced by Sir Ken Dodd OBE

I am honoured to have been asked to introduce this story about Norman Jackson VC. Lest we forget.

As you will see when you read this chapter, Norman pulled himself down onto the wing of a Lancaster bomber to extinguish a fire when it was flying at night over Germany with anti-aircraft flack exploding everywhere around. He was attached to the cockpit by the cords of his parachute twisted into a rope. Night fighters were firing at him as he struggled to put out the flames. He was then shot in the arm by a cannon from one of those fighters and he plunged to earth. It was a miracle that he survived.

His courage in confronting fear and terrifying danger in such a horrific situation; his devotion to duty and his loyalty and compassionate concern for his fellow aircrew comrades was then, and is now, inspirational and very moving.

A great British hero. How this wonderful man displayed such heroism and bravery God only knows.

Anyone who has experienced combat will talk of the importance of camaraderie, and for most it is the greatest of all motivations. Even in the Second World War, a conflict where, for Allied servicemen at any rate, there was a notable belief that theirs was a moral crusade to rid the world of evil Nazism and sadistic Imperial Japanese cruelty, most veterans will claim they were fighting on through bitter hell for their fellows in their platoon, or tank, or fighter squadron. 'I didn't want to let down my mates' is a line I have heard more often than any other about what kept soldiers going through the rain and mountains of Italy, the deserts of North Africa or the jungles of Burma. The intensity of camaraderie is also something most veterans find hard to articulate, but it is a shared experience, a unity of purpose, and a very special – and unique – bond that most agree is what saw them through long and protracted periods of fear and extreme discomfort. It also prompted some astonishing acts of self-sacrifice, as the events of the night of Wednesday 26 April 1944 were to prove.

That night showed that camaraderie can be at its most fundamental in a bomber crew. It took seven men to crew a four-engine Lancaster bomber, and in *Uncle Joe II* all were extremely close. There was no outsider, no clique, no pairing who had an extra special friendship; rather, from the outset, they considered themselves to be held together by that old Alexandre Dumas motto: all for one, and one for all. They really were a band of brothers.

They were by no means alone, although on the face of it this was perhaps surprising considering the way bomber crews were put together. After training, the various pilots, flight engineers, navigators, bomb-aimers and wireless operators were posted to an Operational Training Unit. Typically, they would be sent to a large mess hall and told to sort themselves out into crews. It was an ad hoc system, but it was amazing how well it worked and how, more often than not, crews tended to gel immediately. That was the case for pilot Fred Mifflin and the four other men who managed to get themselves together. Mifflin, or 'Miff' as he was always known, was a Canadian from Catalina, a fishing community in Newfoundland. Like all those in Bomber Command, he was a volunteer, although the difference between him and British servicemen was that, while Brits volunteered to be in the RAF, most could not avoid war service conscription; Canadians, on the other hand, chose to play their part in the war without conscription. Mifflin had volunteered back in June 1940 as soon as he'd left school, and joined the RAF rather than the Royal Canadian Air Force. Trained in Canada, he was then posted to Singapore, although the island had surrendered before he had reached the British outpost, and so was held over in Egypt, where he flew Hurricane fighters with the Desert Air Force. Posted back to England after his tour in early 1943, he then, somewhat unusually, retrained on bombers. By July 1943, he was still only twenty years old; he had had quite a war already.

One of the oldest members of Mifflin's crew was Flight Engineer Norman Jackson, who was twenty-four. A cheery Londoner, Jackson, like his new captain, could have avoided front-line service. Adopted as a baby, he grew up in Ealing, west London, and after school became an apprentice fitter and joiner, which was a reserved occupation. However, with the declaration of war in September 1939, the following month he chose to join the RAF Volunteer Reserve, the air force equivalent of the Territorial Army, and became a fitter – a mechanic and member of the ground crew. He soon found himself being posted overseas to Freetown, Sierra Leone, in West Africa to join 95 Squadron, equipped with Sunderland flying boats. For a Londoner who had never been abroad, this was quite an adventure, albeit one in which he was about as safe as he could ever hope to be.

While serving with 95 Squadron, great events were unfolding closer to home, however: the fall of France, the retreat of the British Army to Dunkirk, then the Battle of Britain. By September, London was being bombed daily. At twenty-one, Jackson decided to move from ground crew to retrain as air crew, initially as a pilot and then as a flight engineer, seated next to the pilot, monitoring and controlling the various systems on the aircraft from fuel gauges to trim – that is, adjusting the angle of the propellers. Effectively, he was the airborne mechanic, a position to which he was well suited from his earlier work as a fitter, and, although not a qualified pilot, if anything happened to the captain the flight engineer would be expected to take over.

So it was that, by the summer of 1943, Jackson had not only returned to England but had completed his training and found himself crewing up with Fred Mifflin, Frank Higgins the navigator, Maurice Toft the bomb-aimer and 'Sandy' Sandelands the wireless operator. From there they were then posted to a Heavy Conversion Unit to train on Lancasters, where they were joined by the last two members of the crew, mid-upper gunner William Smith, the eldest at twenty-nine and known as 'Pops' to the crew, and rear gunner Hugh 'Johnny' Johnson, the youngest at just eighteen.

Operating the Lancaster was challenging. At thirty tons and with a wingspan of 102 feet, it was a beast. Inside, however, it was little more than a tin can; the bomb bays were huge and could take up to ten tons of bombs, but that left little by way of comfort or protection for the crew. Access was via a hatch in the fuselage and to reach the front of the aircraft the pilot, bomb-aimer and flight engineer had to clamber over two wing spars that barred their way. Lancasters were equipped with .303 Browning machine guns, which were little more than pea shooters and, as had been proved early on in the war, when British fighter aircraft had been equipped with these weapons, were not particularly effective for air-to-air combat. The bombers could have been given much larger .50-calibrate machine guns, but these were heavier, caused greater drag and reduced the number of bombs that could be carried. Nor was there any armour plating, which was left off the bomber for the same reasons. This meant that Lancaster crews set off on bombing raids able to pack a big punch in terms of the payload, but with woefully poor protection. Bursts of flak could rip large chunks from the plane; an attack by a German night fighter, armed with 20mm and 30mm cannons, meant almost certain destruction.

The statistics are horrific. During the entire war, 44.4 per cent of all RAF Bomber Command crews were killed, almost one in two. A first tour was thirty operations, and then, if an airman was fortunate enough to survive that, some six months later they would be expected to carry out a further twenty; that is, fifty in total. The average, however, was just fourteen missions. That was less than half of a first tour.

Once in the air, experience helped extend the chances of survival, but really it was a lottery: a chance burst of flak, the decision by a night fighter to home in on one aircraft rather than another, and it could be the end for bomber and crew. All too often, accidents were the cause of premature death. It very nearly did for Mifflin and Jackson and their crew on their first flight in a Lancaster. In July 1943, having successfully taken off and carried out a test flight, they were returning to base and approaching the airfield when the ground controller changed the runway on which they were supposed to land. Suddenly, rather than landing into the wind, they were forced to try and touch down into a crosswind. This was a hazardous operation, because the wind was pushing up under one of the wings as the aircraft was losing speed and at its least stable. In addition, this was Mifflin's first flight in a Lancaster as pilot. He touched down too hard, the undercarriage collapsed and the bomber slewed along the runway, shedding two engines and causing the fuselage to catch fire before finally grinding to a halt. Miraculously, all seven crew managed to get clear of the aircraft, although Jackson broke his right leg and was in plaster for six weeks. He stayed with the crew through the rest of the training, flying with his leg in a plaster cast.

It was the kind of prang that might have signalled the end of both Mifflin's flying career and with it the unity of the crew, but they all decided to stick together: they trusted their pilot and each other, and recognised that they were already forging a special bond. As a result, this disastrous first flight only brought them closer together. Furthermore, once in the air, it was clear that Mifflin was a natural pilot and able to handle the Lancaster superbly. By the end of the course, the rest of the crew knew they had been right to back him.

On 4 August 1943, their Heavy Conversion Unit course completed, they were posted to 106 Squadron at Syerston, Lincolnshire, part of 5 Group. The squadron had one of the best records in Bomber Command and had, under the command of Wing Commander Guy Gibson, been among the first to convert to the new Lancasters the previous year. Gibson had been posted back in March to take over the newly formed 617 Squadron for Operation CHASTISE, the Dams Raid, but the spirit and 'press on' attitude he had forged during his eleven months of command remained; the squadron was justifiably proud of its record.

Their first operation was on the night of 22/23 August 1943. Target: the IG Farben factory at Leverkusen in the Ruhr, the industrial heartland of Germany. They were one of eleven from 106 Squadron and of 467 bombers taking part. Flying over the heavily defended Ruhr was always a particularly tough challenge, but that night the weather was terrible with ten-tenths cloud, some of which rose to 22,000 feet, a height above which bombers would usually not fly. More often, they would be at about 18,000–20,000 feet.

First, however, they had to successfully take off and then climb. Lumbering the heavy Lancaster into the air, weighed down by a full bomb bay of one 4,000lb 'cookie' (a blockbuster bomb) and a mass of smaller incendiaries, was not easy. The pilot had to watch the speed rise, painfully slowly, then lift the tail until, at around 120mph, and with the end of the runway approaching all too fast, it somehow lifted into the air. Then there was the threat of collision: eleven aircraft from Syerston, all taking off within a couple of minutes of each other and joining hundreds more in the inky darkness of night, could easily collide. Such an occurrence was not uncommon.

Then came the journey to the target. Britain might have developed the world's first fully coordinated air defence system, with its radar, observers, ground controllers and means of identifying friend from foe, but since the Battle of Britain the Reich had followed suit with increasingly sophisticated technology to help them. On the ground were thousands of searchlights and, by mid-1943, some 10,000 heavy anti-aircraft guns. German radar would pick up British bomber raids almost immediately and further gun-laying radars would help direct the flak batteries below, while night fighters, bristling with machine guns and cannons, would be guided towards an unsuspecting target.

The first anti-aircraft guns and searchlights picked them up as they crossed the Dutch coast, then increased in intensity as they approached the Ruhr. Bursts of flak bounced and jolted the bomber as though it was being knocked about by a giant fist. On this first op, one burst tore a hole in their wing. They flew on, but, because of the cloud, they were forced to climb higher. Pathfinders had flown ahead of the main bomber stream and marked the target with flares, but when Mifflin and his crew reached what they thought was the target they could see no flares at all and so bombed on a fix from 'Gee', one of the British navigational aids. Bombs dropped, they turned and headed for home, and successfully touched down at 2.15 a.m., a little over five hours after they had first taken off. One mission down, twenty-nine to go.

Three and a half months later, by the beginning of December, the crew had survived fifteen missions – one more than the average – and were now halfway through their first tour and old hands at 106 Squadron. Midwinter meant shorter days and longer nights, which meant longer nights for night-bombing operations, but conversely the weather was also worse, too. Furthermore, it was cold, grey and miserable back at base. Mifflin was now a pilot officer, but Jackson and the rest of the crew were all sergeants and so slept in a twelve-man Nissen hut with a single stove that barely gave off enough heat to keep them warm.

Thursday 2 December was another grey, cold day of heavy cloud, yet, despite this, 458 bombers were to be sent to Berlin, and among them were Mifflin and the crew of *Uncle Joe*. This was just about the worst trip of them all: it was a long journey and the flak and air defences around the capital of the Reich were immense. The crew took off from Syerston at around 5 p.m. and headed out across the North Sea and over the Dutch coast. German radar had already picked up the bomber stream and correctly identified Berlin as the target, so waiting for the attackers were a mass of night fighters. Mifflin and his crew successfully evaded them as other aircraft were shot down in droves. There was still heavy cloud over the city as they began their bomb run. This was the most terrifying part of the entire trip, as they had to fly straight and level and felt at their most vulnerable, no matter how much flak was bursting all around them. Despite the cloud, Maurice Toft the bomb-aimer did manage to spot the Pathfinders' flares and, having dropped their bombs, they quickly climbed and headed for home. Soon after, they were picked up by an enemy night fighter which opened fire and with two passes raked the Lancaster with machine-gun and cannon fire. One engine was shot up, while bullets also knocked out the radio and intercom in the cockpit; both Mifflin and Jackson were extremely lucky not to be hit. The mid-upper turret also jammed. The Lancaster was now a sitting duck as Mifflin and Jackson tried to counteract the loss of an engine. All of them braced themselves, waiting for the *coup de grâce*. They were all too aware that few survived an attack by a night fighter. Fortune was smiling on them, however: the killer blow never came and they droned on into the cloud of that dark December night.

Their troubles were far from over, however. Without an intercom, they could not communicate with one another – the noise of three running Rolls-Royce Merlin engines was deafening – nor could they signal to the control tower at Syerston. They would have to land without warning and pray no one else was landing at the same time. The journey back was long and arduous, but they successfully crossed the North Sea and after circling Syerston landed back down safely without further mishap. They had been among the lucky ones. In all, forty aircraft were shot down that night, more than 8 per cent of the attacking force. Mifflin was awarded the Distinguished Flying Medal for that op, and they required a new Lancaster: *Uncle Joe II*.

Mission sixteen had been successfully completed, however, and as December 1943 gave way to January and a new year, so they continued to notch up one more successful raid after another. On the night of 1/2 March 1944, they attacked Stuttgart. This was a long mission, and although they saw their bombs explode close to the target despite another night of heavy cloud, it was not until seven in the morning, almost eight hours after taking off, that they landed again: eight hours of fear, of cold, of rapidly accumulating physical and mental stress. They were all exhausted but Mifflin especially so. The medical officer, recognising signs of combat stress, grounded him for a fortnight. Sometimes this was enough: a break to get some proper rest and recharge the batteries; the key was to spot the signs before a tipping point had been reached.

One of the difficulties for bomber crews was the stark juxtaposition of daily squadron life and the terror and dangers of flying ops. Crews might go days and sometimes more than a week without a mission, then fly two or three in a cluster. On the ground, they could go to the pub or the cinema, meet girlfriends and play sports and a host of other activities. They were well fed compared with many others, and, although conditions were often spartan, 'normal' daily life was not too bad. Then came the ops and up to eight hours of danger. The reminders of violent death were all too vivid. In the air, bombers exploded, or caught fire, or lost a wing and spiralled out of control to the ground, a fate witnessed by those around them. On the base, after an op the empty beds in a shared Nissen hut were melancholy reminders of the deaths of friends. Flying even a single mission required unimaginable courage.

Mifflin was soon back on ops and his crew's number of completed missions continued to rise. Mission number twenty-five was an eight-hour trip to Berlin and then, by the fourth week in April, they had safely negotiated twenty-nine missions: just one to go to complete their tour. The only one of the crew to have already finished was Norman 'Jacko' Jackson, who had flown a single flight filling in for another crew. He was entirely within his rights to bid the others farewell, but he decided he couldn't let them down; they would start and end their tour together, so, while the others completed their thirtieth, Jackson would be on his thirty-first.

On the morning of Wednesday 26 April 1944 they learned they would be flying their final mission that night. That same day, Jackson received a telegram from his wife, telling him he had a son, the couple's first child.

'Be careful,' his wife had added. Later that afternoon during the pre-flight briefing, they were told the target: Schweinfurt, in central Germany. When the American Eighth Air Force had hit this target the previous October, they had lost sixty bombers outright, with a further seventeen so badly shot up they had been scrapped and another 121 damaged. It had been a slaughter. No one wanted to target Schweinfurt.

They took off from Syerston at 9.35 p.m. into five-tenths cloud, successfully reached the target and dropped their bombs, then with the sudden release of weight seemed to leap upwards as Mifflin turned and headed back west. Fortune seemed to be smiling on them one last time, but if they had felt any surge of hope it was a false one. Again, the German air defence system had correctly picked up the attackers and a gaggle of single-engine Focke-Wulf 190 night fighters were waiting and ready to pounce. Suddenly, out of the darkness, bullets and cannons tore into *Uncle Joe II*. Mifflin immediately took evasive action, but the damage from that first pass was severe. They were in serious trouble. A petrol tank on the starboard wing had been hit and fuel was leaking profusely. Jackson had been hit in the legs by cannon-shell fragments and knocked to the ground, while the rear gunner, Johnny Johnson, had been badly wounded, too. Moments later, the heat from the exhaust stubs caused the fuel to ignite and soon flames were licking across the wing. With all too much fuel still to burn, it was clear the Lancaster was doomed unless the fire could be put out.

Disregarding his own wounds, Jackson now got back onto his feet as Mifflin, beside him, was desperately trying to control the stricken Lancaster. Looking out at the burning wing, Jackson told his skipper he was going to try and put out the fire. Mifflin was incredulous at his flight engineer's suggestion, but, as he grappled with the controls, accepted it was their only possible chance of getting home. Grabbing a fire extinguisher, Jackson pushed it into his Irvin sheepskin jacket and unpacked his parachute. With Toft, Higgins and Sandelands holding onto the parachute cords and twisting them into a rope, Jackson, the emergency axe in one hand, clambered up and out of the hatch. The Lancaster was still travelling at around 200mph, so Mifflin throttled back to around 140mph and tried his best to keep the wounded Lancaster flying straight and reasonably level. By now, Jackson was on the top of the plane, picking his way along the top of the fuselage, the freezing air and slipstream doing its best to pull him away. With the others still holding tightly onto the parachute cord, Jackson successfully slipped down onto the burning starboard wing.

It is hard to imagine what must have been going through his mind. Exposed on the wing, held by rope and a pick and with his legs injured, as the flaming Lancaster hurtled through the night air he inched his way towards the fire. At any moment, the entire aircraft could have exploded, and yet Jackson managed not only to pull out the extinguisher, but release the safety catch and then put out the flames. In so doing, he suffered dreadful burns to his face and arms, while the cords of the parachute had begun to burn, too. His life was held by a thread.

Just as it seemed salvation was at hand, fate took another twist as a Focke-Wulf opened fire again, hitting Jackson in the shoulder and knocking him off the wing. Assuming he had been killed, his friends let go of his lifeline and Jackson disappeared into the night, his parachute opening almost immediately but with the cords now on fire. Meanwhile, on board, the Lancaster was once again in serious trouble and plunging earthwards. Mifflin, still at the controls, now ordered the rest of the crew to bail out. While he desperately tried to maintain control of the aircraft, Toft, Sandelands, Higgins and Smith managed to jump successfully. By the time they were safely floating downwards, however, it was too late for Mifflin and the wounded Johnson. Burning and now out of control, the Lancaster crashed into the ground and exploded with both men still on board. In an act of extraordinary and selfless heroism, Mifflin had given his life so that the rest of crew might survive.

The survivors were picked up and taken to hospital where, to their amazement, they saw Jackson; badly burned and wounded, he was miraculously still alive. Somehow, the cords on his parachute had lasted just long enough, although he had broken both ankles on landing. With his badly burned hands, seventeen bullet and shrapnel wounds, one eye closed and swollen, and his face a mess, he had then dragged himself on his elbows until he reached a nearby village and knocked on the door of a cottage. There he was taunted and abused by the German who opened the door until his two daughters took pity on the injured airman and tried to nurse him. Later, he was picked up and taken to hospital. At no point did he lose consciousness and throughout this appalling ordeal bore the unimaginable pain with extraordinary stoicism.

'Nothing was heard from this aircraft after take-off. MISSING' was all that was written in the 106 Squadron operational record book of Lancaster ME669 and its crew[1]. Thanks to Jackson and Mifflin, however, five were still alive. After ten long months, Jackson had largely recovered and was sent to a POW camp where he and his fellow crewmates remained for the rest of the war. After two escape attempts, he was finally liberated in May 1945.

Only after the war in Europe was over did the astonishing story of Jackson's wing walk emerge as his grateful surviving crew members began to talk about that fateful thirtieth mission; Jackson himself had never mentioned it to anyone. In October 1945, news reached him that he had been awarded the Victoria Cross. He struggled to understand why. 'It was my job as flight engineer to get the rest of the crew out of trouble,' he said later. 'I was the most experienced member of the crew, and they all looked to me to do something.'[2] That bond forged within the crew had made a deep impression on all of them. Neither Mifflin nor Jackson had thought twice about their acts of heroism. For Mifflin, it had ended in early death; for Jackson, it had meant almost certain demise. That he had survived was little short of a miracle.

After the war, Jackson left the RAF and, despite permanent damage to his burned hands, he had a long career as a salesman for Haig whisky and he and his wife brought up six more children in addition to the son he had had to wait two years to see. He died, aged seventy-four, in 1994, as unassuming and modest as he had ever been.

Anyone who flew in a bomber crew demonstrated immense courage. All were heroes, but of all the extraordinary acts of bravery few are more extraordinary than that of Norman Jackson's wing walk. To climb out of a flying, burning Lancaster into the freezing night, already wounded, and with enemy night fighters circling, defies comprehension. It is almost fantastical and yet this otherwise unremarkable young man performed one of the most incredible acts of courage imaginable. He did it for his mates, because of that intense camaraderie they had developed over thirty missions. It was the same reason Mifflin had remained at the controls as *Uncle Joe II* had plunged into the ground. It was what ensured that tens of thousands of young men would continue to fly over Germany right until the end of the war. There is no doubting, however, that amidst all that extraordinary courage, Jackson's actions were among the most remarkable.

17

ASSISTANT SECTION OFFICER
NOOR INAYAT KHAN GC

Introduced by Dame Kelly Holmes DBE

Imagine a young woman, the descendant of an Indian Sultan, who dreamed of writing children's stories and who had been brought up in a loving family that believed in always telling the truth.

Now imagine a Second World War radio operator dropped into occupied France with a heavy suitcase full of wireless equipment, evading capture by the Gestapo while covering the workload of six other operators. Eventually captured, this operator tried to escape whenever the opportunity arose.

These two people were one and the same woman, Noor Inayat Khan, codename Madeleine. Not your classic 'James Bond' spy but someone who demonstrated what is possible with resolute spirit and ceaseless determination.

I find her story inspirational because Noor didn't let anyone else define her or limit her actions by deciding what she was capable of achieving. She risked her life in order to carry out the vital role she had been given. We do not face the same challenges as Noor did today, but I feel we can all learn from her example, by making the most of the freedom she gave so much to preserve.

If history had turned out differently we might have been celebrating the life of Noor-un-nisa Inayat Khan as one of our leading children's authors.

Growing up in France, Noor had always enjoyed writing and each family birthday would see her composing a poem especially for the occasion. Then, after completing her degree in child psychology in 1938, she received an offer from a family friend, Baroness van Tuyll. Van Tuyll, going under the name Henriette Willebeek le Mair, was a children's book illustrator and had a plan for a book project. Growing up, Noor had always been fascinated by the Jataka Tales – a collection of some 500 stories, each involving a previous incarnation of Buddha. In the stories, Buddha is represented by various animals, each of which, by some form of sacrifice, helped his evolution.

Van Tuyll's suggestion was that the two of them should put together a children's book consisting of twenty of these stories: Noor would write and adapt them for a young audience; Van Tuyll would illustrate them. Determined to seize this opportunity, Noor set up a schedule: she would awake at six each morning and work uninterrupted for three hours, before the rest of the household woke up. According to the biography of Noor written by her friend Jean Overton Fuller,[1] Noor felt 'this was the time when she felt her freshest. The cool, slightly damp air of the early morning had a magical quality which it lost later.'

The book wasn't the only children's writing that Noor was working on. Her stories started being featured on the Children's Hour of Radio Paris. In 1938, she also began writing stories for the children's page of *Sunday Figaro*, and became a regular contributor. According to Shrabani Basu, 'Noor had an endearing style that immediately drew in young readers'.[2] In August 1939, her story *Ce Qu'on entend quelquefois dans le bois* (What one hears sometimes in the woods) made the children's page of *Le Figaro*.

From the success of these pieces, Noor began looking into the idea of setting up a children's newspaper, *Bel Age* (The Beautiful Age). She worked up some material with an artist, a Monsieur Pinchon, and pitched the material to the journalist and editor Alexis Danan, hoping he'd publish it. According to Jean Overton Fuller, 'he was charmed with the material she had put together, but feared that the cost of production of anything so beautiful as she had in mind would make it impractical to market. When he explained this to her, she replied naively that in that case it should be sold very expensively to rich children, so that it could be distributed free to poor ones.'[3]

But while Noor's business acumen might not have been her sharpest suit, Danan was neither the first nor the last person to find himself charmed by her persuasive skills. He gave the go-ahead for the newspaper, which, coupled with the English publication of *Twenty Jataka Tales* by George G. Harrap, appeared to set 1939 as the year when Noor's career really began to flourish. But *Bel Age* never reached publication. The first edition got as far as proof stage before the outbreak of war paused publication. Like Noor's literary career, the newspaper was first postponed and then, ultimately, overtaken by events.

* * *

To say Noor Inayat Khan's family tree makes for interesting reading would be something of an understatement. Hers was one rich with Indian history and heritage. She was the great-great-great-granddaughter of the Tiger of Mysore, Tipu Sultan, the last Muslim ruler of southern India – hence the 'Spy Princess' tag. Her father, Hasrat Inayat Khan, was no less substantial a figure. He was a musician and mystic and one of the leading proponents of Sufism, making it his life's work to take these beliefs to the West.

Arriving in New York in 1910, Hasrat met Ora Ray Baker at the house of her guardian, where he was speaking. Ora herself had religious roots of a different kind – she was related to the founder of the Christian Science Church – and when she fell in love with Hasrat, her guardian refused to approve the marriage. The result was that Hasrat left for France with Ora following soon after. Here, they were married in 1913, with Ora now known as the Begum and adopting Indian dress. From France, the couple moved to Moscow, where Hasrat had been invited to teach. It was here, on New Year's Day 1914, that Noor was born.

Noor's early childhood continued this cosmopolitan, country-swapping journey. Her parents exchanged Moscow for first Paris and then London for six years, before returning to the French capital. Here, the family (Noor now had two younger brothers and a sister) lived in a house near the racecourse at Longchamps and then in a larger property in Suresnes, with a walled garden. It was here that Noor spent her teenage years – a time of mixed emotions for her, with the death of her father from pneumonia when she was thirteen, and finding herself forced to step up in the running of the house, as well as continuing her education.

In June 1940, with the Germans closing in on Paris, Noor and her family made the decision to leave for England. Joining the exodus from the French capital, they travelled first to Tours and then to Bordeaux. Here, scenes were chaotic, with authorities announcing the town 'full' and refusing to let anyone disembark from the train. When they did finally get to the city, they learned that there was a wait for several days to get on a boat. Eventually, after an abortive journey to St Nazaire to board a British Red Cross ship, the family found passage on the *Kasongo*, a Belgian cargo boat. This took them to Falmouth in Cornwall, before the family travelled to stay with friends in Southampton and Oxford. Noor, like her brother Vilayat, was determined to do her bit for the war effort.

Noor's cosmopolitan background meant that she was of interest to the British authorities, for better and worse, when it came to her role in the war effort. Her fluent French earmarked her as a potential candidate to join the SOE – the Special Operations Executive (SOE) – a select group of British agents working behind enemy lines in France. Interviewed for a role in 1942, the note of the meeting simply read: 'Has interesting linguistic qualifications which might make her of value for operational purposes.'[4]

An earlier meeting, when Noor was working her way up the WAAF (Women's Auxiliary Air Force), had a somewhat different outcome. Asked her opinion regarding Indian independence, Noor told the board of interviewees exactly what she thought; that Indians should be given the go-ahead to be armed and organise their own defence in the face of potential Japanese attack. Asked what her response would be to Indian leaders taking steps against the British, Noor said she'd back any reasonable Indian leader doing what they thought was needed. Quizzed about her loyalty to the Crown, she told her interviewers that she would remain loyal while Britain was at war with Germany. But once the war was over, supporting India against Britain was a real possibility.

This was not a response likely to go down well with Noor's military superiors: in 1942, the future prime minister Jawaharlal Nehru had launched his 'Quit India' campaign, leading to himself and many leading members of Congress being imprisoned. But perhaps as difficult to take as her views was the fact that Noor had been so upfront with them. Later on, when she had been accepted for the SOE and was being trained, one instructor complained about the influence of her 'crackpot father': 'Do you know what the bastard taught her? That the worst sin she could commit was to lie about anything.'[5] A laudable belief, maybe, but not one best suited to intelligence work.

Noor Inayat Khan does not perhaps sound like traditional spy material. 'If this girl's an agent, I'm Winston Churchill,' said a police superintendent who took her through a mock interrogation. 'Temperamentally unsuitable' for the job read a damning report by Colonel Frank Spooner. Her instructor at the SOE training camp called her the 'potty princess'. Agent Yvonne Cormeau described her as a 'splendid, vague dreamy creature, far too conspicuous – twice seen, never forgotten'.

For all this, she had an absolute drive to take part in the war effort – first training as a nurse after the outbreak of war, she had narrowly escaped to Britain via Bordeaux, fleeing France as the Germans invaded. She did indeed have the linguistic skills that SOE sorely lacked. And as a radio operator, she was one of the best: the fastest of any of the trainees coming through. It was undoubtedly a risk to send her in the field, but such was the need to get agents into France that these concerns were overridden for the good of the greater war effort.

Just before she was sent to France, Noor went to London to meet Leo Marks. Marks was the head of communications at SOE, a crack code-maker and a man with a literary bent of his own: he was the son of Benjamin Marks, the owner of 84 Charing Cross Road, the famous bookshop later to feature in the Helene Hanff novel of the same name. Marks was tasked with giving Noor an extended briefing, helping her to memorise the code conventions once she was in the field.

Marks bought and read a copy of Noor's book, *Twenty Jataka Tales*. He was struck by one particular story, about a monkey chief who sacrificed himself by offering his body as a bridge to allow thousands of other monkeys to escape from the clutches of the evil king Brahmadatta (the monkey chief died after one of the monkeys jumped so hard it broke his back). After Noor made some mistakes in the practice messages Marks had asked her to decode, according to Basu's book Marks told her: ' "Coded messages have one thing in common with monkeys: if you jump too hard on them you'll break their backs – and that's what you have done to this one. I doubt if Brahmadatta himself could decipher it, I know my monkeys in the code room couldn't." Noor looked up in surprise. "You've read my book," she said. Marks recalled that the "intensity of her look reduced him to chutney".'[6]

Continuing the literary theme, Marks told Noor that her book could help her to become a stronger coder: 'Every time you encode a message think of the letters in it as monkeys trying to cross the bridge between Paris and London. If they fall off, they'll be caught and shot . . . but they can't cross themselves, and if you don't help them by guiding them slowly and methodically, one step at a time, giving them all your thoughts and all your protection, they'll never reach the other side.'[7] Having received his pep talk, Noor had another go at the coding tests. This time, she was perfect.

* * *

The average survival time for a radio operator in the field was estimated by the SOE to be just six weeks. The reason for this was twofold: firstly, the fact that the radio operator was broadcasting meant that the Germans were able to place their location. As a result, radio operators needed a number of different locations from which they could broadcast. Travelling around was the second reason why the role was so full of risks: radio operators had to carry their wireless sets with them. These were bulky and heavy pieces of kit, and needed a suitcase to be carried around (they also required seventy feet of aerial in order to work). There would be little chance of outrunning a German patrol while lugging such a set about; equally, a stop and search could lead to immediate arrest.

Up to Noor's departure, SOE agents sent to France were given the role of courier: Noor was the first woman to be sent to France as a radio operator. As well as her wireless kit, she was given two additional items to take with her. The first of these was a new name: Noor was now Jeanne-Marie Renier, a children's nurse. Her cover story skilfully wove fictional detail with facts taken from her own life and upbringing. As well as this identity, Noor also had a codename – Madeleine, a character taken from one of her stories.

The final piece of kit Noor was given was a selection of pills: the first was a sort of sleeping pill that would knock someone out for six hours if slipped into their tea or coffee. The second had the opposite effect: a stimulant to keep Noor awake if she was exhausted in a moment of emergency. The third pill gave the taker a stomach upset, useful if they needed to fake illness. Finally, there was the L pill, which contained cyanide. This was fatal if bitten into, but harmless if swallowed whole. This was given as an option for agents who felt unable to cope with interrogation once captured.

Noor arrived in France in June 1943, tasked with working in Le Mans as a wireless operator for Cinema, a sub-circuit of Prosper, one of the largest and most successful circuits of agents running in the Paris area. Upon arrival, Noor was told to go to 40 rue Erlanger, Paris 16e, the home of Emile Henri Garry, where she was to give her password: *'Je viens de la part de votre ami Antoine des nouvelles au sujet de la société en Bâtiment'* (I have come on behalf of your friend Antoine for news on the building society). Garry would then respond by saying, *'L'affaire est en cours'* (the business is in hand). However, Noor was convinced that her contact was an old lady, so, having been let in by Garry, she didn't give her password but sat and waited instead. It was not an auspicious start.

Worse was to follow. Within ten days of arriving in France, the Prosper network was broken by the Gestapo. Having infiltrated the circuit, the Gestapo were able to arrest both the circuit's leaders and capture all of its equipment. Noor, initially ordered to lie low, was the only one able to break the news of the collapse to London: it transpired that she now had the only transmitter left in Paris. Her handler in the UK immediately ordered Noor to return home, on the grounds that the situation was now too dangerous. But Noor refused: she felt that, as the last link between Paris and London, it was important for her to stay there to let people know what was going on.

Over the next few months, Noor's posts back to the UK were crucial to the war effort. It is difficult to understate either their importance or the risks that she took in sending the information: so often did Noor change her hair colour to avoid detection that it became rough and stiff. Such was the pressure on her that she was carrying out a workload equivalent to that of six radio operators. With the Germans tuning in to her broadcasts and determined to find her, Noor had to find an ever-increasing number of places from which to broadcast. One narrow escape followed another: on one occasion she had her aerial wrapped around a tree outside her apartment. When it fell to the ground, it was picked up by a passing German soldier. Assuming she was innocently trying to tune into some music, the officer helped her put the aerial back up, with Noor doing her best to stay cool.

The number of operations that Noor helped with during these months was countless: these included getting thirty Allied airmen who had been shot down over France out of the country; sorting positions for parachute drops of arms; getting money and weapons to the French Resistance; arranging false papers for various agents and helping others leave for Britain. But all the while the Gestapo net was being drawn in: she was nearly caught out by a plan involving two Germans posing as Canadian agents (the original agents had been arrested and the Germans had been broadcasting as them in their place).

Then, just as she had accepted orders for her to leave and return to Britain, she was betrayed. The Gestapo were tipped off by someone called Renée – assumed (though never confirmed) to be the sister of Henri Garry, her first contact on arrival in France. To begin with, Noor managed to evade the German officers whom she realised were following her. But on returning to her flat she was captured, though not without a fight, attacking and repeatedly biting the person trying to arrest her.

Taken to Gestapo headquarters, Noor remained silent as her interrogator, Ernest Vogt, fired questions at her. Unable to get her to talk, Vogt agreed to Noor's request for a bath. At first, the guards kept the door ajar, until Noor shouted furiously at them to give her some privacy. Once the door was closed, Noor immediately tried to escape, climbing through the window and clambering onto the guttering. Vogt, who had gone to the lavatory next door, was surprised to see her tiptoeing past. Being careful not to surprise her (such was the drop that, if Noor fell, she would have been killed), Vogt chided, 'Madeleine, don't be silly. You will kill yourself. Think of your mother. Give me your hand.'[8] Helping her back in, Noor was escorted back down to her cell.

This wasn't Noor's last attempt to escape. Teaming up with Captain John Starr and Colonel Faye in adjacent cells, the three hatched a plan to break out by loosening the bars on their cell windows with a screwdriver they'd secured. This they succeeded in doing. But just as they were making their escape across the rooftops, an unfortunately timed RAF attack set off the air raid sirens. The trio knew their empty cells would be discovered and took evasive action, using the blankets they had with them as a rope to swing down and break through the windows of the next-door house. When they reached street level, they saw a road cordon already set up and knew they were surrounded.

Her second escape foiled, Noor was now given an ultimatum: either sign a declaration that she would not try and break out again, or she would be transferred to a prison in Germany that could handle her. Noor's response was defiant: if the chance to escape came, she would take it. She was transferred immediately, the first British female agent to be sent to Germany. She was sent to Pforzheim prison, on the northern edge of the Black Forest, where she was categorised as 'highly dangerous' and a '*Nacht und Nebel*' prisoner ('Night and Fog', a term used for prisoners who disappeared into the system, with no information given as to where they were being held). Here, conditions were extremely hard: Noor was kept in solitary confinement on minimal rations and chained both hand and foot, and also by hand to foot.

By September 1944, the tide of the war had turned. Allied troops were now pushing German forces back, and the Germans were turning on those they had already captured. On 11 September, Noor was taken from Pforzheim and, along with three other SOE agents (Eliane Plewman, Madeleine Damerment and Yolande Beekman) was transferred to Dachau by car and train. Their stay there was all too short: arriving just after midnight, the other three SOE agents were taken out of their cells in the early morning and shot beside the crematorium. Noor, meanwhile, was ordered to be given the 'full treatment' and spent her last night being tortured and abused in her cell. But for all the brutality inflicted upon her, Noor's defiance and spirit somehow survived. As the pistol was raised to kill her, she uttered a single word: '*Liberté*'.

* * *

For all the concerns about her character before she was sent to France, Noor surpassed all expectations in terms of her bravery and what she achieved: far from cracking under pressure, she kept a cool head and withstood all the interrogation and torture that the Gestapo and German prison guards tried, never revealing any information of note. In April 1949, three years after the French had awarded Noor the *Croix de guerre* with Gold Star (their highest civilian award), she was also posthumously awarded the George Cross. According to the citation, Noor 'displayed the most conspicuous courage, both moral and physical over a period of more than 12 months'.

On her last day in England back in June 1943, Noor had been picked up in an open car by Vera Atkins, the SOE recruiter, and driven through the Sussex countryside to Tangmere, from where she would be flown to France. Here, at Tangmere Cottage, Noor was taken upstairs to get ready. On one of the chairs in the room was a novel called *Remarkable Women*. Vera Atkins commented to Noor that one day someone should write a book about the 'most remarkable women of all . . . that book will have to be rewritten after these girls have done their stuff'.[9]

There is little doubt that Noor Inayat Khan more than qualifies for inclusion in such a book.

PIPER DANIEL LAIDLAW VC

Introduced by Eddie Redmayne OBE

Hans Christian Andersen once said that 'where words fail, music speaks', At the battle of Loos in 1915, words failed but music spoke above the wailing shells, the repetitive bark of machine guns and the silent, stealthy creep of mustard gas. Music spoke through the bagpipes of Piper Laidlaw, a forty-year-old father of six from a small village outside Berwick-upon-Tweed.

As the King's Own Scottish Borderers prepared to go over the top, they were shrouded in poisonous gas and enveloped in confusion. This risked delaying their attack, but Piper Laidlaw's actions that morning showed a determination and inspiration that rallied his battalion. He faced the German machine guns, artillery and gas armed only with his bagpipes and his courage.

Now over a hundred years after the battle of Loos, it falls to another generation to pass on the story of Piper Laidlaw and the men he fought alongside.

The unique sound of the bagpipes affects the senses in many different ways. Their reedy and baleful moan is by turns haunting and mournful, but also uplifting and inspiring. Theirs is a sound that penetrates the soul, makes the hairs on the back of the neck stand up. To some, however, it grates. Bagpipes make a sound of exquisite beauty to some, to others a terrifying cacophony. Few, however, would doubt there is a more emotive sound. Time and time again through the centuries, the pipers have led men into battle and helped put the fear of God into those on the receiving end. Albert Martin, a London-born rifleman, watched in awe during the Battle of Alamein in Egypt in 1942 as he saw the men of the 51st Highland Division disappear, spectre-like, into the swirling smoke and sand, the sound of the pipes clear through the din of battle. 'It was,' he said, 'the most moving sound I ever heard.'[1] Even in 1967, during the conflict in Aden, the Gordon Highlanders were able to attack without firing a shot; the sound of the pipes alone was enough to make their enemy turn and run.

The history of this extraordinary instrument remains shrouded in myth and obscurity, but it is possible its origins lie in ancient times. Some have suggested it was brought to Scotland by Roman legionaries. Forms of bagpipes were played in Asia and elsewhere across Europe, but for the past 500 years and more they have been rooted in the cultural heritage of Scotland, and by the seventeenth century, and very probably earlier, they had become an essential sound of war. Whether it was clashes between clans or Jacobites against the English, bagpipes were used to inspire and motivate men in battle.

Certainly the pipers were playing at Culloden in April 1746, as the Jacobites made their last stand. James Reid was one of the pipers that fateful day and was among the 558 men captured by the Duke of Cumberland's government forces and brought to England. Put on trial, Reid was accused of high treason, although he argued his innocence. He had, he pointed out, borne no arms and had never taken up sword against the Crown; all he had done all day was play the bagpipes. After a short deliberation, the judges rejected his plea. No Scottish regiment went into battle without its piper, and therefore, they asserted, the bagpipes had to be considered a weapon of war. Reid was found guilty, sentenced and hanged, drawn and quartered. No other piper would suffer such a fate, but plenty more would die playing. Piping men into battle was always, and has remained, a dangerous business. A man needed nerves of steel to play the pipes in battle.

Following the Battle of Culloden, the British government worked hard to stamp out Scottish nationalism. The Disarming Act that same year, 1746, banned the bearing of broadswords, dirks, pistols and other weapons but also the wearing of tartan, plaid and any traditional Highland clothes. Bagpipes were, perhaps surprisingly, not banned, but their use did decline, and nearly fifty years later, in 1794, recruiting sergeants struggled to find enough pipers to fill Scottish regiments being raised to fight Napoleon.

By the mid-nineteenth century, Scotland, and Scottish culture, had become acceptable and even fashionable thanks to the novels of authors like Sir Walter Scott but also in part due to Queen Victoria's love of the country and the Highlands especially. By making a home at Balmoral and embracing the beauty of the landscape and Scotland's traditions and customs, she paved the way for a resurgence that swept away the suspicion and antipathy of the eighteenth century. One of those young Scotsmen who had little hesitation in accepting the Queen's shilling was Daniel Logan Laidlaw. Born in July 1875 in the village of Little Swinton near the border town of Berwick-upon-Tweed, he was one of three boys born to Margaret Laidlaw and her husband, Robert, a local quarryman.

They were poor and working class but Daniel still received an education, albeit across the border in Northumberland and where, after his schooling, he became a miller's apprentice. Later, aged twenty-one, and dreaming of a world beyond the relentless, back-breaking grind of milling, he joined the local regiment, the Durham Light Infantry (DLI), not as a piper but as a foot soldier, and, like so many before him, found himself on a troopship and sailing away from the very small and narrow world of his early upbringing and heading across the oceans to the far reaches of the British Empire.

For the next two years, Laidlaw served in India where for much of the time he was based in Bombay. For the most part, there was little going on – the Black Watch were part of the garrison troops, there to oversee British rule. When bubonic plague broke out in the city, the DLI were among those troops brought in to help contain its spread. India was also where Laidlaw transferred from the DLI to the King's Own Scottish Borderers (KOSB), where his oldest brother, Jim, was Pipe Major. Perhaps it was Jim who encouraged him to pick up the pipes. At any rate, it was at the behest of his second older brother, William, who was then also a Pipe Major in the King's Own Scottish Borderers, albeit back in Scotland. By the end of 1898, Daniel Laidlaw was back in Scotland, had successfully transferred to the home battalion of the KOSB, and had begun his career as a regimental piper.

Marrying in 1906, in Alnwick, Northumberland, Laidlaw and his wife soon started a family – there would eventually be six children, three boys and three girls – and six years later, now thirty-seven, he went onto the reserve list, which meant a return to civvie street, although he remained eligible for a call-up should he be required. For the next couple of years, Laidlaw worked as a canteen manager in the Alnwick Co-operative stores and became an assistant scout master.

He would have presumably assumed his full-time military career was over, partly because of his age but also because the two battalions of the King's Own Scottish Borderers had been absorbed into the militia and the Territorials. In August 1914, Britain went to war in the first pan-European conflict since Waterloo ninety-nine years earlier. By September that year, Laidlaw was back in uniform with the KOSB, his pipes once more dusted down, and both they, and his lungs, recalled to duty. All too soon, he and millions of others would be heading across the English Channel to war.

The regular British Army had been small in August 1914; in fact, Britain had traditionally had small armies. Not for nothing was the Royal Navy known as the Senior Service and it was the navy, not the army, that had been at the heart of Britain's overseas expansion. In any case, a large army made little sense – after all, where would all those men be kept in times of peace? A large army would mean peacetime conscription. Far better to spend a defence budget on creating the world's largest and most modern navy, which had the benefits of ensuring Britannia continued to rule the waves, provided accommodation away from England's green and pleasant land and required less manpower than maintaining a sizeable army. As a result, the British Army stood at just 247,432 regulars on the eve of the First World War, which, with a further almost half a million in militias and territorials, seemed, at the time, plenty. It was well over double the size it is today.

In those opening months of the war, the fighting was highly mobile as the Germans tried to hustle their way into France with a wide, sweeping thrust down along the Belgian coast. This was a time when cavalry still played a vital role and when there was no firm static front line as such. This mobile manoeuvrist war came to a halt in November when the British and French managed to hold the German thrust at Ypres in Belgium. For the Allies, it was a close-run thing – on 11 November 1914, the Prussian Guard, moving swiftly through the autumn mists, punched a big hole in the line that might easily have proved fatal had it not been for a ferocious counter-attack by the Oxfordshire and Buckinghamshire Light Infantry.

The Battle of Ypres – the first of three major battles fought in the war on this low-lying area of Flanders farmland – was a harbinger of what was to come. The small British Expeditionary Force (BEF) had lost more than 58,000 men since the outbreak of war – more than a fifth of its original number – while the Germans had suffered even greater casualties. Ypres was known to the Germans as *Kindermord Zuehlke Ypres:* the Ypres Massacre of the Innocents. Now winter was upon them and the shorter days, and cold, wet conditions, as well as the physical exhaustion of the men at the front, meant both sides went to earth. Traditionally, armies fought in the summer months for a good reason and, despite the advent of heavy calibre artillery and machine guns, the modern age had so far done little to change the difficulties of fighting a year-round battle.

There was a further problem: both sides had gone to war in August 1914 assuming the conflict would be a swift one and certainly over by Christmas. As a result, they were running out of ammunition and especially artillery shells. A pause was needed – one that was characterised by the sound of shovels digging into the soft clay and chalk of Flanders and north-west France.

Piper Daniel Laidlaw reached the Western Front in June 1915, by which time it was abundantly clear that the war was developing into a conflict of bitterness and attrition; there were no obvious ways a decisive breakthrough could be achieved without the sacrifice of a huge number of young men's lives. Now just a few weeks shy of his fortieth birthday, Laidlaw could have avoided being part of the carnage to come; he could have stayed at home with his increasingly large family, but presumably, as a piper and a proud patriot, he believed it was his duty to play his part. As a highly experienced soldier, too, he would not have wanted any of his children to ask him innocently what he had done in the Great War.

By the time of his arrival at the front, the British Army had already suffered a number of hard knocks. The word March comes from Mars, the Roman god of war, and traditionally that was when the campaigning season began again. In March 1915, that had been the case, and a joint Anglo-French offensive had been planned, although this was dependent on the British taking over part of the French line north of Ypres. However, then the British 29th Division, the last of the regular army still to be committed, was posted to Greece instead, which meant a territorial division would have to fill the breach. Field Marshal Sir John French, the British Commander-in-Chief, felt this territorial division was not up to the task originally earmarked for the 29th. Joffre, the French and overall Allied C-in-C, was incensed and called off the offensive. French, however, decided to go ahead with his planned attack anyway.

Over the winter, the Germans had dug just one line of trenches, and the attack at Neuve Chapelle by General Rawlinson's IV Corps on 10 March 1915 nearly worked. The largest barrage of the war so far was followed by a sweeping infantry attack that pushed the Germans back more than a thousand yards. Unfortunately for the British, however, two German machine guns had escaped the barrage and cut to pieces the infantry then attacking in the north of the line. This setback caused a delay that was exacerbated by the fog of war. Rawlinson, unable to understand clearly what was happening, was then unable to exploit what successes had been achieved. The glaring reality of this evolving conflict was suddenly becoming clear: that it was incredibly difficult for attackers to reinforce successfully any gains because there were no effective means of swiftly communicating where and on what scale that reinforcement was needed.

The Germans had also learned lessons from Neuve Chapelle – namely that their defensive positions needed to be deep. One line of trenches was not enough and they soon began digging not only a second line, but increased bands of barbed wire, communications trenches linking one line to the other and further back a line of concrete machine-gun posts. The only way the Allies were going to bulldoze their way through this was by even heavier artillery and even more men. The trouble was that in the spring of 1915 they had neither. In fact, the ammunition shortage was causing a major political crisis back at home.

Meanwhile, the Germans now attacked at Ypres, using gas for the first time in battle on 22 April, which was initially very effective. As with the British at Neuve Chapelle, however, the Germans found they were unable to make the most of their initial success and the Second Battle of Ypres soon descended into an attritional battle in which large numbers of young men were killed and wounded for not very much gain. In May, the British tried to take the initiative again, this time at Aubers Ridge, near La Bassée Canal, but the artillery support was less than it had been at Neuve Chapelle and, once again, the attack achieved little.

Despite these costly failures, both the French and British were determined to keep on the offensive. On 24 June, around the time of Piper Laidlaw's arrival in France, French and Joffre met to discuss future plans. Both were committed to the Western Front and agreed that to go on the defensive would be 'wholly inadmissible'. Over the following weeks, as Laidlaw and his fellows in the King's Own Scottish Borderers began to accustom themselves to trench life, French and British political and military leaders agreed there should soon be a major and combined offensive on the Western Front.

Joffre wanted the British to attack on the left of the French around the mining town of Loos. This was the area of General Sir Douglas Haig's First Army and he wasted no time in pointing out that the location was a bad one in which to attack; the Germans were dug in here using a mass of mining slag heaps, pit-heads and abandoned housing to their advantage. Any infantry attacking would come under sweeping enemy fire. Until there was considerably more artillery to suppress these German positions beforehand, Haig believed any infantry attack would be most likely cut to shreds. 'We should not be helping the French,' Haig told Joffre's liaison officer, 'by throwing away thousands of lives knocking our heads against a brick wall.'[2] Field Marshal French was persuaded by Haig's arguments, but Joffre was the senior commander and insisted the attack go ahead as planned. In August, Field Marshal Lord Kitchener, secretary of state for war, also waded in. On the Eastern Front, the Russians were in retreat and he told French a major effort was needed to draw German troops away from the east.

Planning for the Loos offensive therefore went ahead, against Haig's wishes. A further disagreement broke out between him and French over the use of the reserve. Haig wanted to keep IX Corps, the troops allocated to exploit any success, close at hand, whereas French insisted on keeping them further back where he could maintain his control over when and where they were committed. Tactically, Haig was right; however, French still had major reservations about the entire battle plan and was increasingly aware that Haig was breathing down his neck to take over as C-in-C. Furthermore, he did not trust Haig, concerned that he would throw in the reserve before there was a big enough breach to exploit. French's stance was therefore primarily about control.

Some 533 guns would fire over a quarter of a million shells to launch the British attack at Loos, but the bitter and fruitless fighting so far that year had shown that even such a huge amount was not enough. However, now that the Germans had used gas, the British had few qualms about using it in turn and so hoped that what they lacked in guns they could make good with mustard gas. In 1915, this meant launching it from a large number of canisters rather than by gas shell, a technique fraught with risk: enough wind was needed to ensure it drifted over the enemy lines, but not so much that it then dispersed. What most certainly was not wanted was any sudden change in wind direction; weather and wind direction could, however, be fickle.

Early on the morning of 25 September 1915, as Laidlaw and his fellows readied themselves in their trenches to go over the top and into the attack across no man's land, Haig had to make the difficult decision as to whether or not to use gas – an additional weapon that he recognised might well prove decisive for his attack. His meteorologist advised him the wind direction was favourable, but Haig then carried out his own test. Lighting a cigarette, he watched the tobacco smoke gently drift away. Soon after, he gave the order to launch the canisters.

At 5.50 a.m., as the guns still boomed and shells hurtled over towards the German positions, the gas canisters were switched on. The plan was to shroud the German positions for forty minutes then, at 6.30 a.m., for the infantry to clamber out of their trenches and attack. The King's Own Scottish Borderers were part of 15th Division in the centre of the attacking line.

As the countdown to zero hour continued, British artillery was doing its best to cut the lines of German wire, and gas clouds drifted slowly across no man's land like a curtain that was ghoulishly lit up by the red and orange bursts of shrapnel up ahead. It began to drizzle, the wind died down and, in places, seemed to drop altogether. Then, imperceptibly at first, in a number of places the gas started drifting back.

In the very centre of the line, the guns had done well and much of the wire around the Lens Road Redoubt had been successfully cut. A quarter of a mile away, however, where the King's Own Scottish Borderers waited in their stifling and ill-suited gas helmets, the gas was already over their positions. At 6.30 a.m., as the 6th Cameron Highlanders began their advance, the men of the KOSB held back. Many of the men were struggling with the gas, their gas masks simply not good enough to protect them sufficiently. At that moment, Lieutenant Young, the officer closest to Piper Laidlaw, turned to him and shouted, 'For God's sake, Laidlaw, do something about it!'[3]

Without pause, the piper pulled off his mask, clambered up the ladder and began furiously blowing into his pipes. As machine-gun bullets fizzed and zipped around him, he now began playing the regimental march, 'Blue Bonnets over the Border', striding up and down the parapet as he did so, in full view of both the enemy and his fellows faltering in the trench below.

It was exactly what was needed. Stirred by the plaintive sound of the pipes and Laidlaw's selfless display of courage, the men now hurriedly clambered up the ladders and stumbled out into no man's land. Still Laidlaw played. German artillery shells were now crashing around as well as machine-gun bullets. Laidlaw was hit by shrapnel in the left ankle and leg, but staggered onwards, now playing 'The Standard on the Braes o' Mar'.

Fortunately for the attackers, elsewhere along the divisional front, the wind had been more favourable and the enemy badly hit both by shellfire and the gas. The men of the KOSB, with Laidlaw's pipes still heard above the din of battle, edged their way across the first trench, then the second and on to the third, until they reached the battered remnants of Loos village itself. Only then did Laidlaw, his left leg a bloody mess, stagger back to his own lines.

On the Scots pushed, so that there were reports of German troops running back up the hill behind, fleeing towards their main second line. Almost against expectation, a massive punch had been made in the German positions, in which the reserve now needed urgently to be pushed. Needless to say, these reserves did not arrive as quickly as hoped.

Haig did not have control of IX Corps until 1.20 p.m., more than four hours after the Scottish breakthrough, and even then his reserve troops were still struggling forward along roads clogged with traffic. In fact, they still had a long way to go and were not able to enter the fray until the following day. By this time, the Germans had brought up their own reserves and recovered some of their balance. As the infantry of IX Corps finally attacked on 26 September, they were cut to pieces.

The Battle of Loos continued for a few more days, but ended in failure for the British. Some 43,000 British troops were killed and wounded, including Rudyard Kipling's son John, whose body would lie missing and unidentified until 1992. It also ended the career of Sir John French, who was, just as he had feared, replaced by Douglas Haig. Long years of slaughter followed; tragically, Loos was really just the beginning. Not until the summer of 1918 did the war become mobile again and by that time millions, not tens of thousands, had been killed along the Western Front.

By then, Daniel Laidlaw was long out of the war. In fact, that opening day of the Battle of Loos was his last in action. Nonetheless, that any breakthrough had occurred at all that day was in no small part due to his bravery and inspirational pipe-playing that brought nothing but admiration for both him and the Scottish troops with whom he served. In the Scottish press his heroics were written up and he was dubbed the 'Piper of Loos'. As word spread of his extraordinary playing in the face of chlorine gas and enemy fire, so formal recognition became more likely. So it proved, and on 18 November, as he recovered from his wounds, it was announced that he had been awarded the Victoria Cross. The investiture took place at Buckingham Palace on 3 February 1916, by which time his days as a front-line soldier were over. Instead, he was put to use on morale-boosting and PR drives, playing his pipes at various wartime concerts and although promoted to pipe sergeant in 1917, he was demobilised soon after the war, his long military career finally over. His eldest son was born in December 1920 and Laidlaw remembered the Battle of Loos in his own way, naming him Victor Loos Laidlaw.

Although Laidlaw was one of the more fortunate Victoria Cross recipients who survived their astonishing act of bravery, he struggled after the war, like so many of those returning home. Now a middle-aged man with limited beneficial practical skills, his many years of soldiering counted for little among so many others returning from war. Long periods of unemployment followed, although he did play the pipes in two films and occasionally piped when asked. In the Second World War, he became head ARP warden in Norham and Islandshires in Northumberland. He died in 1950, near Berwick-upon-Tweed and only a few miles from where he had been born and brought up. Poor and largely forgotten, he was buried in an unmarked grave. Not until 2002 was a headstone placed upon his resting place. Being awarded a Victoria Cross has never been a guarantee of lifelong prosperity.

A piece of rare film footage of Laidlaw survives, however, when he was interviewed by the historian Sir John Hammerton, who introduces his guest as 'the famous piper of Loos'. The date is hard to discern, but is perhaps the late 1930s. Laidlaw sits, ramrod-straight, silver moustaches waxed, his bearing resolute and proud. Hammerton asks him to play what he had played that morning in September 1915 and Laidlaw obliges, marching back and forth as he did above the parapet. The sound is eerie and heart-rending. It makes the hairs on the back of the neck stand on end, as it did all those years before.

MALTA GC

Introduced by Joseph Calleja

It is virtually impossible to grow up in Malta – the beautiful island I am so proud to call home – without having the triumphs and scars of this history-drenched rock etched on one's soul.

St Paul was famously shipwrecked on the island, and in the Middle Ages the Knights of Malta successfully repelled the Great Siege of the Ottoman Emperor Suleiman in one of the bloodiest battles in history.

For over 7,000 years Malta has been coveted by different peoples – from the Phoenicians to the Romans, to the French and the British, who remained as friendly occupiers for over 150 years – for its strategic position in the centre of the Mediterranean.

During the Second World War it was Adolf Hitler's turn to fix his dogged gaze on the island.

I vividly recall my family telling stories from that period of the strife and hardship endured by the Maltese, who spent night after night in cramped underground bunkers praying for the intercession of the Sacred Heart of Jesus and Mary to steer the raining bombs out of harm's way. Many lost their homes, their livelihoods and, most tragically of all, their lives, cruelly extinguished by unrelenting air raids. Valletta's famous opera house, in which I would never get the opportunity to sing, was erased, too.

What the people of Malta never lost, however, was their faith, hope and courage, which has been beautifully encapsulated in the essay you are about to read.

The Maltese heroes who lived through those trying times have just reason to be proud of their heroism, and of the George Cross they were awarded in 1942, which to this day is emblazoned on the national flag as a reminder of the nation's valour and indomitable spirit in the moment of truth.

I salute them.

On Wednesday 15 April 1942, King George VI made a historic and unprecedented announcement: the tiny Mediterranean island of Malta, a formal British possession since 1813, was being awarded the George Cross, the highest civilian decoration for gallantry. For John Agius, a young Maltese clerk working in the RAF office in Valletta, this stunning news only reached him two days later, on Friday 17 April, when he read about it in the *Times of Malta*, a newspaper that had stoically and defiantly produced an edition every single day of the war so far. 'To honour her brave people I award the George Cross to the Island Fortress of Malta', the King had written in his own hand, 'to bear witness to a heroism and devotion that will long be famous in History.'[1] The news made front-page headlines around the world, and although there were some hungry mouths on Malta who complained that a George Cross could not be eaten, there was no doubt the majority were thrilled and that it provided a much-needed boost to morale at a terrible moment in the island's history. Certainly, John Agius was delighted and felt both proud and happy at the news.

Nonetheless, by mid-April 1942, the island was slowly dying. The constant air raids and falling bombs were beating the population further into the ground, just as the shortage of food and supplies weakened the appetite for the struggle. Frank Rixon, a British soldier in the Royal West Kents who had married a Maltese girl, found the demoralising job of repeatedly filling in bomb craters on the island's airfields was made all the worse by seeing men blown to smithereens right before his eyes. 'You didn't get counselling then,' he commented, 'for picking up bits and pieces of your mates.'[2] Some 4,000 tons of bombs had fallen on Malta in March 1942; a further 6,782 would hit the island in April. To put that in perspective, 18,000 tons of bombs landed on London during the entire nine-month Blitz and over an area ten times the size. By the time the award of the George Cross was announced, Malta had become the most bombed place on earth.

It was primarily the Luftwaffe, the German air force, that was attempting to pulverise Malta that spring of 1942, although they were joined by the Regia Aeronautica, the air force of their Italian Axis ally. Sicily, just sixty miles away and around fifteen minutes' flying time, was bristling with airfields and was easily able to host the influx of German bombers and fighters of Fliegerkorps II. Malta may have been tiny – around seventeen miles by eight and smaller than the Isle of Wight – but it had always been a place of enormous strategic importance and that certainly held true in this latest world war. Lying some 1,000 miles from Alexandria in Egypt and 900 from Gibraltar in the west, it lay pretty much halfway across the Mediterranean Sea. Traditionally, its deep-water harbours had been home to the Royal Navy's Mediterranean Fleet, but although the navy had relocated its base to Alexandria at the outset of war, Malta remained, first and foremost, an offensive base: from here, British aircraft, ships and submarines could attack Axis supply lines to North Africa.

Italy had declared war on Britain on 10 June 1940 in the mistaken belief that the British, like the French, were on the point of collapse. Benito Mussolini had already conquered Abyssinia in East Africa and Libya was also an Italian colony. With Britain out of the war, he envisaged being handed possessions in between and creating a new Roman Empire in Africa and the Mediterranean in which he was the Caesar. Mussolini, though, much like Hitler, had a narrow world view, with woefully poor geo-political understanding. He completely failed to recognise that Britain's strength lay in naval and air power, and that with the world's largest merchant fleet and access to around 85 per cent of the world's merchant shipping, and to resources all around the globe, she was still in a strong position despite the defeat of the British Army in France.

Nonetheless, Malta had been badly understrength in June 1940. The island was short of anti-aircraft guns and its fighter defence amounted to a handful of crated Fleet Air Arm Gloster Gladiator biplanes. A concerted and decisive attack by the Italians in June 1940 would almost certainly have won them the island and with it a vitally important base which they could deny the British and in turn use themselves.

It was not to be, however. A few desultory raids shocked the islanders and caused individual tragedies, but never threatened the island's safety. By the time the Luftwaffe reached Sicily in December 1940 and began pummelling Malta for the first time, much had changed: the island was by then bristling with anti-aircraft guns and considerable numbers of Hawker Hurricane fighter planes had been flown there. British submarines and bombers were also reaching the island. What's more, elsewhere in the Mediterranean theatre the folly of Mussolini's misguided declaration of war had been fully realised. In North Africa, the 36,000-strong British Western Desert Force had trounced two Italian armies and, by February 1941, more than 130,000 Italians had been taken prisoner. Italy had invaded Greece at the end of October 1940 and what was supposed to have been an easy victory had instead proved a humiliating fiasco. Mussolini, always wary of his Axis partner, had wanted to create an entirely Italian sphere of influence in the Mediterranean while Nazi Germany pursued its own goals. Now, Hitler was sending German forces to help bail out the Italians and ensure there was no threat to the southern flank.

It was no coincidence that Malta was the first target: Germany had recognised what a crucial place it was. Axis shipping in the Mediterranean was limited and the only way to supply North Africa was across the sea. It was therefore imperative that what Axis supplies were sent to Libya reached their destination safely, and not least the two German divisions commanded by Major General Erwin Rommel sent in February 1941. The first Malta 'blitz' was primarily about ensuring that flow of arms was not disturbed.

The level of bombing was unlike anything that had come before. Entire streets in the Three Cities area on the southern side of Grand Harbour were destroyed, and the entire area, as well as Valletta, the capital, was evacuated. Families trudged off to stay with relations away from the harbour areas or began digging down into the limestone. This rock was hard when exposed to sunlight and weather but underground was surprisingly soft and could be dug out comparatively easily using hand tools – and a lot of sweat and hard work.

Nonetheless, although to the Maltese the sight of screaming Stuka dive bombers and hordes of German aircraft over the island appeared to confirm just how unstoppable the enemy was, the Luftwaffe had taken a pummelling of its own during the Battle of Britain and was already overstretched. It could not be everywhere, and, thanks to the ineptitude of the Italian army, had to support German land operations in North Africa, then the Balkans in March 1941, then Greece and finally Crete in May, before transferring almost all its effort to Operation BARBAROSSA, the invasion of the Soviet Union, in June 1941. This meant that for much of the rest of 1941 the responsibility for attacking Malta was left to the Regia Aeronautica. While the bombers still came over, it was not with the same intensity as had been displayed by the Luftwaffe. The Maltese responded stoically – many returned to their homes, or what remained of them, while shops gradually reopened and some semblance of normal life returned. 'We were blasted well out,' ran an advert by a tailors in the *Times of Malta*, 'but we're blasted well open again.'[3]

What's more, the island fortress was becoming stronger and repeatedly proving its value in the ongoing North Africa campaign. In November 1941, for example, Malta-based submarines, ships and aircraft destroyed 77 per cent of all Axis convoys heading across the Mediterranean. British submarines based on Malta, such as HMS *Upholder*, were not only sinking huge numbers of enemy shipping, but also some of the largest supply vessels in the Axis arsenal – ships that could not be replaced. Force K, a group of fast cruisers and destroyers, managed to annihilate one Axis convoy of ten merchant vessels and six Italian destroyers; all but three destroyers were sunk. With this carnage in the Mediterranean, the British Eighth Army then managed to push Rommel's German and Italian army halfway back to Tripoli.

The Germans, now fully committed to the Mediterranean, saw Egypt and the Middle East as a great prize. Oil-starved as they were, the Middle East oilfields also loomed heavily in their thoughts. For 1942, Hitler dreamed of a vast victory: in the east, his armies would sweep down through the Caucasus and capture the oilfields of Azerbaijan, while, from Libya, Rommel's Panzer Army Afrika would thrust into Egypt, capture the Suez Canal Zone and then drive on into the Middle East and link up with German troops from the Eastern Front. It was a grand plan and a tantalising vision but for there to be any chance of success in North Africa that thorn in their side, Malta, had to be neutralised first, as Field Marshal Albert Kesselring, the new commander-in-chief of all Axis forces in the south, was fully aware.

An entire Luftwaffe air corps, Fliegerkorps II, was transferred to Sicily at the end of December 1941, ready to pummel Malta into submission. There was also a plan to invade on the table; it would be primarily an Italian operation but with support from German air and airborne forces. Certainly, Kesselring was keen for this to happen.

The weather in the New Year was miserable – wet and cold – which limited flying, but throughout January and into February the number and intensity of raids began to grow and with it mounting damage. Valletta, and the Three Cities area the other side of Grand Harbour, had been struck hard by the Luftwaffe's first appearance a year earlier but now increasing numbers of homes and buildings were being hit, with rubble flung across the streets. Increasingly, Maltese civilians were being forced underground, digging ever-larger shelters into the limestone.

By the beginning of February, as the weather gradually improved, air raids had become a constant disruption. Although there had been at least one a day since before Christmas, now it felt as though they were arriving every other hour. A new warning device had been devised. If a raid was heading for the harbour areas, a red flag would be raised above Fort St Angelo overlooking the Three Cities and also above the Castile in Valletta. This meant people in these areas could ignore the air raid sirens that blared out for attacks elsewhere on the island. The trouble was, many of the raids were on the harbour areas and the flags were not that easy to see, so most people still found themselves trooping back and forth between the ever-growing number of shelters.

Although John Agius worked in Scott Street in Valletta, he and his family lived in Sliema, the far side of Marsamxett Harbour. There was now a shelter at Victoria Terrace, about fifty yards from their home, and because a large number of the raids were at night, many people, the Agius family included, spent most of their sleeping hours in these underground caverns. The conditions in these roughly hewn shelters were grim. Suzanne Parlby was a twenty-year-old English girl living on the island working as a civilian cipher clerk. Her flat was in Guardamangia, to the north-east of Marsamxett Harbour, and she found herself spending most nights in the local public shelter. Like most others, it was damp, dark and dismal. Candles and dim oil lamps provided the only light while a dark corner was used as a lavatory. Many civilians would pray, babies would cry and all the time there was a warm, damp mustiness and overwhelming stench of urine, cigarette smoke and sweat. 'The stink down there was truly awful,' said Suzanne. 'Life in the shelter really was very unpleasant. You had to take your bedding down every day. If you left it overnight it would soon become damp and mouldy.'[4]

To make matters worse, shortages were starting to make themselves felt – of food, of fuel, of just about everything. Although Malta had some agriculture and market gardening it was not enough to feed a population swollen by servicemen. Consequently, the island was very dependent on the passage of ships for almost everything. In February a much-needed convoy was forced to turn back, so the only supplies now reaching the island were those delivered in small quantities by fast mine-laying submarines from Alexandria and a small amount by air. It was not enough and everyone was going hungry.

It was at this time of growing crisis for Malta that the island needed firm and decisive leadership, but the truth was that the island had so far not attracted appointments from the top drawer. The Governor was Lieutenant General Sir William Dobbie, a devout member of the Protestant Plymouth Brethren (the vast majority of the Maltese were Catholic) and had been posted to Malta from Malaya, even though he had been due for retirement. The Air Officer Commanding was Air Vice Marshal Hugh Pughe Lloyd, who had previously had a staff post at Bomber Command and who had little experience or understanding of fighters, and it was the island's fighter force which was the first line of defence against the enemy air assaults. By the end of January 1942, 340 Hurricanes had been delivered to Malta although only twenty-eight were left. Fifty had been destroyed on the ground in January alone.

The Hurricane had proved a fine aircraft early in the war but its fatal flaw was a slow rate of climb, the one asset needed above all for any fighter operating on Malta. This was because height was a crucial advantage in air combat and the lumbering Hurricanes simply could not get high enough in the time between being scrambled and enemy aircraft reaching the island from Sicily. This meant they were always on the back foot, and, in any case, were no match for the Messerschmitt 109s. Shot-up Hurricanes were patched up time and time again, their engines overused and increasingly temperamental, which in turn meant their performance was even lower. All too often, good pilots were getting themselves injured and killed purely as a result of engine failure. The small rocky fields of Malta with their drystone walls were no place to crash-land.

The answer was to send Spitfires, which were much improved since the Battle of Britain, equipped with more powerful cannons and could climb to 25,000 feet in the same time the Hurricanes could manage just 15,000. They were also in plentiful number by early 1942 – more so than Hurricanes. Lloyd should have pressed to have them sent over at the earliest available opportunity. Luftwaffe resources were not as extensive as they appeared and a steady build-up of Spitfires in the summer and autumn of 1941 could have stopped the attackers in their tracks. Lloyd, however, never once asked for a single Spitfire to be sent. Instead, Air Marshal Arthur Tedder, Commander-in-Chief RAF Middle East, took it upon himself to send an envoy, Group Captain Basil Embry, to see for himself what was needed. Embry's subsequent report was one that should have been delivered by Lloyd himself. He recommended that both Spitfires and a first-class ground controller were needed as a matter of extreme urgency. The first dozen Spitfires duly arrived in early March as did Group Captain 'Woody' Woodhall, a highly experienced Battle of Britain ground controller.

A new convoy was due towards the end of March and enormous effort was made to escort these four ships of precious cargo to the island. One was sunk before reaching Malta and another, *Breconshire*, was hit and had to be towed the last part of the journey. Even so, three out of four made it safely and, even better, a belt of poor weather greeted their arrival, so that for three nights there were no raids whatsoever. It was a much-needed respite and the perfect opportunity for the ships to be swiftly unloaded.

By this time unloading any ship was problematic because the harbours and quaysides were wrecked and the only way to take off the cargo safely was to lower the goods onto lighters first. What was needed was an unloading plan properly thought through before the ships had arrived, one that made provision for all-night unloading and which drafted in the many soldiers stationed on the island to help the Maltese stevedores. Sadly, no such plan had been made. No extra hands were brought in, and nor was there any night-time unloading whatsoever. By the time this was brought to the attention of the Governor and the Administrative Council – which included all three of the island's service chiefs – the weather had improved, the Luftwaffe returned and the three remaining ships were sunk in the harbour with only a fraction of their vital cargoes unloaded. Vast columns of oily smoke rose thousands of feet above the island. Not a single person on the island could have failed to see this rising column, nor recognised what it represented. This failure meant the Maltese people and their defenders faced increased hunger, starvation even, as well as fewer shells, fewer aircraft parts and a gradual erosion of everything on the island.

'The odds against our survival now seemed almost insuperable,' wrote Air Vice Marshal Lloyd, 'but it was a grim and murderous reflection at the time that it was not the fighting which had brought us to our present pass but sheer ineptitude, lack of resolution and bomb-stunned brains incapable of thought.'[5] Lloyd was directing his criticism against Governor Dobbie, but, as a member of the Administrative Council and commander of the RAF on the island, he was equally culpable. Fortunately, because the ships had sunk in shallow water, further supplies were salvaged, but in all only 5,200 tons out of a potential 26,000. It meant Malta could hold out a little longer, but the island was sinking. The harbour installations were a mess. The airfields were frequently unusable. Her offensive capabilities had been brought to a standstill and the island's buildings were being blitzed to smithereens. February and March, however, had been just the warm-up. Worse was to come in April 1942.

By the start of April, the island had already suffered 117 days of continuous attacks; there had been 275 air raid alerts in March alone – nearly ten a day. Already, the Axis air forces had been targeting the island's airfields of Luqa, Hal Far and Takali, and very successfully, too. Takali had been hit by 296 tons of bombs on 20 and 21 March, for example, and although nine more Spitfires had reached the island on the 21st – at Luqa – hardly any were left by the beginning of April. This meant the Luftwaffe and Regia Aeronautica had almost total air superiority. On 7 April they struck the island with a vengeance, particularly Valletta and the harbour areas. Meme Cortis was a Maltese nurse working at the military hospital at Imtarfa, but that Tuesday had been given a day off. She and a friend had crossed Marsamxett Harbour to Valletta from Sliema and had begun climbing the steps up to the heart of the city when the air raid siren rang out yet again. Hurrying to the nearest shelter they still hadn't reached cover when the first bombs started to fall. The Auberge d'Aragon, one of Valletta's most notable buildings, took a direct hit and both Meme and her friend were knocked over by the blast. Quickly, they got to their feet again and ran, reaching safety in the nick of time.

By the time the All Clear rang out and they emerged once more, their first sight was of what had once been the magnificent opera house, and what had been widely considered Valletta's finest building. 'It was just a heap of rubble,' said Meme. 'Not one wall was standing – just a few arches left. I couldn't believe it.'[6]

The home of John Agius and his family was also destroyed that day. They had all taken to the shelter but, once the All Clear had sounded, John had run up the steps and out onto the street. Where his home had once stood was just a cloud of dust which cleared to reveal nothing but a gaping hole. 'I was very upset and started shouting,'[7] he recalled. The following day, Meme Cortis's local church, the Sacred Heart in Sliema, was hit, killing two priests. A cousin was killed, leaving six children; another good friend lost his life during another attack – he had been married with three children under the age of seven. On 9 April, the Rotunda Church in Mosta, in the centre of the island, was struck, but the bomb merely penetrated the dome, hit the church floor and rolled to a halt – without exploding. It had been packed at the time with some three hundred attending an afternoon service, but while the church and its worshippers had been lucky a nearby shelter had suffered a direct hit and twenty-five had been killed and many more injured.

The bombing caused chaos and suffering beyond just the loss of buildings and the deaths of all too many. The electricity supply on the island was invariably cut off, as was the water system. Many telephone lines were down. Distributing food became ever harder. 'When a lorry is sent to take goods from one place to another,' ran a notice in the *Times of Malta*, 'there is no guarantee that it will be able to reach its destination.'[8] The harbours also lay in ruins. Once the pride of the Royal Navy in the Mediterranean, its quaysides were now little more than piles of stone. It was hard not to despair.

On one day that month there were simply no fighter planes available at all, and on several days only one. At other times, the hard-pressed RAF ground crews did their best to get a precious few airborne. Nonetheless, more Spitfires were on their way, courtesy of the large American carrier USS *Wasp*. Two entire squadrons flew off *Wasp* and forty-seven successfully reached Malta. The trouble was, no one had thought to have the radios tuned in, or the guns properly harmonised or to put in place any plan to get them quickly back into the air and so most were destroyed on the ground soon after their arrival. As with the failure of the March convoy, it demonstrated a lack of foresight. Within forty-eight hours of their arrival only seven of the new Spitfires remained serviceable. It was the RAF's lowest ebb on Malta.

If there was one small consolation, however, it was that the island's gunners were doing well. 'Malta is one huge battery of anti-aircraft guns,' reported one Luftwaffe bomber pilot on German radio . 'Heavy and light AA guns are at every important point. Shells come up like a thunderstorm of steel.'[9] This was reported gleefully in the *Times of Malta*, which was not shy about reporting the gunners' mounting score. By 29 April, they had shot down ninety-nine in April alone Could they now make it a neat one hundred? The following day, 30 April, they shot down three more, which made 102 for April. This was a significant number and about a third of the Luftwaffe's force on Sicily.

Kesselring could not keep bombing Malta at this intense rate, not least because Rommel was about to launch an offensive across the sea in North Africa. With the island subdued, 99.2 per cent of Axis supplies had got through that month, and so Rommel planned to attack at the end of May. This meant the Luftwaffe on Sicily would be needed in Libya. As April gave way to May, so they began to move across the Mediterranean.

There had been some high-level arguments among the Axis leaders about future strategy in the Mediterranean. Kesselring and the Italians favoured an invasion of Malta, but Rommel wanted to strike in North Africa before the British could build up too much strength. If he could annihilate British Eighth Army, then his way would be clear to push on into the Middle East and seize the oilfields there. At the time, most British oil came from the USA and Venezuela, but for oil-starved Nazi Germany the Middle East was a tempting prospect. Hitler favoured Rommel and so Malta was spared an invasion – for the time being at least.

On Malta, lessons had been learned, however. A further sixty-four Spitfires flew off *Wasp* on 9 May and this time the island's defenders were ready to receive them. Upon landing, they were led swiftly to protective blast pens where swarms of men refuelled them by hand with precious aviation fuel that had arrived overnight by submarine. Others rearmed them, while the newly landed pilots jumped out and were replaced by those already on the island. Many were ready to fly again in no more than ten minutes. As it happened, the remaining Luftwaffe and Regia Aeronautica barely flew over that day but the next, 10 May, they came over in numbers and this time the faster climbing Spitfires were ready for them. Diving down, they shot down and damaged some sixty-five enemy aircraft. With fewer than two hundred remaining on Sicily, this was a significant blow. Never again would the Axis air forces be able to fly over the island with impunity. May 10 1942 marked a turning point in the siege of Malta.

More Spitfires were on their way, too, suggesting that these aircraft, combined with proper planning and forethought, could have made a

Flight Engineer Norman Jackson VC.
© Illustrated London News Ltd/Mary Evans

Norman Jackson VC with Leonard Cheshire VC
in 1945. © National Portrait Gallery, London

Piper Daniel Laidlaw VC.
© Topical Press Agency/Getty Images

A re-enactment of Piper Daniel Laidlaw VC playing on the parapet of the German trenches.
© George Rinhart/Corbis/Getty Images

Noor Inayat Khan GC's pistol.
© Imperial War Museum

Noor Inayat Khan GC.
© Imperial War Museum

Noor Inayat Khan GC before the war in 1937.
©National Portrait Gallery, London

Children in a bomb-damaged street
in Malta, 1942.
© Mary Evans/Grenville Collins Postcard Collection

German planes over Valetta.
© Roger Viollet Collection/Getty Images

Convoy ship on fire in
Grand Harbour, March 1942.
© Imperial War Museum

Bomb damage in Valetta, May 1942.
© Imperial War Museum

Daphne Pearson GC by
Laura Knight, 1940.
© Imperial War Museum

Daphne Pearson GC after her investiture.
© PNA/Hulton Archive/Getty Images

Rifleman Tul Bahadur Pun VC.

Tul Bahadur Pun VC with Joanna Lumley after the British government
announced settlement rights for former Gurkhas in the UK.
© David Crump/AFP/Getty Images

Field Marshal Frederick Sleigh Roberts,
1st Earl Roberts, VC, KG, KP, GCB,
OM, GCSI, GCIE, KStJ, VD, PC.
© ullstein bild/via Getty Images

Lieutenant Frederick Hugh Sherston
Roberts VC, 1890s.
© National Portrait Gallery, London

Lieutenant William Leefe Robinson
VC. © Hulton Archive/Getty Images

German airship, of a type similar to the SL11, over Maubeuge in occupied France, 1916.
© ullstein bild/ via Getty Images

WO2 Rayene 'Ray' Simpson VC.
© Australian War Memorial

Ray Simpson VC with Keith Payne VC in Saigon, 1969.
© Australian War Memorial

Violette Szabo GC.
© Imperial War Museum

Four-year-old Tania Szabo, after
receiving the George Cross on behalf
of her mother from George VI.
© Imperial War Museum

Investiture of Charles Upham VC and Bar
by George VI, April 1945.
© Kurt Hutton/Picture Post/Hulton Archive/Getty Images

Captain Charles Upham
VC and Bar.
© Imperial War Museum

Charles Upham VC and Bar (right), ready to go with rifle in hand.
© Image kindly provided by the family of Charles Upham VC and Bar

Lord Justice Tasker Watkins VC, wearing his
gown and wig, at the High Court,
London, December 1976.
© Central Press/Hutton Archive/Getty Images

Tasker Watkins VC.
© Imperial War Museum

Lieutenant Colonel the Reverend
Bernard William Vann VC as a
Sherwood Forester officer, c.1916.
© Image kindly provided by the Vann family

massive difference and prevented much suffering had they arrived on the island earlier. Nonetheless, although bombs might no longer have been raining down on the island all day and night, there was now a very real chance Malta might still be forced to surrender, so critical was the lack of supplies becoming. Fast mine-laying submarines could bring in small quantities of precious fuel but not enough food or other essential supplies to feed the entire island. The population was beginning to starve. The Administrative Council now talked of a 'Target Date': the moment at which the island could no longer survive and would be forced to surrender.

On 4 May, General Dobbie had been sacked as Governor and replaced by Field Marshal Lord Gort VC, a man of altogether greater experience and standing and the former Chief of the Imperial General Staff – the most senior British military commander – as well as Commander-in-Chief of the British Expeditionary Force in France in 1940. He was tough, fearless and the kind of calibre of commander the island needed. However, Gort also realised very quickly that the Maltese might well find the increasing food shortages even harder to bear than the bombing. Bread was now rationed to just ten and a half ounces a day. Other staples, such as rice, pasta and tomato paste, were also heavily rationed. Nor were the shortages confined to food. Children went barefoot while others used the rubber from car tyres to resole shoes. By an inevitable process of strangulation, one shortage led to another: when there was no more coal, the power stations faltered and there was no more electricity. People had begun using kerosene with which to cook, but by June that had run out completely. Then the only fuel left was wood, although this mostly came from furniture as there were few trees left on the island. For those who had been left homeless, life was even harder. People had to share homes with relatives or neighbours or remain living underground in shelters. The privations were immense.

Plans were underway to send another convoy, which eventually set sail in mid-June while battle raged in Libya, but so heavy were the attacks on it that it was forced to turn back; the convoy on which they had all been pinning so many hopes had failed. That same day, 16 June, Lord Gort broadcast to the island: 'Every effort will be made to replenish our stocks when a favourable opportunity presents itself,' he told the Maltese. 'Meanwhile, we must stand on our own resources and every one of us must do everything in his or her power to conserve stocks.'[10]

Recently, the papers of the island's Chief Medical Officer have come to light which reveal the situation on Malta that summer of 1942 was even more dire than many appreciated. Such were the shortages of water, new orders were issued to all medical and military units on the island. 'The flushing of lavatory pans after urination to be prohibited,' wrote one order. Washing hands under running water was also forbidden in an effort to preserve water; incredibly, the most basic means of maintaining good hygiene were now being banned. Another order issued to all District Medical Officers urged further economies. 'Savings must be made on every item. As an example I may mention that bandages should not be used once only but washed when necessary and used repeatedly until they are completely unserviceable.'[11] Such were the shortages, this instruction was typed on a half piece of foolscap paper that had already been once used before on the reverse side.

Those left homeless often had little means of feeding themselves and so the solution – of sorts – was the Victory Kitchens, first introduced back in January but now the principal means of feeding a growing proportion of the population. The idea was simple: subscribers forfeited a portion of their rations, or paid sixpence, in return for one hot meal a day. This was all well and good at the start of the year, but by the time of the failed June convoy, the 'hot meal' had become little more than thin, watery gruel. Most loathed the Victory Kitchens but equally, for the majority, there was little choice but to wait in line and eat what was given. By this time, most people were lucky if they were getting 1,100 calories a day.

The only chance of saving Malta now was in the arrival of another convoy. In North Africa, Eighth Army had successful retreated to the Alamein Line in Egypt, where lines of supply were much shorter and had then successfully held Rommel's Panzer Army Afrika. This gave the British a small respite and so, on 10 August, thirteen merchant ships and one fuel tanker set sail from Gibraltar on what was codenamed Operation PEDESTAL heading some 900 miles to relieve the starving island. No convoy of the war ever had a greater escort force: four aircraft carriers, two battleships, seven light cruisers and thirty-two destroyers to protect just fourteen freighters. Along the way, however, the convoy was passing entirely along enemy-occupied or controlled territory, and arrayed against them were no fewer than 659 combat aircraft, six Italian cruisers, fifteen destroyers, nineteen torpedo boats, sixteen Italian submarines and three U-boats. Thanks to an Italian spy in Spanish Morocco, the Axis forces knew the convoy was on its way.

What followed was one of the most epic battles of the entire war, in which nine of the merchant ships were sunk despite the very best efforts of the defending escorts. Fortunately, each ship was carrying a spread of different supplies; the only exception was the Texaco company's oil tanker, the *Ohio*. The first merchant ship managed to enter Grand Harbour on 13 August; the following day, three more made it safely. By this time, the *Ohio* had been hit a staggering ten times and had even had a Stuka dive bomber crash onto its decks, and was now stopped dead in the water with its steering gear wrecked. The ship was even twice abandoned but then reboarded as three destroyers came to its rescue. With one destroyer lashed either side and a third leading the way, they began inching the last fifty miles towards Malta, travelling no faster than walking speed. By this time, it was within range of air protection from the island including from more Spitfires newly flown in at the start of the PEDESTAL convoy.

By 8 a.m. on 15 August, they finally passed safely into Grand Harbour. All along the bastions overlooking the port, crowds of Maltese cheered and waved. 'There were so many people,' recalled Michael Montebello, then a teenager living in a shelter under Valletta's bastions, 'you wouldn't have been able to put a needle between them. Everyone knew exactly what was on the *Ohio* and how important it was.'[12] What's more, by an extraordinary piece of serendipity, 15 August was the Feast Day of Santa Maria, the most important in the Maltese calendar. 'We were all so excited,' remembered Meme Cortis. 'Excited and happy – it was as though a miracle had occurred.'[13]

Some 55,000 tons of supplies had been safely delivered, enough to set back the current Target Date by a couple more months. What's more, the convoy had brought more aircraft, more fuel and more parts and ammunition – enough, in fact, with which to go onto the offensive once more.

* * *

Once again, the fate of Malta was linked to the Allied fortunes in North Africa. Through the second half of August, Malta-based aircraft and submarines were able once more to harry Axis supplies to North Africa; now it was the turn of the Italian and German convoys to feel the full weight of attack. At the same time, Axis air raids on the island were reduced to a trickle, with just fifty-seven occurring during the entire month. At the end of August, Rommel attacked the Alamein Line once more, but, with critical losses of much-needed supplies, his assault was stopped in its tracks and thereafter he went over onto the defensive while Eighth Army gradually but surely built up its strength. In October, Kesselring made a last-ditch attempt to neutralise Malta, but by this time the island was bristling with Spitfires and some 350 Axis aircraft were destroyed or damaged, half the assembled force. 'Our losses,' admitted Kesselring after the war, 'were too high.'[14]

Later that month, Eighth Army attacked at Alamein and routed the Panzer Army Afrika; a week later, a joint Anglo-American force landed in French Vichy-controlled North Africa. Now the Anglo-US First Army was advancing on Tunisia from the west and Eighth Army from the east.

Malta remained perfectly placed to make sure that as few Axis supplies as possible reached North Africa.

Despite this, the Maltese people were facing one of their most difficult phases of the entire war. The PEDESTAL convoy had brought only temporary relief and even then only the most basic of foodstuffs such as flour and potatoes. Of virtually every other basic commodity there was nothing left. On 1 September, the Victory Kitchens' midday meal had to be thrown away in its entirety. 'The meal was composed chiefly of liver in a sort of stew,' reported the *Times of Malta*. 'It was hard and had a bitter taste, which made it unpalatable and uneatable. This suggests that the gall had not been removed either before it was put in cold storage or before it was cooked.'[15]

What was desperately needed was yet another convoy, which reached the island on 15 November: four merchantmen bringing 35,000 tons of supplies. A couple of weeks later, four more ships set sail from Alexandria and arrived in Grand Harbour on 6 December, and, this time, entirely unscathed. The longest siege in British history was finally at an end. The island's misery was still not quite over, however. 'Malta was hit not just by bombs,' Meme Cortis pointed out, 'but by epidemics as well.'[16] The severely malnourished island population were considerably weakened and vulnerable to disease. Dysentery and tuberculosis were rife and then that winter the island was ravaged by a polio epidemic. It also took time for the island to recover from the immense amount of damage suffered during the long siege. The irony is that the George Cross was awarded in April 1942, but back then the population still had so much suffering to come. The stoicism and fortitude with which they faced these appalling hardships was in many ways deserving of a bar to the medal the islanders had already justifiably won.

Life did gradually improve, however, and by July 1943, with North Africa won, Malta had become home to vast numbers of fighter planes and servicemen braced for the invasion of Sicily. In fact, with its airfields heaving with aircraft and harbours wedged with ships of all sizes, the island had become one of the major stepping-off points for the biggest amphibious invasion ever launched. Nowhere in the world had suffered such persistent and concentrated bombing. What had followed had been near-starvation, death and disease, yet, while Malta had been brought to her knees, the island had never fallen into the dust. The collective heroism of her people had been extraordinary.

20

ASSISTANT SECTION OFFICER
DAPHNE PEARSON GC

Introduced by Mary Berry CBE

There is something extraordinary about a person who will confront danger to help a loved one. I remember a photograph of a Swedish woman who was seen racing towards the tsunami of 2005 while everyone else was running, screaming, in the other direction. It transpired her child was sitting on the beach and was in mortal danger. As amazing as that lady was, her actions are explicable, to some at least, on the grounds that she was acting on the instinctive love of a mother. The story of Daphne Pearson that you are about to read tells of a woman who ran towards a burning cauldron, which was about to explode with no other motivation than to try to save the life of a complete stranger. I find it inspiring and I hope you will do so as well.

May 1995. Fifty years after VE Day, London was once more alive with revellers, recalling and remembering the celebrations of the end of the war in Europe half a century before. Back then, to cheers from the crowds gathered in front of Buckingham Palace, King George VI and Queen Elizabeth had come out onto the balcony, together with their daughters, Elizabeth and Margaret. Fast-forward fifty years and Queen Elizabeth was now the Queen Mother and ninety-four years old. As she stepped out onto the Buckingham Palace balcony once again, with a vast crowd waving Union Jacks in front of her, she witnessed a Second World War anniversary flypast overhead.

Over three days of celebrations, events included a thanksgiving service at St Paul's Cathedral and a huge concert in Hyde Park, featuring, among others, Dame Vera Lynn. Hyde Park also boasted an array of everything from Spitfires to air raid shelters, bandstands and stalls selling spam fritters. Those invited to attend included men and women who had been awarded the Victoria Cross or the George Cross, for their actions during the Second World War. Among those presented to the Queen Mother was Daphne Pearson, who had been awarded the George Cross for her actions during the Second World War; she had travelled back to the UK from Australia for the ceremony.

It wasn't the first time they'd spoken; just over fifty years earlier, Daphne had previously met the Queen Mother. She was billeted at RAF Oakington, a bomber station near Cambridge, when word came through that the King, Queen and the two princesses were to visit for an investiture. Daphne was instructed to prepare a large anteroom ready for tea, and went round a nearby village, borrowing tablecloths, teapots and vases to make the room as presentable as possible.

On the day of the visit, Daphne Pearson waited on the steps at the mess, ready to receive the royal party after they had been taken round the hangars. She then took the Queen and her lady-in-waiting to the cloakroom, where the Queen turned to her: 'Oh Flight Commander, how extravagant – *two* tablets of soap, we can share.' Daphne then took the Queen to the anteroom where she sat with her, presenting various WAAF officers who came to be introduced. 'Conversation with Her Majesty' was so easy, Daphne later remembered. The Queen asked for the recipe for the cakes they were eating, and Daphne scuttled off to the kitchen to find who had made them, getting her to write it down before the Queen left.

Half a century later, in the warmth of a glorious day in May, Daphne and the Queen Mother were reacquainted once again. The following day, the press carried photographs of Daphne being presented. For one family especially, the photographs were particularly significant. They realised that this was the person but for whose actions all those years ago they would not be there; Daphne had saved their father and after all this time they were desperate to meet her.

* * *

Daphne Pearson was born in Mudeford, Hampshire, on 26 May 1911. Her father was the Reverend J. H. Pearson and the family spent her early childhood on the Isle of Wight, where he was a parish priest at St Helen's. In many ways, it was a quiet, rural, idyllic childhood; living on a hill facing out across to France, the family had goats and chickens in the garden, and once a week Daphne and her mother would visit a nearby farm to collect fresh butter.

The house had a large garden and the local postman, Coleman, would come and help out after his round. In the winter, they spread seaweed, brought in by the storms, on the fields; in the spring, they would have an abundant crop of asparagus, eating it every day during the season. Accompanying Daphne everywhere was Chinka, the family dog born two weeks before her – a white and chestnut cross between a Pekinese and a Sealyham.

War encroached even on these picturesque surroundings. Daphne remembers lying awake at night, watching the flashes of gunfire and listening to the boom of guns from the battlefields across the Channel. In her autobiography, she describes the war as 'a way of life: young and old men on crutches, some with bandages, others lying around on the grass or sitting in the kitchen'.[1] She remembers the Red Cross cards placed in the windows of houses, which meant that a wife or mother was grieving.

One of Daphne's clearest memories of the war was when she and her parents travelled to Scotland for a working holiday in Dornoch, where her father was taking services. Travelling over the Forth Bridge one night, the train suddenly came to a halt. With German planes overhead, the train was kept in darkness, with the blinds down and no one allowed to light so much as a match, as the guard walked up and down, checking everyone was complying, Daphne and her parents waited anxiously, before, at last, the danger was over and the train continued its journey.

After the war, the family moved back to the mainland, firstly to Twyford in Buckinghamshire and then to Combe in Oxfordshire. It was a difficult period of adjustment: firstly, Daphne was heartbroken when it was decided that Chinka, along with the rest of the family's animals, wasn't coming with them; and then both Daphne and her father suffered bouts of illness. This followed Daphne to school, too; sent away to Clacton-on-Sea, Essex, she was so unwell at the end of one term that she had to be taken back to London by ambulance, before being transferred home.

From here, Daphne got a place at St Brandon's Clergy Daughters' School in Bristol. Although her health improved, school was not a particularly enjoyable experience. Daphne later described it as 'a very well run school, but very strict; about one-third of the girls were Welsh and spoke their language nearly all the time . . . on the whole I did not like school at all. The place was so dark and dreary, with large elms on the terrace with sooty black trunks.'

After finishing school, Daphne hoped to go to the Slade School of Art, but her final drawing exams were not quite good enough to gain her a place. Instead, she turned her attention to photography, getting a place at G. Methven Brownlee's photographic studio as a trainee. As she learned her trade, she began going to the Clifton Arts Club, making friends, including the painter James Floyd, who she would know for the next three decades until his death in the mid-1950s.

In 1929, an opportunity came up in St Ives down in Cornwall. A photographic studio was up for sale or lease – the owner, the only photographer in the town at the time, was advancing in years. The studio would give Daphne a base, allowing her to do regular photographic work and so her father cashed an insurance policy to allow her to take it. Daphne took to life on the Cornish coast – as well as the stock-in-trade photography work, such as weddings and passport photographs, she made money from postcards, and became friends with many local artists, among them the celebrated potter Bernard Leach.

This was a happy period in Daphne's life; sadly, however, during Christmas 1932, her father died: 'my freedom now will end,' she noted in her memoir. Following the funeral, she arranged for her mother to move down to St Ives; the stress of the upheavals and a difficult time at work, with money not coming in, led to what Daphne described as 'feeling very tired and depressed . . . in fact I was near a breakdown'. She travelled to Petersfield, in Hampshire, for a period of recuperation, a home 'dedicated to restoring professional people to work'. After several weeks of recuperation, Daphne went to visit James Floyd, now living in Sussex. Deciding to stay in the area, she got a job, first as a driver, delivering home-made produce, then as a photographic assistant in Petworth. The latter job ended abruptly after the owner tried to take advantage of her in the studio's darkroom: 'the weasel grabbed me, made me turn around and made a pass. One look at him and I gave him a hard slap, shut the door on him and walked through to his Missus and said, "I'm sorry to say, I have to give my notice in. Your husband made advances."' It transpired that this was not the first time this had happened; as Daphne left, 'I remember her saying "I've had trouble before".'

This was how Daphne found herself back at her lodgings at the local butcher's in the middle of the afternoon, the two of them poring over the job vacancies in *The Times*. It was here that she saw an advertisement to become manager of Ditton Court Farm Shop, on the London to Folkestone road, a position that was to take her down to Kent and the defining moment of her life.

* * *

The Women's Auxiliary Air Force (WAAF) was the successor to the Women's Royal Air Force (WRAF), which was founded alongside the

Royal Air Force in 1918. The WRAF was disbanded in 1920, but, with war imminent in summer 1939, the WAAF was formed in anticipation. It came out of the forty-eight RAF companies formed as part of the Auxiliary Territorial Service (ATS), which itself had been established a year earlier, and would go on to be the women's branch of the army during the Second World War.

The WAAF came under the jurisdiction of the RAF. Individuals served as members of RAF commands, rather than being put into a particular unit. WAAF members were not allowed to fly, but took on roles as drivers and medical workers, allowing men to take up more front-line duties. As the war progressed, these roles expanded to include everything from engineering to code interceptors, plane fitters to radar controllers. By 1943, the WAAF had more than 180,000 members, with several thousand women a week signing up.

Daphne Pearson was one of those women who had been involved right from the start. In the late 1930s, she had been inspired to set up a group in Kent to train women interested in first aid, air raid warden training and ambulance-standard driving. Daphne targeted factory workers and shop assistants, going to speak at places such as Aylesford Paper Mills to drum up support. In 1938, she took her mother to France for an extended holiday and in Paris was shocked at the army presence already on the streets. Back in Britain, the threat of war was also coming ever closer; a week before the farm shop's summer crop of raspberries were ready, the army arrived to take it over as a gun site.

Daphne began training at the Maidstone Barracks of the 19th Royal West Kents. As with the other female recruits she was offered the choice of the army or Royal Air Force; she chose the latter. When the call came, she reported to Maidstone Barracks, from where she was transferred to RAF Detling. On 23 September 1939, when war was declared, the air base sirens wailed – Daphne remembers heading down into a deep trench, sitting on school benches, as they waited for the All Clear. There was a scream as a spider appeared: 'It's only a spider,' Daphne said. 'Don't kill him.'

To begin with, jobs for the WAAF were unclear. The base didn't need drivers but cooks – which Daphne refused to do. She turned to the medical side – though she had to be registered as a sick berth attendant since to become a full medical orderly required four years' training. Having undergone training on anatomy and other subjects, Daphne was promoted to the rank of corporal; at the corporals' mess she was subjected to the female initiation rite of downing half a pint of beer (male corporals had a full pint poured over their heads).

RAF Detling had its fair share of casualties: planes having left there for either reconnaissance or bombing missions would often return with casualties suffered under enemy fire. Daphne and her colleagues would be the first call of medical aid, attending to shrapnel and bullet wounds, before the more serious casualties were taken on to nearby Chatham Hospital. As the Battle of Britain began in earnest, planes zigzagging overhead became a regular sight; Daphne was moved closer to the medical facilities so that she could be on call for the sick bay.

On 31 May 1940, Daphne was woken in the middle of the night by the noise of an aircraft in trouble. She knew instinctively that something was wrong; one of its engines was cutting in-and-out and, as the sound grew louder, it appeared to be heading straight for the base. Daphne scrambled to put on her jersey and trousers over her pyjamas, grabbed a pair of Wellingtons and her tin hat and ran outside. In front of her she saw the aircraft descending, smashing through the trees of an adjacent wood and ploughing into the ground. A guard shouted at Daphne to stop, but she ran to the scene of the crash, opening the gates to allow an ambulance through, before herself racing on.

'I remember landing in the nettles in the ditch,' Daphne recalled, 'and the fearsome sight on my right of the plane on fire. I know I was battling with my boots to get there faster; it was terrifyingly hot as two crewmen were coming out of the plane dragging another man out. I turned into them and I realised that something would give.' Daphne shouted at the men, 'Leave him to me – go and get the fence down for the ambulance.'

As the men ran off for help, Daphne continued to pull the injured man away from the blaze by herself. His face was covered in blood and he was clearly in severe pain: 'the fierce scorching light shone on his tooth that had pushed through his cheek,' Daphne remembered. 'It is strange what one does; I pulled the tooth out of the man's cheek and I knew his back or neck was severely injured and he could not be moved by me.'

Both Daphne and the pilot were in great danger: 'Full tank,' the pilot tried to warn Daphne; 'Bombs,' he shouted. Without thinking, Daphne took her tin hat off and placed it over the man's head; then she laid herself over him to offer protection from the blast, digging her elbows into the ground so as not to put any weight on him. Her actions were timely: at that moment a 120lb bomb went off and the plane exploded: 'there was a shocking blast, all the air in my stomach was sucked out, it seemed as if the lining had stuck together.' Splinters and debris showered the site, with several others at the scene knocked clean off their feet.

Picking herself up, Daphne ran down to the ambulance and helped the medical officer with the stretcher, the pair carrying the man over the barbed wire fence into the waiting vehicle. There were further explosions, but Daphne continued to return to the plane, trying desperately to find the fourth member of the crew among the wreckage, but to no avail: he had been killed in the crash. Returning to base, Daphne got out of her bloodied clothes, scrubbed up and immediately went into the sick bay's makeshift theatre area. For the next couple of hours, she and the doctor worked hard, removing metal fragments from the men, and strapping up the injured pilot as best they could, before an ambulance took them on to Chatham Hospital at about 3 a.m.

As the men left, Daphne described herself as feeling numb and worried that she was suffering from night blindness: 'it's quite usual after an explosion that you can't see,' the doctor reassured her. She went back to her quarters, where the cipher officer was up and gave her some hot soup. 'I'll be all right for work,' Daphne told her, knowing that her next shift started at eight the following morning, before finally retiring to bed.

A few hours later, when Daphne turned up to her shift on time, she was told to go straight to see the MO. As she went in, she was greeted by the Commanding Officer (CO) of 500 Squadron and three other officers, who all stood to attention and saluted her. Daphne felt overcome: 'I thought I had better go to my pharmacy closet and fidget with the bottles for a while to get into stride.' But while Daphne wanted to carry on with her work, the CO told her that she had been put up for a commission. Despite her protestations, she was sent to the Air Ministry for training and then posted to West Drayton, a large depot for equipping recruits outside London. It was here that she learned she had been given what she described in a letter to her mother as the 'King's Medal': 'Apparently it will be in the papers in 48 hours. This is very disturbing for my evening work,' she wrote. Two days later, she had a telephone call from Air Commandant Trefusis Forbes, the head of the WAAF: she told Daphne that Winston Churchill was announcing in Parliament her award of the Empire Gallantry Medal, Military Division (this was later changed to the George Cross, when this superseded the award).

Daphne took her mother to the investiture at Buckingham Palace on a scorching hot day – although a proud day, she recalls her frustration that, rather than saluting like the men receiving awards, she had to curtsey to the King. Soon afterwards, she was taken by the Air Ministry to Malvern, where she had her portrait painted by Dame Laura Knight – Knight's studio was in the garden of the celebrated author J. M. Barrie. Originally Daphne was in uniform holding a rifle, but with WAAF members not allowed to bear arms at this point, it was replaced by a gas mask instead. Today, the painting can be seen at the Imperial War Museum, London.

* * *

The plane that came down that day in May 1940 was the first of three significant aircraft to feature in Daphne Pearson's life. The second was the Comet 4 jetliner, which in November 1959 had its inaugural BOAC flight to Australia. One of the passengers on this flight was Daphne.

Following the war, she had set up and run a flower nursery near Kew Gardens but, when advised by her doctor that the cold and wet of London was making her unwell, she decided to move to warmer climes. In Australia, Daphne started a new life and career in landscape design and horticulture. She loved the country and particularly that of Tasmania, where she was part of the Tasmanian Wilderness Society, campaigning to protect the land from development.

The third aircraft of significance in Daphne's life was a helicopter. The man whom Daphne had helped pull from the wreckage in 1940 was Pilot Officer David Bond; following his recovery, he had gone on to set up Bond Helicopters in 1961. By 1995, the company had grown, with a fleet of more than 200 helicopters, and was one of the biggest such firms in the UK. In 2014, it was bought by Babcock International, and today continues to supply flights from Aberdeen to gas and oil installations in the North Sea, and remains the main operator of air ambulances in this country.

When members of David Bond's family saw the photographs of Daphne talking to the Queen Mother at the 1995 VE Day celebrations, everything fell into place. They immediately arranged for Daphne to be flown to Aberdeen, and from there a company helicopter took her to a hotel in Banchory, Deeside, where she met David's family. David had married after the war and had had four sons, one of whom, Stephen, had taken over running the company following his father's death in 1977. Daphne later described the occasion and being able to meet the family as 'so special'.

Daphne died in July 2000, but her legacy lingers on – both in her medals and her portrait on display at the Imperial War Museum, and also in the memories of those who knew her. Writing in a postscript to her memoir, her friend Audrey Jarvis, who knew her well in her later years, puts it well: 'Hers was a rich life filled with diverse experiences, a life that never just marked time. It is hard to put into words the rare being that was Daphne Pearson. Her unquestioning instinctive courage has secured her richly deserved place in history.'

21

RIFLEMAN TUL BAHADUR PUN VC

Introduced by Joanna Lumley OBE

My father showed me a photograph of Tul Bahadur Pun VC when I was six years old. We were sitting on the veranda of our army bungalow in Malaya, and although he never talked about the Chindit campaign in which he and Pun had served, he wanted to tell me about him: 'This is one of the bravest men you will ever see.'

Gurkha soldiers were part of our lives, as we followed my father's regiment around the Far East; but what is it that sets them apart from all other fighting forces? This account of Pun's extraordinary and selfless valour gives a glimpse into the bravery of these legendary men, but his actions on the dreadful day described in this piece, far behind enemy lines in Burma, will live on forever as an example of heroism beyond compare.

Years later, when my father had been dead for nine years, I met Mr Pun VC, just as our Gurkha Justice Campaign gained momentum. I wanted to give him something from my father, and I remembered the little silver figure of a Gurkha piper which Daddy loved and left to me in his will. I knelt down beside Mr Pun's wheelchair – by 2008 he was a frail old man – and gave him the little silver piper. When he heard that my father was dead he put his old hands on my head and said: 'You are my daughter now.' A few months later we laid flowers at the Cenotaph together, in the biting cold of a London winter: this valiant old warrior supported us staunchly on every occasion until the victory came that we had been fighting for, and he was there, immaculately dressed and surrounded by his proud family and fellow soldiers. He was a legend and a hero, and I am so proud and lucky to have known him.

There is a story about Tul Bahadur Pun, retold in a regimental magazine after his death in April 2011, about the time he went duck hunting in north Malaya. Tul Bahadur was a man not only known for his hunting skills but also one careful with his use of ammunition – he was someone for whom every bullet had to count, rather than just shooting indiscriminately.

Malaya, as it was then, was one of the places where Tul Bahadur served after the end of the Second World War before his retirement in 1959. Tul Bahadur was stationed near Ipoh, situated just over 100 miles north of Kuala Lumpur and seventy-five or so miles south-east of George Town, Penang, a place known for its rich mix of natural beauty, offering visitors everything from mangrove swamps to jungles, stunning beaches and sweeping limestone cliffs. That day, Tul Bahadur was less interested in appreciating the nature itself, more the piece of nature that he could bag. Positioning himself in the reeds, thigh-deep in mud and water, he stood and waited. He was there for over an hour, until five ducks moved into his line of sight, and with a single shot, he managed to kill them all.

This anecdote captures many of the characteristics which made Tul Bahadur the person he was: his patience, his precision, his timing, his determination. These were all traits that he needed back in Burma in 1944 – and his role in a campaign that would lead to him being one of thirteen Gurkhas who have been awarded the Victoria Cross, since they were first eligible for it in 1911 (a further thirteen officers attached to Gurkha regiments have also been awarded the medal over the years). They are traits, too, that, as we shall also see, he had to draw on in civilian life as well.

* * *

Tul Bahadur Pun was born in the Nepalese village of Banduk on 23 March 1923. The village is in western Nepal, nestled above the Kali Gandaki River, which flows from Tibet to the Ganges – on one side of its deep gorge are the Annapurna peaks, on the others the Dhaulagiri, the seventh highest mountain in the world. The word Dhaulagiri comes from the Sanskrit, and translates as dazzling mountain. It was on this mountain's lower slopes that Tul Bahadur spent much of his childhood, taking the village sheep and goats to pasture, and often defending them from wild animals with a combination of slingshot and kukri, the iconic, curved Nepalese knife.

It was here that Tul Bahadur's character was forged: that inner strength of hardiness and independence. Certainly, educational opportunities were limited – it wasn't until he enlisted with the Gurkhas in 1940 that he picked up any rudimentary reading and writing. The importance of education, and the opportunities it gave, became a crucial issue for him, and one he would return to, helping others when he left the army two decades later.

The Gurkhas first became part of the British Army 200 years ago, when British troops invaded Nepal on behalf of the British East India Company. They were quickly taken aback by the ferocity of the Gurkhas' defence and the casualties inflicted: as one soldier of the 87th Foot put it, 'I never saw more steadiness or bravery exhibited in my life. Run they would not, and of death they seemed to have no fear, though their comrades were falling thick around them.' The result was that the British not only moved quickly to sign a peace deal, but also offered to pay the Gurkhas to join their army, with an original 5,000 men joining up. In 1857, the Gurkhas became part of the British Indian Army, to which they would belong until 1947: an estimated 200,000 Gurkhas fought in the First World War (20,000 losing their lives) and 250,000 in the Second World War (32,000 being killed). After the partition of India in 1947, so too were the serving Gurkhas split, with four regiments moving across to join the Indian army. Today, their proud relationship with the British Army continues, with an estimated 3,500 Gurkhas currently serving.

265

The Gurkhas originate from the Nepalese region of Gorkha, though their name is thought to come from Guru Gorakhnath, a Hindu warrior saint from the eighth century (according to legend, it was he who gave the Gurkhas their kukri knife). Competition for places is fierce – just 200 a year are available, for which 28,000 apply (recruitment was opened up to women in the mid-2000s). Selected candidates have to be able to do seventy-five bench jumps in a minute, seventy sit-ups in two, and complete the 'doko' – a 5km run up a steep Himalayan track, while carrying a pack containing 25kg of rocks – in less than fifty-five minutes.

The Gurkhas are notoriously tough, summed up by their motto, 'Better to die than be a coward'. Sir Ralph Turner MC served with 2/3rd Queen Alexandra's Own Gurkha Rifles during the First World War, and it is his words that are inscribed on the Gurkha Memorial, near the Ministry of Defence in London: 'As I write these last words, my thoughts return to you who were my comrades, the stubborn and indomitable peasants of Nepal . . . uncomplaining you endure hunger and thirst and wounds; and at the last your unwavering lines disappear into the smoke and wrath of battle. Bravest of the brave, most generous of the generous, never had a country more faithful friends than you.'

After Tul Bahadur enlisted in 1940, he was sent for training in India, before being posted to the 3/6th Gurkha Rifles. This battalion was moved to Lala Ghat, on the Indian border with Burma, where they trained with American aircraft in anticipation of the expedition they were about to take part in. Along with the first battalions of the King's Regiment, the Lancashire Fusiliers and the South Staffordshire Regiment, the 3/6th Gurkhas formed the 77th Indian Infantry, led by Brigadier 'Mad' Mike Calvert, which fought in the second of the Chindit expeditions in Burma in 1944, where Tul Bahadur was to make his name.

* * *

The Chindit expeditions were the brainchild of Major General Orde Wingate, who during the East African Campaign had created Gideon

Force, a unit of troops for Sudan and Ethiopia which he used to disrupt Italian supply lines. When the Commander-in-Chief of the Middle East Command, General Archibald Wavell, moved to become Commander-in-Chief of Indian Command, he tasked Wingate with doing something similar in Burma. The Japanese had captured Burma in 1942, driving British and Chinese forces out of the country. At their occupation of the country, Wingate's plan was to send in troops with the purpose of disrupting lines of communication. The first Chindit expedition, Operation LONGCLOTH, set off in February 1943, and succeeded, albeit temporarily, in disrupting the main Burmese railway.

The second Chindit expedition set out in February 1944, to coincide with General Joseph Stilwell's American/Chinese advance into Burma from India. This incursion was to be behind enemy lines, with the aim of disrupting the lines of communication to the Japanese troops defending, and helping to capture the strategic towns of Mogaung and Myiktana on the Irrawaddy River. This was no easy assignment: because the troops were being dropped behind enemy positions, they only had light arms at their disposal to take out these established Japanese positions. An advance party of 16 Brigade marched 300 miles behind enemy lines to prepare and build a remote jungle airstrip: this strip, known as Broadway, was on the Eastern side of the Indaw–Mogaung railway valley. Once this was complete, Tul Bahadur Pun and the rest of 77 Brigade were flown in by glider to the clearing: in all, 9,000 men, along with mules, ponies, munitions, artillery and anti-aircraft guns were, as Wingate put it, 'inserted into the guts of the enemy'.[1]

In a 2007 interview with the *Daily Mirror*, Tul Bahadur recalled that 'out of 1800 that landed, about 500 hit logs and the pilots were seriously injured'. The harsh realities of war and the need for secrecy meant that the mules 'underwent operations of the throat so they wouldn't bray and give away our position to the enemy'. From Broadway, 77 Brigade moved beyond the railway valley to set another stronghold, called White City. This was fortified, complete with timber dugouts, mined barbed wire, another airstrip and anti-aircraft guns. Conditions were unpleasant: as one account (found in the library at the Gurkha museum) describes it, 'the Japanese made many suicidal attacks, suffering very heavy losses, leading a senior officer to commit suicide on the wire. The place smelt of rotting bodies, with vast clouds of flies, in temperatures of 110 degrees F.'

The 3/6th Gurkhas moved north along the railway valley and spent the next thirteen days trekking until they reached the target of Maluka railway bridge. Conditions were difficult – the march was hot and the country hilly, the men were weighed down with rations as it was unclear when the next supply drop might be able to take place. On top of this, as the regimental history of the 3rd Battalion describes it, 'no one had got accustomed to moving around in enemy territory, and the tendency generally was to expect a Jap behind every tree'.

Attempts to blow the bridge up ran into difficulties. On the first night, gun cotton was fixed onto the bridge to blow it up, but the matches wouldn't work and they couldn't get the fuse to light. The second night, the troops were spotted by the Japanese and had to withdraw. On the third night, the assault was more successful: Chaba Thapa, who was in the 3/6th Regiment alongside Tul Bahadur, described later how they worked together to give covering fire so the attack could take place:

> We went out the next night and blew the bridge up, *barang burung* . . . the OP [operation post] told us where the enemy were and Jemadar Karnabahadur told me, as No 1, on what degree to fire. I went forward and planted the aiming post, went back and fixed the angle and range on the sights. As No 1 that was my job. No 2 put the bomb in the tube. No 3 prepared the bomb for firing by inserting the fuse in the tail, unscrewing the head cap and giving the bomb to No 2. No 4 took the bombs out of the case. No 4 was Rifleman Tulbahadur Pun . . .[2]

As the regiment was successfully blowing up the bridge, a Japanese goods train approached, its brakes screeching when the driver realised it couldn't get across. The sentries ran upon being shot at, leaving the grateful Gurkhas, who had finished their rations that day, to take what supplies they could from the train.

Now the Japanese were aware of the Allied troops and their position, the situation became more difficult. As the troops moved towards Bhamo, the landscape changed from jungle to rice fields and the more open land meant they were easy to pick off. Progress was made, but at the expense of heavy casualties. Chaba Thaba remembers how thirsty the troops were, but so limited were their supplies that no one was allowed to drink from their water bottles without permission from an officer. This led to the desperate measure of trying to drink from a stream, only to discover it was brown from the blood of Japanese casualties further up the river.

The march towards Mogaung continued. With supplies depleted, an attempted drop was made, only for the parachutes to become stuck in the trees in full view of a Japanese OP and the troops were unable to get to them. As June approached, Burma hit the monsoon season; the land was drenched and leeches abounded. As one account quoted in James Lunt's *Jai Sixth!* describes it,

> Mogaung was the very devil of a place to get at. The west side of the town was washed by the Namyin and the north by the Mogaung River, running at six knots. The only approach was from the south-east along a narrow road built up on a causeway, with flooded ground, lakes and marshes right and left and a deep *Chaung* [a waterfall or a deep pool formed by one] bridged only where the road crossed it, barring any flanking movement. From the ridge, Calvert had chosen as his base of attack to the town lay two miles of open country studded with villages, all fortified in the Japanese fashion with bunkers cut underneath them and all able to bring interlocking fire over the front.[3]

Getting over the bridge was obviously crucial. Tul Bahadur was sent out under the cover of darkness to recce the situation: 'Making the slightest noise could spell doom,' he remembered. 'In those days, we had shoes fixed with nails and they made creaking noises, so I wrapped cloth on my feet and inspected the bridge, which had gun posts on top of both ends.' As well as this, there were a number of buildings containing automatic weapons, with one, called Red House, a particular threat.

In the early morning of 23 June, just before dawn, the 3/6th Regiment made their move to capture the bridge and immediately came under heavy fire. Such is the fog of war that the details, from numerous accounts, differ as to what happened next, but the salient facts are well described in the citation of Tul Bahadur's subsequent award:

> Immediately the attack developed the enemy opened concentrated and sustained cross fire at close range from a position known as the Red House and from a strong bunker position two hundred yards to the left of it. So intense was the cross fire that both the leading platoons of "B" Company, one of which was Rifleman Tulbahadur Pun's, were pinned to the ground and the whole of his Section was wiped out with the exception of himself, the Section Commander and one other man. The Section Commander immediately led the remaining two men in a charge on the Red House but was at once badly wounded [Captain Allmand, who died shortly afterwards from his injuries, would also be awarded the Victoria Cross for his actions]. Rifleman Tulbahadur Pun and his remaining companion continued the charge, but the latter too was immediately badly wounded. Rifleman Tulbahadur Pun then seized the Bren Gun, and firing from the hip as he went, continued the charge on this heavily bunkered position alone in the face of the most shattering concentration of automatic fire directed straight at him. With the dawn coming up behind him,

he presented a perfect target to the Japanese. He had to move thirty yards over open ground, ankle deep in mud, through shell holes and over fallen trees.

Despite these overwhelming odds, he reached the Red House and closed with the Japanese occupants. He killed three and put five more to flight and captured two light machine guns and much ammunition. He then gave accurate supporting fire from the bunker to the remainder of his platoon which enabled them to reach their objective.

Interviewed in 2007, Tul Bahadur recalled that eerie moment of being the only person left alive on the battlefield. 'Everyone else was killed but I escaped because I was on the edge . . . I was the lone survivor and it was clear I would also be killed.' In an earlier interview in 1975, he remembered thinking, 'What do I do? I thought. If I go on I will be killed. If I don't go on, I will be called a coward.'[4] But went on he did, and somehow made it across.

Mogaung went on to be captured by 77 Brigade, the first town to be taken back from the Japanese. It took three days of what Tul Bahadur recalled as 'a vicious battle of hand-to-hand combat and flame throwers . . . a whole lot of soldiers who had been taking shelter in the town started escaping by jumping into the river. The water carried about half of them away but the rest managed to reach the other side. For a while the whole river was covered with human bodies.'[5]

Following the capture of Mogaung, the remaining soldiers of 3/6th Regiment marched a further fifty miles to Wazarup, where they were flown back to the headquarters. The mission had been a success but at a heavy cost: Tul Bahadur was one of only two men from his platoon to have survived: the battalion as a whole had suffered 495 casualties. Back at headquarters, Tul Bahadur discovered he had been awarded the Victoria Cross in surprising circumstances:

On one day I had been assigned to bring the rations, which were carried by mules. When I got to headquarters, a message had arrived from the War Office. The clerk on duty took me aside and said, 'Pun, one of the soldiers from your company has done an excellent job. I have collected the message. In all probability he will get a gallantry award. He gave me the message and told me to give it to the company. I glanced at it and saw my name on it.

* * *

One of the men fighting in 3/6th Regiment with Tul Bahadur Pun was Major James Lumley, the father of actress Joanna Lumley. Many years later, in 2006, Joanna Lumley's support would be crucial in helping Tulbahadur settle in the UK.

Following the end of the Second World War and Indian independence, the 6th Regiment was transferred across to the British Army. Tul Bahadur, who had been promoted to havildar (sergeant), went on to serve with the 2nd Battalion in Hong Kong and also during the Malayan Emergency. In 1957, he was appointed regimental sergeant major of the 2nd Battalion, a position he held until he retired from the army in 1959. As well as the Victoria Cross, he was awarded a further ten medals during his army career, including the Burma Star.

Returning to Banduk, he turned his hand to farming and also education. Remembering his own lack of opportunities, he helped to set up two primary schools in the area. In later life, his health deteriorating, he applied for residency in the UK. This was originally turned down on the grounds that, despite his service, he had 'failed to demonstrate strong ties with the UK'. Tul Bahadur's case became something of a *cause célèbre*, and after public pressure from the media and the general public, the government overturned the decision – following an outcry over his case, both the pensions and rights of former Gurkhas to reside in the UK were changed. Tul Bahadur moved to the UK in 2007, living first in Hounslow and then Chiswick: he died in 2011, fittingly, perhaps, on a visit back to Banduk to open a new school.

Tul Bahadur, however, should not be remembered for the bureaucratic wrangles he faced at the end of his life, but for his remarkable actions back in Burma in 1944. As the citation for his Victoria Cross finishes, 'His outstanding courage and superb gallantry in the face of odds which meant almost certain death were most inspiring to all ranks and were beyond praise.'

22

LIEUTENANT
FREDERICK SLEIGH ROBERTS VC

(later Field Marshal Earl Roberts of Kandahar)

Introduced by Geoffrey Palmer OBE

Roberts was born in India into an army family and destined for an army career despite hopes his mother harboured of a Church calling. When reading Roberts' story and that of his son, there seems no doubt that army lineage ran in the family. This gallant and fearless man's actions and those of his son (also awarded a VC, but posthumously) provide a humbling and fascinating story. Remarkably, Roberts and his son form one of only three father and son pairs to be awarded VCs.

For army personnel of his genre Roberts was distinctive in that he was an East India Company officer instead of the more highly regarded Queen's officer in the British Army. Despite this, Roberts' stellar career saw him rise to Commander-in-Chief of the British Army, the first Indian Army officer to do so. He possessed a natural military style and his career spanned India, Abyssinia, the Anglo-Afghan War and the Second Boer War. On his death Kipling wrote 'Lord Roberts', a commemorative poem for his friend who was known affectionately by the British public, quite simply, as Bobs. A true soldier to the last, his story evokes images of a bygone period of gallantry, service and dedication.

'The ground gradually sloped upwards towards Khudaganj,' recalled twenty-five-year-old Lieutenant Fred Roberts, 'and the regiments moving up to the attack made a fine picture. The 93rd [Highlanders] followed the impulsive 53rd [Foot], while Greathed's brigade took a line to the left, and as they neared the village the rebels hastily limbered up their guns and retired.'[1]

It was the morning of 2 January 1858, and Roberts was serving on the staff of Sir Hope Grant's cavalry division, part of the 30,000-strong field force that Sir Colin Campbell, Commander-in-Chief in India, had assembled to put down the armed insurrection known to Britons as the Indian Mutiny.[2]* Barely six weeks earlier, Campbell's army (with Roberts in tow) had relieved the British garrison in the besieged city of Lucknow, thus saving 4,000 lives, including 1,500 non-combatants. Now Campbell's task was to capture Fatehgarh, the last rebel-held city in the Doab, and thereby open land communications between the Punjab and Calcutta, the capital of British India.[3]

En route to Fatehgarh on New Year's Day 1858, Campbell had received intelligence that the main rebel force, under the Nawab of Farrukhabad, had partially destroyed the bridge over the Kali Nadi River near the village of Khudaganj, before withdrawing. He therefore sent forward a force of infantry to repair the damage and secure the bridge. What that force discovered, however, was that the enemy had returned to Khudaganj and were occupying, in Roberts' words, an 'advantageous position' from which they could pour fire onto any troops who tried to cross the river. Campbell at once ordered up the rest of his army – including Hope Grant's cavalry and horse artillery – and prepared to attack.[4]

Covered by artillery fire from heavy naval guns, Campbell's infantry crossed the river, followed by the cavalry and horse artillery: 'a tedious operation,' recalled Roberts, 'as there had not been time to fully repair the bridge, and in one place planks had only been laid for half its width,

---

* Indians remember it as the Great Uprising or the First War of Independence.

necessitating horses being led, and Infantry passing over in sections'. By now the enemy had the exact range of the bridge, 'and several casualties occurred at this spot', including the killing and wounding of six men of the 8th Foot by a single round shot.[5]

Once over, the troops were formed up for an attack on the village. But before Campbell could give the order, the 'advance' was sounded and the 53rd Foot, 'composed of a remarkably fine set of fellows, chiefly Irish', and long jealous of Campbell's apparent preference for the 93rd Highlanders, charged the enemy. Knowing it was futile to call them back, a furious Campbell sent the rest of his infantry in pursuit, and ordered his horsemen to mount.[6]

It was from the saddle that Roberts observed the flight of the enemy from Khudaganj. 'This was,' he noted,

> an opportunity for mounted troops as does not often occur [i.e. the pursuit of a beaten enemy]. It was instantly seized by Hope Grant, who rode to the Cavalry, drawn up behind some sand hills, and gave the word of command, 'Threes left, trot, march.' The words had hardly left his lips before we had started in pursuit of the enemy, by this time half a mile ahead, the 9th Lancers leading the way, followed by Younghusband's, Gough's, and Probyn's squadrons.[7]

Once the gap had narrowed to 300 yards, the charge was sounded and a 'regular mêlée ensued', with many rebels killed and 'seven guns captured in less than as many minutes'. Hope Grant now reformed the cavalry into a long line to continue the pursuit. 'On the line thundered,' recalled Roberts,

> overtaking groups of the enemy, who every now and then turned and fired into us before they could be cut down, or knelt to receive us on their bayonets before discharging their muskets. The chase continued for nearly five miles, until daylight began to fail and we appeared to have got to the end of the fugitives, when the order was given to wheel to the right and form up on the road.

As Roberts was about to make this movement, he and Lieutenant George Younghusband's squadron of the 5th Punjab Cavalry overtook a batch of mutineers who 'faced about and fired into' the horsemen 'at close quarters'. Roberts saw Younghusband shot from his saddle, but was unable to assist him because, nearer at hand, a Punjabi sowar[8] was in 'dire peril from a sepoy[9] who was attacking him with his fixed bayonet'. Had 'I not helped the man and disposed of his opponent' with a sword cut to his face, commented Roberts, 'he must have been killed'.[10]

Roberts had done his bit – and more – and was about to obey the earlier order to reform on the road when he saw in the distance two sepoys making off with a rebel standard. Without hesitation, he determined that the colour 'must be captured', and so rode after the rebels alone. It was an extraordinarily brave – if not foolhardy – act that almost cost Roberts his life. Quickly overtaking the sepoys before they could enter a village, he grabbed the colour staff with one hand, and cut down the man holding it with the other. But as he did so, the remaining sepoy placed the muzzle of his musket close to Roberts' chest and pulled the trigger. Incredibly it misfired – probably because the cap that ignited the charge was faulty – and Roberts was able to get away with the colour. But for this stroke of luck, Victorian Britain would have lost one of its leading soldiers before his career had properly begun. Instead, for these two acts of gallantry – saving the sowar and capturing the colour – Roberts was awarded the Victoria Cross, receiving the medal from Queen Victoria at Buckingham Palace on 8 June 1859.[11]

* * *

Frederick Sleigh Roberts was born in Cawnpore, India, on 30 September 1832, the younger son of Major General (later Lieutenant General Sir) Abraham Roberts, a senior officer in the East India Company's Bengal Army, and his second wife Isabella, both of Anglo-Irish descent. He was educated at Eton College for a year before entering the Royal Military College at Sandhurst. His mother had hoped he might go to Oxford or

Cambridge, and enter the Church. Young Roberts had other ideas. 'I had quite made up my mind to be a soldier,' he wrote later. 'I had never thought of any other profession.'[12] He wanted to join the British Army but his father, on the grounds of expense, persuaded him to enter the service of the Honourable East India Company.[13]

After eighteen months at the Company's military academy at Addiscombe, near Croydon, Roberts passed out ninth in his class and was commissioned into the Bengal Artillery. Within two years he was commanding a troop of the prestigious Bengal Horse Artillery, and by the outbreak of the Indian Mutiny in May 1857 had received a plum appointment on the staff of the Quartermaster-General's Department (in effect the General Staff of the Bengal Army, responsible for operations, planning and intelligence).

Roberts was small of stature – no more than five feet four inches in height – but hard to miss, with his magnificent black moustache and matching pair of mutton-chop whiskers. He was wiry and strong, of robust health, and an excellent horseman.[14] He was also ambitious and saw the Mutiny campaign as an opportunity to gain recognition, and to make up for the fact that he was an Indian Army officer in the employ of the Company, rather than a Queen's officer in what was then considered to be the more pukka British Army. On 24 July 1857, while he was recovering from a minor bullet wound to the spine that he had suffered during the four-month siege of Delhi, he wrote revealingly to his mother back in England of his hopes for the campaign:

> I could not be jollier ... I have got just what I wanted in the Quartermaster-General's Department on service, and service that I enjoy most thoroughly – as far as the results go, helping to exterminate every Sepoy in the Army ... Please God before I write again, I shall have ridden 'thro Delhi, and then I hope to join some Force going either towards Rohilkhand, and Oude or Gwalior – all new countries to me, and all of which I am very anxious to see; and then, if I may

look so far, after the fun is over, to return to Peshawur permanent
in the Department. Won't that be nice, my Mother. I am afraid,
according to the new rules, Brevets[15] can't be promised to Subalterns
as formerly, but there are plenty of other rewards, and what I want
more than any other is the <u>Victoria Cross</u>.[16] Oh! If I can only manage
that how happy I shall be![17]

Just over five months after writing to his mother, Roberts was presented
with his opportunity at the Battle of Khudaganj and, fearful risk or no,
he was not about to let it slip through his fingers. His first account of the
fight, in a letter to his father, was modesty itself. 'The Infantry and guns
advanced on the village,' he wrote on 12 January 1858,

out of which the rebels were soon driven, and then our Cavalry
followed up in two lines led by General [Hope] Grant. I accompanied
the first line, and in the scrimmage captured a very pretty Standard!
which I will send home . . . the first opportunity. A great piece of luck
my getting it, was it not? The evening left 8 guns in our possession, 2
in the village, and 6 were got in the pursuit, besides some 300 dead
on the field. Our own loss was trifling.[18]

He received word of his award in camp near Cawnpore in early February
1858, and promptly informed his mother:

I have such a piece of news for you. I have been recommended
for the '<u>Victoria Cross</u>.' The letter says for 'repeated gallantry in
the field, more especially on the 2nd Jan. 1858, when Lieut. Fred
Roberts captured a rebel standard, killing the Standard Bearer, and
on the same day saved the life of an Irregular Cavalryman by cutting
down a Sepoy who was attacking him with a musket and Bayonet.'
Is not this glorious? How pleased it will make the General. <u>Such a</u>
<u>Medal</u> to wear with '<u>For Valour</u>' scrolled on it. How proud I shall

be, darling Mother, when I show it to you – better than all the other Medals put together. All get Medals when given for a campaign, but few, very few, this glorious Cross . . . My name has also gone in for a Brevet majority on promotion to a Company. Major Fred. Roberts, V.C.! will sound well, will it not.[19]

Roberts returned to Britain on sick leave in April 1858, having participated in the recapture of Lucknow a month earlier, and there married Nora Bews, the daughter of a fellow Bengal Army officer. It was a long and happy marriage, and produced six children (though three died in infancy). A tall and forceful woman, Nora was said to exercise considerable influence over Roberts as he rose to high command, particularly with regard to his choice of subordinates, causing the press to dub them 'Sir Bobs and Lady Jobs'. Roberts, wrote Queen Victoria in 1895, is 'ruled by his wife who is a terrible jobber . . . her notorious favouritism'.[20]

They returned to India in July 1859 – by which time the Mutiny was over and the authority for governing the country had been transferred from the East India Company to the Crown[21] – and Roberts resumed his job with the Quartermaster-General's Department. He briefly saw active service on the North-West Frontier in 1863, and five years later, as Acting Quartermaster-General of the Bengal Brigade, took part in Sir Robert Napier's successful Abyssinia expedition. Roberts was chosen to carry Napier's dispatches to London and received a brevet lieutenant colonelcy.

In 1875, after more good work during the Lushai expedition in Assam (rewarded by a CB – Companion of the Order of the Bath), he reached the top of his department when he became Quartermaster-General of the Bengal Army with the acting rank of major general. But it was during the second Afghan War of 1878–80 that his ability as a field commander became apparent with seminal battlefield victories over the Afghans at Peiwar Kotal in 1878, Charisia and Sherpur in 1879 and Kandahar in 1880. En route to the latter battle, he had covered the 313 miles from

Kabul in just three weeks, a feat of logistics and endurance that turned him into a national hero.[22] Of the march, he wrote:

> When it is remembered that the daily supply for over 18,000 men and 11,000 animals had to be drawn from the country after arrival in camp, that food had to be distributed to every individual, that the fuel with which it was cooked had often to be brought from long distances, and that a very limited time was available for the preparation of meals and for rest, it will readily be understood how essential it was that even the stupidest follower should be able to find his place in camp speedily.[23]

The daily routine was reveille at 2.45 a.m. and by 4 a.m. 'the tents had been struck, baggage loaded up, and everything was ready for a start'. The column – two infantry brigades with mountain artillery, field hospitals, ordnance and engineer parks, treasure and baggage, followed by another infantry brigade with guns – was preceded and flanked by the cavalry to protect against a surprise attack. After every hour there was a halt of ten minutes, and at 8 a.m. this was doubled to allow for breakfast. Roberts took advantage of these stops to have a quick nap, 'awaking greatly refreshed after a few minutes' sound sleep'.[24]

The task of the rearguard, recorded Roberts, 'was to prevent the [camp] followers from lagging behind, for it was certain death for anyone who strayed from the shelter of the column; numbers of Afghans always hovered about on the look-out for plunder, or in the hope of being able to send a Kafir [non-believer, usually a European], or an almost equally detested Hindu, to eternal perdition'. Yet towards the end of the march, so 'weary and footsore' were the camp followers that many of them hid in ravines, 'making up their minds to die, and entreating, when discovered and urged to make an effort, to be left where they were'.[25]

The whole column had to endure extremes of temperature – from freezing point at dawn to 110 degrees Fahrenheit at midday – lack of water, constant sandstorms and 'the suffocating dust raised by the column in its progress'. Roberts was laid up with fever for the last four days of the march, but managed to mount his horse for the entry into Kandahar on 31 August 1880. He was unimpressed by the 'demoralized condition' of the British and Indian garrison troops who seemed to Roberts to be 'hopelessly defeated' and were 'utterly despondent'.[26]

A day later, within sight of the walls of Kandahar, he routed Ayub Khan's Afghan army, reporting to the Viceroy: 'His camp was captured, the two lost guns of E Battery, B Brigade Royal Horse Artillery [lost to Ayub in the recent defeat at Battle of Maiwand] were recovered, and several wheeled guns of various calibre fell to the splendid Infantry of this force; the Cavalry are still in pursuit.'[27]

Roberts' victory was acknowledged with a step in knighthood to GCB (Knight Grand Cross of the Order of the Bath – he had been made KCB or Knight Commander a year earlier) and command of the Madras Army. In 1885 he became Commander-in-Chief in India, remaining in post for an unprecedented eight years, during which time he drew up plans to counter a possible Russian attack through Afghanistan and altered the ethnic composition of the army in favour of the so-called 'martial races' of the north.[28]

With his career winding down, he was created Baron Roberts of Kandahar (in 1892), promoted to field marshal and appointed to the undemanding Irish command (both in 1895). But he hankered for one last field command and was granted his wish in mid-December 1899 when, in the wake of the disastrous 'Black Week' of British defeats by the Boers, he was appointed by Lord Salisbury's government to succeed Sir Redvers Buller as commander of British forces in South Africa. A day later he received word that his only son and namesake Freddie, a lieutenant in the King's Royal Rifle Corps, had died from bullet wounds received at the Battle of Colenso as he tried to rescue a battery of stranded British field guns. 'Tell them,' Freddie wrote to his sister from his deathbed, 'we saved two of the guns.'

Freddie Roberts, perhaps unsurprisingly, had followed his father into military service, joining the King's Royal Rifle Corps in 1891 after Eton and Sandhurst. He was mentioned in dispatches for his contributions during the Waziristan expedition and awarded the Order of the Meijidieh of the Fourth Class after the Nile expedition in 1898. At the Battle of Colenso, he showed great bravery in attempting to save the field guns in the face of intense enemy fire.

Freddie was awarded a posthumous Victoria Cross,[29] thus making him and Roberts senior one of only three pairs of father and son to receive the medal (the others are C. J. S. and J. E. Gough, and W. N.[30] and W. la T. Congreve).[31] A heartbroken Roberts wrote to his wife: 'The rent in my heart seems to stifle all feelings . . . I could not help thinking how different it would have been if our dear boy had been with me [and not Buller].'[32] It is said he never forgave Buller for his son's death.

On reaching South Africa in January 1900, Roberts altered Buller's strategy by putting the major effort into the relief of Kimberley in the eastern Cape. To do this he concentrated a force of 37,000 men (including 8,000 cavalry and mounted infantry), 100 guns and hundreds of supply wagons below the Modder River. He also issued new tactical instructions, in the form of 'Notes for Guidance in South African Warfare', to combat the threat from magazine weapons by urging careful reconnaissance, open order, delegating responsibility to company and battalion officers, precise and accurate messages and better use of cover.[33]

Kimberley was relieved on 15 February, and twelve days later the Boer General Piet Cronje surrendered his force of 4,000 men to Roberts' deputy Herbert Kitchener on the Modder River. The advance continued and the Boer capitals of Bloemfontein and Pretoria fell to Roberts on 13 March and 5 June respectively. Yet he had failed to trap and destroy any significant Boer army or to inflict a major defeat in the field, thus enabling the enemy to continue the war by conducting guerrilla operations. To counteract this Roberts ordered the selective destruction of Boer farms.

Overall, his time in South Africa had been, a biographer wrote, 'dramatically successful'. In just nine months, Roberts 'had advanced about 500 miles, defeated the main enemy armies, and occupied their capitals. Although the war dragged on for another two years, its issue was no longer in doubt . . . Probably no other contemporary British general could have bettered or even equalled Roberts's achievement, at the age of sixty-seven.'[34]

His achievement was recognised by Lord Salisbury, the prime minister, who told Queen Victoria on 19 September that Roberts would soon succeed Lord Wolseley as Commander-in-Chief of the British Army. 'The popularity he has obtained,' wrote Salisbury, 'and the great services he has tendered during this war make it almost impossible that any other nomination should be made.'[35]

Roberts returned to Britain in December 1900 to take up the post of Commander-in-Chief, the first Indian Army officer to rise to the chief command. Additional recognition took the form of the Order of the Garter, an earldom and a grant of £100,000. As the new head of the British Army, he introduced new weapons – including the magazine Lee-Enfield rifle for all troops, including cavalry – ordnance, vehicles and khaki service dress. Army training and education was improved by the creation of a new department. But in February 1904, on the advice of the post-war Esher Commission, Roberts lost his job when the post of Commander-in-Chief was replaced with the Army Council (headed by the Chief of the Imperial General Staff).

He served for a time on the Committee of Imperial Defence (to research and coordinate military strategy), but resigned in November 1905 when Balfour's government refused to introduce compulsory military service which he believed necessary to counter the military threat from Imperial Germany. Instead he became President of the National Service League – founded in 1902 – and campaigned for conscription without success until his death in 1914. It was finally introduced, for the duration of the First World War, in January 1916.

Shortly after the outbreak of war in August 1914, he was appointed Colonel-in-Chief of the Empire ('Overseas') troops in France and died of pneumonia while visiting Indian troops near St Omer on 14 November. He was eighty-two.[36]

* * *

He is buried in the crypt of St Paul's Cathedral, London. The gun carriage that his son died trying to save at Colenso bore the coffin at his funeral. His Victoria Cross is in the National Army Museum in London.[37]

23

LIEUTENANT
WILLIAM LEEFE ROBINSON VC

Introduced by Alexander Armstrong

One of the things that has always intrigued me about pilots flying sorties from East Anglia or Lincolnshire in the First and Second World Wars is that they were based right in the heart of the English countryside. So, when not risking their necks – let's not forget the life expectancy of a Lancaster crew member was estimated at just two weeks or five operations – the airmen would return each day to the strange calm of home: that idyll of honeysuckle-clad cottages, village inns, bike rides down leafy lanes and apple-cheeked country girls that infantrymen could only dream of.

Siegfried Sassoon reflects on how the trauma of war was seldom felt at the front itself where unspeakable horrors were digested often with shocking sangfroid. It is back in Kent, leaning on a gate post in the afternoon sunshine, that Sassoon buckles under the weight of all he has witnessed. Perhaps it's only against the sheer ordinariness of home that the depths of war's depravities can be measured. If so, then what a bizarre life of extremes the pilot's must have been.

William Leefe Robinson's flying operations in the Great War are told through his letters and contemporary accounts. Pilots of Robinson's generation were pioneers, so when he writes to his mother describing the views above the clouds one must remember he is among the very first humans ever to have experienced this phenomenon. The fact of his being able to witness such sights, travel such distances, alone, in unexplored elements at the very forefront of powered flight must have made war a weirdly euphoric affair for Robinson. Throw in his most famous act of heroism and the hugely public arena in which it was performed, and one wonders what kept airmen such as Robinson from thinking they were God-like beings.

Alas, for all the bravery and achievement of Robinson's war, his end was all too human. His story is a colossal one and a worthy addition to this book.

At 10.45p.m. on 25 April 1916, Lieutenant William Leefe Robinson took off from Sutton's Farm airbase in Essex in his BE2c biplane with a single goal in mind – to spot and, if possible, take down one of the German Zeppelins whose attacks on the British mainland had been raining down with little resistance.

The Zeppelin attacks on Britain during the First World War are a part of the conflict that is often overlooked, but had a huge effect on the population at home in terms of morale – particularly as it appeared there was little the home defence could do to stop them. The technology behind airships was still in its infancy: Count Ferdinand von Zeppelin had built his first airship at the turn of the century; a decade later, in 1910, his first passenger airship was built. However, it was its military potential that interested the German armed forces: Zeppelins could be used both for observation and also on bombing raids.

When war broke out in 1914, rumours abounded of sightings of Zeppelins along the British coast. In fact, the Germans lacked the numbers for any raids and were instead in the process of building up their air fleet as quickly as they could. At the same time, the German High Command had a second challenge in the shape of Kaiser Wilhelm, who was set against authorising bombing raids on London – partly because of fears for his cousins, George V and Queen Mary, and partly because of the damage that would be caused. It wasn't until January 1915 that approval was given – it was agreed that military buildings would be attacked, with docks and establishments in the lower Thames and coastal areas the main targets.

Between January 1915 and August 1916, a total of thirty-nine Zeppelin raids were launched: in all, 439 people were killed and a further 980 injured in the strikes. They were called the 'Baby Killers' by the British press, and were seemingly able to attack with impunity. Defences in the shape of a combination of searchlights and anti-aircraft guns suffered from a limited range. Air defences, too, had to make do with insufficient equipment: Sutton's Farm, agricultural land requisitioned by the Royal Flying Corps, had a landing strip marked out by two lines of petrol cans, filled with petrol, paraffin and cotton waste. The planes themselves, the BE2cs, were originally tasked with flying above the Zeppelins in an attempt to drop bombs or explosive darts on them. This was no easy task, and the Zeppelins were able simply to climb out of range. As civilian deaths mounted, matters weren't helped by arguments between the British forces as to who should be in charge of defending the skies: Lord Kitchener saw the expansion of the Royal Flying Corps in France as a more important priority than building up home defences.

It was into that situation that William Leefe Robinson found himself loaned by his Squadron Commander, on Christmas Eve 1915, to be part of the London defences. As well as his skills as a pilot, Robinson was particularly useful because of his experiences as a night flyer, which was something of a rarity. With a lull in the bombing raids over the winter, Robinson took the time to train hard for his new role, and to get to grips with the BE2c aircraft. Originally a reconnaissance plane, BE2cs were converted into single-seater planes, with the front cockpit covered with aluminium. It wasn't particularly fast, but it was steady and reliable, making it suitable for night flying.

On that April night in 1916, Robinson donned his leathers and smeared his face with whale oil to protect his skin from the cold as usual.

His aircraft had no heating, nor indeed any oxygen equipment, radio or parachute. With instructions to patrol at 5,000 feet, he guided his aeroplane up, then, on seeing nothing, decided to continue climbing, this time to 7,000 feet. Robinson noticed a number of spotlights pointing north, and it was then that he saw a Zeppelin looming above him. He immediately turned and headed straight for the enemy aircraft. As he got to within 2,000 feet of it, he opened fire with his Lewis machine gun.

For a moment, Robinson thought he had been successful: 'I distinctly saw a bright flash in the front part of the forward gondola of the Zeppelin,' he wrote in his report afterwards. 'I thought it rather prolonged for the burst of a shell.' Instead, the Zeppelin was unscathed and, despite Robinson's best efforts, the aircraft got away. 'I fired at the Zeppelin three times,' he wrote. 'The machine gun jammed five times and I only got off about twenty rounds. When the Zeppelin made off in a ENE direction, I followed for some minutes, but lost sight of it.'

Robinson wasn't the only member of Sutton's Farm's 'B flight' to engage the Zeppelin; Captain Arthur Harris also spotted and attacked it later with similarly limited success; also returning with tales of fleeting glimpses in the searchlights and a machine gun that jammed when in range. Both noticed, too, the help that the Zeppelin was getting from the ground – flashes of light acting as signals to guide the craft. For Robinson, it was his first encounter with a Baby Killer, and next time the outcome would be different: 'Either the Zepp or I,' he vowed.

* * *

William Leefe Robinson was born at Kaima Betta, in Coorg, southern India, on 14 July 1895. He was the youngest child of Horace and Elizabeth 'Bessie' Robinson, following Ernest, Katherine, Grace, Irene, Ruth and Harold: Leefe, his mother's maiden name, was given to all the children.

Kaima Betta was a coffee estate, which had been bought for Horace by his father. It stood 3,500 feet above sea level, surrounded by mountains and forests. Coffee was a difficult crop to cultivate, but Horace was skilled at it, being one of the last plantation owners to maintain his independence, others being swallowed up the East India Company and Coffee Planters' Association. Even with his cultivation skills, Horace struggled against the changing economic climate: at the turn of the century, the Indian coffee industry faced fierce competition with the arrival of Brazilian exports. For the Robinson family, this meant a temporary return to England in 1901, where the family settled in Oxford and William and Harold were sent to The Dragon School. The family returned to India in 1903, with the two boys going to the Bishop Cotton Boys' School in Bangalore.

In 1909, the two youngest brothers set sail for the UK once more, where they continued their education at St Bees in Cumbria. St Bees had been founded back in the 1580s and since the mid-nineteenth century had taken in boarders. William loved the location and the holidays – many of them spent with local families in Keswick, in the heart of the Lake District – though in 1912 William went to stay with the Reckes in Russia, family friends of the Robinsons and for whom William's sister Katherine was working as an English tutor.

William was not academically gifted, something he was particularly aware of given the success of his elder brother, Horace. Instead, he excelled at sport and music and did well, too, at the Officers' Training Corps (OTC), where he achieved the rank of sergeant. Here, William discovered the direction he wanted to go: 'I think the best plan for me to do,' he wrote to his mother in 1913, 'is . . . to try Sandhurst and get, if I can, into the Indian army. Then, if I find the Indian climate agrees with me, I could either get into the English army or, if luck smiled upon me, and I made a few influential friends I would go – or have a good try to go – into the Egyptian army. It is aiming high, I know, but then it is better to aim at the bull than the outer circle.'[1]

Robinson proceeded to follow through with his plan. On 14 August 1914, ten days after the outbreak of war, he entered Sandhurst. In December, he joined the 5th (Militia) Battalion of the Worcester Regiment as a second lieutenant, and was posted to Fort Tregantle in

Cornwall, where new recruits were completing their training before being sent to the Western Front. Robinson, however, was not among them – his role was overseeing the new arrivals rather than going to fight himself, which he found immensely frustrating. It was this that led to his application to join the Royal Flying Corps in March 1915, which resulted in him seeing action in a different way, as an air observer.

Here, Robinson had found his true vocation, his enthusiasm for flying being clear in a letter he wrote to his mother: 'You have no idea how beautiful it is above the clouds. I have been up at 5 o'clock on a still afternoon – you have no idea how glorious it is to gaze at the earth at 7000 feet or over. But thrilling as that is, the real beauty comes with the clouds. Those rolling wastes of vapour or a hundred shades fading away till they terminate at the horizon in one straight line, or rather circle, which frames your view . . . I love flying more and more every day, and the work is even more interesting than it was.'[2]

The role of air observer was to record enemy artillery positions: once these were reported back to the Battery Commander, they could aim their guns accordingly; the air observer would then use a clock-face code via Morse key to say whether the target had been hit or by how much it had missed. It must have been a strange sight, observing the fighting from the air, but Robinson was quickly up to speed and revelled in the fact that he was finally doing something for the war effort. However, it was a role that carried a risk, and, barely six weeks after starting the position, he found himself invalided back to England: 'It was about 4.50am on Saturday over Lille that the beasts got me,' Robinson wrote to his mother. 'I thought I was bruised at first but went on with my reconnaissance, but after a bit my arm got a bit stiff and the blood dirtied all the maps, so we cut our reconnaissance short at the end and went back to the aerodrome. From there I went to the dressing hospital where they took out the shrapnel bullet and dressed the wound, and sent me off to Boulogne. I arrived there late on Saturday night and was told should probably go to England – great was my joy!'[3]

Back in the UK, Robinson now knew exactly what he wanted to do: to become a pilot. His progress was rapid: he made his first flight under instruction at the end of June, made his first solo flight in mid-July and qualified for the Royal Aero Club ten days later – after just under four hours' flying time. After more training, Robinson got his wings in mid-September, and became a flying officer. It was a position that he relished, and, as the autumn progressed, he mixed business with pleasure as he delivered aircraft and passengers around the country. 'I have a simply ripping time,' he wrote in one letter. 'I landed for lunch near Banbury the other day – you are immediately surrounded by people offering you cars, lunch, tea, bed and the Lord knows what. Of course, if you are wide you generally pick out the grounds of a country house or large villa of some kind to land in. My last landing was at Kenilworth. I had a passenger with me and we had the time of our lives. Talk about autograph books and cameras. By gad, I was positively sick of seeing and signing my own signature.' In another letter to his mother, he signed off, 'I remain your ever loving son, Billy the Birdman'[4].

As autumn turned to winter, so the war became more serious for Robinson. His secondment to the Home Defence Squadron was to see him tackle the deadly threat of the German Zeppelins. Having failed to down one on his first encounter, he was determined not to let the enemy out of his sight the next time.

* * *

That occasion came in the early morning of 3 September 1916. The previous afternoon, a total of sixteen German airships had begun to make their journey towards England and London. It was the first time that the German Naval Airship Division and Army Division had come together for an operation and constituted the largest German air raid of the war so far. By 1700hrs that evening, the first reports that the airships were on their way began to reach Naval Intelligence. The first bombs of the raid were recorded in Bacton on the Norfolk coast at 21.50hrs, as the airships used cloud cover to continue their journey towards their main target: London.

Robinson set off from Sutton's Farm airfield at 23.08hrs, climbing to 10,000 feet in his search for German airships. He got a sighting of his first at 01.15hrs – *LZ98*, which had been dropping bombs on Dartford and Tilbury, mistakenly assuming it was over London docks. *LZ98* proved to be the one that got away: 'I very slowly gained on it for about ten minutes,' Robinson wrote in his report on that night's events, 'I judged it to be about 800 feet below me and I sacrificed my speed in order to keep the height. It went behind some clouds, avoided the searchlights and I lost sight of it.'

As the airship disappeared into the cloud, Robinson thought his moment had gone – especially as his designated flying time was almost up and his plane was beginning to run short of fuel. But then, at 02.10hrs, another airship, the Schütte-Lanz *SL11*, was spotted over Alexandra Palace, in north London, and lit up by the searchlights from Victoria and Finsbury Park. Anti-aircraft guns fired up at it and Robinson hove in on its location, despite the explosions raining up from below. For those watching in the street below it was both an awesome and terrifying spectacle – the huge looming airship and the tiny biplane was an aviation David versus Goliath. It is said that thousands of people watched the battle from the streets, bedroom windows and rooftops.

SL11 was being piloted by a hugely experienced German commander, Hauptmann Wilhelm Schramm; he was using every inch of his airship know-how, dropping his remaining bombs to lighten his load and continually shifting direction in the hope of dodging the spotlights. But William Robinson's aircraft was onto him. He dived under the airship's bows and, flying along underneath, fired his Lewis machine gun up at the underside of the airship. Nothing happened. Having emptied one drum, Robinson clipped on a second. He repeated the attack, but, again, to no effect.

Now Robinson only had one drum of ammunition left. He approached the airship from the rear and focused his attack on an area beneath the hull. To begin with, it looked as if the attack had been as futile as before, but then there came a pale pink glow from inside the airship: this swiftly turned red as the ship caught fire. Robinson turned his plane away as the heat became intense, huge strips of fabric peeling way, the metal hissing and spitting. Such was the brightness that the burning airship could be seen from as far away as Reigate in Surrey. On the London streets below, meanwhile, onlookers were cheering and clapping in celebration.

All but out of fuel, Robinson then brought his BE2 back down to Sutton's Farm. When he landed, it was clear that the attack had left the plane damaged and that its pilot had been lucky it had landed in one piece. The wreckage of the airship, meanwhile, came down near the village of Cuffley, in Hertfordshire, and continued to burn for two days. The army had to put up a cordon to stop people looting the remains of the airship. The sight of *SL11* coming down had really captured the public imagination – the day became known as Zepp Sunday and over the next couple of days more than 10,000 people travelled to the village to visit the wreckage.

Echoing the public mood, William Leefe Robinson found himself swiftly rewarded for his efforts. On 5 September, it was revealed that he had been awarded the Victoria Cross. The report in the *London Gazette* stated: 'His Majesty the King has been graciously pleased to award the Victoria Cross to the undermentioned officer: Lieutenant William Leefe Robinson, Worcestershire Regiment and Royal Flying Corps. For most conspicuous bravery. He attacked an enemy airship under circumstances of great difficulty and danger, and sent it crashing to the ground as a flaming wreck.'

* * *

Life was never quite the same again for Robinson. Travelling to Windsor Castle to receive the medal from King George V on Friday 8 September, he found himself back on duty the following day. This time he didn't even make it into the air – a gust of wind blew his craft towards a hedge as he attempted to take off, and he was lucky to escape with his life as his plane went up in flames.

For a while, the Royal Flying Corps didn't want to risk their newfound national hero being killed, and Robinson found himself put forward into round after round of social events. He was determined to be allowed to fly again and eventually persuaded High Command to transfer him to France. Here, his participation didn't last long: April 1917 became known as 'Bloody April' as one plane after another went down – 150 Royal Flying Corps planes in total. One of those was Robinson's. Caught by German fire, he eventually managed to bring the stricken plane down and landed behind enemy lines. Promptly captured, he was taken prisoner and sent to the POW camp at Freiburg-im-Breisgau, near the Swiss border.

His war was over. Despite several spirited attempts to escape, Robinson was moved to camps at Zorndorf, Clausthal and Holzminden. He was repatriated in December 1918, after the end of the war. Sadly, however, imprisonment had taken its toll on him physically, and almost immediately after returning to the UK he succumbed to a flu epidemic and died on 31 December 1918.

It was a quiet, unassuming death, out of kilter with the bravery and courage shown by Robinson in the skies. For what he had achieved the night of his Victoria Cross action was something special and unique – few such heroics have been witnessed by so many people, one of those events that brought a beleaguered population together, at a time when they needed it the most.

24

WO2 RAYENE 'RAY' SIMPSON VC

Introduced by Kate Adie OBE DL

Ray Simpson never gave up. Toughened by a difficult childhood in Australia, a string of odd jobs, he longed to join the army. An army demands discipline, insists on rank being respected and likes orderly paperwork. Simpson was never entirely at home with such conventions. On the other hand, he was a superb soldier.

He enlisted at eighteen, in 1944, and was finally discharged from the army twenty-six years later. It hadn't been a straightforward career, with numerous run-ins with army regulations, a persistent drive to acquire skills and practical experience in a host of military disciplines from jungle warfare to parachute training, and a single-minded determination to serve where the action was. He joined the Australian Army three times – the second under an assumed name, the third by buying a ticket back to Vietnam and turning up and asking, 'Where's my gear?'

Put briefly like that, it's a story which might suggest a dilettante approach to soldiering. It was anything but. He was tough, had a formidable grasp of the art of warfare, and turned out to be extremely courageous.

Armies have always attracted more than their fair share of buccaneers, oddballs and tough guys. The system copes with them, up to a point. But even when someone shows consistent abilities as a soldier, but fails to toe the very precise points of discipline and respect, the system often tends to spit them out. Only the very determined attempt to return. Ray Simpson was one of them, determined to prove that his qualities and courage were still needed.

His VC was earned in a war which the public found complex and contentious, without patriotic fervour at home. It is testimony to professional soldiering, where the drive to keep going, to save your mates, to disregard your own safety, deserves the recognition 'For Valour'.

In November 1967, Bruce McIlwraith was a warrant officer for the Royal Australian Army Service Corps, serving in Vietnam as part of the AATTV (Australian Army Training Team Vietnam). This was a unit set up in 1962, originally with the role of advising and training South Vietnamese forces in their fight against North Vietnam and the Viet Cong, but one that moved into combat operations as well, as the Australian involvement in the conflict grew.

That November, McIlwraith was at the AATTV headquarters in Saigon, working on some admin, when he found himself with a unique problem. Standing in front of him was an Australian, a former soldier, asking to re-enlist: 'He said, "Well, where am I allotted to?" I said there were no advisers expected today – we meet them on arrival. He replied, "Well, I am here." I asked for his papers . . . He replied, "I don't have any of those." I then realised we had a problem.'[1]

It is somewhat unusual for a civilian to turn up in a war zone to enlist. But, then, Ray Simpson, known to everyone as Simmo, was in many respects no ordinary soldier. In Michael Malone's biography of Simpson, Louise McClymans, widow of another AATTV soldier, Danny McClymans, remembers Simpson's decision to go: 'I think the most fantastic thing the man ever did . . . is he got himself back to Vietnam after he did his first stint over there. They didn't want him to go back . . . And he said to my husband, "I'll get there myself", and Danny said, "Oh, yeah?", not believing a word of it. Could you imagine anyone doing this? And he went straight out, got himself a job to save money for the trip. He worked on a cattle ship, took himself to Vietnam and just walked into the Australian station there, and said, "Where's my gear?"'[2]

Simpson was sent to a safe house in Da Nang while they decided what to do with him. Eventually, after sorting out his security clearance and paperwork, he was assigned a new regimental security number and sent to join the Provincial Reconnaissance Units at Pleiku Base in Kontum province. 'We were amazed,' Louise McClymans recalled. '[Danny] came back in '68 and said I've just been told Simmo walked in over there and straight into action.'[3]

* * *

Rayene (Ray) Simpson was born in Chippendale, Sydney, on 16 February 1926, the fifth child of Robert and Olga Simpson. He had four sisters and a younger brother. Simpson's early life was hard: his mother left when he was just three and his father struggled to find work as the Great Depression bit. The family moved in with Robert's mother in Darlington, but she, too, struggled to look after them. The upshot was that the girls were sent to the Church of England Girls' home in Carlingford, and Simpson and his younger brother to the Dalmar Children's Home in the same Sydney suburb. The aim of the institution was to 'rescue, body and soul . . . those little street urchins who were commonly known as nobody's children'. Many children were there through similar positions of hardship and it cannot have been an easy beginning to life. Simpson's father never visited his children and his mother came only once a year.

Simpson next went to the Carlingford District Rural School, which focused on training the children for a life on the land. When he was eleven he was sent to Dumaresq Island, further up the coast between Newcastle and Port McQuarrie, where he was lodged with a local family, going to the local primary school and working as an indentured labourer, children from orphanages often being put to work in this sway at the time. Simpson was desperate to join the army, especially with the outset of the Second World War, but was too young to join up. Until he was old enough to do so, he spent the next few years doing odd jobs on the wharves. In 1944, as soon as he was eighteen, he signed up.

Simpson began his training at the 14th Australian Infantry Training Battalion at Cowra, New South Wales, before going on to be schooled at the Jungle Warfare Training Course in Canungra, Queensland: although a soldier could join the army at eighteen, he could not be deployed until he was nineteen. Simpson got his first taste of action somewhat earlier when, in August 1944, more than 1,000 Japanese POWs attempted a mass breakout from the Cowra camp where they were being held. With the Japanese overpowering and killing four guards as they escaped, Simpson's battalion was called up to help restore order and bring back the escapees. Simpson himself was positioned on the Vickers Number One gun monitoring the compound fence.

Although he was shaping up to have the makings of an excellent soldier, Simpson also found himself repeatedly in trouble with the authorities. He went absent without leave in early 1945; he then received twenty-eight days' detention for 'using insubordinate language to a superior officer', not the last time he would be charged with such an offence. Once his training was completed, Simpson travelled on board HMS *Kanimbla* to the AIF (Australian Imperial Force) base in Morotai, Indonesia, and from here to, first, Tarakan as part of the 2nd/3rd Pioneer Battalion, and then to Rabaul, in Papua New Guinea, as part of the 26th Infantry Battalion. He returned to Australia in June 1946 and, having got into trouble again with the authorities (a combination of insubordinate language, drunkenness and 'conduct prejudicial to good order and military discipline'), he was demobilised in January 1947.

This, however, was just the beginning of Simpson's army career. After four years working at various jobs (as a tram conductor, labourer, sugar cane cutter and sailor, among others), he re-enlisted at the outbreak of the Korean War in 1950. Such was Simpson's concern that his previous bad behaviour might lead to him being rejected, he initially signed up under his brother's name. He joined 3RAR (the Royal Australian Regiment) as a rifleman shortly after the regiment had been instrumental in winning the Battle of Kapyong in April 1951. Simpson was assigned to A Company, who were based to the south of the Imjin River, a strategically important position which was blocking a Chinese route down towards Seoul.

In order to shore up the position, 3RAR was tasked with taking Hill 317, named Maryang San, which took place as part of Operation COMMANDO in October 1951. It was a successful if brutal battle, described by one historian as 'the greatest single feat of the Australian army during the Korean War' – it left twenty members of the regiment dead and another eighty-nine injured. More than 200 enemy soldiers were killed. Simpson himself, described laconically by his platoon sergeant as 'worth feeding', was promoted to lance corporal in November 1951, to corporal two months later and sergeant the following year (during this period of promotion, he also got married in Tokyo, to Shokai Shakai, whom he had first met on a previous visit to Japan).

Following Korea, Simpson saw action when he was sent to Malaya in 1955 as platoon sergeant for A Company in 2RAR. Australia, along with other SEATO (Southeast Asia Treaty Organization) countries, had committed troops to defend Malaya against communist insurgency; as well as more conventional tactics, the Australian troops also engaged in jungle warfare, employing small patrols. Simpson, enigmatically, was in the thick of the action. His second in command, Ron King, remembers that 'he would go out and leave us in position and then disappear, and he'd just piss off into the jungle. I have no idea what he did. He never explained it and I never asked.'[4]

In 1957, when a new Special Forces outfit was set up – 1st Special Air Service Company (SAS) – it was perhaps no surprise that Simpson was one of its first recruits. He was to serve with the company for five years, among other duties running training courses in unarmed combat. His reputation continued to grow; renowned both for his toughness and choice use of language, it became clear that he was bright and well read, particularly in military tactics and the art of war.

* * *

Since the mid-1950s, following the French withdrawal from Vietnam, the situation in that country had deteriorated. Post-colonial Vietnam found itself split between the communist-led north and the Western-sponsored south, with the latter fighting to retain control against the Viet Cong insurgents trying to overthrow the government. Politically, the struggle quickly took on a Cold War feel, with America and her allies supporting the south and the Soviet Union and China the north.

Following the American lead, in 1962 the Australian government decided to send a team of military advisers to assist the South Vietnamese government. The AATTV originally consisted of thirty men. Over the next decade, more than 900 would serve in the unit, reaching a maximum deployment of 100 at any one time.

Simpson was one of the original thirty sent over. Initially, he was sent to Lao Bao, near the border with Laos, where he helped to train the local people. He was then transferred to the Phu Bai Training Centre at Dong Da and given responsibility for Intelligence, Reconnaissance and what was euphemistically described as 'Special Subjects'. In July 1963 he returned to Australia and the SAS, where he used his experience in Vietnam to train up other possible AATTV recruits. It was a busy time for the company, with the men preparing for their first active service in Borneo.

Rather than heading for Borneo, however, Simpson returned to Vietnam, for his second tour, in 1964. He was sent to Ta Ko, an isolated American camp once again close to the Laotian border. Here he helped train members of the Civilian Irregular Defence Group (CIDG) in weapons handling, tactics and fieldcraft. The area for the base at Ta Ko was cleared in advance by napalming, and by the time Simpson and the others arrived the grass was still smouldering and with a smell similar to burnt sugar. The base was relatively cut off, with cloud and wet weather making it particularly difficult to get in and out.

On the morning of 16 September 1964, Simpson left the base as part of a thirty-man fighting patrol which included Americans, Australians and CIDG men. At 3 p.m. the patrol was ambushed as it approached an enemy camp. As they came under attack, Simpson set about organising the forward members of the patrol into a defensive position, and called for assistance. As he was doing so, he was hit in the leg, the bullet shattering his right femur.

Simpson was to receive both a Bronze Star with V (Valor) from the US Army and a DCM (Distinguished Conduct Medal) for his actions that afternoon. As his citation for the latter states:

> Despite his wounds, he rallied his platoon, formed a defensive position, contacted base by radio and, by personal example and inspiring leadership, held off repeated assaults by the Viet Cong force, until, with ammunition almost exhausted, and himself weak from a loss of blood, the relief force he had alerted arrived at the scene. Even then, not until he was satisfied that the position was secure and the troops of his patrol adequately cared for, did he permit himself to be evacuated.

By the time support arrived, Simpson was extremely weak: he was put on a saline drip and given morphine. Extracting him was no easy task given the isolated location, but once helicoptered out he was taken to hospital first in Nha Trang, and then, because of the seriousness of his injuries, to a US military hospital in Zama, Japan. Simpson was advised that his leg should be amputated, but he refused, saying, 'There are no jobs in the Army for one-legged soldiers'[5]. After many hours in theatre his leg was saved, but he had to undergo seven months of rehabilitation before he was finally allowed to leave hospital.

Simpson returned to hospital but, given his injuries, found himself medically downgraded and assigned to garrison duties only until he returned to full fitness. He was attached to 1 Commando Company, based in Sydney, as a training warrant officer. Little by little, he became requalified in Special Forces skills; officially banned from taking a parachute jump, he slipped in as 'Private Bloggs' to requalify as a paratrooper.

Simpson wanted to return to Vietnam and was on course to do so when, in 1965, he went to Gan Gan, a training camp in New South Wales used by commandos. What happened that night seems to depend a little on who is telling the story, but the essentials seem to be that a number of men were drinking boisterously in the canteen tent in an end-of-camp sort of way. As Michael Malone's biography of Simpson then describes it, 'The Adjutant, in an over-zealous attempt to close down proceedings and get the men to bed, threw a smoke grenade into the tent. The chaos that followed saw Simmo lose his temper and punch the Adjutant, as he saw this as a dangerous act in a confined space.'[6] Simpson might have had right on his side, but punching a senior officer is a difficult act to come back from; he was offered a court martial or a discharge. With tears streaming down his face, Simpson filled out the form for the latter and left the army.

For a brief while, Simpson tried to put the experience behind him and to slip into civilian life. Staying with his brother, Bob, he attempted to work for his company selling Rena Ware (pots and pans), a job at which he was hopeless. As Simpson colourfully described the experience years later, 'I couldn't sell a fuck to a sailor.' He tried, briefly, to join the US Army but they directed him back to the Australian Army. So, in 1967, he followed their advice, catching a flight to Saigon and sitting himself down in front of Bruce McIlwraith.

* * *

His papers sorted out, Simpson's third tour of Vietnam saw him assigned to a PRU (Provincial Reconnaissance Unit) at Pleiku Base in Kontum province. Essentially, the units were there to follow any North Vietnamese unit that entered South Vietnam along the Ho Chi Minh Trail (this jungle trail, in fact a series of trails, ran for 1,000 kilometres along the Vietnamese and Laos/Cambodian borders). The information Simpson's unit gleaned would then be passed to the local Vietnamese commander. Simpson helped with training, showing the units how to track without being spotted, and teaching them about tactics, clothing and equipment.

From here, Simpson moved to Mike Force as Platoon Commander of 232 Company 3rd Battalion, and then Company Commander of 231 Company 3rd Battalion in March 1969. It was for actions on 6 and 11 May while serving here that Simpson was to be awarded the Victoria Cross. In the first incident, Simpson was on what was known as a Search and Clear operation near the Laotian border when his unit came under heavy fire. Simpson led the fightback, during which one of his Platoon Commanders, Warrant Officer Mick Gill, was badly injured. As Simpson's citation reads, 'Warrant Officer Simpson, at great personal risk and under heavy enemy fire, moved across open ground, reached the wounded Warrant Officer and carried him to a position of safety. He then returned to his company where, with complete disregard for his safety, he crawled forward to within ten metres of the enemy and threw grenades into their positions.'

Five days later, as part of the same operation, word came over the radio that another warrant officer, Jock Kelly, was also badly injured. Simpson was one of the officers to respond, following his Battalion Commander, USSF Captain Martin Green, to the scene: tragically, Green was killed and 'at the risk of almost certain death' Simpson tried but failed to recover his body in the face of persistent enemy fire. His citation continues, 'Warrant Officer Simpson alone and still under enemy fire covered the withdrawal . . . until the wounded were removed from the immediate vicinity.'

Summing up, the citation concludes: 'Warrant Officer Simpson's repeated acts of personal bravery in this operation were an inspiration to all the Vietnamese, United States and Australian soldiers who served with him. His conspicuous gallantry was in the highest tradition of the Australian Army.'

* * *

After Simpson had been awarded the Victoria Cross, he became Platoon Commander of the Training Company, 2MSF Battalion at Plaiku, a move possibly intended to keep a Victoria Cross recipient out of harm's way. He left Vietnam in May 1970, received his award from the Queen in an investiture ceremony in Sydney the same month, and was discharged from the army for the final time a few weeks later.

Moving to Japan, Simpson initially found adjusting to civilian life as difficult as he had back in the mid-sixties. He taught English for a time and also tried selling whisky to the US military bases. Once more he flew to Vietnam to try to re-enlist, but this time was firmly turned down. Struggling for work, he returned to Sydney and his former commando unit, where former colleagues fixed him up as a cook's assistant. When the powers that be got wind of this, they decided that it would not make a good news story if it was discovered that a recipient of the Victoria Cross was working in a kitchen.

In 1972 a position was found for Simpson at the Australian embassy in Tokyo as a security guard-cum-admin officer, dealing with diplomatic couriers and managing their stay in the city (which often involved taking them for a drink or three). Not long after taking up his job, Simpson discovered he had a malignant lymphoma, which, it has been suggested, resulted from exposure to Agent Orange, the powerful herbicide and defoliant chemical used to devastating effect by the US Army in Vietnam. For whatever reason, Simpson kept his illness to himself for as long as possible. This, though, was one enemy he was unable to defeat, and he died from cancer in October 1978, aged just fifty-two.

Peter Billingham of the Royal British Legion knew Simpson in Tokyo. As he says in Michael Malone's biography, 'He left a host of saddened drinking buddies and . . . left a happy legacy in the shape of his beloved Bunker Bar in the Australian Embassy. After his death, Embassy members noticed that the Bunker Bar had not been cleaned and they were trying to find out who the cleaners were. It finally dawned on them that Simmo used to clean the bar himself every day with no fuss. A soldier to the last.'[7]

25

ENSIGN VIOLETTE SZABO GC

Introduced by Jeremy Irons

Violette Szabo, a twenty-three-year-old widowed mother, was parachuted twice into Nazi-held France to try to help organise part of the French Resistance shortly after the D-Day landings. When discovered, she kept the enemy at bay while her colleagues escaped; was captured, imprisoned, interrogated, and, having given nothing away, was sent to a labour camp and eventually executed by a bullet in the back of the neck.

I remember as a boy, watching the film of her exploits, being overwhelmed by her bravery and falling for Virginia McKenna who played her.

The courage, bravery and selflessness of this young woman was a lesson to me then, and I hope will be to all who read about her now.

In the spring and early summer of 2017, around the time I was writing this introduction, we witnessed humbling examples of bravery and selflessness by individuals under pressure that earned our admiration and respect. I hope that more of us will be motivated by their and Violette's example, to stand up for what we believe in and let the actions of those fine people encourage us all to become more proactive in our lives, and bear real responsibility both for the world we live in and the changes we must help make to bring about a better one.

In January 1947, four-year-old Tania Szabo was taken by her grandparents to Buckingham Palace. She was wearing, fittingly, a dress brought for her by her mother from Paris, and had been practising hard how to 'skurtsy', as she described it. ('Can't the poor child even say the word properly?' her grandfather had asked.)

As it turned out, Tania's 'skurtsying' was perfectly good. Remembering the occasion in her book *Young, Brave and Beautiful*, Tania recalls:

> I walked into a much larger room, but not huge. I think it was quite
> beautiful in a muted kind of way. And then the King came over to
> me – he was very tall and slim. Perhaps he had a navy-blue suit on.
> I curtsied as I knew so well how to do. And he leant forward and
> pinned the George Cross onto my right-hand side . . . He asked me
> to keep it carefully for my mother, for such a very brave lady, and I
> replied that I would always keep it. It is lovely: a fine massive silver
> cross nestling in a beautiful blue bow.[1]

The actions of Violette Szabo have long captured the public imagination: in the 1950s, a bestselling biography based on her life, *Carve Her Name With Pride*, by R. J. Minney, was turned into an equally successful film of the same name starring Virginia McKenna and Paul Scofield. It is easy to see why her life is one that continues to resonate: one of the first women to be awarded the George Cross, hers is a story that at its heart is about character, charisma and courage in the most desperate of conditions.

* * *

The starting point of the narrative that saw Violette Szabo ultimately awarded the George Cross can probably be traced back to Bastille Day 1940. At the time Violette Szabo was Violette Bushell. She'd been born in Paris in 1921, before her parents (Charles George Bushell and Reine Blanche Leroy) moved to Britain, eventually settling in Brixton, south London, in the early 1930s. Violette had five siblings: an elder brother, Roy, who was born in 1920, and younger brothers, John, Noël, Harry and Dickie (Harry died from diphtheria, aged five). Five foot five tall and striking, Violette left school at fourteen to work as a shop assistant. She was still working in a shop when war broke out.

By summer 1940, the London population had been swelled by the many French citizens who had fled their country and the Nazi occupation. On Bastille Day, the Free French Forces held a parade in the centre of London. Violette's mother, originally a dressmaker from Pont-Rémy and the one responsible for her daughter's fluent French, told Violette to watch the parade and to see if she could find a Frenchman, feeling homesick, who might like to come back and have a meal with the family. Violette did just that, inviting back a member of the French Foreign Legion, *Adjutant-chef* Etienne Michel René Szabo, to supper.

Etienne was a member of the 1st Battalion of the 13e Demi-Brigade de Légion Etrangère (DBLE), who had fought the Germans in Norway, before arriving in Britain via Brest to join the Free French Forces, under the leadership of General Charles de Gaulle. Supper with Violette's family was swiftly followed by a second date alone with Violette, and then a third. Even after Etienne had to return to barracks (Morval, near Farnborough in Hampshire), the courtship continued, the two of them seeing each other whenever they could. It didn't take long for Etienne to ask Violette's father for her hand in marriage. Or try to, anyway: Etienne's English was as limited as Violette's father's French, and the two communicated through a mixture of speaking and sign language. It was all quite sudden and Violette's parents may, too, have had concerns over the age difference: Etienne was thirty and Violette nineteen, which at the time meant that she needed parental approval to marry. Approval, however, was given and the pair married at Aldershot Registry Office on 21 August 1940, just over a month after they had first met.

After a week-long honeymoon, Etienne had to leave, travelling up to Liverpool where, along with the rest of the 13e DBLE, he boarded a ship for West Africa. Their task was to help persuade the forces there loyal to Vichy France to switch sides and join the Free French. Instead, when they arrived in Dakar, the Vichy French forces fought back. Orders changed and the 13e DBLE headed instead for Gabon where another confrontation with Vichy troops occurred, though this time the outcome was more successful. From here, Etienne continued his tour of Africa, heading down to Durban, South Africa, and then up the east side of the continent, fighting in first Eritrea and then Syria. By the time he arrived back in Liverpool, it was more than a year since he'd left England and last seen his wife.

He was met by Violette, by now with a plan of her own to do her bit for the war effort. Originally, Violette had taken a job as a telephonist, until a particularly heavy night's bombing in the Blitz flattened the exchange where she worked (Violette, thankfully, was not working there that night). When Etienne returned to the UK, Violette told him that she wanted to join the Auxiliary Territorial Service (ATS), to which Etienne reluctantly agreed. After training, she worked as part of an anti-aircraft battery until in early 1942, she discovered she was pregnant.

By the time Violette gave birth to Tania that June, Etienne was in Africa again, now stationed at the desert outpost of Bir Hakeim in Libya. Upon learning of Tania's birth, Etienne was desperate to return home, but leave proved impossible as events overtook the situation. In October, Etienne was injured in the Battle of El Alamein and then killed in the ambulance taking him away for medical treatment (records are unclear, but it appears the ambulance was hit by enemy fire or ran over a mine). He died never having seen his daughter. Violette's response was a determination to take the fight to the enemy herself: a desire that was rewarded when she was invited for an interview to join the British Special Operations Executive (SOE).

* * *

On 5 April 1944, Violette was parachuted into occupied France on the first of her missions for the SOE. She was flying in with Philippe Liewer, who was in charge of Salesman, the circuit he ran in Normandy of more than 300 members of the Resistance, carrying out acts of disruption and sabotage across the region. Liewer's circuit, however, was in trouble. His deputy, Claude Malreux, had been arrested in Rouen and it was necessary to discover just what the Germans knew about their activities. It was too high-risk for Liewer to travel there in person, so the job was assigned to his new courier, Violette Szabo.

Violette had completed her SOE training with mixed results. While excelling at some aspects, her assessors were more critical of others. Her general agent grading was a D and the summary of her abilities was varied. On the one hand it described her as 'a quiet, physically tough, self-willed girl of average intelligence. Out for excitement and adventure but not entirely frivolous.'[2] A second report from her paramilitary course, said, 'I seriously wonder whether this student is suitable for our purpose. She seems lacking in a sense of responsibility and although she works well in the company of others, does not appear to have any initiative or ideals.'[3] On the other hand, however, her assessors also noted that she 'has plenty of confidence in herself and gets on well with others. Plucky and persistent in her endeavours. Not easily rattled.'[4]

The more negative comments read as strange assessments in retrospect, for in the field Violette proved to be the very opposite of what these reports suggested: they seem to have been written about a completely different person from the one who risked everything for the war effort. Maybe that is the difference between how someone reacts in training and out in the field. Despite the misgivings about her ability, and further concerns that she spoke French with an English accent, Violette was sent out regardless; with D-Day approaching, information was crucial and the SOE were running desperately short of female couriers.

Violette's drop, from a Consolidated B-24 Liberator bomber, was not without incident. As she landed, she became caught up with the harness and struggled to free herself. As she lay there, in a hedgerow south of Paris, she immediately became aware of voices. Unable to move, she waited in silence, listening for whether they were speaking French or

German. The voices were French and then, to her relief, they walked on, leaving her undiscovered. It was a lucky break and one that balanced out her bad luck in her parachute training: on her first attempt, she had sprained an ankle on landing and had to be sent home to recuperate (an injury that, as we will see later, was to cost her dearly).

Having untangled herself and found Liewer, Violette went first to Paris and then on her own to Rouen by train. She was travelling as Corinne Leroy, a commercial secretary (the latter's mother's name) and the attention to detail was precise. Her clothes were French-designed; her bag, also French, was checked at the airfield to ensure that there was nothing to give away her identity, leaving behind only French money, French keys and her various false papers. Over three weeks, Violette carried out her investigative work to discover what had happened to Malreux and how damaged the Salesman circuit was. The fact that there were wanted posters with Liewer's picture on them was a good indication of how dire the situation was: in all, more than a hundred members of the Resistance had been arrested.

Violette made it back to Paris to inform Liewer of the situation. It must have been quite a shock to see the city of her early childhood so changed, now with food shortages, street signs in a different language and German soldiers on the Champs-Elysées. Violette did allow herself time to go shopping in the shops that were still open, while she waited for her return to England. Among her purchases was the dress that Tania would wear for the George Cross ceremony.

* * *

Six weeks later, Violette was back in France. The success of her first mission had led to her being promoted to Ensign in the FANY (First Aid Nursery Yeomanry, the cover name for female SOE agents). This second mission was, if anything, more hazardous than the first. Together again with Liewer, the aim was to set up a second Salesman circuit, this time between Limoges and Périgueux. Time and events were now pressing:

Violette landed in France on the night of 7/8 June, the day after the start of the D-Day landings.

From the very start, this operation did not go to plan. When Liewer and Violette arrived, the organisation they were expecting to encounter was somewhat lacking. 'When I left London,' Liewer wrote in a later report,

> I was given to understand that I would find on arrival a very well organised Maquis [Resistance fighters], strictly devoid of any political intrigues, which would constitute a very good basis for extending [the] circuit throughout the area. On arrival, I did find a Maquis which was roughly 600 strong, plus 200 gendarmes who joined up on D-Day; but these men were strictly not trained, and commanded by the most incapable people I have ever met; also most decided not to fight, as was overwhelmingly proved by the fact that none of the D-Day targets had been attended to.[5]

Liewer decided he needed help to set up his circuit and wanted to bring in Jacques Poirier, who ran another circuit further south called Digger, to help. To arrange this, he turned to Violette to make contact, sending her along with another agent, Jacques Dufour, and *maquisard* Jean Bariaud (Dufour was described in Tania Szabo's account as 'a risk-taking Pétainist gendarme committed to the Resistance'). Violette's cover was that she was Mme Villeret, the widow of an antiques dealer from Nantes: a cover compromised by the fact that, at her insistence, Liewer had given her a Sten gun with which to defend herself. The car they were driving, a large black Citröen, was also conspicuous in an area where petrol-fuelled cars were extremely rare.

Heading in the opposite direction to the three agents was the 2nd Panzer Division Das Reich, en route to Normandy. On the way, they had been ordered to intervene in a skirmish at the village of Guéret, where local *maquisards* had attacked a German garrison. During the fighting, the troop's commander, Helmut Kämpfe, was captured. The result was that the Germans had put up a number of roadblocks to try and find out what had happened to him: one of these was at Salon-la-Tour, on the route that Violette and her companions were travelling.

According to Liewer's later report, Dufour described what happened to him as follows:

> Nearing the village of Salon, we came, after a bend in the road, to a T junction. At a distance of fifty yards, I saw we were coming to a road block, manned by German soldiers who waved me to stop. I instantly put out my arm and waved back, slowed down and warned Szabo to get prepared to jump out and run. I stopped at thirty yards distance from the road block, jumped flat on the surface by the car, and started shooting – I noticed Bariaud, who was unarmed, running away, but found that Szabo had taken up a similar position to mine on the other side of the car, and was firing, too.[6]

The pair were heavily outnumbered. By how much varies from account to account – Tania Szabo's book suggests there were forty – but the two fell back, retreating into a maize field and heading for a wood about 400 yards away. Violette was nursing an injured arm, having been shot in her left shoulder during the exchange of fire. As Tania Szabo's book describes, 'it was stifling as they weaved between corn stalks, half-crawling or bent double, running and stumbling through sharp stalks, machine guns heavy in their hands, ready to fire. The corn tore at Violette's bare legs. They maintained their tactic of zigzag, turn, aim, shoot then zigzag again.'[7]

According to Tania Szabo's account, Violette 'stumbled into a half-hidden hole',[8] the ankle she had initially hurt in her parachute practice giving way. Mme Montintin, who was living at the nearby farm where Violette headed for, suggests her injury was as a result of being shot. Dufour's own account, meanwhile, makes no mention of the sprained ankle, suggesting instead she was simply exhausted and could go no further. Whatever the case, Szabo told Dufour to go, that she would cover him as he escaped. This she did, bravely keeping the advance troops at bay at a nearby farm for as long as she had bullets left, until Dufour was safe.

Violette was defiant when the Germans captured her. According to Mme Montintin's account, 'a German officer approached and offered her a cigarette. She spat in his face and didn't accept it.' Susan Ottaway's biography says, 'The German in charge of the roadblock is said to have told her that she was the bravest woman he had ever seen. He then saluted her, not a Nazi salute but a smart military salute, before ordering her to be taken away.'[9]

* * *

Violette was taken first to Limoges prison, and then on to Fresnes prison in Paris and 82–85 Avenue Foch, the Gestapo headquarters for the whole of France. She was interrogated in both Limoges and Paris, but held firm and refused to divulge any information. In August, Violette was deported, along with fellow agents Denise Bloch and Lilian Rolfe, and thirty-seven male prisoners to Saarbrücken camp in Germany. On the way, the train they were travelling in was attacked by Allied aircraft. The men, who were locked in a prison carriage, were trapped and fearful of being burned alive: the German guards did not release them but left the train, warning they would shoot anyone who tried to escape. Violette, chained to another prisoner, crawled along the corridor to give the men water as the bombing continued.

Saarbrücken was a transit camp and from here Violette was sent to the concentration camp of Ravensbrück, to the smaller camp of Torgau and the punishment camp of Klein Königsberg. To say the conditions in these camps were appalling would be to do a huge disservice to those who suffered them. Ravensbrück, a concentration camp for 'criminals and enemies of the state', was designed for 7,000 inmates: in fact, 43,000 had been taken there by June 1944, and a further 90,000 by the following March. Overcrowded and disease-ridden, in the camp the inmates were kept close to starvation and made to work hard – Violette was one of many on stone-breaking duties. Roll call for work started at half past three in the morning and an hour later in winter, regardless of the weather. Beatings were common.

At Torgau, essentially a slave labour camp, Violette found herself making munitions: she and her colleagues were ordered to obey or be shot. Despite the conditions, Violette continued her defiance, sabotaging and obstructing the factory's work as much as she could get away with, making plans with others about how they might escape. This was not to happen. At the beginning of January 1945, Violette was returned to Ravensbrück, along with Denise Bloch and Lilian Rolfe. There the three women were summarily executed, shot in the back of the neck by an SS officer and cremated.

Violette Szabo was twenty-three when she was killed, but in her short life her courage and belief shone through – she set out to do her part for the war effort, and did so admirably. Her actions led to her being one of the first women ever to be awarded the George Cross, as well as the *Croix de guerre* by the French government in 1947 – an award also awarded to her late husband – and also the *Médaille de la Résistance*. Violette Szabo's is a story of bravery that has captured the imagination of generations ever since; a story that has been told and retold many times over the years, but one that has never lost its impact or meaning.

26

CAPTAIN
CHARLES UPHAM VC (AND BAR)

Introduced by Tom Ward

'Obstinate, pugnacious, independent, blunt, tactless, hard-swearing, highly strung, careless in his dress.' As a concise summary of the traits the modern parent is urged to excise from their children, this could hardly be bettered. How gratifying, then, that it is in fact a contemporary description of Captain Charles Upham, VC and Bar.

Yes, VC and Bar – that elegantly understated suffix tells you that we are talking about a unique man: the only combat soldier to have been awarded the Victoria Cross twice. And, what's more, he survived – returning, like an old Roman, to live on his farm in peace.

After reading this brilliant account of Upham's exploits, I felt awed, unsurprisingly; painfully inadequate, obviously; and slightly guilty. It is a story that could be straight from the Commando comics I used to love as a ten-year-old: of a no-nonsense New Zealander, dispatching the bad guys with tommy gun and grenade; defying superiors and the enemy alike with insouciant one-liners; exhorting his more circumspect comrades to show their very best. It is a story where a leap into the darkness from a speeding train is little more than an aside. It is utterly thrilling.

Hence, no longer being ten, the self-reproach. This was real. Those grenades did not explode in the five black pen lines of Commando, but in a cloud of blood and bone and noise; the friends dying all around did not

316

get forgotten at the end of the chapter; the bad guys were not always bad, but perhaps young and terrified themselves, with stories of their own.

So, I humbly thank and salute you, Captain Upham, not in celebration of war, but in celebration of your unbelievable courage, resilience and resourcefulness (or obstinacy, pugnacity and independence, if you like), in the face of war's horror.

It's still a thrilling story, though.

Summer 1944, Weinsberg prison. Charles Hazlitt Upham was a prisoner of war with a plan. He'd been at the Black Forest camp for almost a year and was desperate to escape. This time, he thought he'd cracked it. Watching the guards on manoeuvres, patrolling the perimeter fence, Upham had spotted a small but significant change to their routine. Rather than there being three guards patrolling, ensuring enough overlap so that all the fence was in eyesight at all times, now there were only two. With the guard in the tower more interested in watching the young lovers out in the field beyond, there was suddenly a window for escape – a short period, no more than forty-five seconds, when the corner of the fence was unguarded.

To attempt to escape from the prison camp in broad daylight was considered nigh-on impossible. What Upham also had to achieve in those forty-five seconds, day or night, was also challenge enough in itself: first, pass the tripwire and low apron fence to scale the inner of the two main fences; leap from that over the bushes of barbed wire to land on the outer fence; scale that, get down and run before the guards realised what was happening and the machine gun in the tower was turned on him.

Upham, though, was a soldier unafraid of taking risks. Having arranged with some of the other prisoners to create a diversion, he waited for his moment . . . and ran. The first part of his plan went smoothly, and he was up onto the top of the inner fence in no time. But just as he was about to leap across to the outer fence, disaster struck: a staple went on the fence, slackening the wire. His leap lost all impetus and, rather than reaching the second fence, he only made it as far as the bundles of barbed wire in between.

Landing on those was painful enough, but Upham was now stuck and it was only a matter of time before his failed escape was discovered. Sure enough, a shout from outside alerted the guards, who came running for Upham, guns ready. The prisoners who'd been causing the diversion came running over, too, grimly awaiting Upham's inevitable fate. Sure enough, a German corporal appeared, pistol drawn, shouting that he was going to finish off the errant prisoner.

Upham, however, was no ordinary soldier. In front of the assembled crowd he reached into his pocket and took out a cigarette. Then, slowly, deliberately, he lit it. It was a bold, confident move that completely caught the corporal off guard. Gun still raised, he wavered, uncertain of what to do next. Behind the fence, the Senior British Officer had arrived and shouted at Charlie to see what he was going to do. 'Nothing,' he replied, according to the account in his biography, *Mark of the Lion*.[1] 'They can damned well come and get me. And I refuse to be shot by a bloody corporal. Tell 'em to bring an officer.'

The stand-off continued. When an officer finally arrived, he too shouted over at Upham to ask what he was doing. Getting no response, he produced a camera and proceeded to take a series of photographs, to prove to his superiors precisely what he had on his hands here. Then, with a sigh, he said, 'You are a very, very brave man, Captain Upham. Now please come out.' Only when the Senior British Officer ordered him to did Upham finally put his cigarette out, and was escorted down to the cells.

* * *

'Was he New Zealand's greatest soldier of the Second World War?' the journalist T. P. McLean once considered. 'The question,' he concluded, 'is unimportant. He was Charles Hazlitt Upham. Charlie Upham. Unforgettable.'

Unforgettable is certainly the word. Upham was not, in many senses, your model soldier: 'obstinate, pugnacious, independent, blunt, tactless, hard-swearing, highly strung, careless in his dress'[2] was one description. Yet his unswerving loyalty to his men and his absolute bravery without thought to his own safety was absolute. It led to him being one of those extremely rare soldiers to be awarded the Victoria Cross not once, but twice. Such was the unusual nature of this achievement that Upham's superior officer, Major General Howard Kippenberger was called in by King George VI to ask whether he deserved such an award. 'In my respectful opinion,' Kippenberger told the King, 'Upham won the VC several times over.'

Charles Upham was born in Christchurch on 21 September 1908. His father, John, was a prominent barrister and solicitor; his mother, Agatha, was the daughter of a clergyman. Charles was the Uphams' only son (he had three sisters) and in this comfortable upbringing he was described as shy and courteous, but also with an early streak of determination. His nanny recounted a story of Upham's dislike for fish – so much so that after being made to eat it for lunch, he kept it in his mouth for two hours, before finally agreeing to swallow it.

Having been a boarder at Christ's College, Christchurch, Upham resisted following the family path into law, saying, 'I'd always be jealous of my friends on farms.' That was what he wanted to do, and went to Canterbury Agricultural College (also known as Lincoln College), to study for a Diploma in Agriculture. Having achieved this, he began six years of learning his craft on the land as a sheep farmer, musterer and farm manager. He got to know the land inside out, a knowledge of reading the landscape that would prove invaluable later on as a soldier. From here, Upham's life continued its upwards trajectory: he met and proposed to his future wife Molly; joined the government's land valuation department and returned to Lincoln College for further training in valuation and farm management. As with so many other careers and life plans, however, events intervened. When war broke out in 1939, Upham was determined to do his part, and was among the first to volunteer.

The Principal of Lincoln College, Professor Eric Hudson, was moved to write to the military about Upham – the only one of his students for which he did so. 'A young man by the name of Upham has left the College to join your unit,' he wrote to Commanding Officer of Burnham Military Camp. 'I commend him to your notice, as, unless I'm greatly mistaken, he should be an outstanding soldier.'

Right from the start of his training the army discovered a soldier of both strength and strong opinions. On one occasion he went to see Colonel Kippenberger to ask for unscheduled leave in order 'to give a chap a hiding'. The man in question owed Upham money for a car but hadn't paid up. Kippenberger, amused, agreed. On Upham's return he asked whether he'd got the money, to which Upham said no. 'Did you give him a hiding?' Kippenberger asked. 'Yes, sir, I did,' Upham replied with a grin.[3]

Then there was the time that a new lawn needed laying around the Battalion HQ. Upham, with his training, was put forward for the job. 'The war's not going to be won by laying down ruddy lawns,' he told his captain. 'Is it an order?'[4] he asked, before being told it was. When Upham was selected to be put forward for the Officer Cadet Training Unit, he asked Kippenberger if the training might stop him going overseas with the battalion. When Kippenberger said he couldn't make a promise either way, Upham asked to be taken off the list: 'I don't want to be mucking about in New Zealand.' As it happened, Upham's hopes were quickly met: he was subsequently selected for the advance party from New Zealand, one of just fifty-two soldiers drawn from the training camps across the country.

* * *

As part of the New Zealand Division in Egypt, Upham continued both his training and his singular attitude to proceedings. As Kenneth Sandford wrote in *Mark of the Lion*:

Intent on learning the essentials of fighting, and nothing else, he showed no affection for parade-ground niceties, little respect for the conventions of Army life and rank. Indeed, it is a wonder he escaped arraignment for plain insubordination. He would speak bluntly to everyone, whatever their rank. He became quickly intolerant of the many artificialities of the Army system, outspoken about anything that did not immediately appear to help the business of fighting and winning a war.[5]

His bluntness with those higher up was balanced by the loyalty the men in his command held for him. They called him 'boss'; he called them by their first names. Given command of his own platoon, his skills as a farmer of knowing the land came to the fore: he had a natural eye for terrain and how to use it. Not that everyone understood his instinct immediately, however. On one training exercise a supervising officer looked at Upham's planned deployment and told him to move his men. Upham, who thought he was right and the supervising officer wrong, refused – even when the supervising officer told him it was an order and he could be arrested if he didn't follow it. Upham's response was he didn't think that was possible: 'We're out in the desert here, and I'd have a right to insist on two NCOs of equal rank to escort me – and there aren't two other sergeants within three miles.'

Upham was put forward again for officer training, despite his Battalion Adjutant's reservations: 'I doubt if he'd make a good officer. Rough as guts . . . he's the scruffiest we've got, but he's a hell of a good soldier,' he told Kippenberger[6]. This time Upham didn't decline, and the Adjutant's opinion seemed justified: out of the list of those who'd passed the training, Upham's name was right at the bottom. He was assigned to 15 Platoon of C Company, a unit made up of men from the west coast of New Zealand's South Island: 'the isolated, law-unto-itself part of New Zealand', as Sandford describes it.[7] It was a good match: Upham took one look at his rugged new charges and told them, 'You look a pretty tough mob to me. But you don't look fit. In fact, you look like a lot of boozers.' The platoon, in turn, had the tough talking officer they needed to lick them into shape.

Finally, Upham saw the first glimmers of action he'd been desperate to partake in. In March 1941, the New Zealand Division was moved to Greece, to help defend it in the face of German attack. Upham's unit were sent to Katerini, about 300 miles north of Athens, where they were to defend the village of Riakia. Sweeping through Yugoslavia, the German attack, which began on 6 April, was swift. The Katerini defences were in danger of being isolated, and within forty-eight hours Upham's battalion was being pulled back. They were repositioned near Mount Olympus, positioned on a crossroads, monitoring the refugees escaping from the north (the Germans were advancing centrally through the Monastir Gap). After several days of heavy aerial bombardment, Upham's battalion withdrew again, this time to Thermopylae. Here, too, the pattern was repeated: the Greek forces were no match for the Germans, and the New Zealand troops were in danger of being cut off. The decision was made to evacuate. Upham's unit, part of the 4th Brigade, was given the job of being the delaying force at Kriekouki, near Athens, while the 5th and 6th Brigades made good their withdrawal.

For Upham, the pain of withdrawal was reinforced by pain of a more physical nature. He had dysentery and was barely able to eat or walk. All he could get down in terms of food was condensed milk, for which he sent his troops to forage for tins. Unable to travel on foot, he found himself a donkey and rode from section post to section post. It was as ignominious as the Allied retreat itself.

* * *

In total, some 32,000 Allied troops were evacuated from Greece to Crete. The troops were taken here to save time – Crete being only 100 kilometres away from Greece – rather than the longer sea journey back to Egypt. But instead of then being sent straight on, the troops were ordered to stay in Crete, in the hope of repelling the imminent German invasion. The result was another major military miscalculation – 'the Gallipoli of its era', as Glyn Harper described it in *In the Face of the Enemy*.[8] Once again, the Allied troops found themselves unable to stop the German advances, first pulling back and then attempting an evacuation: this time, not all the troops could be taken off, and the campaign ended with some 6,500 men left behind, ending up as POWs.

But while the Battle of Crete was a strategic disaster, the Allied troops on the island itself fought hard and with distinction – and none more so than the example of Charles Upham, one of three soldiers to be awarded the Victoria Cross for his endeavours. As his citation says, 'during the operations in Crete, this officer performed a series of remarkable exploits, showing outstanding leadership, tactical skill and utter indifference to danger'.

Upham's battalion was first involved in attempts to retake Maleme airfield, of which German paratroopers had taken control. As Upham was leading his platoon towards the airfield, they came under heavy fire from a German machine gun. With the rest of the platoon dropping to the ground and edging forwards on their stomachs, Upham crawled his way round to behind the position to attack. As one eyewitness described the incident,

> although it was still dark, we could tell by the way the Jerries were shouting to each other that they didn't like the look of the situation. When he got round behind the tree the platoon officer jumped to his feet and hurled three Mills bombs, one right after another, into the nest and then jumped forwards with his revolver blazing. Single-handed he wiped out seven Jerries with their Tommy guns and another with a machine-gun.[9]

Upham's night was just beginning. Under attack from two more machine guns in a house and shed respectively, Upham ran to the shed under covering fire. Here, he put a grenade in a dead German's hand and shoved him into the shed. Following the explosion, eight German soldiers came out and surrendered. Turning his attention to the machine gun in the house, Upham ran forward again, this time lobbing a grenade in through the open window to silence the enemy fire.

For all Upham's heroics, however, his work was undone by the fact that the counter-attack was ordered too late. By the time they reached the airfield, it was broad daylight and advancing any further was impossible. As the troops began to withdraw, it became clear that D Company had become cut off from the rest of the battalion. Upham took it upon himself to find the missing company, taking his sergeant with him for the journey through 600 yards of open, exposed enemy territory: Upham killed two more Germans for good measure. He then led a small group to retrieve the wounded, using wooden doors as makeshift stretchers to carry them back.

During the withdrawal from Maleme, Upham was hit by mortar shrapnel in the left shoulder, which he first ordered his platoon sergeant to cut out and then was told to have properly treated. Three days later, at his platoon's new defensive position at Galatas, Upham went ahead to observe the enemy. Bringing them forward when the Germans advanced, they killed more than forty enemy soldiers and forced the rest to fall back. When his platoon was ordered to withdraw, it was Upham again who went forward to tell the other troops. Fired on by two Germans, Upham, with only one good arm after the shrapnel surgery, found a tree with a fork in which he could rest his rifle. He killed both his combatants, and just in time: the second German was so close he fell onto the muzzle of Upham's rifle.

By now, the Allied withdrawal was in full swing, with the troops making their way to Sphakia, a forty-mile trek across to the other side of the island. It was here that a group of about fifty Germans had managed to outflank the New Zealanders, getting in a position where they could reach and shoot at the evacuation beach. Upham and his men were given the job of climbing along the ravine and attacking the Germans. It took two hours to get the firing party into position, Upham with his Bren gun on top of the ravine. 'By clever tactics,' Upham's citation explains, 'he induced the enemy party to expose itself and then at a range of 500 yards shot 22 and caused the remainder to disperse in panic.'

As the citation concludes, 'During the whole of the operations he suffered from dysentery and was able to eat very little, in addition to being wounded and bruised. He showed superb coolness, great skill and dash and complete disregard of danger. His conduct and leadership inspired his whole platoon to fight magnificently throughout, and in fact was an inspiration to the Battalion.'

* * *

Upham's second Victoria Cross was awarded for his efforts in North Africa. Having arrived back from Crete, the 2nd New Zealand Division fought as part of British Eighth Army over the next two years. The first battle it took part in, Operation CRUSADER, Upham was not involved, chosen by Kippenberger to be one of the officers LOB (left out of battle). The 20th Battalion was badly overrun and indeed, overall, more than 4,600 of Upham's countrymen lost their lives, the costliest battle for New Zealand in the entire war.

After time in Syria, Upham's unit was ordered back to Egypt in June 1942. Eighth Army were suffering badly at the hands of Rommel, and the New Zealand troops found the army retreating as the Axis forces moved forwards. The 2nd New Zealand Division attempted to set up a defensive position at Minqâr Qaim, but quickly found themselves surrounded on three sides. Upham kept his troops going in near-impossible circumstances: Glyn Harper notes that he was 'inspirational, at one stage standing on the cab of a truck to attract the fire of nearby German infantry so the New Zealand mortars could target them'.[10] The battalion history describes how Upham 'with characteristic coolness, moved around his company on foot, crossing open ground swept by small-arms and mortar fire, steadying one platoon which was under shellfire and encouraging his men'.

Such was the desperate nature of the circumstances that on the following night (27/28 June) the decision was made to break out of the encirclement, with 20th Battalion one of three chosen to punch through the German lines. Upham was in his element – armed with his pistol and a haversack of grenades, he took out one vehicle after another, killing numerous Germans in the process. After the battle, Brigadier Kim Burrows, who was in command of 4 Brigade, told Kippenberger that Upham should be awarded a second Victoria Cross for his actions.

In fact, the citation for Upham's second Victoria Cross states it is awarded for 'commanding a Company of New Zealand troops in the Western Desert during the operations which culminated in the attack on El Ruweisat Ridge on the night of 14th–15th July, 1942'. This latter battle followed swiftly on from Minqâr Qaim, with the 2nd New Zealand Division ordered to take the ridge along with 5 Indian Brigade: the ridge was ten miles long and although not high, dominated the area.

As the battle for the ridge went on ahead, Upham's battalion was one of those held back. Brigadier Burrows told Upham to send someone up to see what was happening before he committed his troops: Upham, typically, insisted on going himself, travelling by jeep through heavy gunfire to recce the situation. With the order to attack that followed, Upham again led the charge. As his citation describes it, 'Captain Upham, without hesitation, at once led his Company in a determined attack on the two nearest strongpoints on the left flank of the sector. His voice could be heard above the din of battle cheering on his men and, in spite of the fierce resistance of the enemy and the heavy casualties on both sides, the objective was captured.'

It came at a cost, however. Upham was badly wounded by machine-gun fire – he was shot through the elbow and his arm was broken. Not that it stopped him carrying on, continuing to lead the charge. The ridge was taken, but with armoured support not arriving and numbers dwindling, the position of Upham and his men was insecure, to say the least. Upham went to the RAP (Regimental Aid Post) for medical treatment, before returning to rejoin his company. Unfortunately, he was hit again – this time in the leg by a mortar shell. Upham was now unable to walk, and, with his company reduced to just six, he and his remaining men were taken prisoner by the advancing Axis forces.

* * *

For Upham, his war – in the fighting sense – was over. Taken from prison camp to prison camp over the next three years, he tried repeatedly to escape. After the 'cigarette' escape described earlier, he was moved to Oflag IVC, more familiar as Colditz, for better security: even on the way here, Upham attempted another escape, locking himself in the lavatory, smashing the window and leaping out of the train, at full speed, and into the pitch black of night. He managed to stay away for the best part of a day and night before he was recaptured. Colditz proved too tough even for Upham to escape from, and he was still there when Allied troops liberated it in April 1945.

The one person who didn't feel he deserved the medals and accolades was Upham himself. Back in New Zealand at the time it was announced he'd been awarded the VC for a second time, Upham's response was, 'It's wrong. They shouldn't give it to me. What about all the others? We all did exactly the same thing.'[11] His response to a letter of congratulations from one friend was even more curt: 'Thanks for your note. Lot of bloody nonsense. Yours, Charles.'[12] Certainly, Upham hated the limelight and the huge publicity that came with such a double honour. A fund was set up to help buy him a farm; although the total was reached, Upham refused to accept the money and it was put to use as a scholarship fund instead.

Upham had been presented with his first VC by the Commander-in-Chief Middle East, General Sir Claude Auchinleck, back in North Africa after the escape from Crete. In front of the whole of 4 Brigade, Auchinleck pinned the medal on him with the words, 'Congratulations,

Upham. New Zealand will be very proud that you've won this decoration.' Upham's reply was, 'I didn't win it, sir.' To which Auchinleck responded, 'Then if you didn't, Upham, I don't know who did.'

As he stood back, his senior officers looked on in horror as he forgot to salute the Commander-in-Chief. It was only after Upham had retreated twenty paces that he remembered and gave a hasty salute. That wasn't Upham's only faux pas: on a day when he was meant to look his smartest, the officers noticed that he'd turned up wearing a pair of yellow socks. As Upham's biographer noted, it summed the man up perfectly: 'On one hand an intense desire to do the correct thing militarily and to fight the war to his utmost; at the same time an innocent indifference to many of the traditions and formalities of military life.'

27

LIEUTENANT COLONEL THE REVEREND
BERNARD VANN VC

Introduced by the Rt Rev and Rt Hon Lord Chartres KCVO

Over 3,000 Anglican priests served as Chaplains during the course of the First World War but more than 500 clergy of the Church of England decided to volunteer in combatant roles.

The Archbishop of Canterbury, Randall Davidson ruled that the role of a combatant was 'incompatible with the position of one who has sought and received Holy Orders'. Other bishops however disagreed and Frank Weston, Bishop of Zanzibar went so far as to raise and command the Zanzibar Carrier Corps which saw active service.

Randall Davidson's view was certainly in harmony with the teaching of the early church but Bernard Vann was determined to share in the dangers faced by the ordinary soldier in what he believed was a war in defence of civilisation against barbarous militarism. The post-war generation, influenced especially by the war poets, came to see the war as largely senseless but it remains true that civilisations die in the night when no one can be found to give their lives for them.

Bernard Vann was utterly committed to what he regarded as a righteous cause. He was a courageous leader who actually led. As one contemporary said of him, 'His convictions were strong. His religion made him happy. His happiness was infectious'. He was repeatedly in the thick of battle. He was wounded many times and was given the ultimate accolade of the

VC but he never forgot that he was a priest. The wording on his headstone reads simply 'A great priest who in his days pleased God'.

A number of photographs survive of Bernard Vann, but the most arresting is a portrait of him staring steadfastly at the camera. It was taken late in 1916 and the ribbon of his first Military Cross is already stitched across his right breast pocket. Vann was twenty-nine at the time. On his head he wears a service cap that is a little battered and which suggests hard-won experience. His face is full, square-jawed and sturdily handsome. Pale blue eyes look down the lens with a mixture of sadness and stoicism. Below the trim military moustache, his mouth curves slightly. Is that a smile? If so, it is one more enigmatic than that of the Mona Lisa. There is something compelling about this photograph; good looks that hint at a lot more. There is a real person there, once flesh and blood. A man who has already seen much in his short life, but who has the resolve and wherewithal to see yet more.

By all accounts, Bernard Vann was an extraordinary man and a truly worthy recipient of the Victoria Cross. So often it is hard to look at the photographs of that First World War generation and be able to see much of the person behind the black and white image. Not so with Vann. His is a portrait of a leader of men, quite palpably someone whom others would always follow into battle. And so his men always did, through three and a half years of brutal war in which he was wounded on more than eight occasions, decorated for valour multiple times, and who rose from subaltern to commanding a battalion. Intelligent, amusing, a superb sportsman, and adored by his men, he was a quite exceptional person in every regard. And, perhaps most surprisingly of all for such a decorated warrior, he was also an ordained priest.

Bernard Vann was born in July 1887 in the Northamptonshire village of Rushden, the fourth son of five. His father, Alfred, was the head teacher at South End Elementary School in the village, where his mother,

Hannah, taught, too. His parents were both from humble backgrounds, but Alfred was clever and ambitious, and between his teaching studied at Oxford University where, a year after Bernard was born, he gained his masters. With this academic qualification to his name, Alfred was able to leave South End Elementary behind and in 1899 became headmaster at Chichele Grammar School in nearby Higham Ferrers. All his sons gained places there, too, providing them with an education they would otherwise have been unable to afford. Bernard excelled at Chichele, both academically and on the playing field, where he had a natural gift. During his time at the school he became captain of football, hockey and cricket.

Tragically for the family, Bernard's father died comparatively young in 1906, when Bernard was nineteen. His mother initially stayed in Higham Ferrers and then in 1908 was appointed headmistress of the National school in Church Stowe Northamptonshire. She left in 1914 to live with her unmarried brother, the Reverend Thomas Simpson, the Rector of Coates, near Cirencester in Gloucestershire. Bernard, who by the time of his father's death had left school, took up his first professional post as a teacher at Ashby-de-la-Zouch Grammar School in Leicestershire. There he quickly gained a reputation for his charismatic approach to teaching and for the profound influence he had upon his pupils. He also continued to play as much sport as he could, including hockey for Leicestershire and football for Northampton Town, along with his brother Harry. The brothers impressed and both were invited to play for Burton United, then a member of the Football League, as amateurs during the 1906–7 season. Vann made his league debut in a 1–1 draw against Barnsley on 16 February 1907. After playing four more games for Burton, he was invited to join Derby County, making his first appearance on 23 March that same year.

Derby County, or the Rams as they are still known today, were already a major club at this time. Although relegated to the Second Division in 1906, they had been runners-up in the First Division in 1896 and had appeared in three FA Cup finals. Vann's career with them was short-lived, however, as in the autumn of 1907 he went up to Cambridge to read history at Jesus College. Nonetheless, by that time he had played against such notable clubs as Aston Villa, Chelsea and Notts County, and scored a goal against Wolverhampton Wanderers.

By all accounts, Bertie, as he was known at university, threw himself into varsity life, co-founding The Roosters debating club where he gained a reputation for his flamboyant speeches. Charismatic and dynamic, he was a highly popular figure within the college. He also continued to play as much sport as possible, captaining Jesus at football and winning a blue for hockey. It seems all this sport and social life came to the detriment of his academic studies, however; he scraped a third in his Part I tripos and a second in his Part II.

Vann had always been a practising Christian and while at Ashby-de-la-Zouch had helped take the New Pilgrim Club on a football tour of Bohemia (part of the modern-day Czech Republic), Austria and Hungary. Even so, pragmatism as much as faith probably influenced his decision to train for the ministry in the Church after leaving Cambridge in the summer of 1910. The family was not at all well off and, financially, he had done well to make it through his time at Cambridge. He had been helped, as a potential candidate for Holy Orders (selected by the Bishop of Peterborough), with some financial support from the Diocese of Peterborough. For a graduate with his modest background, his professional options were limited. By becoming a vicar he was pursuing a respectable and comfortable career for someone of his station in life. He took up a post as assistant curate at St Barnabas in Leicester and was ordained at Peterborough Cathedral. Just over two years later, Vann took up a far more suitable post for someone of his interests as chaplain and assistant master at Wellingborough School, where he also taught history and theology and where he was able to indulge his passion for sport by coaching football and cricket.

Had it not been for the advent of war Vann would most probably have remained a schoolmaster all his life, but no sooner had Britain declared war on Germany and the Central Powers on 4 August 1914 than he rushed to join up, applying to become an army chaplain. Naturally impetuous, when he learned his application to become a chaplain would take some time, he discarded his dog collar and with another of his brothers, Harry, joined up as an ordinary soldier, becoming a private in the 28th (County of London) Battalion, the Artists Rifles. Accepted on 31 August, two days later he was granted a commission and posted as a second lieutenant to the 1/8th Sherwood Foresters.

The regiment was a line infantry regiment, formed only in 1881 from the old 45th and 95th Regiments of Foot in the Nottinghamshire and Derbyshire Militia, the forerunner of the Territorials, so it was as part of the Territorial Force that Second Lieutenant Bernard Vann was obliged to wear the brass 'T' on his jacket lapel beneath the regimental crest. The British Army serving in France in February 1915 – when Vann reached the Continent – was already rapidly expanding but was very much two armies: the old, pre-war professional one and those in the Territorial Force, hurriedly called up for front-line duty now that the country was at war. Perhaps not unsurprisingly, the regulars tended to rather look down their noses at their territorial cousins, with the regular Sherwood Foresters already having a proven track record, having served in India on the North West Frontier and in South Africa during the Anglo-Boer War.

Once out in France, Vann quickly proved that he had not merely swapped the Bible for a rifle. Rather, he continued to help with religious duties whenever he could and remained a devout Christian. He also soon proved himself a fearless soldier who always led from the front and who, like all the very best officers, would never consider asking his men to do anything he was not prepared to do himself.

By the time he had reached the front the days of mobile warfare were already a thing of the past and both sides were hastily constructing the vast network of trenches that would become such a feature of the Western Front for the next three years. Towards the end of April, the Sherwood Foresters were desperately trying to hold their positions around Kemmel, south-west of Ypres, in the face of a major German offensive. By 23 April, they were coming under heavy fire, which was causing terrible damage to the front-line trenches they were holding. As the men furiously tried to repair the parapets at the top of the trenches and dig a new communication trench they were also suffering from the effects of the first ever use of gas, introduced to the battlefield the previous day. Although most of it had dispersed, the men's eyes were still smarting and the smell permeating the battlefield was deeply unpleasant. Without proper gas masks at this stage, the men had to make do with wetted handkerchiefs placed over their eyes and mouths.

At around 6 p.m. the following day, 24 April, another parapet was blown down and two platoons were withdrawn after eight men were killed and a further six wounded. Everyone expected a German assault to follow but it never appeared, and by 8.30 p.m. the parapet had been repaired and the two withdrawn platoons were back at their posts. A little further along the Foresters' line was Lieutenant Vann and his platoon and now it was their turn to come under fire. Suddenly, more shells began whistling over and soon a part of their parapet was blown in, too. Vann was buried in mud and earth but quickly dug himself out and then carried on digging out the other buried men, only for another shell to hurtle down, killing six and wounding eight. Vann was thrown eight yards into the air and, despite being badly bruised and shaken, scrambled to his feet and continued the rescue work. 'All Lt. Vann's platoon behaved splendidly,' noted the duty officer, 'under very trying circumstances.'[1]

The battalion was relieved later that night but, rather than be sent down the line to a field hospital, Vann insisted on remaining with his men and recovered slowly and by sheer willpower. A few days later at Sanctuary Wood, a neighbouring unit, just arrived in France, quickly became confused and disorientated by their first experience of sustained enemy fire and the Germans' use of flame throwers. Vann, armed only with a service revolver, hurried along the line to provide leadership and encouragement, and by his obvious confidence and disregard towards danger was able to restore morale at this critical moment.

Much of life in the front line became a matter of holding positions, going out on patrols, improving trenches and sending wiring parties into no man's land. This was a regular night-time operation in which men stole into no man's land to create fields of barbed wire in an effort to deter the enemy from attacking. Often wire was damaged from shelling so needed repairing, too. Vann provided encouragement, cheeriness and an example of boundless energy to his men. Out of the line, he was always willing to organise and play in football matches, and invested in his men a sense of discipline, hope and the need for constant training. Vann did not tolerate 'slackers' – but such men were few and far between, first in the platoon he commanded, and then, by June 1915, in his company. By this time, he was an acting captain and in August was awarded a Military Cross for his gallantry at Kemmel and at Sanctuary Wood.

Although the war on the Western Front had descended into an attritional stalemate, both the British and French were determined it should not remain that way. A large-scale offensive was planned over the summer, which, it was hoped, would be both large and concentrated enough to create a decisive breakthrough. This was to be the Battle of Loos, and was launched in September, even though there were those among the British commanders, not least General Sir Douglas Haig of First Army, who believed the British did not yet have the weight of artillery fire to enable their infantry to break through.

Haig's fears were soon justified and among the early casualties was Vann's brother, Harry, also by then a captain with the 12th West Yorkshires, who was killed on 25 September 1915. Vann himself was badly wounded during an assault on the Hohenzollern Redoubt, a German strongpoint formed around a series of old slag heaps and pit heads in the coal-mining district north-west of Lens. The main assault on the Redoubt was launched by the 9th Scottish Division on 13 October. They managed to capture it and a number of trenches to the south-east but, as would soon become a regular feature of such offensives, exploiting that initial success proved very difficult and by the end of the day the enemy had counter-attacked and retaken much of the Redoubt itself, although the British still clung onto a trench known as 'Big Willie' and the 'Fosse Trench' to the south-east. The day's fighting had cost the attackers more than 3,600 casualties.

The 1/8th Sherwood Foresters had been in reserve but on the afternoon of 13 October had been ordered up and placed under temporary command of 137th Brigade. They were told to hurry up towards the Redoubt and to start digging a new communication trench between the old British front line and the newly captured Hohenzollern Redoubt. Having been digging for eight hours solidly, they were then told they would probably have to make an attack on Point 60. The Redoubt was shaped like a lozenge jutting out from the rest of the old German line and connected by a series of communication trenches codenamed Little Willie, North Face, South Face and Big Willie. The south-eastern front of the Redoubt was West Face, while where that trench met with South Face and Big Willie was Point 60. It was this feature that the Sherwood Foresters were to attack.

It was 1.45 on the morning of 14 October that orders were received for them to attack West Face and Point 60 and block the connection with South Face and Big Willie. They were to assault by using 'bombs' – hand grenades. They were not entirely on their own as the battalions of 137th Brigade would also be attacking Big Willie at the same time.

Such operations, in the dark and following a day of hard labour and with shells whizzing over constantly, were never straightforward to organise and it wasn't until 4 a.m. that A Company under Major Ashwell and Vann's D Company were ready and in position for the attack. It began at 4.15 a.m., led by the battalion commander, Lieutenant Colonel Fowler. There was heavy mist and only the thin first light of dawn, but by using a flashlight they managed to successfully approach Point 60 and then separated into attack parties. Vann led his men, dashing forward and hurling one grenade after another into the German trenches until badly wounded when a bullet passed clean through his left forearm, causing some paralysis and a line of trajectory the length of his hand from halfway up his forearm to just below his elbow. Being right-handed he got himself back up and continued throwing more grenades until eventually, several hours later, he was ordered to get medical help. His leadership and example helped the battalion achieve all that had been asked of them, but the Foresters had paid a heavy price; casualties among the attacking companies had been high.

And, it seemed, it was all for naught. Of the attack on their right by 137th Brigade there had been no sign, and it was clear the enemy still held far more of Big Willie than the Foresters had been led to believe. New orders arrived instructing them to consolidate their newly taken positions around West Face and Point 60. An enemy artillery barrage and persistent sniping chipped away at the men in their new positions on West Face, however. The following day, Lieutenant Colonel Fowler was killed by a sniper and the day after that the Foresters were pulled into reserve. By 19 October, the attack on the Hohenzollern Redoubt was over and the Loos offensive stalled, a costly and bloody failure, just as Haig had predicted.

Within two months, Vann was back at the front and by June 1916 had been made a substantive captain and acting major. His reputation had continued to rise, and he was known for his fearlessness and disregard of danger. His men adored him in part because of his example, but also because of his natural charisma, positive attitude and partly for the spiritual guidance he was always willing to offer. On more than one occasion he ventured out into no man's land to conduct burial services.

In September 1916, near Bellacourt, south-west of Arras, Major Vann led a raid on the enemy forward lines with dual aims of gathering intelligence and inflicting casualties on the enemy. Around a hundred men were to be used, divided into separate parties labelled A to E Party, each led by a junior subaltern, which was why a senior figure such as Vann was brought in to lead the entire operation. Such operations were not easy. Wire cutting had to be carried out beforehand, then a coordinated artillery bombardment ordered and executed. As evening fell on 21 September, Vann could see that the combination of wire parties, the bombardment and the liberal use of trench mortars all afternoon had created several gaps through which they could later advance. At 8 p.m., Vann sent out a wire patrol who returned and reported there were indeed several gaps, as hoped. Machine guns were set up to cover these while, at 11.15 p.m., wire patrols went up and out into no man's land to lay tape through the gaps, which the raiding parties could then follow.

Finally, at 11.20 p.m., it was time for Vann to lead his men out for the attack. Crossing no man's land went well and by midnight they were all in position in groups at distances of 70–125 yards apart. On cue at 12.15 a.m., the artillery support opened up and shells began screaming across the sky and landing in front of them. Realising they were too close for comfort, Vann now ordered the men back by about twenty yards. The barrage was due to last just thirteen minutes, so, at 12.25, Vann sent word for the men to get ready, and at 12.28, as the last shells whammed down on the German positions, he led the men forward, rushing into the enemy trenches. While his men clambered down into the trenches, throwing grenades forward and setting fire to any dugout they came across, Vann hurried along the parapet with his runner and two buglers to help B Party along their trench. A German grenade burst nearby them, wounding his runner and one of the buglers. It appeared to have been thrown from one of the enemy communication trenches, but Vann hurled a grenade of his own in its direction and that seemed to silence the enemy. He now continued to throw more grenades into the enemy trench ahead of the B Party men until reaching a large dugout. One of the men called for the Germans to come out. Two emerged soon after, carrying rifles with bayonets fixed, so Vann shot the first clean dead with a bullet to the head and a second in the thigh. 'This man was pulled out and four others, including a stretcher-bearer, came out with hands up,' noted Vann, 'shouting "Kamerad, Kamerad!" and crying for mercy. They were very frightened.'[2] They were quickly sent back to British lines for interrogation, but by now flares were lighting up the sky and German artillery had opened up, with shells starting to fall horribly close by. It was time to get back. At 12.49 p.m., Vann ordered his bugler to sound the recall, and they hurried back across no man's land, bullets pinging and hissing around them as they ran. Incredibly, not a single man was hit and every one of the raiding party made it back. Total casualties were eight wounded and only one badly so. It had been a success.

By this time, Vann was already suffering badly from neuritis, a physical rather than a mental condition but one caused by the inflammation of the peripheral nerve system, which in turn led to constant and acute pain as well as pins and needles. This was the result of the number of wounds he had suffered and which he had all too often brushed aside without giving himself a proper chance for recovery. With the Battle of the Somme drawing to a close and the Arras sector quiet, he bade farewell to the battalion he had served for more than two years and was sent back to England. It was while recovering that he learned he had been awarded a bar to his MC for leading the raiding party.

Back in England, Vann met and fell in love with Doris Beck, a Canadian volunteer nurse, and, at twenty, nine years his junior. What followed was a period of rest and recuperation for Vann and it was around this time that he was photographed for the studio portrait already described. He and Doris married in London in December 1916, two days after Christmas, and he was then posted to the Adjutant Command School until July 1917, after which he was given command of the 1/6th Battalion, Sherwood Foresters, and promoted again, this time to acting lieutenant colonel. Fully recovered from his neuritis and wounds, happily married and with a wealth of experience, he was an obvious choice for battalion command.

Back out at the front, Vann took command of the 1/6th Sherwood Foresters in the Neuville-Saint-Vaast sector, near Vimy Ridge to the north of Arras. For the next few months, theirs was a fairly quiet sector, but there were always patrols to be carried out, trench raids and wiring parties to be organised. The battalion continued to suffer its fair share of casualties.

Vann was sent on leave twice, first in December and again in April, and although the Germans launched their last major offensives in March and then again in April 1918, neither was near the 1/6th Sherwood Foresters. In May, Vann left the front again and was back in hospital for a fortnight, although the reason for this is not clear. Soon recovering, he returned to command the battalion once more until late August, when he enjoyed his final leave of the war with Doris, spending ten days with her in Paris.

The war that had been waged for over four years was now entering its end game. Through the summer there had been signs that the Germans had finally shot their bolt. Supplies were struggling to get through; Germany was financially ruined, and manpower and a shortage of arms and ammunition were becoming a serious problem. On 8 August, the British launched an assault along the Amiens sector and captured some 12,000 German troops and 500 guns as the Canadians advanced eight miles. Ludendorff, the German commander, called it 'the black day of the German Army'. The offensive was called off after four days, but Haig, the British Commander-in-Chief, now planned a series of new offensives, which he aimed to launch both consecutively and concurrently in an effort to give the enemy no respite at all.

Throughout August and into September these attacks continued along the front and were then supported by the French and Americans further to the south-east along the Argonne sector. The Germans had now fallen behind the Hindenburg Line, a major defensive position which made the most of the plentiful rivers and canals in the region. Crossing any waterway was a considerable challenge and at the end of September it was left to British Fourth Army to get across the formidable St Quentin Canal and then smash through the German positions on the far side. The canal was only thirty-five feet wide but had wire in the water, brick banks ten feet deep and was supported by concrete emplacements on the far side and a six-line system of trenches and dugouts to a depth of some 6,000 yards. The initial attack was made by two Australian and two American divisions that were still under British command, but the actual crossing itself was to be made by 46th Division, and that included the men of Vann's 1/6th Battalion.

Sunday 29 September 1918 dawned damp and misty. Preparations for the assault had been kept secret but it had still been preceded by a three-day bombardment by 1,600 guns firing 750,000 shells along a 10,000-yard front, and included 18-pounders equipped with shrapnel shells that cut wire far more effectively than had been possible earlier in the war. Vann and his men advanced with difficulty through the mist, made worse by the smoke from the guns, but successfully reached the canal, and by using a combination of collapsible boats, mud mats, ladders and life belts brought in especially from cross-Channel ferries, managed to get across at Bellenglise in just fifteen minutes with only limited casualties.

From the canal, the ground rose gradually and with Vann's old 8th Battalion on their right, they advanced together and cleared the forward enemy trenches codenamed the Yellow Line. As they pressed forward and reached the high ground above the village of Bellenglise, Vann now realised they were leading the assault. Their crossing had been around a bend in the canal and they were now coming under heavy machine-gun and artillery fire from both up ahead and south of the canal around Lehaucourt where the forward German positions had not yet been penetrated.

With no sign yet of the promised tanks, but with heavy enemy suppressing fire threatening to stall the entire attack and hold up rein-forcements, Vann now asked for a smokescreen to be laid down over the ridge south of the canal. Once that had been carried out he then ordered one company to push east along the canal towards Lehaucourt and then personally led a second on a charge up the ridge. Despite com-ing under heavy machine-gun fire, they rushed over the crest and the startled enemy began surrendering in droves.

There was, however, one stubborn enemy gun team that kept firing at the British tanks now, at last, lumbering forward in support. One tank after another was knocked out until five had been hit and put out of action. Again, Vann decided he had to seize the initiative and so charged forward and took the gun almost single-handedly, shooting three of the gunners and wounding two more. It was for his inspired leadership and gallantry at this vital moment in the battle that he was awarded the Victoria Cross. 'By his prompt action and absolute contempt for danger, the whole situation was changed, the men were encouraged and the line swept forward' ran his citation. 'The success of the day was in no small degree due to the splendid gallantry and fine leadership displayed by this officer.'[3]

By 1.15 p.m., Vann and his men had reached their objectives. Away to their right, the enemy continued to try and make counter-attacks across the canal near Lehaucourt, but each time were driven off. 'The third time,' noted Vann, 'an officer on horseback was trying to rally his men, who then rushed up the hill.' Both the officer and the horse were promptly shot and that was the last attempt the enemy made to regain the situation. The day had been emphatically won, and now there was an ever-widening breach across the canal through which more and more men were pouring. The 1/6th Sherwood Foresters' bag for the day was eight field guns, fifteen machine guns, one anti-tank gun and some 400 prisoners.

The praise that followed this attack was effusive. 'The story of the storming of the St. Quentin Canal, the capture of Bellenglise and the subsequent advance,' wrote Major General Geoffrey Boyd, the commander of the 46th Division, 'will make one of the most glorious stories in the history of the war.' More notices of congratulations and praise followed – from the IX Corps commander, even from Haig himself. All recognised this had been a critical and decisive day that had blasted a hole into the mighty Hindenburg Line. The long, brutal war was almost over. Everyone could sense it.

Tragically, the end of the war and the return to peace was not something Vann would enjoy. Just a few days later, on 3 October, while leading the advance yet again, he was shot by a sniper and killed instantly. Few, perhaps, deserved to have survived those last few weeks more than Vann, having battled through more than four years of service. At the time of his death, his Canadian wife was one month pregnant with his only child.

One of his friends and colleagues wrote an appreciation for *The Times*. 'I can think of him only as a fighter,' he wrote, 'not merely against the enemy in the field, but a fighter against everything and everybody that was not an influence for good to his men. Sometimes the strength of his personality and the force of his convictions drove him up against "authority" but he had no fear for himself and nothing on earth would have moved him to do what he felt to be wrong.'[4] The Bishop of Southwell thought of him as 'bright, happy, determined – a true leader of men'.[5] One of his officers described him as 'the best Christian I ever met'.[6]

Doris gave birth to a son, Bernard Geoffrey, who as a young man was awarded a Distinguished Service Cross (DSC) while serving in the Royal Navy in the Second World War, and who, like his father, also married a volunteer nurse. Some of his father's characteristics appear to have been passed on. Bernard Vann VC has not been forgotten. A blue plaque marks his childhood home in Rushen, while his medals are on display in the Imperial War Museum in London. In 2017 Durham University set up the Vann Fellowship in his name to fund post-doctoral research into the relationship between the Church and the armed forces. It is a legacy that is more than deserved, for there is no doubting that Lieutenant Colonel the Reverend Bernard Vann VC, MC and Bar, *Croix de guerre*, was an exceptional man.

28

MAJOR TASKER WATKINS VC

Introduced by The Rt Hon the Baroness Hale of Richmond DBE,
President of the Supreme Court of the United Kingdom

*When I was asked to contribute to this project, it seemed obvious to write
about Sir Tasker Watkins VC. I never met him, but superficially we had
a lot in common: a state school background, a career in education and
training, followed by a career in the law, a particular interest in mental
health law, a first full-time judicial appointment in the Family Division of
the High Court, and even, dare I say it, an interest in rugby union football.*

*But there the similarities end. After the war, Sir Tasker made a highly
successful career as a barrister before becoming a judge. Apart from a capacity
for hard work and attention to detail, both of which he had in abundance,
successful barristers need two qualities: great courage and good judgement.
They must know when to fight and when not to fight, how to fight and how
not to fight, how to get the judge or the jury on their side. And these were just
the qualities which earned him the Victoria Cross on that remarkable night in
Normandy on 16 August 1944. Of course, had radio communication not been
lost, his company would not have continued to advance. But as it had, they
carried on with what they had been told to do. Their leader had the trust and
confidence of his men – he had got them on his side. He had the judgement to
know what needed to be done if they were to gain their objective. And he had,
above all, the courage to carry it out against almost impossible odds.*

*Small wonder, then, that when he was President of the Welsh Rugby
Union, the coach, Graham Henry, used to pin up a copy of his Victoria*

Cross citation in the players' changing room before Six Nations matches – as an example of what the Welsh could achieve if they had the courage to do so.

No wonder, too, that he had such a stellar career when he came to the Bar in 1948. He quickly developed a wide-ranging and very successful practice on the Wales and Chester circuit, doing both civil and criminal as well as public enquiry work. Taking silk in 1965, he moved to London chambers and quickly established a successful practice there, too. Appointed to the Family Division in 1971, he transferred to the Queen's Bench Division in 1974 when a vacancy arose, and was then promoted to the Court of Appeal in 1980, where he took on increasing administrative duties, first as senior Presiding Judge and then as Deputy Lord Chief Justice.

He was known for his wisdom and sensitivity and understanding of humanity on the bench. Lord Judge, speaking when the statue which commemorates him at the Millennium Stadium in Cardiff was unveiled, remembered vividly the case of a burglar who had stolen the husband's war medals from his widow: 'They were her medals too, Igor.' The words of a great war hero as well as a great judge and a great man.

In the Second World War, British casualties were about half what they had been during the four years of the First World War and so there is a perception that, despite the gargantuan casualties suffered by Germany, the Soviet Union and China in particular, Britain got off lightly. Hand in hand with that is a lurking suspicion that somehow Britain did not quite pull her weight. Anyone believing that should think again, however. British strategy in the Second World War was quite deliberately to use 'steel not flesh' wherever possible. Her war leaders understood, quite rightly, that Britain had enormous global reach and that meant access to all the resources needed for a long drawn-out attritional war. British war strategy was to use technology and machinery as far as possible rather than the lives of her young men, and broadly speaking this was incredibly successful. Unlike Nazi Germany, for example, the British Army was, from the start of the war until the end, fully mechanised – that is, it was designed to move its forces from A to B by motorised transport. Germany, less automotive than most other leading nations in the world, was never able to become fully mechanised.

The British dependency on mechanisation and technology led to the huge air fleets of heavy bombers with which the process of grinding down Germany's ability to wage war was carried out. It meant British troops did not have to depend on horse and cart as the Germans did; and it also ensured that Britain could fight its war with fewer troops, which, in turn, inevitably did save lives, while more men could be channelled into British factories to build guns, tanks, aircraft and other war materiel. On the other hand, those unfortunate enough to experience the coalface of war – the front line of fighting – faced truly appalling odds. Those in the British infantry or armoured divisions, for example, who served in the Second World War were less likely to emerge unscathed than those a generation earlier who fought between 1914 and 1918. In Normandy, the combined average daily casualty rate during the seventy-seven-day campaign was a staggering 6,674. That's worse than the Somme, Passchendaele and Verdun. One British tank regiment, the Sherwood Rangers Yeomanry, lost forty-four officers and 175 other ranks in the Normandy campaign alone; they began on D-Day with thirty-six and just over two hundred. In other words, they lost more than 100 per cent of their officers and more than 80 per cent of their crews. Being a front-line British soldier in the war was very, very dangerous indeed and the chances of coming through entirely unscathed were extremely slight.

The vast majority of soldiers did what they were told, kept their heads down and prayed Lady Luck would be with them. They were utterly dependent on a handful of officers and non-commissioned officers – NCOs – who were prepared to go the extra yard and provide the example and leadership to help drive them forward and see them through. These were the exceptional ones – those whose courage and resolve was a cut above the mass and who ensured that a largely conscript army from a democracy in which capital punishment for desertion had long been kicked into touch would still go forward despite barely comprehensible levels of danger. And some – a very, very small minority – would prove truly exceptional. Tasker Watkins was one of those men, as he would prove in August 1944 in Normandy in one of the most astonishing and outrageously courageous actions of the war.

* * *

Out of necessity, the Second World War did much to break down class structures in Britain and was unlike any other conflict, the First World War included, in the degree in which the conflict affected every single man, woman and child in the country. The totality of the national effort was unprecedented and many of the social mores were challenged and even broken down forever by those long six years. It was true that officers had been promoted from the ranks in the 1914–18 conflict, and it was also the case that officers no longer came exclusively from the public schools. However, this was far more frequent in the Second World War, where outstanding leadership was rightly considered far more important than social standing.

This shift in attitude certainly ensured that Tasker Watkins was granted a commission in 1941. Watkins was born in November 1918 in the small mining town of Nelson, near Pontypridd in Wales. His father, like so many in the town, worked in the mining industry, as an underground fitter in one of the deepest of the mines in the area. The family lived in a two-up, two-down terraced house and for the Watkins, as with much of the rest of the town's inhabitants, life was hard physically and economically.

Their son, however, had been born with brains, natural athleticism and a healthy dose of steely determination. Not only did he win a place at the local grammar in Pontypridd, he also excelled at sports, and especially rugby and cricket. In 1931, when young Tasker was still only thirteen, his parents took the decision to leave Wales; his father, Bertram, had managed to secure a job working for the Ministry of Supply in

Dagenham, Essex, and so Tasker moved to Romford County School for Boys, a technical rather than a grammar school. Nonetheless, his brief time at the grammar school in Pontypridd had taught him how to think for himself and to aim high, and so it was that although after school he took a job working for Crookes Laboratories in the chemical industry, he was also able to take up an external place at London University to read law and commerce. It meant for a lot of hard work, but he still managed to find time to play sport, captaining the local cricket and football teams as well as playing what rugby he could.

The outbreak of war changed his life as it did so many others'. Approaching his twenty-first birthday he was swiftly called up and posted to the Duke of Cornwall's Light Infantry. Although he had been con-scripted as a private, Watkins' obvious leadership potential, physicality and intelligence were soon picked up. He was granted an emergency commission and posted to the Welch Regiment as a second lieutenant in May 1941, having completed an Officer Cadet Training Unit (OCTU) commissioning course earlier that month. Almost immediately he was posted to the 19th Battalion, the Welch Regiment, which was currently training in Northern Ireland and protecting that part of the United Kingdom from any potential German invasion. In truth, the invasion scare had receded before Lieutenant Tasker Watkins joined the battalion and in November 1941 the Welch Regiment, along with the entire 53rd (Welsh) Division, returned home to the Welsh border counties.

Much has been made of the quality of German training but for the vast majority of British troops fighting in the war training was far longer and more extensive than it was for those of the Wehrmacht. The main difference was that German recruits went through basic training, then further training while carrying out occupation duty, and were then posted to the front. Those who survived swiftly built up combat experience, something that was lacking for the 53rd Division, which had been re-formed on 1 September 1939 and had been training within the United Kingdom ever since.

Tasker Watkins soon proved his ability within the Welsh regiment. Always leading from the front, he was physically extremely fit, made sure all his men followed suit, and had the wit and technical intelligence to excel at all aspects of training. By the autumn of 1943 he had been promoted to acting captain and posted to the War Office Battle School at Llanberis in North Wales, where he became an instructor at the Rifle Wing of the Advanced Handling and Fieldcraft School. Within a couple of weeks, he had been made the Chief Instructor. Nor were his pupils ordinary soldiers, but officers and senior NCOs. He was, by all accounts, and his own admission, a hard taskmaster who really drove the men in his charge. 'We trained everywhere,' he later recalled, 'as far away as Blaenau Ffestiniog and Cader Idris, and were engaged in pretty ferocious activity.'[1] He laid especial emphasis on testing his charges' stamina, as well as intense weapons training, whether it be rifles, machine guns, sub-machine guns and even mortars. Fieldcraft, he said, was also of vital importance. 'When I served in the sniper-school under him,' recalled Tom Edwards, who later served in the 1/5th Welch Battalion, 'he gave me the works. I was glad to see the day over, to get back to billets. It was the most arduous scheme that I ever was on.'[2] Watkins later drily observed that there had to be 'a fair amount of sadism'[3] in being an instructor. But the old adage 'train hard, fight easy' invariably paid off.

The 53rd Division was posted to Normandy and arrived on 28 June 1944; the day before, Watkins had been also called to action, sent from Llanberis to the 103rd Reinforcement Group and then, a month later, on 25 July, he was posted to 1/5th Welch Regiment as a substantive lieutenant. He joined them to the south-west of Caen along with the rest of XII Corps, one of three, along with XXX and then VIII Corps on their right, in British Second Army. To their left, on their eastern flank was the multinational Canadian, British and Polish Second Canadian Division.

Watkins arrived at the front at a key moment in the campaign. For more than six weeks, the British and Canadian armies had been facing the bulk of the ten German panzer divisions in Normandy. These were the finest enemy divisions in the West: the best trained, with the most motivated and even fanatical men, and certainly the best equipped. At no point anywhere in the world did Allied forces face such a concentration of German panzer units. It has often been depicted that it was the British who were banging their heads against a brick wall of panzer divisions, but, in fact, it was rather the other way around, as the Germans were unable to ever successfully counter-attack and were being relentlessly worn down by British and Canadian firepower. One of the reasons the conduct of the Normandy campaign has come in for criticism – and the command of Field Marshal Montgomery especially – is because the campaign did not pan out how it had been envisaged beforehand. The Allied experience of fighting German armies was that the enemy tended to retreat behind a series of defensive lines. This had been the case in North Africa, Sicily and mainland Italy. During the build-up to the Allied invasion, there was little reason to suggest the German response would be any different this time around.

However, Hitler had insisted his men defend every yard. Normandy was the only theatre where all three services of the Wehrmacht could still operate; once they lost the French coastline, for example, they would also lose U-boat and torpedo boat bases, as well as vital airfields. By fighting close to the front, however, they played into Allied hands. British and American lines of supply were shorter and for much of the campaign German troops remained within range of a mass of offshore warships and their large-calibre guns.

Much of the fighting after D-Day had been around the city of Caen. This was the largest town in Normandy and the hub of a network of roads, railways, rivers and even a canal. Beyond, to the south-east, lay the higher ground of the Bourguébus Ridge, a key piece of territory and one suitable for airfields. This was effectively the hinge around which the Americans, to the west, would swing, and from where Allied forces would launch their sweep eastwards across France and up towards the Low Countries and the German border.

Although the British had been unable to push on and gain the Bourguébus Ridge, they had been successfully wearing down the German defences. On 18 July, they had launched Operation GOODWOOD, a major armour thrust to the east of Caen, and although they had gained only seven miles rather than a decisive breakthrough, 75 per cent of the British tank losses were back in action within days, thanks to the incredibly efficient repair and maintenance organisation, while the Germans were finally nearing the point of collapse. This appeared to happen largely when Operation COBRA, the American second part of the two-fisted offensive, proved highly successful.

Tasker Watkins arrived at the front just as General Dempsey, the commander of British Second Army, launched Operation BLUECOAT, the drive by VIII and XXX Corps to the west in support of the American First Army's COBRA around St-Lô. Again, BLUECOAT did not achieve all that had been hoped of it, but certainly in VIII Corps' sector the German defences were on the point of complete disintegration. Where German resistance remained most stubborn was further to the east of the line and precisely where Watkins and the Welsh units of 53rd Division were now positioned. Furthermore, hurrying forward to precisely this hinge part of the line were the II SS Panzer Corps under General Wilhelm Bittrich, whose men were among the most determined and fanatical of the entire German forces in Normandy.

The campaign was now increasingly fluid, however. General Patton's US Third Army had arrived in Brittany at the beginning of July and now began to sweep eastwards to the south as the US First Army and the British troops of VIII Corps also began turning south and east. As part of this campaign, the role of the Welshmen was to keep up the pressure to the south of Caen against the armour of the 10th Waffen-SS Panzer Division and the infantry of the 271st Division. Watkins and his men in B Company reached the shattered village of Grimbosq on 7 August. Five days later, they were in battle, advancing behind a heavy British artillery barrage to take the village of Fresney-le-Vieux, some five miles south-east of Grimbosq and some twelve miles north-west of the key objective of Falaise. Watkins was second in command of B Company, on the left of the attack, and he and his men managed to capture all their objectives swiftly. The same could not be said along the right, and it was only when reserve troops were sent forward along with tanks and flamethrowers that a stubborn enemy strongpoint was finally overcome.

This had been Watkins' first time in combat. All those long years of training had paid dividends; and he had led his men well. When his company commander had been wounded, Watkins had immediately stepped into the breach and been promoted back up to captain. He also recognised the importance of comradeship. 'The infantry soldier lives very close to the earth, literally,' he commented later, 'and the dependence of one soldier upon another is extremely intimate.'[4] It was doubly important that he understood this and gained the swift trust of his men because he had only joined them a couple of weeks earlier.

The battalion was back in action just four days later, by which time the surviving Germans were bottled up in a long finger of land running west from Falaise. Only a narrow corridor to the east of the town would allow them to escape at all, but despite this the flanks of this narrow bulge were still being tenaciously defended. The 1/5th Welch Battalion, part of 160th Brigade, were ordered to push south and try and cut the D511, the ancient Roman road that led east into Falaise.

Here, the Normandy countryside gently drops into a low, wide valley. From the north, thick woods masked the British and Canadian advance; what was to become known as the 'Falaise Gap' lies spread out, like a shallow hollow. Ancient roads crisscross fields thick with hedgerows; this is *bocage* country, difficult through which to attack because the hedges and small villages offer excellent cover for the defenders, while the network of roads still provided the only real route along which Allied tanks, trucks and other vehicles could move. The Allied way of war was to use their immense firepower as much as possible, but it was still the poor bloody infantry, alongside the armour of the tank regiments, who had to do the probing forward to try and get the enemy to show their heads. They were, in effect, the bait.

Orders to cut the D511 reached the battalion in the early hours of Wednesday 16 August 1944. As they neared the small village of Leffard, six miles to the north-west of Falaise, they came under heavy and persistent shellfire, but, leaving their trucks and carriers, took cover in the thick woods to the east and about a mile north of the road. From the woods they inched forward into the village of Martigny-sur-l'Ante, where they linked up with tanks of the 155th Regiment of the Royal Armoured Corps. By this time, enemy troops had been spotted to the south where they were holding not only the road but a railway line, too. To the immediate south of both was a narrow winding stream lined with trees and hedgerows as well as a parallel running track also lined with thick hedges and trees.

A plan was now hatched to attack these positions and capture the road and enemy positions beyond that same evening. D Company was to remain behind in the high ground by the woods along with battalion headquarters; A Company was to be in reserve and C and B Companies were to provide the attacking force, with Watkins' B Company on the left-hand side. To attack the road frontally, they would have to cross the open fields to the north of the D511, although with the support of the tanks, who would effectively act as artillery and offer suppressing fire from the high ground in the woods.

Watkins and his men cautiously crept forward as dusk began to fall, with the tanks blasting away at the enemy positions. The 75mm guns of the Sherman and Churchill tanks were excellent for hitting machine-gun positions and keeping the heads of the enemy down, as were the battalion's mortars. However, a German 88mm anti-tank gun was lurking hidden in further woods to the south. With a velocity of nearly 3,000 feet per second and far greater range than the 75mm tank guns, this weapon was soon proving very effective. At this point, Watkins' B Company lost all radio contact with both C Company and Battalion HQ. Soon after, Brigade sent a message for the two attacking companies not to advance beyond the road, but because of the loss of radio communications it was an order

Watkins never received. From Battalion HQ in the woods to the north of Martigny, B Company were seen pressing forward, dark figures stealing across the road. The battalion commander and his staff feared the worst and could only watch with a mounting sense of tension and helplessness.

Night was now falling. Completely ignorant of the change of orders, Watkins and his men pressed on, over the road and railway and began stealing their way over the fields between the road and the brook. Here they began to get into trouble; the fields had been mined and booby-trapped and German machine guns opened fire. These Spandaus, as they were known, had their problems – they quickly overheated and soon lost accuracy – but with a firing rate of 1,400 rounds a minute could lay down a murderous quantity of bullets in the initial engagement and it was this weight of fire that killed and wounded a number of Watkins' men and which left him as the only officer standing in the company.

They were certainly in a predicament. There was no sign of C Company or any support. The tanks had stopped firing, they had no means of communicating for help, and the enemy appeared to be closing in on them as further small-arms and machine-gun fire opened up. After weighing up the situation, Captain Watkins decided there was only one course now open to them: to fight their way out. Leading from the front, he ordered his men to charge the nearest enemy strongpoint. By keeping moving and firing from the hip with his Sten gun, he managed to personally kill a number of Germans and silenced the Spandau. Their problems were far from over, however, because they now came under attack from a nearby anti-tank gun. Watkins now ran forward and single-handedly took out the gun crew, although just as he was about to shoot the last of the gunners his Sten jammed. Hurling it at the German, it hit the man in the face, knocking him off balance and giving Watkins a chance to draw his pistol and shoot him. Now hurrying back to his men, they began falling back across the fields to the road, but by this time the Germans were counter-attacking. Dropping down, they fired back and, when the enemy attack seemed to be faltering, Watkins led his men forward once more in a bayonet charge on a third enemy position. A further enemy machine gun now began pinning them down once more so Watkins again ordered his men to scatter then personally crept up on the Spandau and killed the gunners.

By this time, his B Company had achieved all their objectives. Watkins ordered his men to hold their position and await reinforcements, but after a while, when it became increasingly apparent that no support was coming, and, with signs of the Germans moving up to surround them, he decided his only option was to try and withdraw around one of the enemy's flanks. It was by now quite dark but with enemy flares occasionally fizzing up into the sky and lighting up the ground. Moving stealthily through the cornfields they were then challenged by a German outpost. Once again, Watkins told his men to scatter, then, taking a Bren gun, charged the enemy position, killing them all. Now gathering up the remains of his company, he led them back to their own lines along with a number of prisoners from the 271st Infantry Division. Only twenty-seven out of sixty had made it back, but Watkins was unscathed, despite personally storming four enemy positions and three entirely on his own.

The following day, the enemy cut and ran, fleeing through the narrow channels that led them out of the Falaise Gap. These roads became known as the 'Corridors of Death'. By the end of the Normandy campaign, two entire German armies had been utterly routed; from the panzer divisions only around 1,300 men and two dozen tanks managed to escape – they had had some 2,500 panzers at the height of the Normandy battle. The carnage of that final flight was appalling. 'At times we had to hold our breath rather than take in the air which reeked with the stench of rotting flesh of men and horse,' noted one witness from the regiment. 'Splashed all over the countryside were the dismembered remnants of all types of German Army vehicles and stores. To those who did not see this, it is frankly impossible to convey the picture of the massacre.'[5]

The Normandy campaign was over and although it had not taken the form Montgomery had predicted before D-Day, the German collapse, when it came, had done so in a flood and, overall, the pre-invasion objectives had been achieved in just seventy-seven days rather than the ninety that had been estimated. The victory was an enormous one, and, as the actions of the 1/5th Welch Battalion had shown on that night of 16/17 August, the British Army could be as good and effective as any soldiers in the world.

What followed was the pursuit: a rapid Allied sweep east and north, across the Seine and then into Belgium and Holland. By September the advance had slowed, however, as the Germans began gradually to regain their balance and as Allied lines of supply grew ever longer. By the third week of the month, the Welshmen were finding themselves embroiled in one minor skirmish after another and inching forward both cautiously and more slowly. Watkins, now a major, continued to lead his men from the front and it was as they entered the town of 's-Hertogenbosch with its many canals that his luck finally ran out. It was perhaps inevitable; very few in an infantry battalion in north-west Europe emerged unscathed. Crossing a canal and advancing towards the railway station, he was hit in the right leg and abdomen by shrapnel when a mortar shell exploded nearby. Taken to Brussels, he nearly lost his leg, but he was stabilised and evacuated to the Queen Elizabeth Hospital in Birmingham. Thankfully, there his leg was saved.

Tasker Watkins was still recovering in hospital when the news arrived that he had been awarded the Victoria Cross for his truly outstanding leadership and breathtaking bravery near Falaise. He was the first Welshman of the war to receive the award and was presented his medal by the King at Buckingham Palace on 8 March 1945, accompanied by his wife, Eirwen, who he had married back in 1941, and his young daughter, Mair. His fighting days were over, however, and he returned to instructing, this time at the Royal Engineers Battle School at Penmaenmawr in North Wales.

With the war over, Watkins was demobbed and once again took up his law studies, enrolling at a crammer in Cardiff. Not only did he pass his exams, he was, in 1948, called to the Bar, taking up chambers in Cardiff where he soon excelled as a barrister of both civil and criminal law. What followed was a long and highly successful career in which he rose to the very top of his profession: he gained silk in 1965, and became a bencher of Middle Temple five years later. Deputy to the Attorney General as counsel to the inquiry into the Aberfan disaster, he later became a judge in 1971, the year he was also knighted, and rose to become Senior Presiding Judge in 1983 and Deputy Chief Justice of England in 1988. It is hard to imagine how the son of a coal mine fitter could possibly have achieved more. Nor was that all, because on retiring from the law he was able to become President of the Welsh Rugby Union. It was rugby, above all sports, that he loved the most and had continued to play during his time in the army and beyond, and had later headed up the Welsh Rugby Union Charitable Trust. As President of the WRU, he oversaw a period of transition from the amateur to the professional game, which included a lengthy and detailed review that became known as the Watkins Report. It was a post he kept for eleven years and in which he brought good judgement, wisdom, fairness and humanity to what was always a demanding and challenging role. Rightly, he remains revered by those within the Welsh Rugby Union and in Wales as a whole.

Sir Tasker Watkins died, aged eighty-eight, in September 2007. He was a truly exceptional man who, despite such humble beginnings, used his intelligence, drive, sporting skills, charm and innate leadership to achieve great things. He rarely spoke of his Victoria Cross but a few years before he died he was asked about it and, for once, reflected on what had happened that night in August 1944 and how it had affected his life. 'You must believe me when I say it was just another day in the life of a soldier,' he told his interviewer. 'I did what needed doing to help colleagues and friends, just as others looked out for me during the fighting that summer. I didn't wake up the next day a better or braver person, just different. I'd seen more killing and death in twenty-four hours – indeed, been part of that terrible process – than is right for anybody. From that point onwards, I have tried to take a more caring view of my fellow human beings, and that, of course, always includes your opponent, whether it be in war, sport or just life generally.'[6]

APPENDIX

VC AND GC CITATIONS FROM *THE LONDON GAZETTE*

The following citations appear exactly as they were first published in *The London Gazette*.

Date	VC/GC recipient
1858	Frederick Roberts

Citation

Frederick Sleigh ROBERTS VC (later Earl ROBERTS OF KANDAHAR VC)
Lieutenant, Bengal Artillery, Attached Hope Grant's Cavalry Division, Honourable East India Company Forces

War Office, 24th December 1858
Bengal Artillery Lieutenant Frederick Sleigh Roberts
Date of Act of Bravery, 2nd January, 1858

Lieutenant Roberts' gallantry has on every occasion been most marked.
On following up the retreating enemy on the 2nd January, 1858, at Khodagunge he saw in the distance two Sepoys going away with a standard. Lieutenant Roberts put spurs to his horse, and overtook them just as they were about to enter a village. They immediately turned round, and presented their muskets at him, and one of the men pulled the trigger, but fortunately the caps snapped, and the standard-bearer was cut down by this gallant young officer, and the standard taken possession of by him. He also, on the same day, cut down another Sepoy who was standing at bay, with musket and bayonet, keeping off a Sowar. Lieutenant Roberts rode to the assistance of the horseman, and, rushing at the Sepoy, with one blow of his sword cut him across the face, killing him on the spot.

(*The London Gazette* of 24 December 1858, Numb. 22212, p. 5516)

APPENDIX

Date | **VC/GC recipient**
1857 | William Edward Hall

Citation
Thomas James YOUNG VC[1]
William Nelson HALL VC
War-Office, February 1, 1859, Naval Brigade
Lieutenant (now Commander) Thomas James Young
William Hall, A.B.
Date of Act of Bravery, 16th November 1857

Lieutenant (now Commander) Young, late Gunnery Officer of Her Majesty's ship "Shannon", and William Hall, "Captain of the Foretop" of that Vessel, were recommended by the late Captain Peel for the Victoria Cross, for their gallant conduct at a 24-Pounder Gun, brought up to the angle of the Shah Nujjiff, at Lucknow, on the 16th of November, 1857.

(*The London Gazette* of 1 February 1859, Numb. 2225, p. 414)

Date | **VC/GC recipient**
1879 | Henry Hook

Citation
John WILLIAMS VC[2] (born John FIELDING)
Alfred Henry HOOK VC
War Office, May 2, 1879.
2nd Battalion 24th Regiment, Private John Williams
2nd Battalion 24th Regiment, Private Henry Hook

Private John Williams was posted with Private Joseph Williams, and Private William Horrigan, 1st Battalion 24th Regiment, in a distant room of the hospital, which they held for more than an hour, so long as they had a round of ammunition left: as communication was for the time cut off, the Zulus were enabled to advance and burst open the door; they dragged out Private Joseph Williams and two of the patients, and assegaied them. Whilst the Zulus were occupied with the slaughter of these men a lull took place, during which Private John Williams, who, with two patients, were the only men now left alive in this ward, succeeded in knocking a hole in the partition, and in taking the two patients into the next ward, where he found Private Hook.
These two men together, one man working whilst the other fought and held the enemy at bay with his bayonet, broke through three more partitions, and were thus enabled to bring eight patients through a small window in the inner line of defence.

(Supplement to *The London Gazette* of 2 May 1879, 2 May 1879, Numb. 24717, pp. 3177–78)

Date   **VC/GC recipient**
1899   Charles Fitzclarence

Citation
Charles FITZCLARENCE VC
Captain, The Royal Fusiliers (City of London Regiment), attached to D Squadron, The Protectorate Regiment

War Office, July 6, 1900
The Royal Fusiliers (City of London Regiment)
Captain Charles FitzClarence

On the 14th October, 1899, Captain FitzClarence went with his squadron of the Protectorate Regiment, consisting of only partially trained men, who have never been in action, to the assistance of an armoured train which had gone out from Mafeking. The enemy were in greatly superior numbers, and the squadron was for a time surrounded, and it looked as if nothing could save them from being shot down. Captain FitzClarence, however, by his personal coolness and courage inspired the greatest confidence in his men, and, by his bold and efficient handling of them, not only succeeded in relieving the armoured train, but inflicted a heavy defeat on the Boers, who lost 50 killed and a large number wounded, his own losses being 2 killed and 15 wounded. The moral effect of this blow had a very important bearing on subsequent encounters with the Boers.
On the 27th October, 1899, Captain FitzClarence led his squadron from Mafeking across the open, and made a night attack with the bayonet on one of the enemy's trenches. A hand-to-hand fight took place in the trench, while a heavy fire was concentrated on it from the rear. The enemy was driven out with heavy loss. Captain FitzClarence was the first man into the position and accounted for four of the enemy with his sword. The British lost 6 killed and 9 wounded. Captain FitzClarence was himself slightly wounded. With reference to these two actions, Major General Baden-Powell states that had this Officer not shown an extraordinary spirit and fearlessness the attacks would have been failures, and we should have suffered heavy loss both in men and prestige. On the 26th December, 1899, during the action at Game Tree, near Mafeking, Captain FitzClarence again distinguished himself by his coolness and courage, and was again wounded (severely through both legs).

(*The London Gazette* of 6 July 1900, Numb. 27208, p. 4196)

Date   **VC/GC recipient**
1899   Walter Congreve

Citation
Walter Norris CONGREVE VC (later Sir Walter Norris CONGREVE VC)
Captain, 2nd Battalion The Rifle Brigade (Prince Consort's Own),
attached Staff 4th Infantry Brigade

War Office, 2 February, 1900.
The Rifle Brigade (The Prince Consort's Own)
Captain W.N. Congreve

At Colenso on the 15th December, 1899, the detachments serving the guns of the 14th and 66th Batteries, Royal Field Artillery, had all been either killed, wounded, or driven from their guns by Infantry fire at close range, and the guns were deserted.

About 500 yards behind the guns was a donga in which some of the few horses and drivers left alive were sheltered. The intervening space was swept with shell and rifle fire.

Captain Congreve, Rifle Brigade, who was in the donga, assisted to hook a team into a limber, went out, and assisted to limber up a gun. Being wounded, he took shelter; but, seeing Lieutenant Roberts fall, badly wounded, he went out again and brought him in. Captain Congreve was shot through the leg, through the toe of his boot, grazed on the elbow and the shoulder, and his horse shot in three places.

(*The London Gazette* of 2 February 1900, Numb. 27160, p. 689)

Date   **VC/GC recipient**
1914   Thomas Crean

Citation
Chief Stoker William LASHLEY, R.N.[3]
Petty Officer (First Class) Thomas CREAN, R.N.

The KING was pleased, on Saturday, the 26th instant, at Buckingham Palace, to present to Chief Stoker William Lashley, R.N., and Petty Officer (First Class) Thomas Crean, R.N., Albert Medals[4] of the Second Class, which had been conferred upon them by His Majesty in recognition of their gallantry in saving life as detailed below:

At the end of a journey of 1,500 miles on foot, the final supporting party of the late Captain Scott's expedition towards the South Pole, consisting of Lieutenant Edward Ratcliffe Garth Russell Evans, R.N., (now Commander Evans C.B.), Chief Stoker William Lashley, R.N., and Petty Officer (First Class) Thomas Crean, R.N., were 238 miles from the base when Lieutenant Evans was found to be suffering from scurvy. His condition rapidly became worse. When 151 miles from the base he was unable to stand without support on his ski sticks, and after struggling onward on skis in great pain for four days, during which Lashley and Crean dragged their sledge fifty-three miles, he collapsed and was unable to proceed further.

At this point Lieutenant Evans requested his two companions to leave him, urging that eighty-three miles lay between the party and the nearest refuge hut, at that unless they left him three lives would be lost instead of one. This, however, they refused to do and insisted in carrying him forward on the sledge.

Favoured by a southerly wind, Lashley and Crean dragged Lieutenant Evans in the sledge for four days, pulling for thirteen hours a day, until, on the evening of February 17, 1912, a point was reached thirty-four miles from a refuge hut, where it was thought possible that assistance might be obtained. During the following twelve hours, however, snow fell incessantly, and in the morning it was found impossible to proceed further with the sledge.

As the party now only had sufficient food for three more meals, and both Lashley and Crean were becoming weaker daily, it was decided that they would separate, and that Crean would endeavour to walk to the refuge hut, while Lashley stayed to nurse Lieutenant Evans.

After a march of eighteen hours in soft snow Crean made his way to the hut, arriving completely exhausted. Fortunately Surgeon Edward L. Atkinson R.N., was at the hut with two dog teams and the dog attendant. His party, on February 20, effected the rescue of Lieutenant Evans and Lashley.

But for the gallant conduct throughout of his two companions Lieutenant Evans would undoubtedly have lost his life.

(*The London Gazette* of 29 July, 1913, Numb. 28741, pp. 5409–10)

Date **VC/GC recipient**
1914 Maurice Dease

Citation
Maurice James DEASE VC
Lieutenant, 4th Battalion The Royal Fusiliers, (City of London Regiment) 9th Brigade

War Office 16th November, 1914.
Lieutenant Maurice James Dease,
4th Battalion, The Royal Fusiliers

Though two or three times badly wounded he continued to control the fire of his machine guns at Mons on 23rd August until all his men were shot. He died of his wounds.

(Third Supplement to *The London Gazette* of 13 November 1914, 16 November 1914, Numb. 28976, p. 9374. Repeated in *The London Gazette* of 17 November 1914, Numb. 28977, p. 9403)

Date **VC/GC recipient**
1915 Martin Dunbar-Nasmith

Citation
Martin Eric NASMITH VC (later Sir Martin Eric DUNBAR-NASMITH VC)
Lieutenant Commander, HM Submarine *E11*, Royal Navy

Admiralty, 24th June, 1915.
Lieutenant-Commander Martin Eric Nasmith, Royal Navy

For most conspicuous bravery in command of one of His Majesty's Submarines while operating in the Sea of Marmora. In the face of great danger he succeeded in destroying one large Turkish gunboat, two transports, one ammunition ship and three storeships, in addition to driving one storeship ashore. When he had safely passed the most difficult part of his homeward journey he returned again to torpedo a Turkish transport.

(*The London Gazette* of 25 June 1915, Numb. 29206, p. 6166)

Date   **VC/GC recipient**
1915   The 6 Victoria Crosses "before breakfast" at Gallipoli

Citation
Richard Raymond WILLIS VC
Alfred Joseph RICHARDS VC
William KENEALLY VC

War Office, 24th August, 1915
Captain Richard Raymond Willis, 1st Battalion, The Lancashire Fusiliers.
No.1293 Serjeant Alfred Richards, 1st Battalion, The Lancashire Fusiliers.
No.1809 Private William Keneally, 1st Battalion, The Lancashire Fusiliers.

On the 25th April, 1915, three Companies and the Headquarters of the 1st Battalion Lancashire Fusiliers, in effecting a landing on the Gallipoli Peninsula to the West of Cape Helles, were met by a very deadly fire from hidden machine guns which caused a great number of casualties. The survivors, however, rushed up to and cut the wire entanglements, notwithstanding the terrific fire from the enemy, and, after overcoming supreme difficulties, the cliffs were gained and the position maintained.

Amongst the many very gallant Officers and men engaged in this most hazardous undertaking, Captain Willis, Serjeant Richards and Private Keneally have been selected by their comrades as having performed the most signal acts of bravery and devotion to duty. (*The London Gazette* of 24 August 1915, Numb. 29273, p. 8395; repeated in the Third Supplement to *The London Gazette* of 13 March 1917. 15 March 1917, Numb. 29985, p. 2619)

Cuthbert BROMLEY VC
Frank Edward STUBBS VC
John Elisha GRIMSHAW VC
War Office, 15th March, 1917.
Capt. (temp. Maj.) Cuthbert Bromley (since drowned).
No. 1506 Sjt. Frank Edward Stubbs (since died of wounds).
No. 2609 Cpl. (now Sjt.) John Grimshaw.

On the 25th April, 1915, headquarters and three companies of the 1st Battalion, Lancashire Fusiliers, in effecting a landing on the Gallipoli Peninsula to the West of Cape Helles, were met by very deadly fire from hidden machine guns, which caused a great number of casualties. The survivors, however, rushed up to and cut the wire entanglements, notwithstanding the terrific fire from the enemy, and after overcoming supreme difficulties, the cliffs were gained and the position maintained.

Amongst the many very gallant officers and men engaged in this most hazardous undertaking Captain Bromley, Serjeant Stubbs and Corporal Grimshaw have been selected by their comrades as having performed the most signal acts of bravery and devotion to duty. The above awards of the Victoria Cross are to be read in conjunction with those conferred on the undermentioned for most conspicuous bravery on the same occasion:-
Capt. Richard Raymond Willis, 1st Bn., Lan. Fus.
No. 1293 Sjt. Alfred Richards, 1st Bn., Lan. Fus.
No. 1809 Pte. William Keneally, 1st Bn., Lan. Fus.
See *London Gazette*, dated 24th August, 1915.

NOTE: Consequent on the award of the Victoria Cross, the award of the Distinguished Conduct Medal to No. 2609 Sjt. John Grimshaw, 1ˢᵗ Bn., Lan. Fus., which was published in the London Gazette dated 16ᵗʰ November, 1915, is hereby cancelled.

(Third Supplement to *The London Gazette* of 13 March 1917. 15 March 1917, Numb. 29985, p.2619)

Date   **VC/GC recipient**
1915   Daniel Laidlaw

Citation
Daniel Logan LAIDLAW VC Piper,
7ᵗʰ Battalion The King's Own Scottish Borderers, 46ᵗʰ Brigade, 15ᵗʰ Scottish Division

War Office, 18ᵗʰ November, 1915.
15851 Piper Daniel Laidlaw, 7ᵗʰ Battalion, The King's Own Scottish Borderers.

For most conspicuous bravery prior to an assault on German trenches near Loos and Hill 70 on 25ᵗʰ September, 1915.
During the worst of the bombardment, when the attack was about to commence, Piper Laidlaw, seeing that his company was somewhat shaken from the effects of gas, with absolute coolness and disregard of danger mounted the parapet, marched up and down and played his company out of the trench. The effect of his splendid example was immediate, and the company dashed out to the assault. Piper Laidlaw continued playing his pipes until he was wounded.

(Third Supplement to *The London Gazette* of 16 November 1915. 18 November 1915, Numb. 29371, pp. 1144–50)

Date   **VC/GC recipient**
1916   Donald Bell

Citation
Donald Simpson BELL VC
Temporary Second Lieutenant, 9ᵗʰ Battalion Alexandra, Princess of Wales's Own (The Yorkshire Regiment), 69ᵗʰ Brigade, 23ʳᵈ Division

War Office, 9ᵗʰ September, 1916.

Temp. 2ⁿᵈ Lt Donald Simpson Bell, late York. R.

For most conspicuous bravery. During an attack a very heavy enfilade fire was opened on the attacking company by a hostile machine gun. 2ⁿᵈ Lt. Bell immediately, and on his own initiative, crept up a communication trench and then, followed by Corpl. Colwill and Pte. Batey, rushed across the open under very heavy fire and attacked the machine gun, shooting the firer with his revolver, and destroying gun and personnel with bombs.

This very brave act saved many lives and ensured the success of the attack.
Five days later this gallant officer lost his life performing a very similar act of bravery.

(Supplement to *The London Gazette* of 8 September 1916. 9 September 1916, Numb. 29740, p. 8870)

Date   VC/GC recipient
1916   William Robinson

Citation
William Leefe ROBINSON VC
Lieutenant, 5th Battalion The Worcestershire Regiment and No 39 Squadron, Royal Flying Corps

War Office, 5th September, 1916.
Lt. William Leefe Robinson,
Worc. R. and R.F.C.

For most conspicuous bravery. He attacked an enemy airship under circumstances of great difficulty and danger, and sent it crashing to the ground as a flaming wreck.
He had been in the air for more than two hours, and had previously attacked another airship during his flight.

(*The London Gazette* of 5 September 1916, Numb. 29735, p. 8704)

Date   VC/GC recipient
1916   William Congreve

Citation
William La Touche CONGREVE VC
Brevet Major, 3rd Battalion The Rifle Brigade (Prince Consort's Own) 76th Brigade, 3rd Division

War Office, 26th October, 1916.
Bt. Maj. William La Touche Congreve, D.S.O., M.C., late Rif. Brig.

For most conspicuous bravery during a period of fourteen days preceding his death in action.
This officer consistently performed acts of gallantry and showed the greatest devotion to duty, and by his personal example inspired all those around him with confidence at critical periods of the operations. During preliminary preparations for the attack he carried out personal reconnaissance of the enemy lines, taking out parties of officers and non-commissioned officers for over 1,000 yards in front of our lines, in order to acquaint them with the ground. All these preparations were made under fire.
Later, by night, Major Congreve conducted a battalion to its position of employment, afterwards returning to it to ascertain the situation after assaults. He established himself

in an exposed forward position from whence he successfully observed the enemy, and gave orders necessary to drive them from their position. Two days later, when Brigade Headquarters was heavily shelled and many casualties resulted, he went out and assisted the medical officer to remove the wounded to places of safety, although he was himself suffering severely from gas and other shell effects. He again on a subsequent occasion showed supreme courage in tending wounded under heavy shell fire.

He finally returned to the front line to ascertain the situation after an unsuccessful attack, and whilst in the act of writing his report, was shot and killed instantly.

(Fourth Supplement to *The London Gazette* of 24 October 1916. 26 October 1916, Numb. 29802, pp. 10393–94)

Date   VC/GC recipient
1918   Arthur Harrison

Citation
Arthur Leyland HARRISON VC
Lieutenant Commander, HMS *Vindictive*, Royal Navy

Admiralty, 17th March, 1919,
Lieutenant-Commander Arthur Leyland Harrison, R.N.

For most conspicuous gallantry at Zeebrugge on the night of the 22nd–23rd April, 1918. This officer was in immediate command of the Naval Storming Parties embarked in "Vindictive."

Immediately before coming alongside the Mole Lieut.-Commander Harrison was struck on the head by a fragment of a shell which broke his jaw and knocked him senseless. Recovering consciousness he proceeded on to the Mole and took over command of his party, who were attacking the seaward end of the Mole. The silencing of the guns on the Mole head was of the first importance, and though in a position fully exposed to the enemy's machine-gun fire, Lieut.-Commander Harrison gathered his men together and led them to the attack. He was killed at the head of his men, all of whom were either killed or wounded.

Lieut.-Commander Harrison though already severely wounded and undoubtedly in great pain, displayed indomitable resolution and courage of the highest order in pressing his attack, knowing as he did that any delay in silencing the guns might jeopardise the main object of the expedition i.e., the blocking of the Zeebrugge-Bruges Canal.

(Sixth Supplement to *The London Gazette* of 14 March 1919. 17 March 1919, Numb. 31236, pp. 3590–91)

Date   VC/GC recipient
1918   Bernard Vann

Citation
Rev Bernard William VANN VC
Acting Lieutenant Colonel

1/8th Battalion The Sherwood Foresters (The Nottinghamshire and Derbyshire Regiment) commanding 1/6th Battalion, 139th Brigade, 46th Division

War Office, 14th December 1918
Capt. (A./Lt.-Col Bernard William Vann M.C.,
late 1/18th Bn, attd. 1/16th Bn. Notts. & Derby.R. (T.F.).

For most conspicuous bravery, devotion to duty and fine leadership during the attack at Bellenglise and Lehaucourt on September 29th, 1918.

He led his battalion with great skill across the Canal Du Nord through a very thick fog and under heavy fire from field and machine guns.

On reaching the high ground above Bellenglise the whole attack was held up by fire of all descriptions from the front and right flank.

Realising that everything depended on the advance going forward with the barrage, Col. Vann rushed up to the firing line and with great gallantry led the line forward. By his prompt action and absolute contempt for danger the whole situation was changed, the men were encouraged and the line swept forward.

Later, he rushed a field-gun single-handed and knocked out three of the detachment. The success of the day was in no small degree due to the splendid gallantry and fine leadership displayed by this officer.

Lt.-Col. Vann, who had on all occasions set the highest example of valour, was killed near Ramicourt on 3rd September, 1918, when leading his battalion in attack.

(Second Supplement to *The London Gazette* of 13 December 1918, 14 December 1918, Numb. 31067, p. 14774)

Date   **VC/GC recipient**
1940   Daphne Pearson

Citation
Joan Daphne Mary PEARSON EGM/GC
Corporal, Women's Auxiliary Air Force

St. James's Palace, S.W.1, 19th July 1940.

The KING has been graciously pleased to approve the following Awards:

The Medal of the Military Division of the Most Excellent Order of the British Empire, for Gallantry:

880538 Corporal (now Assistant Section Officer) Joan Daphne Mary Pearson, Women's Auxiliary Air Force.

On the 31st May, 1940, at 0100 hours an aircraft crashed near the Women's Auxiliary Air Force quarters, the pilot being seriously injured, another officer killed outright and two airmen slightly injured. Upon hearing the crash Corporal Pearson rushed out to it and, although the aircraft was burning and she knew there were bombs aboard, she stood on the wreckage, roused the pilot, who was stunned, and assisted him in getting clear, releasing his parachute harness in doing so. When he was on the ground about 30 yards away, a 120 lb. bomb went off. Corporal Pearson at once threw herself on top of the pilot to protect from blast and splinters. Her prompt and courageous action undoubtedly helped to save the pilot's life.

(*The London Gazette* of 19 July 1940, Numb. 34900, p. 4434)

Date   VC/GC recipient
1941/42   Charles Upham

Citation
Charles Hazlitt UPHAM VC*
Second Lieutenant, 20th Battalion, 2nd New Zealand Division, 2nd New Zealand Expeditionary Force

War Office, 14th October, 1941.
Second-Lieutenant Charles Hazlitt Upham (8077), New Zealand Military Forces.

During the operations in Crete this officer performed a series of remarkable exploits, showing outstanding leadership, tactical skill and utter indifference to danger.
He commanded a forward platoon in the attack on MALEME on 22nd May and fought his way forward for over 3,000 yards unsupported by any other arms and against a defence strongly organised in depth. During this operation his platoon destroyed numerous enemy posts but on three occasions sections were temporarily held up.
In the first case, under a heavy fire from a machine gun nest he advanced to close quarters with pistol and grenades, so demoralising the occupants that his section were able to "mop up" with ease.
Another of his sections was then held up by two machine guns in a house. He went in and placed a grenade through a window, destroying the crew of one machine gun and several others, the other machine gun being silenced by the fire of his sections.
In the third case he crawled to within 15 yards of an M.G. post and killed the gunners with a grenade.
When his company withdrew from MALEME he helped to carry a wounded man out under fire, and together with another officer rallied more men together to carry other wounded men out.
He was then sent to bring in a company which had become isolated. With a Corporal he went through enemy territory over 600 yards, killing two Germans on the way, found the company, and brought it back to the Battalion's new position. But for this action it would have been completely cut off.
During the following two days his platoon occupied an exposed position on forward slopes and was continuously under fire. Second Lieutenant Upham was blown over by one mortar shell, and painfully wounded by a piece of shrapnel behind the left shoulder, by another. He disregarded this wound and remained on duty. He also received a bullet in the foot which he later removed in Egypt.
At GALATOS on 25th May his platoon was heavily engaged and came under severe mortar and machine-gun fire. While his platoon stopped under cover of a ridge Second-Lieu-

tenant Upham went forward, observed the enemy and brought the platoon forward when the Germans advanced. They killed over 40 with fire and grenades and forced the remainder to fall back.

When his platoon was ordered to retire he sent it back under the platoon Serjeant and he went back to warn other troops that they were being cut off. When he came out himself he was fired on by two Germans. He fell and shammed dead, then crawled into a position and having the use of only one arm rested his rifle in the fork of a tree and as the Germans came forward he killed them both. The second to fall actually hit the muzzle of his rifle as he fell.

On 30th May at SPHAKIA his platoon was ordered to deal with a party of the enemy which had advanced down a ravine to near Force Headquarters. Though in an exhausted condition he climbed the steep hill to the west of the ravine, placed his men in positions on the slope overlooking the ravine and himself went to the top with a Bren gun and two riflemen. By clever tactics he induced the enemy party to expose itself and then at a range of 500 yards shot 22 and caused the remainder to disperse in panic.

During the whole of the operations he suffered from dysentery and was able to eat very little, in addition to being wounded and bruised.

He showed superb coolness, great skill and dash and complete disregard of danger. His conduct and leadership inspired his whole platoon to fight magnificently throughout, and in fact was an inspiration to the Battalion.

(Second Supplement to *The London Gazette* of 10 October 1941. 14 October 1941, Numb. 35306, pp. 5935–36)

Charles Hazlitt UPHAM VC*
Second Lieutenant, 20th Battalion 2nd New Zealand Division, 2nd New Zealand Expeditionary Force

War Office, 26th September, 1945,
Captain Charles Hazlitt UPHAM, V.C. (8077),
New Zealand Military Forces

Captain C.H. Upham, V.C., was commanding a Company of New Zealand troops in the Western Desert during the operations which culminated in the attack on El Ruweisat Ridge on the night of 14th–15th July, 1942.

In spite of being twice wounded, once when crossing open ground swept by enemy fire to inspect his forward sections guarding our mine-fields and again when he completely destroyed an entire truck load of German soldiers with hand grenades, Captain Upham insisted on remaining with his men to take part in the final assault.

During the opening stages of the attack on the ridge Captain Upham's Company formed part of the reserve battalion, but, when communications with the forward troops broke down and he was instructed to send up an officer to report on the progress of the attack, he went out himself armed with a Spandau gun and, after several sharp encounters with enemy machine gun posts, succeeded in bringing back the required information.

Just before dawn the reserve battalion was ordered forward, but, when it had almost reached its objective, very heavy fire was encountered from a strongly defeated enemy locality, consisting of four machine gun posts and a number of tanks.

Captain Upham, without hesitation, at once led his Company in a determined attack on the two nearest strongpoints on the left flank of the sector. His voice could be heard above the din of battle cheering on his men and, in spite of the fierce resistance of the enemy and the heavy casualties on both sides, the objective was captured.

Captain Upham, during the engagement, himself destroyed a German tank and several guns and vehicles with grenades and although he was shot through the elbow by a machine gun bullet and had his arm broken, he went on again to a forward position and brought back some of his men who had become isolated. He continued to dominate the situation until his men had beaten off a violent enemy counter-attack and consolidated the vital position which they had won under his inspiring leadership.

Exhausted by pain from his wound and weak from loss of blood Captain Upham was then removed to the Regimental Aid Post but immediately his wound had been dressed he returned to his men, remaining with them all day long under heavy enemy artillery and mortar fire, until he was again severely wounded and being now unable to move fell into the hands of the enemy when, his gallant Company having been reduced to only six survivors, his position was finally over-run by superior enemy forces, in spite of the outstanding gallantry and magnificent leadership shown by Captain Upham.

The Victoria Cross was conferred on Captain Upham for conspicuous bravery during operations in Crete in May, 1941, and the award was announced in *The London Gazette* dated 14th October, 1941.

(Supplement to *The London Gazette* of 25 September 1945. 26 September 1945, Numb. 37283, p. 4779)

Date   **VC/GC recipient**
1942   Malta

Citation
THE ISLAND OF MALTA GC
The Governor
Malta

To honour her brave people I award the George Cross to the Island Fortress of Malta to bear witness to a heroism and devotion that will long be famous in History.

George R.I.
15th April 1942.

(Letter from HM King George VI to Lieutenant General Sir William Dobbie, Governor of Malta)

Date   **VC/GC recipient**
1942   Eugene Esmonde

Citation
Eugene ESMONDE VC
Lieutenant Commander, Royal Navy, No 825 Squadron, Fleet Air Arm

APPENDIX

Admiralty, Whitehall.
3rd March, 1942.
The late Lieutenant-Commander (A) Eugene Esmonde, D.S.O.,
Royal Navy.

On the morning of Thursday, 12th February, 1942, Lieutenant-Commander Esmonde, in command of a Squadron of the Fleet Air Arm, was told that the German Battle-Cruisers SCHARNHORST and GNEISENAU and the Cruiser PRINZ EUGEN, strongly escorted by some thirty surface craft, were entering the Straits of Dover, and that his Squadron must attack before they reached the sand-banks North East of Calais.
Lieutenant-Commander Esmonde knew well that this enterprise was desperate. Soon after noon he and his squadron of six Swordfish set course for the Enemy, and after ten minutes fight were attacked by a strong force of Enemy fighters. Touch was lost with his fighter escort; and in the action which followed all his aircraft were damaged. He flew on, cool and resolute, serenely challenging hopeless odds, to encounter the deadly fire of the Battle-Cruisers and their Escort, which shattered the port wing of his aircraft. Undismayed, he led his Squadron on, straight through this inferno of fire, in steady flight towards their target. Almost at once he was shot down; but his Squadron went on to launch a gallant attack, in which at least one torpedo is believed to have struck the German Battle-Cruisers, and from which not one of the six aircraft returned.
His high courage and splendid resolution will live in the traditions of the Royal Navy, and remain for many generations a fine and stirring memory.

(Third Supplement to *The London Gazette* of 27 February 1942. 3 March 1942, Numb. 35474, p. 1007)

Date   **VC/GC recipient**
1943   Guy Gibson

Citation
Guy Penrose GIBSON VC
Wing Commander
Royal Air Force
Air Ministry, 28th May, 1943.
Acting Wing Commander Guy Penrose GIBSON, D.S.O., D.F.C. (39438). Reserve of Air Force Officers, No. 617 Squadron

This officer served as a night bomber pilot at the beginning of the war and quickly established a reputation as an outstanding operational pilot. In addition to taking the fullest possible share in all normal operations, he made single-handed attacks during his "rest" nights on such highly defended objectives as the German Battleship *Tirpitz*, then completing in Wilhelmshaven.
When his tour of operational duty was concluded, he asked for a further operational posting and went to a night-fighter unit instead of being posted for instructional duties. In the course of his second operational tour, he destroyed at least three enemy bombers and contributed much to the raising and development of new night-fighter formations.
After a short period in a training unit, he again volunteered for operational duties and

returned to night bombers. Both as an operational pilot and as leader of his squadron, he achieved outstandingly successful results and his personal courage knew no bounds. Berlin, Cologne, Danzig, Gdynia, Genoa, Le Creusot, Milan, Nuremberg and Stuttgart were among the targets he attacked by day and by night.

On the conclusion of his third operational tour, Wing Commander Gibson pressed strongly to be allowed to remain on operations and he was selected to command a squadron then forming for special tasks. Under his inspiring leadership, this squadron has now executed one of the most devastating attacks of the war – the breaching of the Moehne and Eder dams.

The task was fraught with danger and difficulty. Wing Commander Gibson personally made the initial attack on the Moehne dam. Descending to within a few feet of the water and taking the full brunt of the anti-aircraft defences, he delivered his attack with great accuracy. Afterwards he circled very low for 30 minutes, drawing the enemy fire on himself in order to leave as free a run as possible to the following aircraft which were attacking the dam in turn.

Wing Commander Gibson then led the remainder of his force to the Eder dam where, with complete disregard for his own safety, he repeated his tactics and once more drew on himself the enemy fire so that the attack could be successfully developed.

Wing Commander Gibson has completed over 170 sorties, involving more than 600 hours operational flying. Throughout his operational career, prolonged exceptionally at his own request, he has shown leadership, determination and valour of the highest order.

(Supplement to *The London Gazette* of 25 May 1943. 28 May 1943, Numb. 36030, p. 2361)

Date **VC/GC recipient**
1944 John Baskeyfield

Citation
John Daniel BASKEYFIELD VC
Lance Sergeant, 2ⁿᵈ Battalion The South Staffordshire Regiment,
1ˢᵗ Airlanding Brigade, 1ˢᵗ Airborne Division
War Office, 23ʳᵈ November, 1944.
No. 5057916 Lance-Sergeant John Daniel Baskeyfield, The South Staffordshire Regiment (1ˢᵗ Airborne Division) (Stoke-on-Trent).

On 20ᵗʰ September, 1944, during the battle of Arnhem, Lance-Sergeant Baskeyfield was the N.C.O. in charge of a 6-pounder anti-tank gun at Oosterbeek. The enemy developed a major attack on this sector with infantry, tanks and self-propelled guns with the obvious intent to break into and overrun the Battalion position. During the early stage of the action, the crew commanded by this N.C.O. was responsible for the destruction of two Tiger tanks and at least one self-propelled gun, thanks to the coolness and daring of this N.C.O., who, with complete disregard for his own safety, allowed each tank to come well within 100 yards of his gun before opening fire.

In the course of this preliminary engagement Lance-Sergeant Baskeyfield was badly wounded in the leg and the remainder of his crew were either killed or badly wounded. During the brief respite after this engagement Lance-Sergeant Baskeyfield refused to be carried to the Regimental Aid Post and spent his time attending to his gun and shouting encouragement to his comrades in neighbouring trenches.

After a short interval the enemy renewed the attack with even greater ferocity than before, under cover of intense mortar and shell fire. Manning his gun quite alone Lance-Sergeant Baskeyfield continued to fire round after round at the enemy until his gun was put out of action. By this time his activity was the main factor in keeping the enemy tanks at bay. The fact that the surviving men in his vicinity were held together and kept in action was undoubtedly due to his magnificent example and outstanding courage. Time after time enemy attacks were launched and driven off. Finally, when his gun was knocked out, Lance-Sergeant Baskeyfield crawled, under intense enemy fire, to another 6-pounder gun nearby, the crew of which had been killed, and proceeded to man it single-handed. With this gun he engaged an enemy self-propelled gun which was approaching to attack. Another soldier crawled across open ground to assist him but was killed almost at once. Lance-Sergeant Baskeyfield succeeded in firing two rounds at the self-propelled gun, scoring one direct hit which rendered it ineffective. While preparing to fire a third shot, however, he was killed by a shell from a supporting enemy tank.

The superb gallantry of this N.C.O. is beyond praise. During the remaining days at Arnhem stories of his valour were a constant inspiration to all ranks. He spurned danger, ignored pain and, by his supreme fighting spirit, infected all who witnessed his conduct with the same aggressiveness and dogged devotion to duty which characterised his actions throughout.

(Supplement to *The London Gazette* of 21 November 1944. 23 November 1944, Numb. 36807, p. 5375)

Date   **VC/GC recipient**
1944   Tul Bahadur Pun

Citation
TUL BAHADUR PUN VC
Rifleman, 3rd Battalion 6th Gurkha Rifles, 77th Indian Infantry Brigade, 3rd Indian Division

War Office, 9th November, 1944.
No. 10119 Rifleman Tul Bahadur Pun, 6th Gurkha Rifles, Indian Army.

In Burma on June 23rd, 1944, a Battalion of the 6th Gurkha Rifles was ordered to attack the Railway Bridge at Mogaung. Immediately the attack developed the enemy opened concentrated and sustained cross fire at close range from a position known as the Red House and from a strong bunker position two hundred yards to the left of it.

So intense was the cross fire that both the leading platoons of "B" Company, one of which was Rifleman Tulbahadur Pun's, were pinned to the ground and the whole of his Section was wiped out with the exception of himself, the Section Commander and one other man. The Section Commander immediately led the remaining two men in a charge on the Red House but was at once badly wounded. Rifleman Tulbahadur Pun and his remaining companion continued the charge, but the latter too was immediately badly wounded. Rifleman Tulbahadur Pun then seized the Bren Gun, and firing from the hip as he went, continued the charge on this heavily bunkered position alone, in the face of the most shattering concentration of automatic fire, directed straight at him. With the dawn coming up behind him, he presented a perfect target to the Japanese. He had to move for thirty yards over open ground, ankle deep in mud, through shell holes and over fallen trees.

Despite these overwhelming odds, he reached the Red House and closed with the Japanese occupants. He killed three and put five more to flight and captured two light machine guns and much ammunition. He then gave accurate supporting fire from the bunker to the remainder of his platoon which enabled them to reach their objective.

His outstanding courage and superb gallantry in the face of odds which meant almost certain death were most inspiring to all ranks and were beyond praise.

(Supplement to *The London Gazette* of 7 November 1944, 9 November 1944, Numb. 36785, p. 5129)

Date   **VC/GC recipient**
1944   Leonard Cheshire

Citation
Geoffrey Leonard CHESHIRE VC (later Lord CHESHIRE VC)
Wing Commander, Nos 35, 76 and 617 Squadrons, Royal Air Force Volunteer Reserve

Air Ministry, 8th September, 1944
Wing Commander Geoffrey Leonard CHESHIRE, D.S.O., D.F.C. (72021)
Royal Air Force Volunteer Reserve, 617 Squadron.

This officer began his operational career in June, 1940. Against strongly-defended targets he soon displayed the courage and determination of an exceptional leader. He was always ready to accept extra risks to ensure success. Defying the formidable Ruhr defences, he frequently released his bombs from below 2,000 feet. Over Cologne in November, 1940, a shell burst inside his aircraft, blowing out one side and starting a fire; undeterred, he went on to bomb his target. About this time, he carried out a number of convoy patrols in addition to his bombing missions.

At the end of his first tour of operational duty in January, 1941, he immediately volunteered for a second. Again, he pressed home his attacks with the utmost gallantry. Berlin, Bremen, Cologne, Duisburg, Essen and Kiel were among the heavily-defended targets which he attacked. When he was posted for instructional duties in January, 1942, he undertook four more operational missions.

He started his third operational tour in August, 1942, when he was given command of a squadron. He led the squadron with outstanding skill on a number of missions before being appointed in March, 1943, as a station commander.

In October, 1943, he undertook a fourth operational tour, relinquishing the rank of group captain at his own request so that he could again take part in operations. He immediately set to work as the pioneer of a new method of marking enemy targets involving very low flying. In June, 1944, when marking a target in the harbour at Le Havre in broad daylight and without cloud cover, he dived well below the range of the light batteries before releasing his marker-bombs, and he came very near to being destroyed by the strong barrage which concentrated on him.

During his fourth tour which ended in July, 1944, Wing Commander Cheshire led his squadron personally on every occasion, always undertaking the most dangerous and difficult talks of marking the target alone from a low level in the face of strong defences. Wing Commander Cheshire's cold and calculated acceptance of risks is exemplified by his conduct in an attack on Munich in April, 1944. This was an experimental attack to test out the new method of target marking at low level against a heavily-defended target situated deep in Reich territory. Munich was selected, at Wing Commander Cheshire's request, because of the formidable nature of its light anti-aircraft and searchlight defences. He was obliged to follow, in bad weather, a direct route which took him over the defences of Augsburg and thereafter he was continuously under fire. As he reached the target, flares were being released by our high-flying aircraft. He was illuminated from above and below. All guns within range opened fire on him. Diving to 700 feet, he dropped his markers with great precision and began to climb away. So blinding were the searchlights that he almost lost control. He then flew over the city at 1,000 feet to assess the accuracy of his work and direct other aircraft. His own was badly hit by shell fragments but he continued to fly over the target area until he was satisfied that he had done all in his power to ensure success. Eventually, when he set course for base, the task of disengaging himself from the defence approved even more hazardous than the approach. For a full twelve minutes after leaving the target area he was under withering fire but he came safely through.

Wing Commander Cheshire has now completed a total of 100 missions. In four years of fighting against the bitterest opposition he has maintained a record of outstanding personal achievement, placing himself invariably in the forefront of the battle. What he did in the Munich operation was typical of the careful planning, brilliant execution and contempt for danger which has established for Wing Commander Cheshire a reputation second to none in Bomber Command.

(Fifth Supplement to *The London Gazette* of 5 September 1944. 8 September 1944, Numb. 36693, pp. 4175–76)

Date   **VC/GC recipient**
1944   Noor Inayat Khan

Citation
Noor-un-Nisa INAYAT KHAN GC
Ensign, Women's Auxiliary Air Force, seconded Women's Transport Service (FANY), attached Special Operations Executive

St. James's Palace, S.W.1., 5th April, 1949.

The KING has been graciously pleased to approve the posthumous award of the GEORGE CROSS to:

Assistant Section Officer Nora INAYAT-KHAN (9901),
Women's Auxiliary Air Force.

Assistant Section Officer Nora INAYAT-KHAN was the first woman operator to be infiltrated into enemy occupied France, and was landed by Lysander aircraft on 16th

June, 1943. During the weeks immediately following her arrival, the Gestapo made mass arrests in the Paris Resistance groups to which she had been detailed. She refused however to abandon what had become the principal and most dangerous post in France, although given the opportunity to return to England, because she did not wish to leave her French comrades without communications and she hoped also to rebuild her group. She remained at her post therefore and did the excellent work which earned her a posthumous Mention in Dispatches.

The Gestapo had a full description of her, but knew only her code name "Madeleine". They deployed considerable forces in their effort to catch her and so break the last remaining link with London. After 3 ½ months she was betrayed to the Gestapo and taken to their H.Q. in the Avenue Foch. The Gestapo had found her codes and messages and were now in a position to work back to London. They asked her to co-operate, but she refused and gave them no information of any kind. She was imprisoned in one of the cells on the 5th floor of the Gestapo H.Q. and remained there for several weeks during which time she made two unsuccessful attempts at escape. She was asked to sign a declaration that she would make no further attempts but she refused and the Chief of the Gestapo obtained permission from Berlin to send her to Germany for "safe custody". She was the first agent to be sent to Germany.

Assistant Section Officer INAYAT-KHAN was sent to Karlsruhe in November, 1943, and then to Pforsheim where her cell was apart from the main prison. She was considered to be a particularly dangerous and unco-operative prisoner. The Director of the prison has also been interrogated and has confirmed that Assistant Section Officer INAYAT-KHAN, when interrogated by the Karlsruhe Gestapo, refused to give any information whatsoever, either as to her work or her colleagues.

She was taken with three others to Dachau Camp on the 12th September, 1944. On arrival, she was taken to the crematorium and shot.

Assistant Section Officer INAYAT-KHAN displayed the most conspicuous courage, both moral and physical over a period of more than 12 months.

(Supplement to *The London Gazette* of 1 April 1949. 5 April 1949, Numb. 38578, p. 1703)

Date   VC/GC recipient
1944   Norman Jackson

Citation
Norman Cyril JACKSON VC
Sergeant, No 106 Squadron, Royal Force, Royal Air Force Volunteer Reserve
Air Ministry, 26th October, 1945.
905192 Sergeant (now Warrant Officer) Norman Cyril Jackson,
R.A.F.V.R., 106 Squadron.

This airman was the flight engineer in a Lancaster detailed to attack Schweinfurt on the night of 26th April, 1944. Bombs were dropped successfully and the aircraft was climbing out of the target area. Suddenly it was attacked by a fighter at about 20,000 feet. The captain took evading action at once, but the enemy secured many hits. A fire started near a petrol tank on the upper surface of the starboard wing, between the fuselage and the inner engine.

APPENDIX

Sergeant Jackson was thrown to the floor during the engagement. Wounds which he received from shell splinters in the right leg and shoulder were probably sustained at that time. Recovering himself, he remarked that he could deal with the fire on the wing and obtained his captain's permission to try to put out the flames.

Pushing a hand fire-extinguisher into the top of his life-saving jacket and clipping on his parachute pack, Sergeant Jackson jettisoned the escape hatch above the pilot's head. He then started to climb out of the cockpit and back along the top of the fuselage to the starboard wing. Before he could leave the fuselage his parachute pack opened and the whole canopy and rigging lines spilled into the cockpit.

Undeterred, Sergeant Jackson continued. The pilot, bomb aimer and navigator gathered the parachute together and held on to the rigging lines, paying them out as the airman crawled aft. Eventually he slipped and, falling from the fuselage to the starboard wing, grasped an air intake on the leading edge of the wing. He succeeded in clinging on, but lost the extinguisher, which was blown away.

By this time, the fire had spread rapidly and Sergeant Jackson was involved. His face, hands and clothing were severely burnt. Unable to retain his hold, he was swept through the flames and over the trailing edge of the wing, dragging his parachute behind. When last seen it was only partly inflated and was burning in a number of places.

Realising that the fire could not be controlled, the captain gave the order to abandon aircraft. Four of the remaining members of the crew landed safely. The captain and the rear gunner have not been accounted for.

Sergeant Jackson was not able to control his descent and landed heavily. He sustained a broken ankle, his right eye was closed through burns and his hands were useless. These injuries, together with wounds received earlier, reduced him to a pitiable state. At daybreak he crawled to the nearest village, where he was taken prisoner. He bore the intense pain and discomfort of the journey to Dulag Luft with magnificent fortitude. After 10 months in hospital he made a good recovery, though his hands require further treatment and are only of limited use.

This airman's attempt to extinguish the fire and save the aircraft and crew from falling into enemy hands was an act of outstanding gallantry. To venture outside, when travelling at 200 miles an hour, at a great height and in intense cold, was an almost incredible feat. Had he succeeded in subduing the flames, there was little or no prospect of his regaining the cockpit. The spilling of his parachute and the risk of grave damage to its canopy reduced his chances of survival to a minimum. By his ready willingness to face these dangers he set an example of self-sacrifice which will ever be remembered.

(Fourth Supplement to *The London Gazette* of 23 October 1945. 26 October 1945, Numb. 37324, p. 5233)

Date **VC/GC recipient**
1944 Tasker Watkins

Citation
Tasker WATKINS VC
(later Sir Tasker WATKINS VC)
Lieutenant, 1ˢᵗ/5ᵗʰ Battalion The Welch Regiment
War Office, 2ⁿᵈ November, 1944.
Lieutenant Tasker Watkins (187088), The Welch Regiment (Dagenham)

In North-West Europe on the evening of 16ᵗʰ August, 1944, Lieutenant Watkins was commanding a company of the Welch Regiment. The battalion was ordered to attack objectives near the railway at Bafour. Lieutenant Watkins' company had to cross open cornfields in which booby traps had been set. It was not yet dusk and the company soon came under heavy machine-gun fire from posts in the corn and farther back, and also fire from an 88 mm. gun; many casualties were caused and the advance was slowed up.

Lieutenant Watkins, the only officer left, placed himself at the head of his men and under short range fire charged two posts in succession, personally killing or wounding the occupants with his Sten gun. On reaching his objective he found an anti-tank gun manned by a German soldier; his Sten gun jammed, so he threw it in the German's face and shot him with a pistol before he had time to recover.

Lieutenant Watkins' company now had only some 30 men left and was counter-attacked by 50 enemy infantry. Lieutenant Watkins directed the fire of his men and then led a bayonet charge, which resulted in the almost complete destruction of the enemy.

It was now dusk and orders were given for the battalion to withdraw. These orders were not received by Lieutenant Watkins' company as the wireless set had been destroyed. They now found themselves alone and surrounded in depleted numbers and in failing light. Lieutenant Watkins decided to rejoin his battalion by passing round the flank of the enemy position through which he had advanced but while passing through the cornfields once more, he was challenged by an enemy post at close range. He ordered his men to scatter and himself charged the post with a Bren gun and silenced it. He then led the remnants of his company back to battalion headquarters.

His superb gallantry and total disregard for his own safety during an extremely difficult period were responsible for saving the lives of his men and had a decisive influence on the course of the battle.

(Supplement to *The London Gazette* of 31 October 1944. 2 November 1944, Numb. 36774, pp. 5015–16)

Date **VC/GC recipient**
1945 Violet Szabo

Citation
Violette Reine Elizabeth SZABO GC
Ensign,
Women's Transport Service (First Aid Nursing Yeomanry), attached Special Operations Executive

St. James's Palace, S.W.1. 17th December, 1946.

The KING has been graciously pleased to award the GEORGE CROSS to: Violette, Madame SZABO (deceased), Women's Transport Service (First Aid Nursing Yeomanry).

Madame Szabo volunteered to take a particularly dangerous mission in France. She was parachuted into France in April, 1944, and undertook the task with enthusiasm. In her execution of the delicate researches entailed she showed great presence of mind and astuteness. She was twice arrested by the German security authorities but each time managed to get away. Eventually, however, with other members of her group, she was surrounded by the Gestapo in a house in the south west of France. Resistance appeared hopeless but Madame Szabo, seizing a Sten-gun and as much ammunition as she could carry, barricaded herself in part of the house and, exchanging shot for shot with the enemy, killed or wounded several of them. By constant movement, she avoided being cornered and fought until she dropped exhausted. She was arrested and had to undergo solitary confinement. She was then continuously and atrociously tortured but never by word or deed gave away any of her acquaintances or told the enemy anything of value. She was ultimately executed. Madame Szabo gave a magnificent example of courage and steadfastness.

(Fourth Supplement to *The London Gazette* of 13 December 1946. 17 December 1946, Numb. 37820, p. 6127)

Date   VC/GC recipient
1968   Barbara Jane Harrison

Citation
Barbara Jane HARRISON GC
Stewardess, British Overseas Airways Corporation (BOAC)

St. James's Palace, London S.W.1., 8th August 1969.

The QUEEN has been graciously pleased to make the undermentioned award.

GEORGE CROSS
Miss Barbara Jane HARRISON (deceased),
Stewardess, British Overseas Airway Corporation.

On April 8th 1968, soon after take-off from Heathrow Airport, No. 2 engine of B.O.A.C. Boeing 707 G-ARWE caught fire and subsequently fell from the aircraft, leaving a fierce fire burning at No. 2 engine position. About two and a half minutes later the aircraft made an emergency landing at the airport and the fire on the port wing intensified. Miss Harrison was one of the stewardesses in this aircraft and the duties assigned to her in an emergency were to help the steward at the aft station to open the appropriate rear door and inflate the escape chute and then to assist the passengers at the rear of the aircraft to leave in an orderly manner. When the aircraft landed Miss Harrison and the steward concerned opened the rear galley door and inflated the chute, which unfortunately became twisted on the way down so that the steward had to climb down it to straighten it before it could be used. Once out of the aircraft he was unable to return; hence Miss Harrison was left alone to the task of shepherding passengers to the rear door and helping them out of the aircraft. She encouraged some passengers to jump from the machine and pushed out others. With flames and explosions all around her and escape from the tail of the machine impossible she directed her passengers to another exit while she remained at her post. She was finally overcome while trying to save an elderly cripple who was seated in one of the last rows and whose body was found close to that of the stewardess. Miss Harrison was a very brave young lady who gave her life in her utter devotion to duty.

(Supplement to *The London Gazette* of 7 August 1969. 8 August 1969, Numb. 44913, p. 8211)

Date   **VC/GC recipient**
1969   Ray Simpson

Citation
Rayene Stewart SIMPSON VC
Warrant Officer Class II, Australian Army Training Team,
attached 232nd Mobile Strike Force Company, 5th Special Forces Group

St James's Palace, London S.W.1., 29th August 1969.

The QUEEN has been graciously pleased, on the advice of Her Majesty's Australian Ministers, to approve the award of the Victoria Cross to the undermentioned:
(To be dated 28th August 1969)
Warrant Officer Class II Rayene Stewart SIMPSON, D.C.M., 217622,Royal Australian Infantry.

On 6th May 1969, Warrant Officer Simpson was serving as Commander of 232nd Mobile Strike Force Company of 5th Special Forces Group on a search and clear operation in Kontum Province, near the Laotion border. When one of his platoons became heavily engaged with the enemy, he led the remainder of his company to its assistance. Disregarding the dangers involved, he placed himself at the front of his troops, thus becoming a focal point of enemy fire, and personally led the assault on the left flank of the enemy position. As the company moved forward, an Australian Warrant Officer commanding one of the platoons was seriously wounded and the assault began to falter. Warrant Officer Simpson, at great personal risk and under heavy enemy fire, moved across open ground, reached the wounded Warrant Officer and carried him to a position of safety. He then returned to his company where, with complete disregard for his safety, he crawled forward to within ten metres of the enemy and threw grenades into their positions. As darkness fell, and being unable to break into the enemy position, Warrant Officer Simpson ordered his company to withdraw. He then threw smoke grenades and, carrying a wounded platoon leader, covered the withdrawal of the company together with five indigenous soldiers. His leadership and personal bravery in this action were outstanding.
On 11th May 1969, in the same operation, Warrant Officer Simpson's Battalion Commander was killed and an Australian Warrant Officer and several indigenous soldiers

were wounded. In addition, one other Australian Warrant Officer who had been separated from the majority of his troops was contained in the area by enemy fire. Warrant Officer Simpson quickly organised two platoons of indigenous soldiers and several advisers and led them to the position of the contact. On reaching the position the element with Warrant Officer Simpson came under heavy fire and all but a few of the soldiers with him fell back. Disregarding his own safety, he moved forward in the face of accurate enemy machine gun fire, in order to cover the initial evacuation of the casualties. The wounded were eventually moved out of the line of enemy fire, which all this time was directed at Warrant Officer Simpson from close range. At the risk of almost certain death, he made several attempts to move further forward towards his Battalion Commander's body, but on each occasion he was stopped by heavy fire. Realising the position was becoming untenable and that priority should be given to extricating other casualties as quickly as possible, Warrant Officer Simpson alone and still under enemy fire covered the withdrawal of the wounded by personally placing himself between the wounded and the enemy. From this position he fought on and by outstanding courage and valour was able to prevent the enemy advance until the wounded were removed from the immediate vicinity. Warrant Officer Simpson's gallant and individual action and his coolness under fire were exceptional and were instrumental in achieving the successful evacuation of the wounded to the helicopter evacuation pad.

Warrant Officer Simpson's repeated acts of personal bravery in this operation were an inspiration to all the Vietnamese, United States and Australian soldiers who served with him. His conspicuous gallantry was in the highest tradition of the Australian Army.

(Supplement to *The London Gazette* of 25 August 1969. 29 August 1969, No. 44925, p. 8873)

Appendix

1 This citation is published jointly with that of Lieutenant Thomas Young, as he and William Hall were awarded the VC in the same action.

2 This citation is published jointly with that of Private John Williams, as he and Private Henry Hook were awarded the VC in the same action.

3 This citation is published jointly with that of Chief Stoker William Lashley, as he and Petty Officer Tom Crean were awarded the Albert Medal in the same life-saving action.

4 Although he was awarded the Albert Medal, which was later to be translated to the George Cross, Tom Crean was not alive at the date of the translation (15 December 1971). According to the Royal Warrant for the translation of the Albert Medal to the George Cross, only those who were alive at the date of that warrant 'should be regarded as if they had been awarded the George Cross'.

NOTES

Chapter 1 *(written by Saul David)*

1 John Daniel Baskeyfield, VC, in Christopher Wright and Glenda M. Anderson (eds), *The Victoria Cross and the George Cross: The Complete History*, 3 vols (London: Methuen, 2013), III, pp. 584–5.

2 Lloyd Clark, *Arnhem: Jumping the Rhine 1944 and 1945* (London: Headline, 2008), p. 66.

3 Ibid., p. 87.

4 Ibid., p. 89.

5 Ibid., p. 83.

6 William F. Buckingham, *Arnhem 1944: A Reappraisal* (Stroud: Tempus, 2002), p. 18.

7 http://ww2talk.com/index.php?threads/l-sgt-j-d-baskeyfield-2nd-airbourne-bn.58681/

8 Buckingham, *Arnhem 1944*, p. 18.

9 Ibid., pp. 31–7.

10 Ibid., pp. 38–9.

11 Ibid., p. 38.

12 Buckingham, *Arnhem 1944*, pp. 54–7; Saul David, *Military Blunders: The How and Why of Military Failure* (London: Robinson, 1997), p. 119.

13 Buckingham, *Arnhem 1944*, pp. 61–2; David, *Military Blunders*, p. 120.

14 David, *Military Blunders*, pp. 120–21.

15 Buckingham, *Arnhem 1944*, pp. 66–8.

16 David, *Military Blunders*, pp. 123–6.

17 http://www.pegasusarchive.org/arnhem/william_hewitt.htm

18 David, *Military Blunders*, pp. 126–8.

19 http://www.pegasusarchive.org/arnhem/william_hewitt.htm

20 http://www.pegasusarchive.org/arnhem/jack_bird.htm

21 Ibid.

22 Buckingham, *Arnhem 1944*, p. 154.

23 http://www.pegasusarchive.org/arnhem/jack_bird.htm

24 ://www.pegasusarchive.org/arnhem/john_baskeyfield.htm

25 Baskeyfield, in *The Victoria Cross and the George Cross*, III, p. 584.

26 War Diary of the 2nd South Staffs, Airborne Forces Archive, https://paradata.org.uk/media/3941?mediaSection=Post-combat%20reports&mediaitem=82281

27 David, *Military Blunders*, pp. 130–32.

28 Baskeyfield, in *The Victoria Cross and the George Cross*, III, p. 584.

Chapter 2 *(written by Tom Bromley)*

1 Alexander Jackson, 'The Sadness of the Master Builder', *The Blizzard*, issue 23 (2016), p. 130.

2 Ibid.

3 Ibid.

4 From A. A. Thompson, *The Exquisite Burden*, quoted in Richard Leake, *A Breed Apart* (Scarborough: Great Northern Publishing, 2008), p. 18.

5 Ibid., p. 25.

6 Quoted in Clive Harris and Julian Whippy, *The Greater Game: Sporting Icons Who Fell in the Great War* (Barnsley: Pen and Sword Military, 2008), p. 55.

7 Quoted in Leake, *A Breed Apart*, p. 27.

8 Harris and Whippey, *The Greater Game*, p. 60.

9 Quoted in Leake, *A Breed Apart*, p. 53.

10 Harris and Whippey, *The Greater Game*, p. 61.

11 Quoted in Leake, *A Breed Apart*, p. 77.

Chapter 3 *(written by Tom Bromley)*

1 Leonard Cheshire, *Bomber Pilot* (London: Hutchinson, 1943).

2 Ibid.

3 Squadron Leader R. C. Rivaz, *Tail Gunner* (London: Jarrolds, 1943).

4 Richard Morris, *Cheshire: The Biography of Leonard Cheshire*, VC, OM (London: Viking, 2000).

NOTES

Chapter 4 *(written by Spencer Jones)*

1 L. G. Thornton, *The Congreves: Father and Son* (London: John Murray, 1930), p. 29.
2 Ibid., p. 30.
3 Staffordshire Record Office, Walter Congreve Papers, D1057/R/5/7/2, Congreve to wife, 14 February 1900.
4 Thornton, *Congreves*, p. 61.
5 Staffordshire Record Office, Walter Congreve Papers, D1057/R/5/7/3, Congreve to H. Montagu Butler, 1 October 1900.
6 Thornton, *Congreves*, p. 135.
7 Terry Norman (ed.), *Armageddon Road: A VC's Diary 1914–16* (London: Walter Kimber, 1982), p. 175.
8 Ibid., p. 188.
9 Ibid., p. 195.
10 Hampshire Archives, Walter Congreve Papers, 170A12WD3731, Diary, 20 July 1916.
11 Thornton, *Congreves*, p. 164.
12 Private Collection, L. G. Thornton Papers, Congreve to Thornton, 15 June 1925.

Chapter 5 *(written by Tom Bromley)*

1 Although he was awarded the Albert Medal, which was later to be translated to the George Cross, Tom Crean was not alive at the date of the translation (15 December 1971). According to the Royal Warrant for the translation of the Albert Medal to the George Cross, only those who were alive at the date of that warrant 'should be regarded as they had been awarded the George Cross'.
2 Michael Smith, *Crean: An Unsung Hero* (Collins Press, 2009).

Chapter 6 *(written by Paul Garlington)*

1 Peter Daybell, *With a Smile and a Wave* (Barnsley: Pen and Sword Aviation, 2005), p. 20.
2 Dease family records quoted in Mark Ryan, *The First VCs* (Stroud: The History Press, 2014), p. 20.
3 *The Stonyhurst War Record* (London: Bemrose and Sons Ltd, 1927), p. xiii.
4 Richard Holmes, *Tommy: The British Soldier on the Western Front, 1914–1918* (London: HarperCollins, 2004), p. 378.
5 Quoted by Ryan, *The First VCs*, p. 94 and p. 107.

6 Dease family records quoted in Ryan, *The First VCs*, pp. 61–2.
7 Ibid., p. 68.
8 Quotations from Captain Tower, Lieutenants Cooper and Steele in Ryan, *The First VCs*. pp 70, 88, 99, 102
9 Lyn Macdonald, *1914: The Days of Hope* (London: Penguin Books, 1989), p. 97.
10 BBC TV, *Timewatch, 1914 – The War Revolution*, 2002–3.
11 Lyn Macdonald, *1914: The Days of Hope* (London: Penguin Books, 1989), p. 99.
12 Richard Holmes, *War Walks*, Series 1, Episode 3, BBC TV, 1996.

Chapter 7 *(written by Tom Bromley)*

1 http://www.edinburghs-war.ed.ac.uk/Moray/People-Morays-VCs/Admiral-Sir-Martin-Eric-Dunbar-Nasmith-VC-KCB-KCMG
2 Ibid.
3 Ibid.
4 Edwyn Gray, *British Submarines at War, 1914–1918* (Barnsley: Pen and Sword Military, 2016), p. 120.

Chapter 8 *(written by Tom Bromley)*

1 Chaz Bowyer, *Eugene Esmonde* (London: William Kimber, 1983).
2 Ibid., p. 30.
3 Ibid., p. 69–70.
4 Ibid., p. 89.
5 Ibid., p. 141.
6 Ibid., p. 150.
7 Ibid., p. 152.
8 Ibid., p. 167.
9 Ibid., p. 66.

Chapter 9 *(written by Spencer Jones)*

1 Spencer Jones, 'The Demon: Brigadier-General Charles FitzClarence VC' in Spencer Jones (ed.), *Stemming the Tide: Officers and Leadership in the British Expeditionary Force of 1914* (Solihull: Helion & Co., 2013), pp. 240–41.
2 Ibid., p. 243.
3 The National Archives, War Office Papers [WO] 98/8, Boer War Victoria Cross Citations, Captain Charles FitzClarence Citation.
4 Ibid.

5 Private Collection, FitzClarence Papers, Diary, 27 October. I am grateful to Mrs Elizabeth Scott, a descendant of FitzClarence, for allowing me to quote from these papers.

6 Jones, 'The Demon', p. 244.

7 FitzClarence Papers, Letter, 14 October.

8 H. W. Wilson, *With the Flag to Pretoria* (London: Harmsworth Bros, 1901), pp. 606–7.

9 The National Archives, WO 98/8, Captain FitzClarence Citation.

10 Jones, 'The Demon', p. 245.

11 Ibid., pp. 247–8.

12 Anthony Farrar-Hockley, *Death of an Arm* (London: Arthur Barker, 1967), p. 164.

13 James Edmonds, *Military Operations: France and Belgium 1914*, Vol. 2 (London: Macmillan, 1925), p. 304.

14 F. Loraine Petre, Wilfrid Ewart and Cecil Lowther, *The Scots Guards in the Great War 1914–1918* (London: John Murray, 1925), p. 51.

15 The National Archives, Cabinet Office Papers [CAB], 45/140, 'A Short Account of the Action of Gheluvelt 31 October 1914' by Major B. C. S. Clarke, 6 June 1922.

16 Mercian Regiment Archive, 'Gheluvelt: A Transcript of Notes by Major E. B. Hankey.'

17 Ibid.

18 Jack Sheldon, *The German Army at Ypres 1914* (Barnsley: Pen & Sword, 2010), pp. 173–4.

19 Ibid., p. 349.

Chapter 10 *(written by Tom Bromley)*

1 Stephen Snelling, *VCs of the First World War: Gallipoli* (Stroud: The History Press, 1995), loc. 345.

2 Ibid., loc. 335.

3 Alan Moorehead, *Gallipoli* (London: Aurum Press, revised edn, 2015), Chapter 7, loc. 1950.

4 Ibid., Chapter 7, loc. 1977.

5 Snelling, *VCs of the First World War: Gallipoli*, loc. 355.

6 Michael Ashcroft, 'Gallipoli Landing VCs', *Daily Telegraph*, 1 February 2014.

7 Snelling, *VCs of the First World War: Gallipoli*, loc. 364.

8 Ibid., loc. 413.

9 Ibid., loc. 412.

10 Ibid., loc. 435.

11 Quoted in 'Gallipoli: Six Tales of Valour and a Missing Victoria Cross', BBC News Website, 23 April 2015, http://www.bbc.co.uk/news/magazine-32416382.

Chapter 11 *(written by James Holland)*

1 Cited by Eric 'Winkle' Brown, author interview.

2 Author interview.

3 James Holland, *The War in the West: Germany Ascendant, 1939–1941*, Vol. 1 (London: Bantam Press, 2015), p. 74.

4 James Holland, *Dam Busters: The Race to Smash the Dams 1943* (London: Corgi, 2013), p. 129.

5 TNA AIR 4/37.

6 Holland, *Dam Busters*, p. 130.

7 Richard Morris, *Guy Gibson* (London: Viking, 1994), p. 127.

8 Ibid., p. 141.

9 Guy Gibson, *Enemy Coast Ahead* (London: Pan Books, 1956), p. 238.

Chapter 12 *(written by Tom Bromley)*

1 Saul David, *The Indian Mutiny 1857* (London: Viking 2002), p. 53.

2 Ibid., p. 54.

3 Charles Bruce Fergusson, 'William Hall VC', Journal of Education, Nova Scotia, December 1967.

4 Ibid.

5 Ibid.

6 David W States, 'William Hall VC of Horton Bluff, Nova Scotia', Collections of the Royal Nova Scotia Historical Society, Vol. 44, p. 73.

7 Fergusson, 'William Hall VC', Journal of Education, Nova Scotia, December 1967.

8 Phyllis Blakeley, 'William Hall, Canada's First Naval VC', The Dalhousie Review, Vol. XXXVII.

9 Ibid.

10 Ibid.

Chapter 13 *(written by James Holland)*

1 Philip Warner, *The Zeebrugge Raid*, loc. 1961 (Barnsley: Pen & Sword, 2008); C. Sandford Terry and Keble Howard, *The Raids on Zeebrugge and Ostend*, 1918, loc. 714 (Naval & Maritime Series, 2010).

2 Philip Warner, op. cit.

NOTES

3 https://www.rmg.co.uk

4 *London Gazette*, 17 March 1919.

Chapter 14 *(written by Tom Bromley)*

1 Susan Ottaway, *Fire Over Heathrow:
The Tragedy of Flight 712* (Barnsley: Pen and
Sword Aviation, 2008), p. 44.

2 Ibid., p. 4.

3 Ibid., p. ix.

4 Ibid., p. 47.

5 'The Crash by The Pilot', *Evening News*,
9 April 1968.

6 Ottaway, *Fire Over Heathrow*, p, 136.

7 Ibid., p. 139.

Chapter 15 *(written by Saul David)*

1 'An Account by 1373 Private Alfred Henry
Hook, VC, 2/24th Regiment', *Royal
Magazine*, February 1905, edited and
transcribed for publication by Walter Wood.

2 Saul David, *Military Blunders: The How and
Why of Military Failure* (London: Robinson,
1997), pp. 251–67.

3 Earlier that day, on receiving news that Zulus
had been seen in the vicinity of Isandlwana
camp, Major Henry Spalding, the original
commander at Rorke's Drift, had ridden ten
miles to the settlement at Helpmekaar to
hurry forward reinforcements. He left Chard
in command.

4 Knocked small holes in the walls through
which a rifle could be fired.

5 London, National Army Museum (NAM),
6309–115, 1st Chard Report, 25 January
1879.

6 'An Account by 1373 Private Alfred Henry
Hook', op. cit.

7 Ibid.

8 Saul David, *Zulu: The Heroism and Tragedy
of the Zulu War of 1879* (London: Penguin,
2004), p. 159.

9 Alfred Henry Hook VC, in *The Victoria Cross
and the George Cross: The Complete History*,
3 vols (2013), III, pp. 393–4; David, *Zulu*,
p. 163.

10 1st Chard Report, op. cit.; 'An Account by
1373 Private Alfred Henry Hook', op. cit.;
David, *Zulu*, p. 159.

11 'An Account by 1373 Private Alfred Henry
Hook', op. cit.

12 David, *Zulu*, pp. 166–9.

13 1st Chard report, op. cit.

14 'An Account by 1373 Private Alfred Henry
Hook', op. cit.

15 1st Chard Report, op. cit.

16 'An Account by 1362 Private Frederick
Hitch, VC, 2/24th Regiment', in Norman
Holme, *The Noble 24th: Biographical
Records of the 24th Regiment in the Zulu
War and the South African Campaigns
1877–1879* (London, 1999), p. 284.

17 Interview with Roger Lane, Sergeant
Gallagher's great-grandson, 'Zulu – The
True Story', *Timewatch*, BBC2, 24 October
2003.

18 'An Account by 1373 Private Alfred Henry
Hook', op. cit.

19 David, *Zulu*, p. 170.

20 2nd Chard Report, 21 February 1880, in
Holme, *The Noble 24th*, p. 274.

21 Ibid.; 'An Account by 1373 Private Alfred
Henry Hook', op. cit.

22 2nd Chard Report, op. cit.

23 'An Account by 1373 Private Alfred Henry
Hook', op. cit.

24 In his account of the battle, Hook says
Robert Cole 'went outside and was instantly
killed by the Zulus'. In fact Cole was later
rescued from the hospital by a Lance
Corporal McMahon. Hook may have
confused him with Private Thomas Cole
of Monmouth whose death was witnessed
by Lieutenant Chard. (Privates Robert and
Thomas Cole, in Holme, *The Noble 24th*,
p. 329.)

25 Ibid.

26 Ibid.

27 Account by Private John Waters,
The Cambrian 13 June 1879.

28 Ibid.

29 Ibid.

30 Account by Private John Waters, *The
Cambrian*, 13 June 1879.

31 'An Account by 1373 Private Alfred Henry
Hook', op. cit.; David, *Zulu*, p. 175.

32 Account by Private R. Jones, *Strand*,
January–June 1891.

33 'An Account by 1373 Private Alfred Henry
Hook', op. cit.

34 David, *Zulu*, pp. 177–9.

35 They collected 100 rifles and guns, and
around 400 assegais.

36 'An Account by 1373 Private Alfred Henry
Hook', op. cit.

37 2nd Chard Report, op. cit.

38 An Account by 1373 Private Alfred Henry Hook', op. cit.

39 David, *Zulu*, pp. 183–4.

40 Lieutenant Gonville Bromhead, VC, in Holme, *The Noble 24th*, p. 320.

41 After lobbying by senior officers and the press, a further three Victoria Crosses were awarded to Surgeon James Reynolds, Commissary Dalton and a Corporal Christian Schiess who had performed prodigious deeds during the defence of the inner line. The total of eleven VCs is the most awarded for a single action.

42 *The Victoria Cross and the George Cross*, III, pp. 392–4.

43 Ibid.; Hook, in Holme, *The Noble 24th*, pp. 339–40

44 Letters from the Assistant Secretary at the British Musuem to Mrs Ian Pratt, 19 May 1954, VC-GC Association Archives; Transcription of Testimonials sent to the British Museum on behalf of Hook, VC-GC Association Archives.

45 *The Victoria Cross and the George Cross*, III, pp. 393–4.

Chapter 16 *(written by James Holland)*
1 TNA AIR 27834.

2 *Daily Telegraph*, 26 March 1994.

Chapter 17 *(written by Tom Bromley)*
1 Jean Overton Fuller, *Noor-un-nisa Inayat Khan* (East-West, 1988), p. 72.

2 Shrabani Basu, *Spy Princess: The Life of Noor Inayat Khan* (Stroud: The History Press, 2011), Chapter 2, loc. 731.

3 Overton Fuller, *Noor-un-nisa Inayat Khan*, p. 84.

4 Internal SOE Memo, 21 October 1942.

5 Basu, *Spy Princess*, Chapter 6, loc. 1805.

6 Ibid., Chapter 6, loc. 1827.

7 Ibid., Chapter 6, loc. 1836.

8 Overton Fuller, *Noor-un-nisa Inayat Khan*, p. 209.

9 Hugh Verity, *We Landed by Moonlight* (Manchester: Crecy, 1998), p. 94.

Chapter 18 *(written by James Holland)*
1 Author interview.

2 Richard Holmes, *The Western Front* (London: BBC Book, 2008), p. 76.

3 Edward M. Spiers, 'Laidlaw, Daniel Logan (1875–1950)', *Oxford Dictionary of National Biography* (Oxford: Oxford University Press, 2008).

Chapter 19 *(written by James Holland)*
1 *Times of Malta*, 17 April 1942.

2 Author interview.

3 *Times of Malta*, 12 June 1941.

4 Author interview.

5 James Holland, *Fortress Malta: An Island Under Siege 1940–1943* (London: Cassell Military Paperbacks, 2009), p. 259.

6 Author interview.

6 Author interview.

7 *Times of Malta*, 10 April 1942.

8 Ibid., 24 April 1942.

9 *Times of Malta*, 14 May 1942.

10 Official medical documents in possession of Mr Simon Cusens.

11 Author interview.

12 Author interview.

13 Albert Kesselring, *The Memoirs of Field-Marshal Kesselring* (New York: Skyhorse Publishing, 2016), p. 135.

14 *Times of Malta*, 1 September 1942.

15 Author interview.

Chapter 20 *(written by Tom Bromley)*
1 Daphne Pearson, *In War and Peace* (London: Thorogood Publishing, 2001). All other excerpts quoted in this piece are also from this memoir.

Chapter 21 *(written by Tom Bromley)*
1 Roger Arnett, *Drop Zone Burma* (Barnsley: Pen and Sword Books, 2008), p. 105.

2 J. P. Cross and Buddhiman Gurung (eds), *Gurkhas at War* (Barnsley: Greenhill Books, 2002), pp. 107–8.

3 James Lunt, *Jai Sixth!* (Barnsley: Pen and Sword Books, 1996), p. 67.

4 Tul Bahaldur Pun, 'My War', *Daily Mirror*, 2 June 2007.

5 Ibid.

Chapter 22 *(written by Saul David)*
1 Lord Roberts of Kandahar, *Forty-One Years in India* (London: Macmillan, 1898), p. 214.

2 Indians remember it as the Great Uprising or the First War of Independence.

3 Saul David, *The Indian Mutiny: 1857*
(London: Penguin, 2002), p. 333.
4 Roberts, *Forty-One Years in India*, pp.
212–13.
5 Ibid., p. 213.
6 Ibid., pp. 213–14.
7 Ibid., p. 214.
8 General term for an Indian cavalry trooper.
9 General term for an Indian infantry private.
10 Ibid., pp. 214–15; Lieutenant Frederick
Sleigh Roberts, VC, in *The Victoria Cross
and the George Cross: The Complete History*,
3 vols (London: Methuen, 2013), I, p. 243.
11 Roberts, *Forty-One Years in India*, p. 215;
Roberts, in *The Victoria Cross and the
George Cross*, I, pp. 243–4.
12 Fred Roberts, *Letters Written During the
Indian Mutiny* (London: Macmillan, 1924),
Preface, p. xvii.
13 Officers in the East India Company army
were paid twice the salary given to their
equivalent ranks in the British Army, and
did not have to purchase their commissions.
14 Brian Robson, 'Frederick Sleigh Roberts,
first Earl Roberts', in *Oxford Dictionary
of National Biography* (Oxford: OUP,
2004–16).
15 Nominal promotion for gallantry or
meritorious conduct, without the
corresponding increase in authority and pay.
16 A month earlier, on 26 June 1857, the
Queen had personally awarded the first
sixty-two Victoria Crosses to veterans of
the Crimean War in a public ceremony in
Hyde Park.
17 Roberts, *Letters Written During the Indian
Mutiny*, pp. 28–9.
18 Ibid., pp. 122–3.
19 Ibid., pp. 134–5.
20 Robson, 'Frederick Sleigh Roberts', op. cit.
21 At which point the East India Company
Armies became the Indian Army.
22 Robson, 'Frederick Sleigh Roberts', op. cit.
23 Roberts, *Forty-One Years in India*, pp.
478–9.
24 Ibid., p. 479.
25 Ibid.
26 Ibid., pp. 479–92.
27 Ibid., p. 492.
28 Robson, 'Frederick Sleigh Roberts', op. cit.
29 Prior to the Boer War, Victoria Crosses
could not be awarded posthumously.

Freddie Roberts' death helped to change
this policy, though the Royal Warrant was
not amended until 1920.
30 Also awarded for attempting to save the guns
at Colenso.
31 Ibid.
32 Rodney Attwood, *The Life of Field Marshal
Lord Roberts* (London: Bloomsbury, 2015),
p. 188.
33 Ibid., p. 192.
34 Robson, 'Frederick Sleigh Roberts', op. cit.
35 Attwood, *The Life of Field Marshal Lord
Roberts*, p. 214.
36 Robson, 'Frederick Sleigh Roberts', op. cit.
37 Roberts, in *The Victoria Cross and the
George Cross*, III, pp. 393–4.

Chapter 23 *(written by Tom Bromley)*
1 Letter from Robinson to his mother, 23
January 1913. Quoted in Raymond Laurence
Rimell, *The Airship VC* (Birmingham: Aston
Publications, 1989), p. 21.
2 Letter from Robinson to his mother, quoted
in Leslie William Bills, *A Medal for Life*
(Staplehurst: Spellmount, 1990).
3 Ibid., p. 37.
4 Rimell, *The Airship VC*, pp. 34, 37.

Chapter 24 *(written by Tom Bromley)*
1 Michael J. Malone, *Simmo* (Perth:
Imprimatur Books, 2015)
2 Ibid., p. 161.
3 Ibid., p. 161.
4 Ibid., p. 51.
5 Ibid., p. 124.
6 Ibid., p. 147.
7 Ibid., p.215

Chapter 25 *(written by Tom Bromley)*
1 Tania Szabo, *Young, Brave and Beautiful*
(Stroud: The History Press, 2015), p. 383.
2 Susan Ottaway, *Violette Szabo* (Barnsley: Pen
and Sword Books, 2002), p. 73.
3 Ibid., p. 80.
4 Marcus Binney, *The Women Who Lived for
Danger* (London: Hodder & Stoughton,
2002), Chapter 9, loc. 3280.
5 Ibid., Chapter 9, loc. 3443.
6 Ibid., Chapter 9, loc. 3490.
7 Szabo, *Young, Brave and Beautiful*, p. 307.
8 Ibid.
9 Ottaway, *Violette Szabo*, p. 154.

Chapter 26 *(written by Tom Bromley)*
1 Kenneth Sandford, *Mark of the Lion* (London: Hutchinson, 1962), chapter 3, The Impatient Sergeant, loc. 443

2 C. E. Lucas Phillips, *Victoria Cross Battles of the Second World War* (London: Heinemann, 1973), pp. 15–16.

3 Direct speech from Sandford, *Mark of the Lion*, chapter 2, loc. 342–50 (Penguin ebook edition) (adapted by the author of this essay).

4 Ibid., chapter 2, loc. 368.

5 Sandford, *Mark of the Lion*.

6 Direct speech from Sandford, *Mark of the Lion*, chapter 3, loc. 495 (adapted by the author of this essay).

7 Sandford, *Mark of the Lion*.

8 Glyn Harper and Colin Richardson, *In the Face of the Enemy* (London: HarperCollins, 2007).

9 D. J. C. Pringle and W. A. Glue, *Official History of New Zealand in the Second World War 1939–1945: 20 Battalion and Armoured Regiment* (Wellington: War History Branch, Department of Internal Affairs, 1957), p. 108.

10 Harper and Richardson, *In the Face of the Enemy*, chapter 12, North Africa 1941-43, loc. 3750.

11 Direct speech from Sandford, *Mark of the Lion*, chapter 19, Desert Echo, loc. 4614 (adapted by the author of this essay).

12 Ibid., chapter 19, loc. 4655

Chapter 27 *(written by James Holland)*
1 TNA WO 95/2694.

2 Ibid.

3 Bernard Vann VC, in Christopher Wright and Glenda M. Anderson (eds), *The Victoria Cross and the George Cross: The Complete History*, 3 vols (London: Methuen, 2013), II, p. 766.

4 *The Times*, 19 December 1918.

5 Ibid.

6 Charles Beresford, *The Christian Soldier* (Solihull: Helion, 2016), p. xvi.

Chapter 28 *(written by James Holland)*
1 IWM 32045.

2 W. Alister Williams, *Heart of a Dragon: The VCs of Wales and the Welsh Regiments, 1914–82* (Exeter: Bridge Books, 2008), p. 398.

3 IWM 32045.

4 Williams, *Heart of a Dragon*, p. 398.

5 Ibid., p. 399.

6 IWM 32045.

ACKNOWLEDGMENTS

The Sebastopol Project is a registered UK charity (charity number: 1166265).

There are many individuals who have very generously given The Sebastopol Project their support. Some of those who have either provided their time or sponsored the project wish to remain anonymous; we are most grateful for everything they have done.

We would like to name others who have worked for, encouraged, or supported the project in so many ways:

Nick Aldridge, John Alexander, John de Bono QC, Richard Collins, Richard Connaughton, Dave Davis, The Dragon School, Laura Entwhistle, Dr. Colin Ferrett, Ollie Hawken, Tommy Hutchinson, Dr Hyde-Dunn, Philip Jeans, Lady Dodd, Helen Pike, Magdalen College School, Felicity McCallum, Gary Middlebrook, Rose Montgomery, The National Army Museum, Major General James Shaw CBE, Gary Smith, Stonyhurst College, Paul Tucker QC and Richard Wilson.

Charles Merullo for sourcing a wide array of images. Victoria Cook for her efficient and thorough research, and for also helping to find images.

Tom Bromley, Saul David, Paul Garlington, James Holland and Dr. Spencer Jones for bringing these stories to life.

John Bond, George Edgeller and the team at whitefox for their belief in the project and their expert advice, support and guidance throughout.

We would also like to thank the families of the Victoria Cross and George Cross recipients included in the book, for adding their personal touch to the chapters and providing an insight into the fathers, grandfathers, sisters, grandmothers and others behind the stories.

Lastly, our deep gratitude to Rebecca Maciejewski as secretary and to the trustees of The Victoria Cross and George Cross Association, without whom this book would not have been possible.